Psychology Revivals

Children's Peer Relations

The relationships children form with each other are important not only to childhood happiness but also to healthy adult functioning. Originally published in 1998, Phillip Slee and Ken Rigby presented an up-to-date overview of the latest findings in this area at the time, with reviews of current theory, research and intervention strategies across a wide range of topics from an international group of researchers and clinicians.

Children's Peer Relations includes sections on peer status, gender and ethnicity, disability, illness and loneliness with particular attention to the question of how children's peer relations can best be described and evaluated. There is also critical examination of methods of intervention to improve children's relations with others in school, family and community. *Children's Peer Relations* provided social researchers, school counsellors, psychologists and students of child development with a comprehensive handbook on this crucial topic. Today it can be read in its historical context.

Children's Peer Relations

Edited by
Phillip T. Slee and Ken Rigby

Routledge
Taylor & Francis Group
LONDON AND NEW YORK

First published in 1998
by Routledge

This edition first published in 2026 by Routledge
4 Park Square, Milton Park, Abingdon, Oxon, OX14 4RN

and by Routledge
605 Third Avenue, New York, NY 10158

Routledge is an imprint of the Taylor & Francis Group, an informa business

A Library of Congress record exists under ISBN: 9780415153928

ISBN: 978-1-041-23051-9 (hbk)
ISBN: 978-1-003-73553-3 (ebk)
ISBN: 978-1-041-23144-8 (pbk)

Book DOI 10.4324/9781003735533

Children's Peer Relations

Edited by Phillip T. Slee
and Ken Rigby

London and New York

First published 1998 by Routledge
11 New Fetter Lane, London EC4P 4EE

Simultaneously published in the USA and Canada, by Routledge
29 West 35th Street, New York, NY 10001

Reprinted 2001 by Routledge
27 Church Road, Hove, East Sussex, BN3 2FA
29 West 35th Street, New York, NY 10001

Routledge is an imprint of the Taylor & Francis Group

Typeset in Times by
J&L Composition Ltd, Filey, North Yorkshire
Printed and bound in Great Britain by
TJI Digital Ltd, Padstow, Cornwall

British Library Cataloging in Publication Data
A catalogue record for this book is available from the British Library

Library of Congress Cataloging in Publication Data
Children's Peer Relations/edited by Phillip T. Slee and Ken Rigby.
p. cm. - (International library of psychology)
Includes bibliographical references and index.
I. Interpersonal relations in children. I. Slee, Phillip T.
II. Rigby, Ken. III. Series.
BF723.1646C47 1998
155.4' 18–dc21 98–13903
CIP

ISBN 0-415-15392-1

Contents

Figures

Tables

Contributors

Nina Bazarskaya: Head of the Foreign Language Department at Voronezh Forestry Institute, Voronezh, Russia.

Roland W. B. Blonk: Coronel Institute, Academic Medical Centre, Meidergdroef, 15, 1105AZ, Amsterdam, Netherlands.

Verity Bottroff: School of Special Education and Disability Studies at the Flinders University of South Australia, GPO Box 2100, Adelaide, South Australia 5001.

Sue Finch: Researcher in the School of Psychological Science at La Trobe University, Bundoora, Victoria, 3083, Australia.

Craig H. Hart: Professor in the Department of Family Sciences at Brigham Young University, Provo, Utah USA 84602.

Kym Irving: The Centre for Applied Studies in Early Childhood, Faculty of Education, Queensland University of Technology, Locked Bag No. 2, Red Hill, Queensland Australia, 4059.

Shenghua Jin: Professor and Vice-director of Department of Psychology, Beijing Normal University, Beijing 100875, P.R. China.

Ari Kaukiainen: Doctoral candidate at the Department of Psychology at the University of Turku, SF-20014, Turku, Finland.

Gregor Kennedy: Doctoral candidate in the Department of Psychology at the University of Melbourne, Parkville, Victoria 3052 Australia.

Kirsti Lagerspetz: Professor in the Department of Psychology at the University of Turku, SF-20014, Turku, Finland.

Helen McGrath: School of Scientific and Developmental Studies, Faculty of Education, Burwood Campus, Deakin University, Burwood, Victoria, 3125. Australia.

Colin MacMullin: School of Special Education and Disability Studies at the Flinders University of South Australia, GPO Box 2100, Adelaide, South Australia 5001.

Mary Kay McNeilly-Choque: Doctoral Student and Research Assistant in the Department of Family Sciences at Brigham Young University, Provo, Utah 84602, USA.

Barbara L. Mandleco: Associate Professor in the College of Nursing, 534 SWKT, Brigham Young University, Provo, Utah 84602, USA.

Elaine Sorensen Marshall: Associate Professor in the College of Nursing, 444 SWKT, Brigham Young University, Provo, Utah 84602, USA.

Elizabeth Matjacic: Postgraduate student at the Royal Melbourne Institute of Technology, GPO 2476V, Melbourne, Victoria, 3001 Australia.

Jacquelyn Mize: Department of Human Development and Family Studies, Auburn University, Auburn, Alabama, 36849-5604 USA.

David B. Moore: Co-Director of Transformative Justice Australia (TJA), 115 Curlewis St, Bondi NSW 2026 Australia.

David A. Nelson: Doctoral Fellow and Research Assistant at the Institute of Child Development, University of Minnesota, 51 East River Rd, Minneapolis, MN 55455.

Larry Nelson: Doctoral Student and Research Assistant at 3304 Benjamin Building, Department of Human Development, University of Maryland, College Park, MD 20742-1131.

Susanne Frost Olsen: Assistant Professor in the Department of Family Sciences at Brigham Young University, Provo, Utah 84602, USA.

Gregory S. Pettit: Professor at the Department of Human Development and Family Studies, Auburn University, Auburn, Alabama, 36849-5604 USA.

Peter Randall: Family Assessment and Support Unit, University of Hull, Hull HU6 7RX UK.

Ken Rigby: Adjunct Associate Professor of Social Psychology, University of South Australia, Underdale Campus, Holbrooks Rd, Underdale, South Australia, 5032.

Clyde C. Robinson: Associate Professor in the Department of Family Sciences at Brigham Young University, Provo, Utah 84602, USA.

Julie Ann Robinson: School of Psychology at the Flinders University of South Australia. GPO Box 2100. Adelaide. South Australia 5001.

Alan Russell: Dean of Education at the Flinders University of South Australia, GPO Box 2100, Adelaide, South Australia 5001.

Christina Salmivalli: Department of Psychology at the University of Turku, SF-20014, Turku, Finland.

Ann Sanson: Professor in the Department of Psychology at the University of Melbourne, Parkville, Victoria 3052 Australia.

Barry H. Schneider: School of Psychology, University of Ottawa, Ottawa, Canada K1N 6N5.

Rosalyn H. Shute: School of Psychology at the Flinders University of South Australia, GPO Box 2100, Adelaide, South Australia 5001.

Phillip T. Slee: School of Education at the Flinders University of South Australia, GPO Box 2100, Adelaide, South Australia 5001.

Keith Sullivan: Director of Postgraduate Studies, School of Education, Victoria University of Wellington, PO Box 600, Wellington, New Zealand.

Marian Tulloch: School of Social Sciences and Liberal Studies, Charles Sturt University, Mitchell, Bathurst, NSW, 2795, Australia.

Chongming Yang: Doctoral Student and Research Assistant in the Department of Family Sciences at Brigham Young University, Provo, Utah, USA 84602.

Peixia Wu: Doctoral Student and Research Assistant in the Department of Family Sciences at Brigham Young University, Provo, Utah, USA 84602.

Xinzi Wu: Doctoral Student and Research Assistant in the Department of Psychology at the University of Virginia, Charlottesville, Virginia, USA 22903.

Preface

The idea for this volume grew out of the 1994 University of South Australia's 'Children's Peer Relations' conference in Adelaide co-ordinated by Ken Rigby, which brought together researchers and educators from around the globe to address the issue of children's relationships with their peers. At that time in Australia the issue of children's peer relations had not been addressed in such a focused or co-ordinated fashion. The conference considered the significance of peer relations not only in terms of the happiness and misery they bring to particular children but because they lay the foundation for healthy functioning in women, men and families.

The book content addresses current issues in peer relations while providing some indication of newly emerging fields of research. The international flavour of the book is reflected in the contributions made from Australia, Canada, China, England, Finland, The Netherlands, New Zealand, Russia, and the United States of America. The book provides a blend of current conceptual and methodological issues in research involving peer relations along with a consideration of contemporary thinking around the topic of intervention. To that end it has been developed around major themes including family, school and culture, peer status, gender and ethnicity, disability, illness and isolation and interventions.

The first section takes up the manner in which extrafamilial and parenting practices fashion and shape children's social competence and peer relations. The diverse content explored in this section presents some new developments, research and thinking around the manner in which broader family and cultural influences present in children's lives influence and mould the nature of their peer relations.

The second major component of the book takes up the challenge of understanding the impact of gender and ethnicity on children's peer relations. The effect of sex differences on the nature of peer relations, particularly where conflict is involved, provides a sharp focus for this section. Consideration is given to the important, albeit little researched, question of how race and ethnicity mediate relations between children.

In the third major section peer relations are explored in connection with illness, disability and isolation. Here are included a number of health issues which have hitherto received little or no research attention.

The section on peer status addresses the broad developmental task facing children in terms of the way in which they develop and maintain positive relations with their peers. The extent to which this important task is achieved has significant implications for children's overall well-being. Critical consideration is given to methodological and conceptual issues in assessing peer status and some strong directions for future research are indicated.

In the fifth section the problematic issue of the efficacy of interventions to promote harmonious peer relations is considered. The issues addressed are provocative in terms of the conceptual and methodological challenges they present in relation to the effectiveness of peer relations interventions. This section is especially practical in its orientation providing an overview of contemporary and innovative intervention programmes.

Acknowledgements

We would like to acknowledge sincerely all our contributors for their patience and commitment to this volume. At all times we were reliant on their enthusiasm and professionalism in relation to the important topic of children's peer relations and to their dedication to the ideal of helping to make a difference in children's lives.

Professor Peter Smith provided encouragement and advice in the development of the book. We would also like to thank Ms Robyn Cunningham for proofreading and assisting in editing the manuscript. We were greatly assisted in the development and production of the manuscript by the Aboriginal Research Institute of the University of South Australia. Our thanks also go to the many individuals at Routledge whose efforts behind the scenes helped bring this work to fruition.

Phillip T. Slee and
Ken Rigby

Part I

Culture and family

Chapter 1

Peer contact patterns, parenting practices, and preschoolers' social competence in China, Russia, and the United States

Craig H. Hart, Chongming Yang, David A. Nelson, Shenghua Jin, Nina Bazarskaya, Larry Nelson, Xinzi Wu and Peixia Wu

Research over the past decade has focused on ways that parents enhance or constrain the quantity and quality of their children's interactions with peers outside of the immediate family context (e.g., Ladd and Hart 1992; Mize *et al.* 1995; Profilet and Ladd 1994; Russell and Finnie 1990). Much of this work indicates that parenting works in concert with a host of personality, familial, and extrafamilial variables in ways that facilitate or diminish children's socially competent behaviour with peers (Hart *et al.* 1997).This line of research is important given evidence suggesting that the quality of peer relations stemming from familial and extrafamilial interpersonal relationships is linked to children's social/psychological adjustment throughout their lives (e.g., Ladd and Kochenderfer 1996; Rubin *et al.* 1998).

Our goal in this chapter is to explore ways that extrafamilial peer contact patterns and parenting practices are associated with children's social competencies in different cultures. In order to provide a meaningful context for this discussion, we begin by highlighting important distinctions between parenting styles and parenting practices that have relevance to cultural understandings. This is followed by an overview of the research on peer relationships and parenting practices associated with them. We conclude the chapter by exploring similarities and differences in peer contact patterns and parenting practices associated with social competencies across different cultural contexts in Beijing, China; Voronezh, Russia; Baton Rouge, Louisiana, USA; and Provo/Orem Utah, USA using data gathered from these diverse settings.

Parenting styles and practices

The focus of Mize *et al.* (this volume) is on stylistic features of parenting as linked to social competencies in young children. Conceptual similarities and distinctions between parenting styles and parenting practices (the focus of our chapter) are well articulated there. In summary, parenting styles are currently defined as 'aggregates or constellations of behaviours that describe parent–child interactions over a wide range of situations and that are presumed to create a pervasive interactional climate' (Mize and Pettit 1997). This climate creates a context that likely moderates how receptive children might be to certain parenting practices which are enacted in specific contexts noted below (cf. Baumrind 1996; Darling and Steinberg 1993; Grusec and Goodnow 1994; Jaffe 1997; Kochanska 1997; Smetana 1994). Stylistic features of parenting (e.g., authoritative, authoritarian) have been linked in similar ways to children's social/psychological functioning in Chinese, Russian, and North American cultural contexts (e.g., Chen *et al.* 1997; Hart *et al.* 1992; Hart *et al.* 1998a; Hart *et al.* in press).

Despite increasing knowledge concerning stylistic features of parenting, little is known about ways that parents may *directly* influence their children's social development by making explicit, intentional efforts to help children attain specific socialization goals in varying cultural contexts (cf. Darling and Steinberg 1993; Garcia Coll *et al.* 1995; Mize and Pettit 1997). Darling and Steinberg (1993: 494) postulate that parenting styles may be 'equally effective in socializing children across all cultural contexts, but that the goals toward which children are socialized, and thus parents' practices, vary across these very same ecologies'. The contrast between parenting styles and parenting practices parallels the etic/emic (culture-general/culture-specific) distinction found in cross-cultural research (e.g., Berry 1989; French *et al.* in press).

Parenting practices across situations and cultures

Parental goals and subsequent actions for facilitating changes in children's social behaviour often depend on the nature of the situation or transgression and may vary by culture and age of the child. Thus, certain practices may not be pervasive in overall styles of parent–child interactions but are rather specific to discrete events (cf. Barber 1996). As an illustration, different practices (which often include specific behaviours associated with styles noted in Mize *et al.*, this volume) have been found to be used more frequently by parents of young children in Western samples when responding to specific situations (e.g., Grusec and Goodnow 1994; Smetana 1994). These include predominantly authoritarian responses to noncompliance or high arousal child behaviour (e.g., not going to bed; noisy, disruptive play), and involve reasoning-oriented persuasion that is sometimes accompanied by authoritarian techniques for moral (e.g., physical and/or psychological harm to self or others) or conventional transgressions (e.g., bad table manners or not cleaning one's room).

However, similar situational events may evoke different sets of parenting practices depending on cultural norms for what constitutes conventional behaviour (e.g., slurping at the dinner table – acceptable in Japan) or what defines children's freedom and self-expression (e.g., children should be seen, but not heard). Likewise, parents are prone to hold older children more responsible for negative behaviours and enact authoritarian practices in contexts where social skills are expected to have matured with age (Dix *et al.* 1989; Geller and Johnston 1995; Rubin and Mills 1992).

Practices can also define specific strategies that parents use directly to promote academic, athletic, or social competence in specific contexts (cf. Darling and Steinberg 1993; Ladd and Hart 1992; Mize and Pettit 1997). These practices may receive greater emphasis in different cultural contexts depending on the domain of socialization. For example, the Chinese cultural notion of 'training' or *chiao shun* lends itself to Chinese mothers endorsing a higher level of behavioural control (that appears authoritarian to Westerners) for promoting academic competence. This practice, coupled with supportive involvement, appears to promote children's academic success in the Chinese culture and is more valued by Chinese mothers than European–American mothers (Baumrind 1996; Chao 1996).

Less is known, however, about similarities and differences in cultural practices that can exert direct influence on young children's social competence. Moreover, little is known about how children arrange their own social environments when there is less parental involvement, particularly as children grow older. Before turning to our exploration of cross-cultural differences concerning these issues, a brief review of the literature on peer contact patterns as linked to social competence and parenting practices derived from the Western literature is needed. This will establish the framework and introduce many of the variables used in cultural comparisons to be presented later.

Peer contacts and social competence

As illustrated in research by Lieberman (1977) and Howes (1983, 1988), children who participate in stable peer relationships develop more complex and sophisticated forms of social interaction and are better adjusted in school later on (Ladd 1990). Access to agemates provides children with greater autonomy and control over their social experiences. This appears to foster higher levels of social interaction, relationship formation, and a host of other interpersonal skills essential for the development of social competence and later school adjustment (see Berndt and Ladd 1989; Hart *et al.* 1997; Ladd *et al.* 1992; Rubin *et al.* 1998). However, the extent of these advantages appears to vary according to child age and gender, whether or not peers are perceived as friends or acquaintances, positive and negative features of peer influence, and the level of conflict or victimization that is experienced (Berndt and Keefe 1995; Hartup and Laursen 1993; Ladd *et al.* 1996; Kochenderfer and Ladd 1996; Parker and Gottman 1989; Rubin and Coplan 1992).

In general, North American studies have pointed to social advantages for young children who experience more nonschool peer contacts across the early and middle childhood years. During the preschool years (ages 3.5 to 5.6 years), research by Ladd and Hart (1992) indicated that children who initiated more peer contacts displayed lower levels of anxious playground behaviour and were better accepted by peers. Mothers in another study of 5- and 6-year-old kindergarteners were also found to rate higher contact initiating children as having better social skills (Prinstein 1997). Yet other research findings have suggested that 3.4 to 4.6-year-old preschoolers who spent more time playing in network members' homes were more accepted by peers in preschool (Ladd *et al.* 1988). They also received higher school adjustment scores from teachers and higher acceptance ratings from peers if their nonschool peer networks were comprised of a greater proportion of same-age peers (cf. Ellis *et al.* 1981). Additional research supporting positive outcomes associated with peer contacts indicated that informal, unsponsored meetings help children from smaller families become more tolerant and accepting of peers during middle childhood (Bryant 1985). These types of social opportunities and social skills appear to be enhanced when parents are involved in facilitative ways.

Parenting practices that facilitate peer relations

During the early and middle childhood years, parents (particularly mothers) vary in the degree to which they enroll children in organized activities, chauffeur them from one house or social event to another, arrange play interactions with playmates who may or may not be children of parents in the parent's own social networks, and supervise interactions with peers (e.g., Rubin and Sloman 1984). Parents in North American samples engage in many of these activities more for younger versus older children (Bhavnagri and Parke 1991; Ladd *et al.* 1992). Although siblings also play an important role in the socialization process (see Hart *et al.* 1997), contacts with siblings are less likely to be arranged by parents. The focus of the next two sections is on how parents manage their children's peer relations by *designing* their social environments and *mediating* access to peers (Ladd and Le Sieur 1995), as well as on the *supervising* and *advising/consulting* roles that are embodied in the educational functions that parents play.

Managerial practices

Designer

As designers, parental choice of neighbourhood, decisions about enrolling children in preschool or day care, and providing access to community or religious activities (e.g., soccer, pools, libraries, Cub Scouts, church activities) are all avenues that can enhance or diminish children's experiences with peers. For example, parents often consider the availability of playmates when making living arrangements. The immediate neighbourhood can present a wide array of social opportunities since children spend much of their time close to home. Opportunities for peer interaction may occur on playgrounds, on footpaths, in school yards, in vacant lots, and within or around each other's homes (Moore and Young 1978). Neighbourhoods that have large child populations, are perceived to be safe and are characterized by features such as the presence of footpaths and playgrounds, and short distances between homes appear to provide the greatest access to peers (Berg and Medrich 1980; Medrich *et al.* 1982). In contrast, homes that are widely spaced, physically isolated, inaccessible, or relatively dangerous appear to inhibit peer contact opportunities (Cochran and Riley 1988; Medrich *et al.* 1982). Some of these factors may have implications for children's social adjustment. Recent research indicates that stressful life events are strong predictors of childhood aggression only under conditions of high neighbourhood disadvantage (Attar *et al.* 1994). In contrast, life stressors related to childhood aggression appear to be mitigated by advantaged neighbourhood settings (Kupersmidt *et al.* 1995).

Although peer relations may only be one of many considerations for parents choosing to involve their children in community and religious activities, extant data suggests that these settings can serve to enhance children's peer relations and school adjustment. Data gathered from a midwestern US sample indicate that preschoolers who regularly participated in these settings were less anxious and had fewer absences in kindergarten (Ladd and Price 1987). Similarly, Bryant (1985) found that 10-year-old children who participated in unstructured community activities appeared to benefit with higher perspective-taking abilities (i.e., recognizing when others think, feel, or perceive things differently than themselves).

Mediator

Parents vary in the degree to which they become involved or allow their children to take the initiative in facilitating relationships with peers. In the *mediating* role, research findings indicate that preschoolers who had mothers who bridged between their child and playmates by orchestrating child-peer engagements had a larger number of playmates and more consistent play companions in their informal nonschool networks (Ladd and Golter 1988). Children with higher initiating mothers have also been found to spend more time playing in peers' homes, which, as noted earlier, was associated with better classroom adjustment and acceptance by peers (Ladd *et al.* 1988). Parental initiations have also been linked to more child prosocial behaviour and less nonsocial behaviour in preschool classrooms (Ladd and Hart 1992), and to greater classroom peer acceptance among boys, but not girls (Ladd and Golter 1988; Ladd and Hart 1992). Similar findings have been obtained for German grade-schoolers (Krappman 1989), with closer, more stable, and less difficult friendships being associated with parents actively arranging and stimulating peer relations.

The parental mediating role is also associated with maternal beliefs about the importance of social skills and perceptions of their children's sociability (Hart *et al.* 1997), as well as with maternal sociability (Prinstein 1997). For example, recent findings indicate that mothers who perceived their preschoolers as more sociable not only believed social skills were important, but also believed they should play an active role in the socialization of these competencies (Mize *et al.* 1995; Rubin *et al.* 1989). Additional data have indicated that when compared to mothers who perceived their children as less sociable, those who saw their children as more sociable facilitated more informal peer activities (Profilet and Ladd 1994; Prinstein 1997). Further evidence suggests that mothers who involved their children in the process of arranging informal play activities (e.g., scaffolding play arrangements) tended to have children who initiated more of their own play dates (Ladd and Hart 1992). This ability on the part of mothers has also recently been linked to higher levels of maternal sociability (Prinstein 1997). These findings support the notion that parental mediating practices help empower children with the abilities to initiate, communicate, and manage their own peer relationships, particularly as parent involvement in this regard diminishes as children grow older (Bhavnagri and Parke 1991; Ladd and Hart 1992).

Educational practices

Supervising and *advising/consulting* comprise the educational roles that parents play. Both practices can serve to educate children about ways to negotiate the peer milieu, using interactions with peers as teaching opportunities for how to get along when playing with peers.

Supervision

The supervision function includes interactive and directive interventions (Lollis *et al.* 1992) and also includes monitoring (Ladd and Le Sieur

1995). *Interactive interventions* involve parents being actively present and participating in their child's play by proactively regulating or 'scaffolding' social interaction. This type of supervision is typically used with toddlers (Bhavnagri and Parke 1985), although it does occur with older children as well (Bhavnagri and Parke 1991). *Directive interventions* involve parents operating from outside the context of children's play, in terms of being aware of activities and becoming involved as needed. This is more typical when supervising older rather than younger preschool-age children (see Lollis *et al.* 1992), and tends to be reactive to events in children's play (Ladd and Le Sieur 1995). Higher levels of directive intervention have been linked to more rejection by peers, suggesting that mothers might be responding more to children who are exhibiting behaviour problems (Ladd and Golter 1988; Prinstein 1997). Research also indicates that higher levels of maternal involvement in the supervision context, coupled with less skilled directive interventions involving irrelevant or disruptive communicative behaviours, are related to less socially competent childhood behaviour (Mize *et al.* 1995). Alternatively, Finnie and Russell (1988) and Russell and Finnie (1990) obtained evidence suggesting that more relevant, group-oriented maternal communication in this context lent itself to children being more liked by peers.

Finally, tracking children's whereabouts, partners, and play activities that included minimal direct parental involvement is referred to as *monitoring*. This typically applies to older children who are more self-directing and tend to play in settings less accessible to parents. Lack of parental monitoring has generally been linked to child externalizing behaviour problems and adolescent delinquency (e.g., Barber 1996; Parke 1994). More parental monitoring, on the other hand, appears to engender a feeling of control over life circumstances and self-efficacy in children's lives, even for those living in high-crime neighbourhoods (Coley and Hoffman 1996).

Advising/consulting

Advising/consulting consists of 'decontextualized discussions' about how to initiate friendships, manage conflicts, identify solutions to interpersonal problems, deflect teasing, repel bullies, and so on (cf. Flannagan 1996; Flannagan and Baker-Ward 1996). These may occur during dinner, after school, before bedtime, during travel in a car, or in a variety of other settings (Ladd *et al.* 1992; Lollis *et al.* 1992; Laird, *et al.* 1994). Consulting may be proactive, designed to prepare children for future social activities. It may also be reactive, taking the form of parents giving advice for how to negotiate new or unfamiliar aspects of the peer culture (Ladd and Le Sieur 1995), or taking the form of acting as a sounding board for children's self-generated solutions (Kuczynski 1984). Taken together, research concerning this involvement indicates that higher levels of quantity (e.g., number of conversations) and quality (e.g., of advice offered, warmth and positivity) are linked to positive social/communicative peer group outcomes (Laird *et al.* 1994; Profilet and Ladd 1996; Russell and Finnie 1990). Alternatively, blaming-oriented maternal consulting has been associated with childhood withdrawal (Profilet and Ladd 1996).

Cross-cultural investigation

To our knowledge, with the exception of a German study noted earlier (Krappman 1989) and work in Australia (e.g., Russell and Finnie 1990) and India (Balda 1998), the literature is silent as to how most aspects of peer contact patterns, parental management, and parental education/supervision practices might be similar or different across cultures. In an effort to begin assessing these constructs in different cultures we expanded a paper–pencil measure designed by Ladd *et al.* (1988) to include more parental management and supervision variables. Our aim was to have it translated for use in countries such as China where systematic phone log methodologies used in prior work would be impossible to carry out due to most families having limited access to telephones (cf. Ladd and Hart 1992). Dimensions of this measure were correlated with teacher behaviour ratings and peer sociometric data gathered in nursery school and day care settings in ways that are outlined below.

Samples

Four samples comprised of 703 children and their parents from four diverse cultural contexts participated in the study. Sample one included 207 children attending three nursery schools and their ethnic Russian families in Voronezh, Russia, a provincial city of one million inhabitants located approximately 250 miles south of Moscow. Foreign visits were strictly regulated by Soviet officials until 1990 when foreigners gained free access to the city. Voronezh is unique in that, even today, it is relatively isolated from Western influence due to its southern location. Sample two included 196 children attending one of two nursery schools in Beijing, China. Beijing is the capital and cultural centre of China, with a population of approximately ten million people.

Sample three was located in urban Provo/Orem, Utah (population approximately 120,000) in the western part of the United States. It consisted of 186 children attending a university-based preschool laboratory or a Head Start community-based early childhood programme. One of the unique features of this sample was that 96 per cent of the families were affiliated with the Church of Jesus Christ of Latter Day Saints (Mormon). This provided a unique opportunity to explore peer contact patterns in a community where familial and child social networks are highly integrated with neighbourhood-based Church congregations. Sample four included 114 children enrolled in one of four centre-based preschool programmes in Baton Rouge, Louisiana, a southeastern metropolitan area with a population of approximately 500,000 people. Families in the sample represented diverse religious backgrounds (e.g., Catholic, Protestant, no affiliation). Both US samples were comprised of families from predominantly European-American backgrounds, with a good portion of the Louisiana sample being comprised of French-European descent.

Data was gathered in China in 1996, Russia in 1995, and Utah in 1994 and 1995. The Louisiana data was gathered several years earlier. As noted in Table 1.3 (p. 18), only a portion of the data was gathered in Louisiana as measures were further developed later on to reflect the emerging literature in this area. Demographic comparisons of the four samples based on maternal responses to a questionnaire are shown in Table 1.1. Parents in all samples were relatively well educated and were generally in their thirties. Children in China had no siblings (as expected due to the one-child policy). Russian and Louisiana families were also small relative to Utah where larger families are more the norm. Children in China and Russia also spent considerably more time in nursery school than did Utah or Louisiana children. However, nonschool peer contacts were perceived by mothers to be relatively important in all cultures, with Utah and Russian mothers attaching somewhat more value to this. Finally, Chinese and Russian mothers perceived their neighbourhoods to be less safe when compared to US mothers.

Table 1.1 Demographic comparisons

	China	*Russia*	*Utah*	*Louisiana*
Father's education (in years)*	14.06 (3.01)	14.53 (2.42)	15.10 (2.50)	17.16 (2.71)
Mother's education (in years)*	13.78 (2.31)	14.95 (2.34)	14.23 (2.59)	16.41 (2.13)
Child's age (mean months)	60.99 (7.66)	60.95 (7.89)	60.15 (6.84)	54.32 (8.76)
Father's age (in years)	34.76 (5.39)	32.40 (7.09)	32.22 (5.57)	35.94 (4.57)
Mother's age (in years)	33.09 (3.34)	30.65 (5.62)	30.30 (5.61)	34.00 (4.16)
Out-of-home care (mean hours per week)	45.00 (0.00)	45.00 (0.00)	15.00 (8.86)	14.89 (9.99)
Number of children in family	1.00 (0.00)	1.33 (0.54)	3.22 (.38)	1.12 (0.98)
Perceived importance of nonschool peer contact (5pt scale: 5 = extremely important)	3.68 (0.98)	4.12 (0.83)	4.12 (0.81)	3.84 (0.86)
Perceived safety of neighbourhood (1–5 scale: 5 = extremely safe)	2.63 (0.92)	2.54 (0.96)	3.98 (0.79)	3.91 (0.80)

Note
* Twelve years equals high school graduation.

Method

All measures noted below were successfully forward- and back-translated by Chinese and Russian linguists who were fluent in English and their native languages, with input from the investigators for difficult-to-translate items. The following procedures and methods were employed in all four cultural settings and are only briefly described due to space limitations.

Peer contacts measure

The peer contacts questionnaire was completed for each target child by the parent who felt they were most aware of children's nonschool peer contacts. Similar to past research (e.g., Ladd *et al.* 1988; Ladd and Hart 1992), this was primarily mothers (approximately 98 per cent in all cultures). The instrument consisted of a grid upon which parents were asked to list their child's nonschool network members. From there, parents were asked to respond to a series of questions for each network member and to record their estimated response on the grid (e.g., frequency of contact, how they supervise when the playmate is present, who typically initiates contacts) after selecting from designated categories that were explained on the questionnaire (e.g., frequency: daily, weekly; supervision: directive, monitoring; initiates: parent, child, playmate). Variables derived from the instrument are briefly described in the left column of Table 1.3 (p. 18). Scores were calculated representing the proportion of children in each target child's nonschool peer network that fell into each category shown in Table 1.3 (with two exceptions for nonproportional mean scores noted at the bottom of the table). A comprehensive taxonomy of these variables along with the questionnaire is available upon request.

Teacher behaviour ratings

Teachers completed a battery of measures that tapped into subtypes of children's aggressive, sociable, and withdrawn behaviours. How these behavioural dimensions tie into definitions of social/communicative competence (or lack thereof) are described in Hart *et al.* (1997). All measures with the exception of the Gresham and Elliott (1990) internalizing and externalizing behavioural dimensions were derived from extensive pilot testing, psychometric evaluations, and item refinement in the United States (e.g., McNeilly-Choque *et al.* 1996; Nelson *et al.* 1998). Due to space limitations, a taxonomy of these measures along with sample items is provided in Table 1.2 (p. 16). Instrument items were accompanied by a three-point scale anchored by never (0) and very often (2).

These behavioural measures were designed to reflect recent research indicating, for example, that there are subtypes of aggression (e.g., Crick *et al.* 1997) and withdrawal (e.g., Coplan and Rubin 1998) that carry different social/psychological meanings in the peer group. For example, our research on withdrawn subtypes noted in Table 1.2 with preschoolers suggests that the reticent behavioural subtype is related to children's peer rejection in each of the Chinese, Russian, and US cultural settings (Hart *et al.* 1998b). Both relational and overt forms of aggression are also related to preschoolers' peer rejection across different cultural contexts (e.g., Hart *et al.* 1998c; McNeilly-Choque *et al.* 1996). Prosocial and friendly children are typically more accepted by peers (e.g., Chen *et al.* 1995a; Hart *et al.* 1993). All measures noted in Table 1.2 yielded similar factor structures for each culture that clearly delineated behavioural dimensions one from another within each measure of aggression, withdrawal, and sociability (e.g., eigen values > 1, minimal cross-loadings, Cronbach's alphas > 0.70 for each behavioural dimension). Copies of each measure and associated factor structures are available upon request.

Peer sociometric assessments

Standard peer sociometric nomination procedures where children identify up to three classmates they most like to play with and three classmates they least like to play with from photographs on a picture board were administered to children in the study (McCandless and Marshall 1957). Positive and negative nomination scores were created by summing the 'votes' each child received for each criterion. These scores were then standardized by classroom (cf. Coie *et al.* 1982). Peer nomination procedures were administered in a counterbalanced fashion with rating scale procedures (Asher *et al.* 1979). Children assigned classmates' pictures into one of three boxes depicting either a happy face ('children you like to play with a lot'), a neutral face ('children you kinda like to play with') or a sad face ('children you don't like to play with'). Average ratings received from all the raters in each class were then standardized by classrooms. More description of these procedures as well as pros and cons from a reliability and validity standpoint for preschool samples can be found in Wu *et al.* (1998). A minimum of 70 per cent of children participated in the study from each classroom.

Results

The results are organized into four sections. These include (a) cultural comparisons, (b) peer contact patterns and social competence, (c) parental management practices and social competence, and (d) parental educating/supervising practices and social competence. Within each section, variables representing peer network structural features, parental management design practices, parental management mediating practices, and parent education/supervision practices are shown in Table 1.3 (p. 18). Given the general lack of cross-cultural peer contact and parenting practices information to draw from for formulating specific hypothesis, all analyses were *exploratory* in nature and interpreted in light of current cultural understandings. Arc-sine transformations were applied to proportional scores shown in Table 1.3 prior to analysis to control for the possibility of covariance between the means and variances of the proportional data (see Winer 1971: 399).

Cultural comparisons

For the cultural comparison analyses, one-way ANOVAs were conducted to assess significant differences between cultures regarding the variables shown in Table 1.3. *Post hoc* tests (Student–Newman–Keuls) were used to compare all possible pairs of group means.

Network structural features

It was of interest to note that in China, Louisiana, and Russia, where families had fewer children (see Table 1.1), peer networks (range of partners) were smaller than in Utah (see Table 1.3). The larger peer networks in Utah likely reflected the greater number of children in families that children have to choose from relative to the other three cultural sites.

With the exception of Louisiana, results indicated that the preschoolers comprising the China, Russia, and Utah samples had networks predominantly consisting of same-age peers. Anomalous Louisiana findings for relatively younger preschoolers (see Table 1.1) favouring older playmates were not dissimilar to that found in prior work conducted in Indiana. Younger preschoolers there were also found to have proportionally more older children in their networks (Ladd *et al.* 1988). Although proportionally more playmates in each culture were identified by parents as friends rather than as relatives or cousins, Chinese children had proportionally more cousins in their networks. This finding makes sense given the one-child policy that would likely facilitate more contacts with close relatives (cf. Yang *et al.* 1995).

Children in all locations tended to have more playmates of the same sex (cf. Feiring and Lewis 1988, 1989), and more playmates whom they had known for more than one year. Children in Russia knew peers somewhat longer, perhaps reflecting little mobility due to extreme economic circumstances accompanied by little flexibility in living arrangements (i.e., apartments are at a premium). Play bouts in most cultures lasted for one-to-two hours on average, although slightly longer in

Russia. Interestingly, only a small proportion of peer networks in all cultures was comprised of playmates known at nursery school or day care.

Chinese children had relatively less frequent contact with peers outside of school. It was also striking to note the relative similarities for peer contact frequency across the Louisiana, Russia and Utah cultures in light of the disproportionate amount of time children spent in nursery school each week in Russia (see Table 1.1). Possible reasons for these contact frequency findings are explained in the next section.

Parental management (designing practices)

Although parents rarely have complete control over the design of their children's social environment, cultural variations in where parents live appear to be associated with the degree to which children have access to peers. As seen in Table 1.3, there was less neighbourhood propinquity to playmates for Chinese children when compared with other cultures. This may also partially explain why there were fewer fostering/introductory meetings in Chinese community and neighbourhood settings, fewer peers (range of partners), and less frequent daily contacts relative to what is shown in Table 1.3 for the other cultures.

More specifically, children in Louisiana, Russia, and Utah were more likely to have the majority of playmates in their immediate neighbourhoods. Likely denser populations of playmate choices in neighbourhoods due to larger families accompanied by less time spent in preschool or day care may account for the relatively higher daily peer contact frequency in Utah (Table 1.3). Interestingly, only a small proportion of fostering/initial meetings occurred in religious settings. Given the Utah religious culture, it would seem more likely that children would have met in their neighbourhood church. However, because Utah neighbourhood and church's are tightly interwoven, it is not surprising that parents attributed the fostering of more first meetings with playmates to the neighbourhood context where most children attend the same church congregation together.

Finally, surrounding neighbourhoods represented relatively small proportions of play venues in all cultural settings for preschoolers (Table 1.3), and were perceived by mothers to be more dangerous in China and Russia than in Utah (Table 1.1). Although the majority of play occurred in homes in all cultural settings, Chinese mothers perceived their children to play in home settings significantly more than did their Russian or Utah counterparts. More will be said about this later.

Parental management (mediating practices)

The data also indicated that Chinese children were allowed to take more initiative in fostering initial meetings and relationships with peers than

Table 1.2 Taxonomy of child behavioural measures (sample items)

Aggression

Overt:

- intimidates or threatens to get something he/she wants;
- hits or kicks others for the sake of doing it;
- uses hostile means to keep others from getting what he/she has

Relational:

- says, 'I won't be your friend' to peers 'if you don't do things my way';
- tells other children not to play with or be a peer's friend;
- tries to get others to dislike a peer (e.g., whispering mean things about the peer)

Withdrawal/inhibition

Solitary passive:

- would rather play alone;
- plays with toys by self;
- does constructive activities alone (e.g., builds things, does puzzles, reads books)

Modest inhibition:

- humbly acknowledges compliments;
- doesn't brag and boast;
- doesn't appear overconfident

Solitary active:[a]

- does dramatic/pretend play by self;
- animates toys by self;
- talks aloud or sings dramatically around peers but does not interact with them

Reticent:

- appears to be doing nothing;
- is unoccupied even when there is plenty to do;
- wanders aimlessly during free play

Anxious/fearful:

- doesn't talk much with other children;
- is fearful when approaching other children;
- shies away when approached by other children

Actively isolated:

- other children tell him/her that he/she cannot play with them;
- is told to go away by other children;
- other children exclude him/her

Sociability

Friendly/amicable:

- has many friends;
- other children like to be with this child;
- likes to talk with peers

Impulse control:

- is slow to anger;
- controls temper in conflict situations;
- receives criticism well

Prosocial:

- helps other children who are feeling sick;
- comforts a child who is crying or upset;
- offers to share materials

Table 1.2 Continued

Leadership/assertiveness:
- introduces self to new people without being told;
- leads out in peer group activities;
- can get activities going with other children

Externalizing and internalizing (Gresham and Elliott 1990)[b]

Externalizing:
- disturbs activities;
- argues with others;
- has temper tantrums

Internalizing:
- acts sad;
- appears lonely;
- says nobody likes him or her

Notes

a Loaded with solitary passive items in the Chinese sample when included as part of a larger measure of withdrawal/inhibition in this report (cf. Hart *et al.* 1998b).

b Only externalizing, internalizing, and peer sociometric measures were gathered in Louisiana.

were children in Russia, Utah, and Louisiana (Table 1.3). However, likely because Louisiana children were younger to start with (see Table 1.1), their mothers played a larger fostering role. With regard to reasons stated for fostering peer relationships, mothers cited friendship as the primary reason for fostering peer contacts in all cultures (particularly in China) along with intellectual stimulation being more of a secondary reason in China. Again, the one-child policy limiting sibling contact, along with traditions promoting academic competence from a cultural training standpoint, may be the operative mechanism here (Yang *et al.* 1995; Chao 1994).

In terms of initiating regular contacts with peers, relative to other possibilities (e.g., siblings, child and playmate together), Chinese children themselves, and to a lesser extent their mothers and cousins, were more responsible for contact initiations and activity planning than were children, mothers, and cousins in Russia and Utah. This may be due, in part, to children being relatively less available in Beijing neighbourhoods and further away in other parts of the city (Table 1.3, propinquity section), resulting in fewer spontaneous mutual peer contact initiations. This may further result in more effortful planning and initiation on the part of children, cousins, and mothers for peer activities when arrangements need to be made for children to come from further away to play. In contrast, Russian and Utah children and playmates were more likely to live in the immediate neighbourhoods and were more prone to mutually initiate their own contacts, along with some help from playmate's parents.

Results for other fostering, initiating, and planning variables were remarkably similar across cultures. For example, the older preschoolers

Table 1.3 Cross-cultural mean comparisons of network structural features, managerial practices and educational/supervisory practices

	China	*Russia*	*Utah*	*Louisiana*
Network structural features				
Range of partners (means)*	4.24^{a} (4.23)	5.66^{b} (3.33)	7.79^{c} (3.91)	5.55^{b} (2.82)
Composition				
Age				
Older	0.09^{a} (0.20)	0.11^{a} (0.19)	0.25^{b} (0.25)	0.52^{c} (0.32)
Same-age (within 1 year)	0.50^{a} (0.38)	0.52^{a} (0.30)	0.50^{a} (0.27)	0.23^{b} (0.28)
Younger	0.41^{a} (0.38)	0.37^{a} (0.30)	0.25^{b} (0.24)	0.25^{b} (0.25)
Relationship				
Siblings	0.00^{a} (0.17)	0.09^{a} (0.20)	0.19^{b} (0.21)	0.15^{b} (0.21)
Relatives (cousins)	0.38^{b} (0.37)	0.15^{b} (0.21)	0.17^{b} (0.23)	0.10^{b} (0.21)
Friends	0.62^{a} (0.38)	0.76^{b} (0.26)	0.64^{a} (0.27)	0.75^{b} (0.27)
Gender				
Same sex	0.63^{a} (0.28)	0.62^{a} (0.28)	0.64^{a} (0.22)	0.68^{a} (0.24)
Opposite sex	0.37^{a} (0.28)	0.38^{a} (0.25)	0.36^{a} (0.22)	0.32^{a} (0.24)
School playmates (% in network)	0.14^{a} (0.29)	0.08^{b} (0.17)	0.08^{b} (0.14)	—
Duration of relationship				
Short (< 1 year)	0.21^{a} (0.34)	0.12^{b} (0.22)	0.25^{a} (0.28)	0.22^{a} (0.30)
Long (> 1 year)	0.79^{a} (0.34)	0.88^{b} (0.22)	0.75^{a} (0.28)	0.78^{a} (0.30)
Contact frequency				
Daily (5–7 times per week)	0.12^{a} (0.25)	0.36^{b} (0.36)	0.41^{c} (0.30)	0.28^{b} (0.29)
Weekly (once per week)	0.31^{a} (0.38)	0.31^{a} (0.31)	0.31^{a} (0.28)	0.36^{a} (0.35)
Biweekly (once per 2 weeks or less)	0.57^{a} (0.40)	0.33^{b} (0.31)	0.28^{b} (0.28)	0.36^{b} (0.33)
Contact time (mean hours)*	1.59^{a} (1.04)	2.09^{b} (1.30)	1.93^{b} (0.90)	1.78^{a} (1.02)
Management (designing practices)				
Propinquity to peers				
Neighbourhood (within walking)	0.31^{a} (0.37)	0.61^{b} (0.33)	0.65^{b} (0.30)	0.54^{c} (0.34)
Within city	0.59^{a} (0.39)	0.33^{b} (0.32)	0.22^{c} (0.26)	0.36^{b} (0.34)
Outside city	0.10^{a} (0.23)	0.06^{b} (0.13)	0.13^{a} (0.20)	0.13^{a} (0.21)
Play location				
Child's home/yard	0.44^{a} (0.43)	0.32^{b} (0.38)	0.35^{b} (0.33)	—
Playmate's house/yard	0.20^{a} (0.33)	0.11^{b} (0.23)	0.11^{b} (0.20)	—
Equal	0.15^{a} (0.30)	0.40^{b} (0.40)	0.43^{b} (0.36)	—
Surrounding neighbourhood	0.21^{a} (0.33)	0.17^{a} (0.29)	0.11^{b} (0.22)	—
Fostering location (where children mutually met)				
Mutual religious setting	0.00^{a} (0.00)	0.00^{a} (0.00)	0.05^{b} (0.12)	0.02^{c} (0.08)
Neighbourhood/community	0.08^{a} (0.21)	0.27^{b} (0.32)	0.22^{b} (0.28)	0.17^{b} (0.23)
Mutual school setting	0.04^{a} (0.15)	0.02^{a} (0.09)	0.07^{b} (0.15)	0.09^{b} (0.18)
Public location	0.01^{a} (0.03)	0.02^{a} (0.10)	0.01^{a} (0.03)	0.00^{a} (0.03)

Table 1.3 Continued

	China		*Russia*		*Utah*		*Louisiana*	
Management (mediating practices)								
Fostering agent (when a location did not foster a mutual meeting)								
Child	0.47[a]	(0.43)	0.16[b]	(0.29)	0.26[c]	(0.35)	0.16[c]	(0.23)
Child's parents	0.21[a]	(0.36)	0.20[a]	(0.30)	0.15[a]	(0.25)	0.33[b]	(0.39)
Others (siblings and playmates)	0.20[a]	(0.31)	0.33[b]	(0.34)	0.24[a]	(0.36)	0.23[a]	(0.28)
Fostering reasons (parents only)								
Friendship	0.68[a]	(0.41)	0.43[b]	(0.39)	0.38[c]	(0.39)	0.52[b]	(0.32)
Intellectual stimulation	0.16[a]	(0.33)	0.06[b]	(0.19)	0.01[b]	(0.01)	0.07[b]	(0.05)
Convenience	0.03[a]	(0.14)	0.05[a]	(0.16)	0.01[a]	(0.06)	0.02[a]	(0.12)
No particular reason	0.13[a]		0.45[b]		0.60[c]		0.39[b]	
Initiation sponsor								
Child initiates play contact	0.44[a]	(0.42)	0.29[b]	(0.35)	0.26[b]	(0.35)	—	
Child and sibling initiate	0.00[a]	(0.00)	0.06[a]	(0.17)	0.09[a]	(0.19)	—	
Child and playmate (mutual)	0.18[a]	(0.34)	0.27[b]	(0.35)	0.29[b]	(0.36)	—	
Child's cousins initiate	0.10[a]	(0.14)	0.02[b]	(0.08)	0.02[b]	(0.08)	—	
Child's mother initiates	0.09[a]	(0.25)	0.03[b]	(0.13)	0.06[b]	(0.17)	—	
Child's father initiates	0.03[a]	(0.11)	0.01[a]	(0.03)	0.01[a]	(0.04)	—	
Mother and child together	0.04[a]	(0.16)	0.13[b]	(0.24)	0.06[b]	(0.19)	—	
Playmate initiates	0.09[a]	(0.22)	0.06[a]	(0.16)	0.09[a]	(0.20)	—	
Playmate's parents initiate	0.03[a]	(0.13)	0.14[b]	(0.27)	0.14[b]	(0.27)	—	
Initiation strategy								
Parent invites	0.13[a]	(0.29)	0.14[a]	(0.25)	0.11[a]	(0.24)	—	
Parent scaffolds (e.g., helps child with invitation strategies)	0.21[a]	(0.36)	0.22[a]	(0.25)	0.28[a]	(0.37)	—	
Playmate/playmate parents invites	0.07[a]	(0.20)	0.05[a]	(0.14)	0.09[b]	(0.19)	—	
Child contrives strategy	0.59[a]	(0.44)	0.59[a]	(0.41)	0.52[a]	(0.40)	—	
Activity Planning								
Parent plans	0.05[a]	(0.18)	0.02[a]	(0.12)	0.03[a]	(0.03)	—	
Parent scaffolds (e.g., helps child decide what, where when)	0.14[a]	(0.15)	0.14[a]	(0.15)	0.14[a]	(0.14)	—	
Playmate/playmate parents	0.01[a]	(0.05)	0.07[b]	(0.19)	0.10[b]	(0.26)	—	
Child plans	0.34[a]	(0.40)	0.16[b]	(0.28)	0.19[b]	(0.32)	—	
Child and playmates plan together (including siblings)	0.47[a]	(0.41)	0.62[b]	(0.36)	0.54[a]	(0.40)	—	
Educational practices (supervision)								
Interactive interventions (parent actively present and regulating)	0.07[a]	(0.21)	0.09[a]	(0.20)	0.08[a]	(0.20)	—	

Table 1.3 Continued

	China	*Russia*	*Utah*	*Louisiana*
Directive interventions (parent overseeing and aware, regulates as needed)	0.40^a (0.40)	0.55^b (0.37)	0.71^c (0.36)	—
Monitoring (parent aware but not involved)	0.53^a (0.43)	0.37^b (0.36)	0.19^c (0.33)	—

Notes
Non-identical letters indicate where means were found to be statistically different across rows.

* All means with the exception of range of partners and contact time means are proportional score means. Similar results were obtained when arc sine transformations were applied to proportional scores. Standard deviations are in parentheses.

comprising the Chinese, Russian and Utah samples were more active in initiating and planning play activities than were their parents, supporting earlier studies indicating that parents become less involved as children grow older (Bhavnagri and Parke 1991; Ladd and Hart 1992).

Parental education/supervision practices

Findings presented in Table 1.3 indicate that Utah mothers saw themselves as participating more in directive interventions, with Russian and particularly Chinese mothers being somewhat less involved in this way. In contrast, Chinese mothers engaged in more monitoring behaviour relative to Russian and Utah mothers. As will be seen later, a closer examination of the supervision data revealed some interesting patterns associated with child social competence that shed further light on these findings.

SUMMARY: CULTURAL COMPARISONS

Substantive findings thus far indicate that larger families in Utah neighbourhoods may facilitate more peer contact opportunities for young children when compared to the other cultural contexts. Structural features with regard to same-age and same-sex peers as well as play contact durations were quite similar across cultures. However, for Chinese children, peers (including more cousins) living further away in other parts of Beijing appeared to limit more frequent access to peers, relative to Louisiana, Russia, and Utah. This appeared to lend itself to more effortful peer contact initiations and planning, primarily on the part of Chinese children, with help from mothers and cousins. Finally, the data suggests that parents are relatively less involved in mediating functions for older preschoolers across diverse settings.

Peer contact patterns and social competence

In the next set of analyses, correlations were run to explore relations among network structural features, child contact initiations, and social competence. The major purpose was to investigate whether peer contacts were associated with positive social competencies in diverse cultural settings as has been found in prior research conducted in North America.

Peer networks, contact initiations, and age composition

Somewhat mirroring prior work with US samples discussed in the introduction, boys in Utah with larger peer networks received more positive peer nominations ($r = 0.29$, $p < 0.01$) and were rated by teachers as being more friendly ($r = 0.25$, $p < 0.05$) and as having more leadership skills ($r = 0.29$, $p < 0.01$). Similarly, boys in Louisiana with larger peer networks received fewer negative nominations from peers ($r = -0.28$, $p < 0.05$). Although the number of different playmates was not related to any classroom social competency indices in China or Russia, it was associated with more frequent peer contacts initiated by Chinese children ($r = 0.28$, $p < 0.01$). Although not directly linked to social competency indices, child initiations in China and Russia were also associated with higher proportions of same-age children in their networks (r's = 0.38 and 0.25, p's < 0.01). This was not found to be the case in Utah. It was of interest to note that Chinese children were more likely to seek out same-age peers outside their neighbourhoods in the city ($r = 0.28$, $p < 0.01$). This was not the case in Louisiana, Russia, or Utah where more peers were available in their own neighbourhoods (see propinquity section in Table 1.3).

Involvement with same-age peers appears to be important for social development in all three cultures. Consistent with findings of Ladd *et al.* (1988), networks comprised of largely same-age companions (within 1 year) appeared to enhance children's opportunities to develop age-appropriate social skills reflected in different measures across cultures. In Utah, having more same-age peers was related to less relational aggression ($r = -0.30$, $p < 0.01$) and to less modest inhibition ($r = -0.35$, $p < 0.01$). In Russia, it was associated with less overt aggression in boys ($r = -0.26$, $p < 0.01$). In China, it was linked to more positive peer ratings ($r = 0.28$, $p < 0.01$) and to fewer negative peer nominations ($r = -0.25$, $p < 0.01$). In contrast, Chinese children with more younger peers in their networks were rated by teachers as being more anxious ($r = 0.26$, $p < 0.01$) and as being more modestly inhibited ($r = 0.25$, $p < 0.01$). Girls in Utah with more younger peers also received fewer positive sociometric nominations in the classroom ($r = -0.26$, $p < 0.05$). Similarly, Louisiana children with more younger peers received lower sociometric ratings ($r = -0.25$, $p < 0.05$).

Contact frequency and duration

Frequent peer contacts (more than once per week) and length of play contacts were associated with more positive social outcomes for children. Boys in Russia with more frequent contacts were rated by teachers as being less anxious ($r = -0.31, p < 0.01$), less reticent ($r = -0.21, p < 0.05$), and as having fewer internalizing disorders ($r = -0.23, p < 0.05$). Russian boys who spent more time together in their peer contacts were also rated by teachers as being less passive withdrawn, less modestly inhibited, and less reticent with peers (r's = −0.22, −0.21, and −0.23; p's < 0.05). Russian girls were also more accepted by peers if they spent more time together in their peer contacts ($r = 0.33, p < 0.01$).

Chinese boys with more frequent contacts were also rated by teachers as being more friendly ($r = 0.22, p < 0.05$) and more prosocial ($r = 0.21, p < 0.05$), while girls with contacts less than once per week were rated as being more passive withdrawn ($r = 0.21, p < 0.05$) and more reticent ($r = 0.23, p < 0.05$). Chinese girls who spent more time together during their play contacts were also rated by teachers as being more friendly and leadership-oriented as well as less anxious and fearful with peers (r's = 0.29, 0.35, and −0.27; p's < 0.01). In Utah, frequent contacts were associated with less teacher-rated relational aggression for boys ($r = -0.25, p < 0.01$) and with more modest inhibition for girls ($r = 0.25, p < 0.05$). Although length of contact time was not linked to social competence in Utah children, it was related to higher levels of peer acceptance for girls in Louisiana ($r = 0.29, p < 0.01$).

SUMMARY: PEER CONTACT PATTERNS AND SOCIAL COMPETENCE

Taken together, this pattern of findings is consistent with the notion that more frequent and longer exposure to peers, as well as contact with same-age companions, facilitates positive social competencies across diverse cultural contexts. However, these findings should be cautiously regarded. It may also be the case that more sociable and less inhibited and less aggressive children are those who foster more frequent peer contacts and who are more attractive to same-age peers. However, little support was obtained in the current data sets for this alternative view. None of the child peer contact initiation/fostering measures were related to any of the teacher-rated social competency indices (cf. Ladd and Hart 1992). Nor were they associated with children being the recipients of more contact initiations from playmates.

Parental management and social competence

The focus of the next set of analyses was on parental management practices. These included design and mediating functions.

Parental designing practices

The majority of significant correlations involving design functions revolved around child play locations as related to parental management (mediating variables) and children's social competence. Mirroring findings of Ladd *et al.* (1988), mothers who initiated more peer contacts saw their children as spending more time playing at playmate's homes in Utah ($r = 0.26$, $p < 0.01$) and in Russia ($r = 0.30$, $p < 0.01$). Utah children who spent more time in playmate's homes were, in turn, rated by teachers as being less relationally aggressive ($r = -0.27$, $p < 0.01$) and received higher classroom acceptance ratings ($r = 0.27$, $p < 0.01$) and fewer negative nominations from peers ($r = -0.23$, $p < 0.05$). Similar findings applied to Russian females who spent more time in playmate's homes. They received more positive nominations from peers ($r = 0.28$, $p < 0.05$).

In contrast, Chinese children who planned activities or initiated contacts on their own or who had mothers who planned, initiated, and scaffolded initiations spent more time playing with peers in their own homes (r's = 0.29, 0.27, 0.25, 0.22, 0.23; p's < 0.01). Peer interactions for children in their own homes were associated with less modest inhibition at school ($r = -0.29$, $p < 0.01$).

SUMMARY: PARENTAL DESIGNING PRACTICES

The findings for Utah and Russia are consistent with the premise that parental facilitation of peer-play in extrafamilial surroundings (e.g., families and homes of network members) may *directly* bolster children's abilities to handle the many interpersonal demands of school (Ladd *et al.* 1988).

Alternatively, the path to social competence associated with parental design functions may be *less direct* in the Chinese culture. In accordance with Chinese cultural training traditions, it appears that Chinese mothers may be prone to mediate peer contacts in ways that foster less independence from home than do their Russian or American counterparts (cf. Chao 1994). This is not surprising given that Chinese mothers are prone to encourage their young children to stay close to them (Ho 1986; Wu 1985), and are less likely to encourage independence and exploration (Lin and Fu 1990). However, Chinese mothers appeared to grant their children more autonomy (compared to US and Russian mothers) when it came to allowing them to foster, initiate, and plan their own peer activities, even though a greater proportion of the actual play interactions that ensued occurred in their own homes (Table 1.3). Although these findings might reflect Ho's (1986) description of Chinese parents being highly lenient and indulgent towards young children under age 6 years (in contrast to the strictness that they impose on older children), this may have payoffs for social skill development. As noted earlier, Chinese children's contact initiations outside of school were linked to contact with more same-age peers. Same-age peer contacts, in turn, were associated with greater acceptance by classmates at school.

Parental mediating practices facilitating social competence

For the three samples in which parental mediation practices were measured, parental fostering, initiation, and initiation scaffolding practices were unrelated to the number of playmates, frequency of contact, or child initiation measures. Nor were these variables directly related in positive ways to social competence and peer acceptance outcomes in ways found in prior research explained in the introduction (cf. Ladd and Golter 1988; Ladd and Hart 1992; Krappman 1989).

However, findings did suggest that mothers in Utah who initiated more peer contacts were more likely to have boys who planned their own activities with peers ($r = 0.21$, $p < 0.05$). Utah girls with mothers who involved them more in planning activities (planning scaffolding) were also more prone to sponsor and initiate their own peer contacts ($r = 0.30$, $p < 0.01$). Similarly, mothers in Russia who more often involved their sons in initiating contacts (initiation scaffolding) had boys who were more likely to plan their own activities with peers ($r = 0.27$, $p < 0.01$). These findings are consistent with the notion that some parental mediational involvement may facilitate children's abilities to manage their own peer relationships, at least in US and Russian cultures (e.g., Ladd and Hart 1992). However, no parallel findings were obtained in China, and may reflect the greater autonomy that Chinese mothers give their children in initiating and planning contacts.

Parental mediating practices stemming from problematic peer relations

Maternal mediating practices also appeared to stem from problematic peer relations. Although the direction of effects cannot be certain, a somewhat parallel pattern of findings emerged across cultures suggesting that mothers become more active socialization agents if their young children are less socially competent. Mothers in Utah were more likely to take it upon themselves to call and invite other children over to play if their boys were rated by teachers as being more overtly ($r = 0.27$, $p < 0.01$) or relationally aggressive ($r = -0.33$, $p < 0.01$), more externalizing ($r = 0.25$, $p < 0.01$), less modestly inhibited ($r = 0.22$, $p < 0.05$), or actively isolated by peers ($r = 0.22$, $p < 0.01$). The same applied to mothers of girls who were rated as more overtly aggressive ($r = 0.30$, $p < 0.05$) or more internalizing ($r = 0.24$, $p < 0.05$). These mothers were also more likely to involve their children in planning play activities (i.e., planning scaffolding) if their child was rated by teachers as being more overtly aggressive ($r = 0.29$, $p < 0.01$), reticent ($r = 0.30$, $p < 0.01$), less friendly ($r = -0.25$, $p < 0.05$), less leadership skilled ($r = -0.24$, $p < 0.05$) or actively isolated by peers ($r = 0.31$, $p < 0.01$). Mothers were less prone to have their children plan activities on their own if they were rated by teachers as being more solitary active ($r = 0.25$, $p < 0.05$) or, in the case of boys, as having fewer leadership skills ($r = -0.29$, $p < 0.01$).

A similar but less pervasive pattern involving significant relationships was found in China, but with different variables supporting views that Chinese parents are intolerant towards inept, disruptive, and aggressive behaviours (cf. Ho 1986). Mothers were less likely to leave it to their child to initiate play dates if they were rated by teachers as being more externalizing ($r = 0.24$, $p < 0.05$) and less co-operative with peers ($r = -0.21$, $p < 0.05$). Instead, they were more likely to initiate and sponsor their child's peer contacts themselves if their sons were perceived by teachers as being more externalizing ($r = 0.34$, $p < 0.01$) and overtly aggressive ($r = 0.24$, $p < 0.05$). Mothers also had greater tendencies to scaffold contact initiations if their sons were perceived by teachers as engaging in solitary active/passive activities ($r = 0.33$, $p < 0.01$). For daughters, Chinese mothers were more likely to take it upon themselves to invite friends over if girls were rated by their teacher as being more relationally ($r = 0.28$, $p < 0.01$) or overtly aggressive ($r = 0.23$, $p < 0.05$). They were also prone to involving their daughters in planning activities (scaffolding) if their girls were rated as being more anxious and fearful with peers ($r = 0.20$, $p < 0.05$).

Contrary to findings in the US and China, Russian mothers were more likely to take it upon themselves to invite playmates over if their sons were perceived by teachers as being more friendly ($r = 0.22$, $p < 0.05$), more prosocial ($r = 0.30$, $p < 0.01$), less modestly inhibited ($r = 0.24$, $p < 0.05$) and as possessing more leadership skills ($r = 0.21$, $p < 0.05$). However, reflecting findings in the US and China, Russian mothers were more likely to scaffold their son's contact initiations if their child was rated by teachers as being more anxious ($r = 0.30$, $p < 0.01$), passive withdrawn ($r = 0.23$, $p < 0.05$), and internalizing ($r = 0.25$, $p < 0.05$). They also tended to scaffold activity planning when their sons were rated by teachers as being more anxious ($r = 0.24$, $p < 0.05$), internalizing ($r = 0.28$, $p < 0.05$), and as having fewer leadership skills ($r = -0.21$, $p < 0.05$). Russian maternal activity planning with daughters (scaffolding) was a more frequent occurrence when daughters were rated as having more externalizing problems by teachers ($r = 0.27$, $p < 0.05$). Russian girls were also less likely to be left to themselves to plan activities if they were perceived by teachers as being more solitary active ($r = 0.20$, $p < 0.05$), more reticent ($r = 0.23$, $p < 0.05$), less friendly ($r = -0.24$, $p < 0.05$), less prosocial ($r = -0.20$, $p < 0.05$), less co-operative ($r = -0.21$, $p < 0.05$), and as possessing fewer leadership skills ($r = -0.21$, $p < 0.05$).

SUMMARY: PARENTAL MEDIATING PRACTICES

Surprisingly, with the exception of the Russian sample, little support was obtained for past research suggesting that parents are more likely to facilitate peer activities for their children during early childhood if they are perceived as being more sociable (cf. Rubin *et al.* 1989; Profilet and Ladd 1994; Prinstein 1997). However, Utah and Russian children were more likely to be involved in planning and facilitating their own peer activities if their mothers were involved in some type of mediating function.

The overall pattern of significant correlations in all three cultures indicated that mothers were more involved in the mediating role when their children were perceived by teachers as being less socially adept. One interpretation of these findings is that mothers may be attempting to provide remedial socialization opportunities for their children through their mediational practices. However, it is difficult to know for sure without taking into account maternal perceptions of whether their children had crossed a threshold of incompetence, thus simulating more parental involvement (Bell and Chapman, 1986). As demonstrated in Mize *et al.* (1995), parental mediating functions associated with positive or negative childhood behaviours may be moderated by parental perceptions of their child's behaviour and beliefs about the importance and modifiability of social skills. This is a topic for further investigation in diverse cultural contexts.

Educating/supervising practices and social competence

This final section explores relations between parental supervision practices and social competence. Most of the significant findings revolved around problematic peer relations and play locations.

Supervision interventions and problematic peer relations

Consistent with findings of Ladd and Golter (1988), Utah mothers engaged in more interactive supervision interventions when their children were perceived by teachers as being more overtly aggressive ($r = 0.23$, $p < 0.05$). Similarly, Russian mothers were more likely to intervene interactively if their children (particularly girls) were perceived to be less co-operative with peers ($r = -0.22$, $p < 0.05$), and if their daughters received more negative peer sociometric nominations ($r = 0.21$, $p < 0.05$).

In China, mothers perceived themselves as enacting more interactive interventions when their children (particularly boys) were rated by teachers as being more solitary active/passive in their play ($r = 0.28$, $p < 0.01$). It may be recalled that they were also prone to scaffold contact initiations for sons who were viewed as engaging in more solitary activities. These maternal practice associations with solitary play patterns may be a result of heightened cultural salience based on parental perceptions that autonomous and immature solitary behaviour runs counter to cultural norms that prize collective values which are facilitative of group processes (Ho 1986).

No findings emerged in this set of analyses regarding directive interventions. However, the Chinese data indicated that mothers were less present in a monitoring capacity when their children (particularly girls) were perceived by teachers as being less externalizing ($r = -0.23$, $p < 0.05$), more friendly ($r = 0.22$, $p < 0.05$), more prosocial ($r = 0.21$, $p < 0.05$), less modestly inhibited ($r = -0.21$, $p < 0.01$), more leadership oriented ($r = 0.22$, $p < 0.05$), as having more impulse control ($r = 0.21$, $p < 0.05$), and if they received fewer negative nominations from peers ($r = -0.24$, $p < 0.01$). Utah mothers were also less involved in monitoring when their children (particularly boys) were rated as being more relationally aggressive ($r = -0.21$, $p < 0.05$), perhaps because it is a less salient form of aggression.

Play location and supervision practices

Supervision and monitoring practices were also tied to play location and social competency outcomes in Russia and China, but not in Utah. Russian children who played more in the neighbourhood rather than in homes or yards were rated by teachers as having less impulse control ($r = -0.24$, $p < 0.01$), being less prosocial ($r = -0.22$, $p < 0.01$), and being more reticent ($r = 0.28$, $p < 0.01$). Children who played more in the neighbourhood were also more likely to have parents who were less likely to monitor their whereabouts and activities ($r = -0.26$, $p < 0.05$).

In contrast, although Chinese boys involved in more neighbourhood play were also rated by teachers as being more reticent ($r = 0.21$, $p < 0.05$) and less prosocial ($r = -0.22$, $p < 0.05$), mothers were more directive in their supervision as their son's levels of neighbourhood peer activity increased ($r = 0.28$, $p < 0.01$). Although not tied to any specific child behaviour, Chinese mothers were also more likely involved in directive interventions for peer-play when it occurred in their own homes ($r = 0.25$, $p < 0.05$), which, as noted earlier was more often than not.

Play location was unrelated to social competency indices in Utah, but was linked to directive interventions and monitoring practices. Utah mothers engaged in more directive interventions and monitoring relative to mothers in China and Russia (see Table 1.3). A closer examination of these findings revealed that Utah mothers were less likely to be directive in their supervision and to monitor their children's activities and whereabouts when they played in the neighbourhood (r's = -0.24 and -0.25;

p's < 0.01). However, they were more vigilant in directive supervision when their children were playing in their own homes or yards ($r = 0.24$, $p < 0.05$).

SUMMARY: PARENTAL SUPERVISION PRACTICES

As noted earlier, general patterns of findings suggested that *prior to peer-play*, mothers in all three cultures became more involved in mediating functions (e.g., initiating contacts, planning activities) when their children were rated by teachers as being less sociable, more aggressive, or more withdrawn. When actually supervising children *during peer-play*, however, interesting cultural distinctions emerged. A pattern of teacher-rated child nonaffiliation and 'conducting play by oneself' appeared to engender more *interactive* supervision on the part of Chinese mothers, perhaps as a means of encouraging more social involvement with playmates during play. However, due to the limited nature of our data gathering techniques, little is known about the educational content of these interactive interventions (cf. Russell and Finnie 1990; Mize *et al.* 1995).

Less affiliative behaviour on the part of boys may be particularly salient to Chinese mothers, since this runs counter to collectivistic notions of maintaining social order and interpersonal harmony (King and Bond 1985). More specifically, Chinese children are encouraged to develop a collectivistic ideology through participating in organized group activities in a facilitative and co-operative manner (Chen, in press). In line with these cultural expectations, Chinese children who did not support these collective values by being actively involved with peers in the classroom appeared to have mothers who were more concerned, as reflected in their interactive supervision practices during nonschool, peer-play interactions.

The lack of similar parental interactive interventions for withdrawn behaviour in the other two cultures may reflect a diminishing of collectivist values that were once more the norm in Russia (Hart *et al.* 1998a), and may represent more individualistic values in the Utah, Western culture. However, in support of past research (Ladd *et al.* 1988; Prinstein 1997), teacher-rated aggressive behaviour appeared to heighten Utah mothers' interactive involvement with their children. Similarly, less co-operative behaviour and peer rejection engendered more interactive interventions for Russian mothers on behalf of their daughters during nonschool peer-play.

In contrast to interactive interventions, *directive* supervision and *monitoring* practices were more tied to behaviours that occurred in specific play locations. Children who played more in Chinese neighbourhoods (boys only) and Russian neighbourhoods (boys and girls) were rated by teachers as being more reticent and less prosocial. As the reticent construct would suggest, this may reflect a pattern of more unoccupied and aimless patterns of wandering that teachers seemed to be noticing at school, which may be carried over into home/neighbourhood based behaviours as well. Of course, this assumes that some children may be spending more time in reticent behaviour than actively playing when engaged in neighbourhood contacts with peers (data that we don't have). For reasons just noted, however, such behaviour appears to engender heightened concern for Chinese mothers, as reflected in their higher levels of direct input and oversight during neighbourhood play interactions on behalf of these children that was not apparent in Russia.

Utah findings suggesting that mothers used less direct supervision and monitoring during neighbourhood play may reflect the relative perception of safety in Utah neighbourhoods (see Table 1.1). The fact that they were also more actively involved in supervising home or yard play could be a reflection of proportionally less play in Utah neighbourhoods as compared to more play in homes or yards (see Table 1.3). Less neighbourhood play in Utah relative to Russia and China shown in Table 1.3 may be a function of larger yards and play spaces associated with homes located in suburban areas. These settings are quite different from the high-rise apartment living that is more common in Beijing, China and Voronezh, Russia, or in any other large metropolitan area of the world, for that matter.

Finally, parenting practice findings reported here support two divergent views of Chinese parenting. More directive interventions in home peer-play and more monitoring oversight in neighbourhood play for Chinese children with less affiliative behavioural orientations support the view that Chinese mothers are more controlling and protective (Kriger and Kroes 1972; Lin and Fu 1990). Alternatively, findings displayed in Table 1.3 indicate that Chinese mothers are less likely than Russian and US mothers to use directive interventions during peer-play overall, and allow more autonomy in child contact fostering, initiation, and planning. This supports the notion that Chinese parents may be more lenient in their parent–child interactions with children under 6 years of age (Ho 1986). One task of future research would be to delineate the contextual domains of parent–child interaction in which these seemingly opposing views of Chinese parenting occur.

General conclusions

Although the exploratory findings associated with peer contact patterns and parenting practices described above are limited to maternal perceptions (cf. Ladd *et al.* 1988), and may be prone to type 1 error due to the many correlations run, the pattern of results paints a relatively coherent picture of similarities and differences across cultural contexts. This should set the stage for hypothesis driven studies that more closely examine the insights gleaned from this investigation. In order to be more certain about the validity of these cross-cultural findings, future research could improve upon the current methodology by utilizing multiple agent, multiple methods, and multiple construct approaches recommended by French *et al.* (in press) for comparisons between cultures. Doing so will help move us further beyond the edge of the frontier in our understanding of peer contact patterns, parenting practices, and children's social competence in diverse cultural contexts.

Given space limitations, we refer readers back to the summaries within the results section for specific findings and interpretations. In broad strokes, it appears that there are many similarities regarding peer group age and sex compositions, contact durations, less mediational involvement of parents for older preschoolers, and heightened parental mediational and supervisory involvement associated with childhood behavioural difficulties in these diverse locations. Frequent associations with same-age peers also appeared to facilitate positive social competencies in all cultural contexts. However, a multitude of cultural nuances stemming from governmental policy (e.g., one-child families in China), cultural norms (e.g., family size, individualistic versus collectivistic norms; maternal closeness versus autonomy), and neighbourhood features (e.g., perceived safety) were also apparent in the data (cf. Edwards 1992; Krappman 1996). These were linked in different ways to cultural variations involving peer contacts with cousins versus friends, to play location preferences, to same-age playmate availability, and to parenting practices with regard to peer contact initiation and supervision functions in different cultures.

In support of our introductory remarks for this chapter, these exploratory findings support the notion that parenting practices may vary across different ecologies, given the different goals representing cultural norms towards which children are socialized (Darling and Steinberg 1993). We also found many similarities. Thus, both etic and emic cultural perspectives were reflected in our data (Berry 1989). In sum, the data gathered from China, Russia and the United States are supportive of both universal and cultural variations in peer contact patterns and parenting practices across diverse cultural contexts for older preschool-age children.

Note

The authors express gratitude to the Center for Studies of the Family, the Kennedy Center for International Studies, the Camilla Eyring Kimball Endowment, and the College of Family, Home, and Social Sciences at Brigham Young University for financial support of this work.

Chapter 2

Further explorations of family–peer connections

The role of parenting practices and parenting style in children's development of social competence

Jacquelyn Mize, Alan Russell and Gregory S. Pettit[1]

Over the past decade, two major research themes in child development – children's peer relationships and parent–child relationships – have converged to become a fertile ground for research and theory. Among the catalysts for the study of linkages between parent–child relationships and children's peer relationships is evidence that individual differences in children's interactions with peers are apparent and somewhat stable even among toddlers (Howes 1988), and that by preschool there are clear differences among children in their peer interaction patterns and the degree to which they are liked by peers (e.g., Mize and Ladd 1990). In light of the early emergence of stable individual differences in children's peer interaction skills, researchers have reasoned that experiences in the family must be important in shaping nascent social competencies. The fact that the extent and quality of children's early peer relationships are associated with current and future indices of adjustment (Ladd and Kochenderfer 1996) makes the study of family–peer system linkages relevant for clinicians and educators, as well as for researchers. In this chapter we provide a framework for considering how two aspects of parenting may influence young children's peer relationship competence and we review research related to the two modes of influence that we propose. In order to provide some context for this discussion we first briefly summarize some of the research on the developmental significance of young children's peer relationships.

The emergence and significance of young children's peer relationships

Over the past two decades, researchers have made considerable progress in describing the emergence of peer relationships in the toddler and preschool years. A few examples of findings from this body of research provide evidence of the significance of young children's peer relationships.

Given the continued opportunity for interaction, toddler friendships are stable over several years. In one study, 80 per cent of toddlers who continued to attend the same centre maintained friendships for three years (Howes and Phillipsen 1992), and these early, stable friendships appear to provide the best arena for the development of early social skills (Howes 1983). Although developmental changes occur in the complexity and sophistication of children's play and problem-solving skills from toddlerhood to preschool, individual differences in children's success in entering peer groups, aggression, and the ability to engage in elaborate interaction sequences are fairly stable. These differences among young children's peer interaction styles have critical implications for their adjustment, both in preschool and during the transition to primary school.

By preschool, even casual observation of a group of young children reveals a great deal of diversity in children's styles of relating to peers. The most socially skilled preschoolers – that is, those who are well-liked by peers and whom teachers agree are competent – engage in elaborate co-operative play that they and their peers find fun and exciting (Gottman 1983). They tend to 'fit in', and tend to be positive and responsive toward peers, rather than aggressive or disruptive (Hazen and Black 1989; Mize 1995). Even when problems arise, they usually are able to manage their emotions (Gottman *et al.* 1996), and often can resolve disagreements constructively (Gottman 1983). Less competent preschoolers (i.e., those who are less well-liked by peers and whom teachers judge to be less competent) often have problems with one or more of the domains of behaviour described above; for instance, they may misread social situations and so intrude inappropriately in peers' play or engage in disjointed, nonsynchronous exchanges (Dodge *et al.* 1990); they may engage in high levels of aggressive behaviour (Dodge *et al.* 1990), or they may spend their time watching, rather than interacting with, their classmates (Rubin *et al.* 1990). Preschool children's behavioural style with peers is associated with both their current and subsequent peer and school adjustment, e.g., liking of school (Ladd and Kochenderfer 1996).

In a series of longitudinal studies, it was found that children's initial adjustment to kindergarten (the first year of public school in the US) was predicted by both the number and quality of friendships (Ladd 1990). Children who maintained their friendships developed more positive attitudes toward school over the course of the year. Children who developed new friendships with classmates in their first year of school also benefited from these relationships in that their academic performance improved. Furthermore, children whose friendships were conflictual became less involved in and more avoidant of school over the course of the school year, and were less happy and more lonely while at school (Ladd *et al.* 1996). Ladd suggests (Ladd and Kochenderfer 1996) that peer relationships in early childhood function as either supports or stressors, depending on whether or not they foster competence and feelings of worth, security, and belongingness. Young children who are unable to form rewarding relationships are often excluded from the peer culture and the opportunity to learn social norms and social skills. Positive peer relationships, especially those with friends and consistent playmates, are a key developmental context and provide young children with instrumental support (e.g., help with school tasks), opportunities to learn and practise increasingly complex social skills, intimacy and emotional support, and satisfying interactions.

Parenting influences on young children's peer relationships

Given the importance of peers in young children's development, it is understandable that researchers, clinicians, parents and teachers are concerned about what factors influence early peer relationships. Research and theory have focused on three broad classes of influences on young children's interaction styles with peers: constitutional factors such as affective responsivity (e.g., Fox *et al.* 1995), experiences with peers or siblings (e.g., Howes 1988; Sinclair *et al.* 1994), and parenting. Ample empirical evidence suggests that each type of factor is associated with children's social competence and relationships, but the largest body of research addresses parenting correlates of children's peer acceptance and behavioural styles. Although our focus in this chapter is on parenting influences we recognize that temperament and experiences with agemates also play powerful roles in children's peer relationships, and may, in fact, interact with parenting in complex ways.

Much of the extensive literature on parenting and young children's social competence is concerned with parenting styles, as reflected in affective aspects of parenting, discipline patterns, and overall qualities of parent–child interaction. Findings from this large body of research suggest that parents who are affectively positive, warm and responsive, who set firm limits that are enforced rationally, especially through the use of reasoning, and who avoid coercion and other forms of harsh discipline produce children who are socially competent (see Cohn *et al.* 1991).

A few recent studies will serve as illustrations of the findings about the role of parenting style in children's social competence. Martha Putallaz (1987) observed first-graders and their mothers as they played a game; mothers of more popular children were more agreeable and less demanding than mothers of less popular children. In their interactions with peers, children's behaviour mirrored that of their mothers: more competent children were positive, whereas less competent children were more disagreeable. A large number of studies link harsh or power-assertive discipline to lower social competence. For instance, Weiss *et al.* (1992) found that harsh parental discipline was associated with higher rates of aggression toward peers in kindergarten. Similarly, Hart *et al.* (1992) report that parents who are power assertive in disciplinary encounters tend to have aggressive and/or unpopular preschool children, whereas parents who use inductive methods are more likely to have prosocial and popular children.

Recently, some researchers have focused on parent–child dyadic interaction style as a predictor of children's social competence. The premise here is that the quality of parent–child interaction reflects the history of the relationship and also provides children with an opportunity to learn and practice behaviour patterns and ways of relating to others that may generalize to peer relationships. Dishion (1990) suggests, for instance, that participation in aversive, disorganized interactions with parents teaches children to use aversive patterns as a way of gaining some control over others, including peers. A powerful construct that has emerged from efforts to describe the dyadic qualities of parent–child interaction is that of interactional synchrony (Isabella and Belsky 1991; Mize and Pettit 1997; Pettit and Harrist 1993; Pettit and Mize 1993). Interactional synchrony can be thought of as the extent to which dyad members' behaviours are positive, reciprocal, and mutually responsive (Mize and Pettit 1997). Although synchrony is dyadic in that it reflects the fit or meshing of the partners' behaviours, most researchers assume that it reflects a history of parental positive responsiveness (Isabella and Belsky 1991; Rocissano *et al.* 1987).

Overall, in examining the link between parenting and children's behaviour problems, it appears that parent–child interactional synchrony is among the best predictors of child adjustment. Interactional synchrony is associated with more secure mother–child attachment relationships (Isabella and Belsky 1991), with children's more willing compliance to mothers' requests (Rocissano *et al.* 1987), and with preschool children's competence in relating to peers both concurrently (Mize and Pettit 1997) and later in kindergarten (Harrist *et al.* 1994). It is possible that positive, mutually responsive or synchronous interactions between parent and child provide the child with opportunities to learn and practise effective interaction skills, such as attention to social cues, turn-taking, and responsiveness (Harrist *et al.* 1994; Mize and Pettit 1997; Pettit and Mize 1993). In subsequent sections interactional synchrony will be examined further as a correlate of children's peer competence, with special emphasis on its role in parent–child play.

Although positive parenting style clearly is linked to children's social competence, it is doubtful that most parents intentionally set out to foster their children's peer relationship skills when they respond warmly or discuss issues rationally. Many parents, however, do undertake actions that specifically are designed to foster their children's peer relationships or their social skills. For instance, parents may arrange play dates or enrol children in playgroup or preschool in order to ensure that they get to experience peer interaction in a supervised setting (Ladd *et al.* 1992), or they may coach children about relationships by talking or problem-solving about peer dilemmas and interaction (Mize and Pettit 1997). Explicit efforts to encourage the development of a particular set of skills have been referred to as parenting practices (Darling and Steinberg 1993; Mize and Pettit 1997).[2]

Although researchers only recently have begun to delineate those parenting practices that might be most closely associated with children's social development, there is accumulating evidence that many of these practices 'pay off' in terms of greater social competence for young children. Several studies in which parents have described their involvement provide evidence that parents do engage in practices that promote peer relationships and that these practices often have the intended effect. Ladd and Golter (1988) found that preschool children whose parents said that they arranged more play contacts had more playmates and a greater number of consistent playmates than did children of parents who were less involved. Not only does orchestrating contacts with agemates seem to facilitate the development of peer relationship skills, but parent–child discussions of peer issues appear to be beneficial as well. In a study in which parents of kindergarteners were interviewed on several occasions by phone, children whose parents more often discussed peer relationship issues at home were found to be better liked by peers and more socially skilled at school than were their classmates whose parents engaged in fewer such conversations (Laird *et al.* 1994).

In the following sections we highlight specific aspects of parenting style and practices that are associated with young children's competence with peers. Within the parenting style section we will discuss in greater detail one important context in which stylistic features of parent–child relationships may be particularly relevant for children's emerging social skills – that of parent–child play. We then will consider a context in which parenting practice may be instrumental in children's social skill development – social and emotional 'coaching'. In both of these sections, we also will speculate on why certain parenting behaviours may function to increase children's competence. That is, we will address the question of mediating mechanisms: what exactly do children learn when parents are responsive or when they give advice about peer relationships?

Parenting style as an influence on children's peer relationships: the case of synchrony during parent–child play

We already have mentioned the significant role that parenting style, and especially the nature of the parent–child relationship as reflected in dyadic synchrony, serves in children's development of competence. Although the quality of parent–child interaction across a range of contexts (e.g., caretaking, comforting, discipline) likely has implications for children's social adaptation, some researchers have suggested that the style of interaction during parent–child play may have special significance for young children's developing peer competence. Part of the impetus for considering parent–child play as a key socializing context is the widespread acceptance of the importance of play as a critical element in children's development. Students of child development long have recognized that play is a vehicle for cognitive and social development (Rubin *et al.* 1983). Increases in play sophistication parallel the growth of competence in other areas such as symbolic and communicative skills, knowledge of cultural patterns, and peer interaction abilities (Ugiris and Raeff 1995). Moreover, for preschool children, it is their play with peers, more than their behaviour in any other context, that defines their social competence in relationships with agemates. Socially successful preschool children are adept at negotiating play themes, they have interesting play ideas, and they are positive and responsive to their peers' ideas (Hazen and Black 1989; Mize 1995).

Some researchers have suggested that during parent–child play, especially physical play, children learn (or fail to learn) skills in emotion recognition and emotion regulation (e.g., MacDonald 1987; MacDonald and Parke 1984). Others have suggested that during parent–child play children may develop templates for playful interaction with peers (Lindsey *et al.* 1997). The first hypothesis, that parent–child play provides a context in which children can learn and practise emotion understanding and emotion regulation, has been explored by Parke and MacDonald and their colleagues. In the first study, MacDonald and Parke (1984) observed preschool children playing at home with their mothers and with their fathers. Parents were asked to play physically if this was something they normally did. Popular children and their parents engaged in more physical play than did dyads involving less popular children. Dyads containing a less competent child were less engaged and less positive. In a replication and extension of this study, but this time using only boys as subjects, MacDonald (1987) again found that popular children engaged in more physical play and expressed more positive emotion during play with their parents than did rejected children. Also, parents of rejected children tended to be more directive. MacDonald described the play sessions of rejected children and their parents as being characterized by more overstimulation and avoidance of stimulation than that of popular children. That is, rejected children were more likely to get overexcited, become upset, and then withdraw. These researchers suggest that the ability or inability to regulate affect during parent–child play may transfer to peer interaction contexts, but they did not directly test the link between quality of parent–child play and children's emotion regulation. However, one recent study found that 2-year-olds who engaged in more reciprocal joint attention during play with their mothers were better able to regulate their emotions, as assessed by children's strategies for distracting themselves during a delay of gratification task (Raver 1996).

Lindsey *et al.* (1997) propose an alternative mechanism for links between parent–child play and children's social competence with peers. They suggest that when the play style of young children and their parents is synchronous and mutually responsive, children learn skills in initiating play ideas, in attending to the play partner, and in responding to partners' initiations, skills that are essential for success in play with peers (see also Mize 1995). These researchers observed preschool children playing with their mothers and with their fathers in a laboratory playroom. Some parent–child dyads were quite balanced in the extent to which they complied with one another's play suggestions; the play of these dyads resembled that of two peers, or equals. More balanced dyads also were rated as being higher in interactional synchrony. Other dyads were less balanced. In many unbalanced dyads the parent issued a great many directives and the child usually did as the parent suggested. In other less-balanced dyads the parents complied with children's suggestions but offered few of their own. Children from more mutually balanced and synchronous dyads were judged to be more socially competent by teachers and were better liked by their classroom peers. Thus, children in parent–child dyads in which both partners were fairly equally engaged in propelling the play forward and each was responsive to the other's suggestions were more competent with peers. Lindsey *et al.* (1997) suggest that during mutually balanced and responsive parent–child play, children may learn to expect that social partners will be responsive to their ideas. So children develop confidence and skill in offering new ideas, and they practise attending to and being responsive to social partners as well.

It is possible, or course, that more socially competent preschoolers are able to establish mutually responsive patterns of play with both parents and with their peers, and that this accounts for the association between parenting and children's peer competence. Resolving questions of direction of effect will require longitudinal designs in which early patterns of parent–child play are used to predict subsequent peer interaction style and/or interventions in which parents are taught to play in responsive ways with children, and the consequences for children's peer relationships are then observed.

Parenting practices that facilitate children's peer relationships: the case of coaching

We define social coaching as providing information and feedback to children about relationships. This definition is consistent with the use of the term in the social skills coaching research (e.g., Mize and Ladd 1990). Evidence from several lines of research suggests that it may be especially useful to consider not just whether parents talk to children about relationships, but what 'substance' or messages parents convey to children during their relationship-related discussions. This issue was examined in a pair of studies conducted with Australian children and their mothers (Finnie and Russell 1988; Russell and Finnie 1990). In the first study (Finnie and Russell 1988), mothers of preschoolers were asked to help their children enter a dyad of children who already were engaged in playing together. Mothers of children who were well-liked by their classroom peers (and thus, presumably highly socially skilled) tended to actively and skilfully involve themselves in helping their children join the dyad, by, for instance, making statements about what the other children were doing and encouraging the child to fit in with the ongoing play. The mothers of children who were not well-liked by their classroom peers tended to avoid giving advice or otherwise assisting their children, but the advice they did offer was less skilful and more disruptive. In a later study (Russell and Finnie 1990), the researchers again asked mothers to help their preschool children enter into play with a pair of unfamiliar children, but this time the mother was given a five-minute period to instruct her child prior to trying to enter the play of the dyad. Mothers of children who were well-liked by their classmates often made relevant, group-oriented statements, both during the initial instruction period and during the entry attempt itself. Mothers of children who were not well-liked were more often disruptive of the play, doing things such as taking charge of the activity.

It is noteworthy that the behaviour and advice of the mothers of well-liked children mirror the behaviour that socially skilled preschoolers use during peer-play. Observational studies of preschool and kindergarten children suggest that when well-liked, socially skilful children attempt to enter the play of other children they try to sensitively 'fit in' rather than disrupt play. For instance, they may ask questions about the play, make positive comments about the play, or they may take on a role that enhances the play (Hazen and Black 1989; Mize 1995; Putallaz 1983). Less socially successful children, on the other hand, may immediately try to take charge or change the course of play, or they may make irrelevant statements, such as talking about themselves (Putallaz 1983). Behaving in ways that are relevant to peers' interests obviously requires attention to what other children are doing and some awareness of human nature, albeit at an elementary level. The studies by Russell *et al.* suggest that perhaps parents of children who are socially successful model and instruct their young children in these important lessons about initiating relationships.

In addition to learning strategies for initiating relationships and negotiating other social situations, children also must learn how to read emotional signals and how to regulate and convey their own emotions.

According to Thompson (1994), emotion regulation consists of monitoring, evaluating and modifying emotional reactions in pursuit of one's goals. Regulating emotion involves experiencing emotions appropriate to the context (e.g., sympathy when another is hurt; guilt when you have harmed another), managing the appropriate expression of emotion, modulating or amplifying emotion depending on circumstances (e.g., calming your own excitement when you need to concentrate), and understanding the emotions of self and others (Cole *et al.* 1994). Because it is critical to adaptive functioning, the development of children's emotion regulation ability is of intense concern to researchers and clinicians.

Scholars who study emotions believe that it is largely within the parent–child relationship that children learn about the importance of emotion regulation for attaining goals (Cassidy 1994; Thompson 1994). Many of the messages children receive from parents about emotions are inadvertent or unintentional, and might be thought of as a by-product of parenting style. By the time a child can understand parents' intentional communication he or she already has acquired a rudimentary understanding of emotion and some skills in emotion regulation as a result of development and through interactions with parents (Cassidy 1994). Although the child learns powerful lessons about emotion by observing how his or her parents express affect or suppress emotional displays, and from parents' sensitive or insensitive responding, here we are concerned primarily with parents' intentional communications about emotions as an aspect of coaching.

Several research programmes have focused on understanding how parent–child communication about emotion can enhance children's understanding of, and ability to regulate, affect (Denham *et al.* 1994; Dunn *et al.* 1991; Eisenberg *et al.* 1992; Gottman *et al.* 1996). Findings from this research suggest that there is considerable variation in how, and how much, parents talk to children about emotions; moreover, these discussions appear to influence children's emotion understanding and regulation abilities. A series of studies conducted by Dunn and her colleagues has provided extensive documentation regarding parents' roles as 'emotion coaches' and faciltators. In a study of British families, Dunn *et al.* (1991) observed 3-year-old children and their mothers and siblings at home as they talked about feelings. In some families this sort of 'emotion talk' occurred rarely, whereas in other families it was quite frequent. Parents who talked often about emotions were not lecturing their children; rather, they were commenting on or explaining events or guiding children's behaviour by reference to emotions in the course of normal family interactions such as arguments, discipline, discussion, or play. Children from families in which talk about feelings was a frequent event showed better understanding of the affective perspective of others at age 6 years. Similar results have been obtained by researchers working in the

United States (e.g., Denham *et al.* 1994; Eisenberg *et al.* 1992). The importance of affective perspective-taking is highlighted by the fact that children who can better understand others' emotions respond more sympathetically and prosocially to others' distress (Eisenberg 1986).

Gottman *et al.* (1996) have asserted that parents' coaching about emotion not only teaches children to recognize and understand emotion but also affects children's ability to calm themselves. These researchers found that children of parents who reported during an interview that they engaged in what Gottman terms 'emotion coaching' when their children were 5 years old (e.g., talking about a situation and the emotion when the child is upset, educating the child about the nature of emotion, teaching the child how to sooth him/herself) behaved in socially competent ways at age 8 years. Gottman suggests that children whose parents engage in emotion coaching become more aware of their own emotions, and can regulate their feelings and behaviour when they are upset. These emotionally skilled children can marshal their resources to attend to important aspects of the social situation (rather than becoming too upset or excited), and so they can behave more appropriately.

The joint effects of style and practice: do they make unique contributions?

One important question that has arisen about parenting style and practices is how they might work together or separately to influence children's development. Is it the case, for instance, that a responsive style and practices that promote a specific domain of development are simply reflections of good, or competent, parenting? If this were the case, one would expect to find that parents who are responsive also tend to engage in facilitative practices. Or are responsive style and practices really independent, such that some parents engage in one but not the other, some parents do neither, and other parents do both? If so, are children whose parents are *both* responsive *and* engage in facilitative practices better off (in terms of their acquisition of social skills) than are children whose parents do one or the other but not both? What about children whose parents engage in competence promoting practices (for instance, they encourage children to share and take turns), but their own relationship with the child is not very warm or mutually responsive? Does the nonoptimal relationship style negate the positive message? Only one research programme has addressed the question of how parenting style and parenting practices work together to influence children's peer relationship skills.

A pair of studies conducted in the US by Mize and Pettit address this question and also further illuminate the lessons parents convey in their coaching, both in regard to emotion-laden situations and in regard to strategies for handling peer interaction situations (Mize and Pettit 1997). In both of these studies mothers and their preschool children were first observed playing together with a set of toys in order to assess parent–child interaction style, including interactional synchrony (some of these mothers were the same mothers in the Lindsey *et al.* 1997 study). The mothers and their children then watched a set of videotaped vignettes depicting peer interaction situations. Mothers were to pretend that their children were the protagonists in each story and to talk to the child about how to handle the situation.

In the first study, the protagonists in each vignette were victims of some sort of negative action by a peer (e.g., a peer knocks over a child's toys). The researchers coded videotapes of the mother-child discussions about the peer interaction dilemmas for the content of coaching, operationalized as whether the mother endorsed prosocial strategies for handling the situation, and whether the mother 'framed' the conflict in a positive way. Mothers who used positive framing tried to depict the situation in as positive a light as possible, for instance by attributing non-hostile intentions to the peers and/or by encouraging a resilient, 'bounce-back' attitude for children to adopt. The measures of constructive coaching and responsive style were relatively independent; that is, a mother who engaged in highly responsive play with her child did not necessarily engage in highly constructive coaching. However, both synchronous parent–child interaction style and constructive coaching content were associated with higher levels of children's social competence with classroom peers.

The second study was similar to the first, except that videotapes depicting a wide range of peer interaction situations were used (e.g., a child in need of help, a child who was new to school, and conflict situations). As before, the mother-child conversations about the vignettes were coded for mothers' endorsement of prosocial strategies, but because positive interpretation of negative events was a less salient issue than it had been in the first study, the researchers coded mothers' elaboration, or the extent to which they engaged in problem-solving about the situation. Consistent with the results of the first study, responsive style and constructive coaching were not significantly correlated, but each was significantly related to measures of children's social competence. In follow-up analyses, using the two samples combined, interactional synchrony and constructive coaching were found to additively and uniquely contribute to the prediction of competent functioning in the peer group, as defined by high levels of peer acceptance and social skills and low levels of aggressiveness.

The Mize and Pettit (1997) studies are the only ones to date to address the question of whether positive parenting style and practices that promote children's peer relationship competence are really reflections of a single dimension of 'good' parenting or whether they are, in fact, separate dimensions of parenting. The findings suggest that parenting style does not necessarily covary with parenting practices, and that both style and practice, at least as operationalized as interactional synchrony and constructive coaching, make independent contributions to children's social competence.

Further issues related to parenting style and practices

In some ways, the distinction we (and others) have drawn between parenting style and parenting practice is an artificial one. After all, all parenting practices are delivered with some style. For instance, a parent may angrily explain that a child is never to hit a peer (perhaps even spanking the child for hitting), the parent may express concern and support while telling a child not to hit, or a parent may convey the 'don't hit' message with so little emotion that it has little impact. In addition, categorizing one set of behaviours as reflecting parenting style and another set as reflecting parenting practices can seem arbitrary. Many features of parenting behaviour that we might consider stylistic are, in fact, undertaken with specific goals in mind. To what extent is sending a child to time-out (usually considered a reflection of discipline style) as a way of expressing displeasure at the child's taking a peer's toy, an explicit message or just a stylistic feature? Thus, closer scrutiny of the style versus practice distinction reveals that the dichotomy may be more illusory than it at first appears. None the less, the style versus practice notion has provided a useful heuristic, especially for encouraging researchers to think about how different aspects of parenting may make unique or overlapping contributions to children's development.

Implications for intervention

Evidence that questions about young children's peer relationships are of concern to parents can be found in a few quick glances through the table of contents of magazines and journals aimed at members of these audiences (e.g., van der Meer 1996). To our knowledge, however, there are no parent education programmes designed specifically to help parents whose children are experiencing peer relationship difficulties, although behaviour management programmes for oppositional children or children with conduct problems are viewed as benefiting these children's peer relationships. In this section, we will address implications of the research findings we have presented for parent education and intervention programmes.

Findings that parents of socially competent preschool children engage their children in discussions about peer relationships have rather straightforward and obvious implications for parent interventions. Parents could be encouraged to problem-solve about peer relationship issues when children describe peer-related events or express peer-related concerns. Parents should be encouraged to view their role as one of facilitating constructive problem-solving and thinking about relationships, rather than one of providing answers or solutions to children's problems. The research evidence reviewed previously suggests that it may be important to accept and discuss emotions, to encourage children to interpret others' behaviour in positive ways, to consider alternative strategies and their consequences, and to endorse more prosocial options (Mize and Abell 1996).

There also are implications of findings linking synchronous, mutually responsive parent–child interaction during play with children's peer competence. Recently, several behaviour management programmes, which traditionally have relied on reinforcement paradigms to reduce children's aggressive and oppositional behaviour (McMahon and Forehand 1984; Patterson 1986), have begun incorporating components to train parents to be responsive during parent–child play (Cavell in preparation; Wahler and Bellamy 1997). Recent inclusions of parent responsiveness training in treatment programmes stem from recognition that healthy families are characterized by a system of positive reciprocity or synchrony (Cavell in preparation; Wahler and Bellamy 1997). Some interventions employ responsive parent play as the primary component (e.g., Guerney and Guerney 1987), whereas others use responsive play as one component of several (e.g., Cavell in preparation; Wahler and Bellamy 1997). In responsive play training, parents are taught to follow the child's lead during play, to reflect the child's activities and feelings, and in general, to avoid controlling children's behaviour through commands, disapproval, or approval (although there are differences among programmes in the extent to which the parent is allowed, or encouraged, to offer suggestions when he/she perceives the child needs it). So far, empirical support for the effectiveness of parent responsive play training is limited (Cavell in preparation). However, one recent study found evidence that responsive parent training increased the compliance of school-age boys with conduct problems (Wahler and Bellamy 1997).

Additional evidence for the importance of parent–child play style comes from an experimental study in which Parpal and Maccoby (1985) taught some mothers to play with their preschoolers in a responsive manner. Children of these mothers were subsequently more compliant to mothers' requests to clean up the playroom than were children of mothers who played in their normal fashion. Parpal and Maccoby suggest that maternal responsiveness established a system of mutual co-operation that made children more willing to be socialized. Thus, responsive or synchronous parent play offers a potentially powerful technique for increasing children's peer relationship competence. Not only is parent–child interactional synchrony during play associated with preschool children's social competence, there is evidence that parent responsive play may increase children's overall co-operativeness and compliance. We believe that parent–child mutual responsiveness inculcates children into a relationship based on mutual co-operation (Maccoby 1992) and helps them learn skills essential for forming positive, satisfying relationships with peers (Lindsey *et al.* 1997).

Conclusions

Current evidence suggests that synchronous, mutually balanced and responsive parent–child play style and parental coaching about peer relationships both contribute to children's competence in the peer group. As yet, however, there is little empirical evidence about how these two distinct aspects of positive parenting operate to increase children's competence. It is possible that synchronous parent–child play provides children with a context for practising skills that are critical in peer interaction – skills such as attending and responding positively to others' suggestions, reading emotional cues, and offering ideas that fit with the play theme. Synchronous play also may give children confidence in their abilities as a play partner. That is, success in playing with a parent as an equal (i.e., in a 'peer-like' way; Russell *et al.* in press), may help prepare children for successful play with their true equals. Parental coaching may help children learn to attend carefully to important social cues, to construe social situations positively, to understand others' feelings, to regulate their emotions, and to engage in problem-solving when they encounter difficulties. Further illumination of the processes through which synchronous parent–child play and parent coaching about social skills influence children's competence will require studies in which children's social information processing, emotional competencies, and behaviour style with peers are examined in conjunction with multiple modes of parental influence.

Notes

1 Preparation of this chapter was supported by a grant to the first and third authors from the Agricultural Experiment Station (10-004).

2 In discussing parenting effects on children's peer relationships, Ross Parke uses the term 'indirect' to refer to coincidental influences such as parenting style, attachment and spousal relationships, and the term 'direct' to refer to intentional influences such as coaching and management (i.e., what we call practices).

Part II

Gender and ethnicity

Chapter 3

Gender and bullying in schools

Ken Rigby

Introduction

Most of the early work on bullying in schools was concerned with boys as bullies and boys as victims. Girls were mainly ignored. This was partly because bullying was conceived as mainly physical, and partly because public interest in bullying which developed in England in the mid-nineteenth century focused upon bullying at boys' private boarding schools such as Rugby and Eton. The nature of such bullying was captured in *Tom Brown's School Days*, a novel written in 1856 by an English lawyer, Thomas Hughes, who drew upon his own experiences as a schoolboy at Rugby. The villain of the story is Flashman, a 17-year-old bully who, together with his cronies, engaged in bullying younger students at the school, including Tom Brown. The bullying was commonly physical; for instance, Tom was held by other boys close to a fire until he was badly scorched. He was also ritually tossed in a blanket, the aim of this cruel exercise being to cause the victim to rise ever higher until he crashed painfully against the ceiling.

Yet despite this, it would not be true to say that bullying was conceived at this time entirely as victimization by physical means. We read in Thomas Hughes's novel that

> Flashman was adept in all ways, but above all in the power of saying cutting and cruel things, and could often bring tears to the eyes of boys in this way, which all the thrashings in the world wouldn't have wrung from them.
>
> (Hughes [1856] 1968: 142)

And again:

> Flashman left no slander unspoken and no deed undone, which could in any way hurt his victims and isolate them from the rest of the house.
>
> (Hughes [1856] 1968: 143)

Thus although the early emphasis was on boys and physical bullying, already in nineteenth-century England the concept of bullying had accommodated verbal and indirect forms of bullying too, and in due course these aspects were to be seen as equally applicable to girls.

Nevertheless, interest continued to focus on problems of peer abuse involving boys. In Sweden, Peter-Paul Heinnemann (1972) popularized the term 'mobbing' (borrowed from Lorenz 1965) to describe collective violence against individual children at school, perpetrated by boys on boys. Subsequently when his compatriot, Dan Olweus began a more systematic and rigorous study of bullying, the term 'mobbing' was abandoned; Olweus recognized that a great deal of peer abuse was conducted by individuals, not groups. But the very title of his highly influential book, published in 1978, *Aggression in Schools: Bullies and Whipping Boys*, shows that the bias in favour of studies of boys remained. It is only in the last few years that researchers (including Olweus) have begun to pay equal attention to boys and girls involved in bully/victim problems.

In this chapter, I shall briefly review contributions to the question of whether boys and girls are bullied equally by their peers in schools and whether, as has been claimed, the nature of the bullying they experience is different. In addition, I shall consider several further issues as yet barely touched upon in the research literature – namely, whether there are significant differences in the reactions of boys and girls to being bullied; whether boys and girls are differently motivated to engage in bullying; and finally whether boys and girls differ in what they are prepared to do to counter peer abuse in schools. In examining these questions I shall present some results from recent studies involving boys and girls in Australian schools.

Are boys and girls equally bullied?

Large scale surveys by Olweus involving more than 40,000 boys and 40,000 girls in Norwegian schools led to the conclusion that 'there is a trend for boys to be bullied more often than girls' (1993a: 15). Defining bullying as occurring 'when a person is exposed repeatedly and over time, to negative actions on the part of one or more persons', Olweus found that for every grade, from grade two to nine, more boys than girls reported that they were bullied 'now and then'. The gender differences between the older students were quite large with more than twice as many boys as girls reporting being bullied in grades seven to nine. Similar findings on sex differences were reported by O'Moore and Hillery (1991) in their study of bullying in schools in Dublin, Ireland.

However, survey research undertaken in England by Peter Smith and his associates at the University of Sheffield has led to a different conclusion.

Members of his team of researchers have expressed concern that both teachers and peers in schools in England have very much underestimated the extent to which girls were being bullied by their peers. They state that:

> The recognition of boys who have been victims of bullying is contrary to the equal numbers of boys and girls reporting being bullied in general surveys.
>
> (Sharpe and Cowie 1994: 124)

This is clearly not the case in the results provided in the Olweus survey, but it is more consistent with results from their own enquiries undertaken in Sheffield, England. Their method was in fact similar to that used by Norwegian schoolchildren. The researchers used essentially the same definition of bullying as Olweus, employing a similar questionnaire adapted, with slight modifications, from that used in Norway. One minor difference was that the criterion of being bullied 'at least once a week' replaced that of 'now and again'. Results from the Sheffield study, provided by Whitney and Smith (1993) based upon questionnaire responses from 2,623 schoolchildren suggest virtually no differences between the incidence of self-reported victimization of boys and girls in junior and middle school; in the senior school there is only a slight tendency for boys to report being bullied more often.

Surveys undertaken in Australia by Rigby and Slee between 1992 and 1996 using the Peer Relations Questionnaire or PRQ (Rigby and Slee 1993a) have provided results bearing on this and other matters addressed in this chapter. It should be noted that the schools taking part in these surveys, 60 in all, were not randomly selected but were those approaching the authors with requests to take part in the study. Hence the bias is towards schools willing to acknowledge the problem of bullying. However, a wide range of schools throughout Australia were sampled, both primary and secondary, private and state, coeducational and single sex. In total 15,418 boys and 10,476 girls with ages ranging from 8 to 18 years have answered questions contained in the PRQ. That instrument was adapted, in part, from the Olweus/Smith questionnaires, but also included a range of questions on many other aspects of children's peer relations. (Details of breakdowns of responses by age and gender to all the questions are given in the *Technical Manual for the Peer Relations Questionnaire* in Rigby 1996c.)

The question of whether boys or girls are bullied more frequently in Australian schools was examined in a number of ways. One approach was simply to compare percentages of boys and girls of the same age in coeducational schools who reported being bullied by peers at least once a week, using a similar definition of bullying to that proposed by Smith and Sharp (1994: 13). Comparing results for children between the ages of 9 and 17 years for which data was available from ten or more schools led to the conclusion that gender differences in reported victimization were minimal among children under 12 years of age, but strongly favoured boys being more subject to bullying thereafter: for example, at age 14 years, 22.7 per cent of boys (N = 1,675) reported being bullied weekly, compared with 13.2 per cent of girls (N = 1,600), the results being drawn from 36 coeducational schools (Rigby 1996b). These results generally support conclusions drawn by Olweus (1993a) regarding overall gender differences in victimization by peers rather than those of Sharp and Cowie (1994).

A second approach to comparing the incidence of reported victimization of boys and girls involved using a multi-item scale which contained items relevant to different kinds of bullying. But before presenting the results for this measure, it is best first to consider the question of whether comparisons using such a measure are, in fact, justified.

Are girls and boys bullied differently?

One of the explanations offered by Sharp and Cowie (1994) for the alleged underestimation by teachers and peers of the extent of bullying of girls at school is that girls are more likely to be bullied by indirect means, such as exclusion, which are more subtle and harder to detect. The evidence that girls are often bullied in schools in qualitatively different ways has accumulated from a variety of sources; for example, Norway (Olweus 1993a); Finland (Lagerspetz *et al.* 1988; Björkqvist *et al.* 1992a); the United States (Batsche and Knoff 1994); England (Rivers and Smith 1994); and in Australia (Owens 1996; Rigby 1997a). Boys have been reported as more frequently the targets of direct physical aggression and girls more often the targets of indirect aggression, with little or no differences found with respect to direct verbal aggression.

Relevant Australian data using the PRQ were derived from answers to five questions asking whether students had been bullied during the current year in different ways: 'often', 'sometimes' or 'never'. The results are given in Table 3.1 according to gender and age-group. Some of these results are consistent with those reported in studies conducted in other countries: that is, boys reported being bullied physically more often, but less often indirectly. There was a slight tendency for cruel teasing and name-calling to be reported more by boys, a result not always reported in other studies outside Australia. For example, Ahmad and Smith (1994a) reported that girls were more likely to be the victims of nasty name-calling in their study in England.

Generalized gender differences in victimiztion revisited

These gender differences apparent in the Australian results, inconsistent as some are in direction, do raise the question of whether it is appropriate

Table 3.1 Reported frequencies, given as percentages, with which children report being bullied by their peers in different ways

	Age groups					
	8–12 years			*13–18 years*		
	Never	*Sometimes*	*Often*	*Never*	*Sometimes*	*Often*
Being teased						
Boys	50.1	38.0	11.9	52.6	38.8	8.6
Girls	52.6	38.8	8.6	58.1	33.5	8.4
Hurtful names						
Boys	49.7	36.4	13.9	56.0	33.1	10.8
Girls	49.6	38.4	12.0	56.7	33.2	10.1
Left out						
Boys	65.9	26.9	7.3	75.7	18.8	5.5
Girls	58.7	32.3	9.0	69.0	24.4	6.6
Threatened						
Boys	71.5	22.7	5.8	74.4	19.8	5.9
Girls	84.9	12.6	2.5	87.8	9.7	2.5
Hit/kicked						
Boys	63.5	28.5	8.0	72.4	21.3	6.3
Girls	77.2	18.9	3.9	88.5	9.3	2.2

to make comparisons between boys and girls with respect to being bullied in the general sense, given that they tend to experience bullying somewhat differently. One way of addressing this issue is to examine the reliability or internal consistency of scales containing a mixed set of items, as derived from samples of boys and girls who answer these questions. Table 3.2 gives results for one such analysis using as items those given in Table 3.1.

The results show that for each sex the item–total correlations are adequate for each item to be included in a five-item scale of acceptable reliability, with alpha values ranging from 0.77 to 0.83. However, it is noticeable that the alpha values are slightly but consistently higher for boys. Evidently the set of items is a better measure of self-reported bullying of boys than of girls. Perhaps it is simply that bullying has a greater coherence and centrality to the lives of boys. Nevertheless, the validity of the measure has been supported for each sex. Correlations between scale scores and a measure of peer victimization derived from peer nominations that were provided by a sample of Australian secondary school students of 'who tends to be bullied at school' were as follows: for boys, $r = 0.45$, $df = 392$; for girls, $r = 0.41$, $df = 345$; in each case, $p < 0.001$ (Rigby 1996b).

If we are prepared to accept the five items as used in a Likert scale as constituting a psychometrically valid measure for comparing the extent to which boys and girls experience bullying in general, we have a relatively

Table 3.2 Reliability of the victim scale

Item	Boys: 8–12 yrs (N = 3,300)	Boys: 13–18 yrs (N = 10,665)	Girls: 8–12 yrs (N = 2,564)	Girls: 13–18 yrs (N = 7,006)
Being teased in an unpleasant way	0.63	0.68	0.63	0.67
Being called hurtful names	0.61	0.67	0.63	0.68
Being left out of things on purpose	0.52	0.60	0.52	0.53
Being threatened with harm	0.57	0.64	0.50	0.54
Being hit or kicked	0.55	0.58	0.48	0.44
Total scale (alphas)	0.80	0.83	0.77	0.78

Note
Table contains item – total correlations in relation to each of the five items, and alpha coefficients for the total scale.

Table 3.3 Mean scores on the self-report peer victimization scale

	Coeducational		*Single-sex schools*	
	Boys	*Girls*	*Boys*	*Girls*
Age 8–12 years	0.87 (1,726)	0.84 (1,760)	0.84 (1,387)	0.82 (629)
Age 13–18 years	0.83 (5,086)	0.82 (4,756)	0.83 (4,726)	0.79 (1,296)

Note
Numbers of students in sub-samples are given in parentheses.

sensitive way of examining overall gender differences. The Australian data provide us with the opportunity of taking into account the possible influence of type of school; that is, single sex or coeducational. Because of the severe positive skewness of the distribution of scores on the scale a logarithmic transformation was applied prior to the computation of means and results for ANOVA (see Tabachnick and Fidell 1983: 84). The mean scores are given in Table 3.3.

Statistically significant results at the 0.001 level by two-way ANOVA can be summarized as follows. For both gender comparisons (within coeducational schools and between single-sex schools) boys reported being bullied by peers more often than was the case for girls. Girls reported being bullied more in coeducational schools than in single-sex schools. The level of reported bullying was higher for boys at the coeducational than at the boys schools. For every comparison a higher degree of peer victimization was reported by the younger age group. In only one case was there a significant interaction effect with age. This was in the comparison of boys in coeducational schools with boys in single-sex schools. An examination of group means shows that the significant difference in reported bullying can be attributed to the higher rate of bullying of younger boys in coeducational schools; among the older students the means were identical.

In interpreting these results it should be emphasized that they are not based upon a random selection of schools, but rather are derived from schools that chose to be in the study. Nevertheless, to the best of my knowledge they provide the only figures currently available for making gender comparisons, at least in the Australian context. They clearly support the hypothesis that boys are bullied by their peers more than girls are. Effects of type of school are suggested with girls appearing to be less likely to be bullied in single-sex schools than in coeducational schools. The absence of boys, who typically contribute significantly to the bullying of girls in Australian coeducational schools (see Tulloch 1995), is a likely explanation for this effect. That boys should also appear to experience less bullying in the boys' schools selected for this study than in coeducational schools is perhaps more difficult to explain. But both findings indicating more bullying in coeducational schools are in direct contradiction to an earlier assertion in the research literature that 'it is incontestable that . . . the presence together of boys and girls in a school has a powerful effect in reducing bullying and unpleasantness' (Dale 1991: 151). One alternative and plausible hypothesis could be that bullying of boys by boys is actually encouraged by the presence of girls whom the more dominant males wish to impress.

Do the reactions of girls and boys to bullying tend to be different?

Three questions can be addressed. Do boys and girls react emotionally to being bullied in similar or dissimilar ways? Second, are boys and girls likely to take similar actions when they are bullied? Third, are boys and girls similarly predisposed to help solve the problem of bullying in schools?

Surveys conducted in Australia using the PRQ have addressed each of these questions. To assess the immediate and perceived effects of being bullied, children who reported being victimized by peers at school were asked whether they generally felt 'mostly angry', 'mostly sad' or 'not bothered'. In addition they were asked to indicate how they felt about themselves afterwards, given the alternatives of 'feeling better', 'feeling much the same' and 'feeling worse'. Results are given in Table 3.4.

Table 3.4 Emotional reactions and self-perceptions of students after being bullied by their peers (percentages reporting)

	Bullied less than once a week		*Bullied once a week or more often*	
	8–12 yrs	*13–18 yrs*	*8–12 yrs*	*13–18 yrs*
(A) Emotional reactions				
Not bothered				
Boys	61.4	62.1	28.7	35.0
Girls	44.4	46.7	19.8	22.6
Mostly angry				
Boys	27.1	28.3	43.1	41.1
Girls	25.0	26.9	28.1	36.1
Mostly sad				
Boys	11.5	9.6	28.2	24.0
Girls	30.6	26.4	52.1	41.3
(B) Perceptions of the self				
Felt better about self				
Boys	6.5	5.3	6.5	7.0
Girls	4.3	3.6	6.9	5.2
Felt much the same				
Boys	68.8	69.2	41.6	44.2
Girls	56.7	53.0	32.3	32.3
Felt worse about self				
Boys	24.7	25.5	51.9	48.8
Girls	39.0	43.5	60.7	62.5

Source: Rigby 1996.

It is apparent that boys were much more likely to say they were 'not bothered'. Where they reacted emotionally they were more likely to say they felt angry than sad. These results complement findings reported in Finland where in one study boys were much more likely than girls to say that they typically reacted in a nonchalant manner, or fought back rather than acting in a helpless way (Salmavalli *et al.* 1996a). Further, results in Table 3.4 also suggest that boys are much less inclined than girls to admit that their self-esteem has been damaged as a result of bullying under conditions of both low and high levels of bullying. Arguably, males more often feel obliged to present themselves (even through an anonymous questionnaire) as resilient, and to deny being hurt.

Gender differences were also found regarding actions children report after being bullied. Informing someone was more common among girls, especially as far as friends, teachers and mothers were concerned, but not fathers (see Table 3.5). One may suspect that 'telling' is often inconsistent

Table 3.5 Percentages of children who have been bullied and have told about it

	Bullied less than once a week		*Bullied once a week or more*	
	8–12 yrs	*13–18 yrs*	*8–12 yrs*	*13–18 yrs*
Person(s) told				
Mother				
Boys	52.9	34.1	62.6	48.0
Girls	64.0	53.4	71.0	64.6
Father				
Boys	41.4	25.8	50.0	37.5
Girls	40.3	28.3	48.6	37.6
Teacher/school counsellor				
Boys	34.0	22.0	49.2	43.4
Girls	43.4	29.1	61.3	52.7
Friend/friend(s)				
Boys	59.3	53.7	62.1	58.1
Girls	76.9	77.9	74.7	79.5

Source: Rigby 1996.

with the macho image of boys. From another question asked in the PRQ it was apparent that informing about bullying by boys was more likely to have adverse consequences for the informant than was the case for girls: 9 per cent of boys aged 13 to 18 years reported that after telling 'things got worse', compared with 6 per cent of girls in this age group. A further difference concerned reporting staying away from school because of bullying. Among the older age group, some 6.3 per cent of boys and 9.1 per cent of girls said they had stayed away for this reason at least once, some many times. These results suggest that reactions to bullying of 'telling' and also staying away from school may be more acceptable for girls.

Do boys and girls bully for different reasons?

There is general agreement in the research literature that boys are more likely to engage in bullying than girls, a view supported in the Australian survey, no matter whether we examine the results for individual or group bullying. But the extent of the difference does not appear to be large in the Australian data. Some 8.6 per cent of boys claimed to engage in bullying others 'often' in one-to-one situations compared with 6.3 per cent of girls; the corresponding estimates for bullying in groups were 7.3 per cent of boys and 6.5 per cent of girls. An inquiry into why children bully others showed that boys and girls tended to give similar explanations. The order of 'popularity' in a list of possible reasons from most endorsed to least endorsed was the same for boys and girls, namely: they annoyed me; to get even; others were doing it; to show how tough I am; for fun; because they are wimps; for money. Thus, based upon responses to suggested reasons for bullying, the Australian data do not suggest marked differences in the reasons why boys and girls bully.

It has been suggested that boys bully to achieve greater power and dominance, and that this is not the case for girls (Besag 1989). It is perhaps more true to say that given the more intimate nature of girls' social networks and the greater emphasis girls tend to place upon close personal relations, girls often have different opportunities from boys to engage in bullying (see Chapter 4, this volume). The means of hurting others may differ, but the underlying motive of exercising power and control over one's peers, which distinguishes the school bully from others, may be much the same for either sex.

Do boys and girls respond differently to the issue of bullying?

Results from assessments of Australian children's attitudes towards bullying suggest that there are gender differences in ways in which boys and girls are predisposed to respond to bullying in schools as an issue. Girls tend to be more pro-victim in their attitudes (Rigby and Slee 1993b; Tulloch 1995). Boys have been found to view the consequences of bullying others in a more favourable light, (e.g., 'makes you feel better than others', 'show others you're the boss'); whilst girls were more likely to indicate that they would feel 'ashamed of themselves' if they bullied others (Rigby 1997c).

Given these differences, it is not surprising that at all ages girls tend to be somewhat more supportive than boys of measures to counter bullying. In both age groups – as indicated in Table 3.6, based on responses to questions in the PRQ – it is evident that girls were more concerned about countering bullying, as reflected by higher proportions of girls supporting the idea of intervention to stop bullying, whether through the efforts of teachers, the efforts of students or by teachers and students working together, or by discussing options with other students. As we have seen, this more proactive approach on the part of girls cannot be because girls are bullied more: they appear to be bullied less. It is not because more girls than boys feel that they could personally use help to stop being bullied: in fact slightly more boys than girls say they could personally use help. Yet this outcome will not surprise many people. As in many other social situations girls are generally prepared to act in a more collaborative and conflict-mitigating manner (see Miller *et al.* 1986).

Table 3.6 What children think should be done about bullying

		Percentages responding			
		Boys		*Girls*	
		8–12 yrs	*13–18 yrs*	*8–12 yrs*	*13–18 yrs*
Teachers and students should be concerned about stopping bullying	Yes	79.9	70.0	83.0	76.4
	DK	17.3	22.2	15.5	19.7
	No	2.8	7.8	1.4	3.8
Teachers should try to stop it	Yes	85.3	75.9	88.8	80.6
	DK	11.6	16.8	9.4	15.2
	No	3.1	7.3	1.8	4.2
Students themselves should help to stop it	Yes	65.6	64.1	69.9	73.0
	DK	24.6	25.0	22.2	21.6
	No	9.8	10.9	7.9	5.4
Students and teachers should work together to stop it	Yes	64.4	54.2	71.2	61.8
	DK	27.6	33.0	24.5	30.9
	No	8.1	12.8	4.3	7.2
Could personally use help to stop being bullied	Yes	47.3	34.1	46.5	32.1
	DK	29.6	31.5	36.6	36.1
	No	23.1	34.5	16.9	31.8
Would be interested in talking about the problem of bullying with other students	Yes	36.0	24.9	46.7	34.2
	DK	40.7	40.0	39.3	42.3
	No	23.3	35.1	14.0	23.5

Source: Rigby 1996.

Discussion

Although schoolchildren are bullied by their peers in a variety of ways, with some of these having implications for gender differences, it is nevertheless reasonable to speak of 'bullying in general', since that concept has a coherence supported by substantial intercorrelations between reports provided by schoolchildren, both boys and girls, of the different ways in which they may be bullied at school. At this general level, the results support the claim made by Olweus (1993a) that boys are bullied more often than girls, especially beyond the age of 12 years. However, when specific aspects of bullying were examined in the Australian sample, in keeping with other results of gender differences reported from Norway, England, Finland and the United States, it was evident that whilst boys are bullied more often physically, girls are more often the target for indirect bullying. Because indirect bullying is more subtle and harder to detect, one would expect observers to underestimate bullying among girls – but this does not mean that girls and boys are, in general, equally bullied, at least not in the Australian context.

Gender differences in bullying are clearly influenced by the social context in which victimization may occur. This is most apparent when comparisons are made between the incidence of reported bullying of girls in single-sex schools and girls in coeducational schools. The presence of boys (who bully girls more often than girls bully boys) in coeducational schools evidently leads to an increase in girl victimization. On the other hand, coeducational schools do not seem to have a moderating effect on the victimization of boys, as Dale (1991) suggested was the case, since the available evidence does not suggest a higher incidence of bullying in 'boys-only' schools.

Research conducted in Australia strongly suggests that particular attention should be paid to differences in the emotional reactions of boys and girls to bullying. As we have seen, girls appear more likely to respond with sadness and boys with anger. These differences should be considered in the light of other findings by Rigby (1995a) that reporting feeling 'sad' after being bullied at school (as opposed to being 'angry' or 'not bothered') was for both sexes associated with reporting (i) reduced self-esteem following being bullied, (ii) having fewer friends, (iii) seeing themselves as less popular than others, (iv) being absent from school more often. Because girls tend to respond more often with sadness to being bullied, perhaps, as some have suggested, blaming themselves more for any show of social ineptitude (see Deaux 1984), the consequences for girls of peer victimization may, in some respects, be more serious.

However, in another respect girls may be advantaged. It was evident that among the most severely bullied Australian students (bullied at least once a week), it was girls rather than boys who told 'someone' about it. This is consistent with the prevailing 'macho' philosophy in Australian schools that you just don't inform or 'dob' other people, which affects boys more than girls. Boys are evidently less likely to look for help when they need it. This is consistent with statistical information provided by Kids Helpline in Australia who claim that over their five years of operation of the 554,000 calls relating to personal problems, only 28 per cent of the calls were from males (Kids Helpline 1996: 1).

Girls were more prepared to take more constructive actions in dealing with the problem of bullying in their schools than their male counterparts. They appeared to be more strongly attracted to the idea of teachers and students working together on the problem, and more interested than boys in discussing the matter with their peers. According to research currently being undertaken by the Education Department of New South Wales in Australia much of the leadership in promoting collaborative methods of solving disputes in schools through peer mediation is being undertaken by girls.

In conclusion, I have concentrated mainly on identifying areas in which there are gender differences relating to the issue of bullying in schools. It should be emphasized however that in many respects the differences are small and that there is a very considerable overlap in the nature of bullying experienced in schools by boys and girls; in the reactions to bullying of victimized children of either sex; in the motives these children have for bullying; and in the actions boys and girls want to take to counter bullying in their schools. Perhaps the time has come when we can take as given the now well-replicated findings – that is, that boys tend to bully others and are bullied by others more frequently, and that girls are more prone to bully and be bullied indirectly and less physically – and concentrate on the newer issues of how children of each sex typically react to bullying, the reasons why they bully and why girls are overall more constructive in their responses to the issue. From such studies we might hope to learn how more effective coping and responding to the issue of bullying can be developed for both boys and girls.

Chapter 4

Aggression in the social relations of school-aged girls and boys

Christina Salmivalli, Ari Kaukiainen and Kirsti Lagerspetz

Introduction

One of the developmental tasks for children is to achieve and maintain positive relationships with peers. In these relationships they seek shared understanding, acceptance, relaxation and pleasure, but also self-enhancement and dominance. Lack of close relationships has been shown to be associated with feelings of loneliness, low subjective well-being, and non-adjustment. Meaningful social relationships constitute a kind of 'safety net' in the course of life and personal development. But as important as social relations are, they sometimes turn into scenes of aggression and displeasure. Conflicts are an unavoidable constituent of human relations.

In this chapter we describe anger and aggression in the social relations of school-aged girls and boys, focusing especially on everyday aggression as it takes place in such commonplace settings as the school environment. One specific type of such aggression is bullying, which will be looked at in the latter half of the chapter. Before that, we address the issues of sex differences and developmental changes in regard to aggression, which have been of central interest in our research group.

Girls, boys and aggression

Girls can also be naughty

In their well-known review, Maccoby and Jacklin (1974) consider it more or less self-evident that males are more aggressive than females. However, their conclusion was almost exclusively based on observational studies in kindergarten and school yards, and rough-and-tumble play was in many of the reviewed studies regarded as aggression. Later reviews on sex differences in aggression (Frodi *et al.* 1977; White 1983; Hyde 1984; Eagly and Steffen 1986; Björkqvist and Niemelä 1992) have been more cautious and have considered sex differences to be qualitative rather than quantitative.

It is true that pushing, hitting, and kicking among children, or such extreme forms of physical violence as murder and assault in the adult world, are committed more by males than females. Male violence is more damaging, and males are more often perpetrators of crimes of violence than females. However, aggression is usually defined as 'any form of behaviour that is intended to injure someone either physically or psychologically' (Berkowitz 1993: 3). Aggression thus manifests itself in a variety of acts, in which girls and women are certainly involved.

Furthermore, one should consider whether aggression takes place between groups, or in interpersonal relations within a group or between two persons. For instance, gang fights and wars are typically male encounters. In addition, both males' and females' aggression changes in form and in intensity depending on the sex of the opponent (see, for instance, Miller *et al.* 1986; Cairns and Cairns 1994).

Gender roles and cultural norms may lead females to avoid direct physical expressions of aggression. Björkqvist *et al.* (1982) found that aggressive girls wished to be less domineering while aggressive boys wanted to be even more domineering than they already were. This result seems to reflect the idealization of aggression amongst males but not amongst females.

If direct aggression is discouraged in girls and women, it is likely that they have to develop alternative styles to physical or direct aggression, styles which are more socially acceptable for them: they resort to indirect forms of aggression. In the studies by Lagerspetz *et al.* (1988) and Björkqvist *et al.* (1992a) indirect aggression was regarded as noxious behaviour, in which the target person is attacked in a roundabout way. This allows the perpetrator to go unidentified, and not to be accused of aggression. Often it is a kind of social manipulation, like spreading malicious rumours about the target person or trying to persuade others not to associate with him/her. In fact it turned out that girls used more of this type of aggression than boys did.

Faces and forms of indirect aggression

It is true that different connotations have been given to the concept of indirect aggression. In 1961 Buss used the term to denote behaviour in which identifying the aggressor is rendered difficult. According to him, 'Gossip is indirect in that the victim is not present, and the noxious stimuli are delivered via the negative reactions of others; the victim gets into trouble at the end of a chain of mediating events and people' (Buss 1961: 8). We have kept this description in mind when studying indirect aggression. However, the questionnaire by Buss and Durkee (1957) had a subscale called 'indirect aggression', which to some extent deviated from the spirit of the above description by Buss himself. For example, the scale contained items about practical jokes, taking and breaking things, etc. In the new version of the questionnaire (Buss and Perry 1992), the scale of indirect aggression was left out.

Since Buss, the term has been used with somewhat different contents in empirical studies. Feshbach (1969) operationalized indirect aggression as active rejection (ignoring, avoiding and excluding) of another person in a face-to-face situation. This kind of aggression was typical for girls aged 6–7 years. With an older age group, 12–13 years, Feshbach and Sones (1971) studied negative reactions on the verbal level toward newcomers in a pair. The hostility could be inferred from the verbal interaction between the children, even when no direct aggression took place. This type of indirect aggression was also more typical for girls than for boys.

Social alienation studied by Cairns *et al.* (1985) also comes close to indirect aggression in a Bussian sense. It includes 'slander and defamation of reputation by gossip'. On this variable, girls scored significantly higher than boys in the fourth and seventh grades, especially in the same sex conflict situations.

Pulkkinen and Pitkänen (1993) found no gender differences in peer-nominated indirect aggression among 8- and 14-year-old children and adolescents. However, their measure of it included items describing both displaced aggression ('kicking furniture') and aggressive behaviours we would define as direct rather than indirect, like facial aggression.

Crick and Grotpeter (1995) introduced the term 'relational aggression'. It refers to social manipulation and it is mostly the same kind of behaviour, which was earlier called indirect aggression by Lagerspetz *et al.* (1988). Crick and Grotpeter also found that this type of aggression was more typical for girls than for boys.

Indirect aggression in girls and boys of different ages

Lagerspetz and Björkqvist and their research group decided to investigate the prevalence and development of indirect aggressive strategies in both sexes. The studies were conducted with children and adolescents of different ages (age groups 8, 11, 15 and 18 years). It is not easy to admit to being aggressive, and since indirect aggression is quite likely used in order to cover one's harmful intentions, self-reports about it are especially unlikely to be honest. For this reason, a peer-rating technique has been used in the studies to find out the prevalence of aggression. Self-ratings were, however, used as a complementary source of information.

An instrument for the measurement of both direct (physical and verbal) and indirect strategies of aggression among schoolchildren was developed through a number of studies. The latest version of this instrument is referred to as the Direct–Indirect Aggression Scales (DIAS) (Björkqvist *et al.* 1992b).

In the DIAS procedure children are asked to rate all their classmates and themselves on the basis of fixed options of behaviour. Aggression is usually defined as a response the intent of which is to injure another organism. Therefore, the behaviours described in the items of the scales were such that they were *likely to harm the target person.* Although anger is not the same as aggression, it is the emotional state most commonly connected with aggression. Therefore, we asked our subjects to rate how often their peers and they themselves behaved in the ways described in the items when they *were angry at* some classmate.

To use exactly the same items for all age groups has its advantages: it enables us to see how the answers to the items change as a result of increasing age. The disadvantage is that all items must be simple enough to be understood by the youngest age group and, of course, the behaviour described in the items should be such that it takes place in all age groups. Therefore, we chose a midway solution: we retained nine items in all age levels, but added age-appropriate items to each age level. The questionnaire for the 8-year-olds was rather simple. The older cohorts' questionnaires contained descriptions of more complicated behaviours and situations. Thus, the number of items increased as a function of age.

Summed variables were constructed on the basis of a factor analysis. Depending on the age group, three or four factors emerged: direct verbal aggression (yelling, swearing, abusing, etc.), direct physical aggression (hitting, kicking, pulling, etc.), indirect aggression (gossiping, excluding from the group, telling bad or false stories, etc.) and peaceful means of conflict-solving (trying to talk, going away, managing to calm down the situation, etc.). The items of these subscales and their alphas have been presented in detail in Lagerspetz *et al.* (1988) and Björkqvist *et al.* (1992a).

The use of indirect aggression (as well as withdrawal and peaceful means) was more common among the girls than among the boys in all age cohorts, with the exception of the youngest cohort, in which girls did not yet use significantly more indirect aggression than boys did. The behaviour of boys, in all age groups, was characterized by direct forms of aggression.

Some antecedents of indirect aggression

Social intelligence

It seems that indirect aggression is not yet fully developed among the youngest girls, who show generally less aggression than boys of the same age. It is conceivable that some degree of social maturation is required for skilful use of indirect aggression.

On the basis of a series of studies (Lagerspetz *et al.* 1988; Björkqvist *et al.* 1992a, 1992b; Lagerspetz and Björkqvist 1993; Kaukiainen *et al.* 1996), a stage theory of the development of aggression has been elaborated. According to it, among young children lacking verbal skills, aggression is predominantly physical. When verbal skills develop, they are not only used for peaceful interaction, but also for aggressive purposes. Along with the development of social skills, even more sophisticated strategies, like indirect aggression, become possible, with the aggressor being able to harm a victim without even being identified.

As a matter of fact, a positive association has been found between social intelligence and the use of indirect aggression (Kaukiainen *et al.* in press), whereas the relation of social intelligence with the use of verbal and physical aggression (always controlling the two other forms of aggression) are non-existent or even negative (Table 4.1). Social intelligence was defined as one's ability to make accurate observations of the social world and to use this knowledge in order to put over one's aims and opinions: that is, knowing how to 'pull the strings' in social interactions. It seems that the use of indirect aggression requires a certain level of social intelligence, as one would assume on the basis of the stage theory of aggression.

Social networks as context of indirect aggression

Since indirect aggression takes advantage of the social setting, children may use the relations between peers in the school class as vehicles of their aggression. Gender role expectations and cultural norms, along with females' physical weakness compared to males', to some extent explain the less frequent use of direct aggression by females. In addition, it seems that the nature of girls' social networks further promotes the use of indirect, rather than direct means of aggression.

The friendship groups of girls differ in size from the boys' groups, the latter being usually larger (Lagerspetz *et al.* 1988). The friendship ratings in our own studies (Lagerspetz *et al.* 1988; Björkqvist *et al.* 1992a) also showed that there was more agreement among the raters about which girls belonged to which group or pair, than there was about the boys' groups.

Table 4.1 Partial correlations between different types of aggression and social intelligence among 10- to 14-year-old girls and boys (N = 526)

Variables controlled	*Aggression type*	*Correlation with social intelligence*
Indirect and verbal aggression	Physical	−0.09*
Indirect and physical aggression	Verbal	−0.04
Physical and verbal aggression	Indirect	0.42†

Note
* = $p < 0.05$, † = $p < 0.001$

When the social networks are known to others, exclusion from the group or conflicts with your friends may hurt more and be more embarrassing than when the friendships are not so commonly known.

In addition, boys' groups are typically units for elaborate games and team sports. In contrast, girls prefer dyadic interaction which offers opportunity for emotional intimacy. Girls disclose themselves more than boys do (Erwin 1993).

In an unpublished study by our research group, we investigated what sixth grade girls and boys expected from a friend and from their relationship with him/her. Three scales, describing different expectations, were used: intimacy (items like 'I can tell my worries to my friend', 'My friend and I share our feelings with each other'), loyalty ('My friend defends me if others are bullying me', 'I trust my friend in every situation') and dependency ('I miss my friend if he or she is away a long time'). The girls expected from their friendships more intimacy, loyalty, and dependency than the boys did (Figure 4.1). It can be argued that such high expectations also offer opportunities for betrayal. Betrayal in such a relationship must be especially hurtful, and therefore an effective means of aggression. Learning this, the girls might also become aware of how to use these behaviours on others. Girls' social networks give them the necessary set of tools to practise indirect aggression. In fact, Green *et al.* (1996) found that tight and dense social networks more readily form a social context suitable for the exhibition of indirect aggression than less dense networks do.

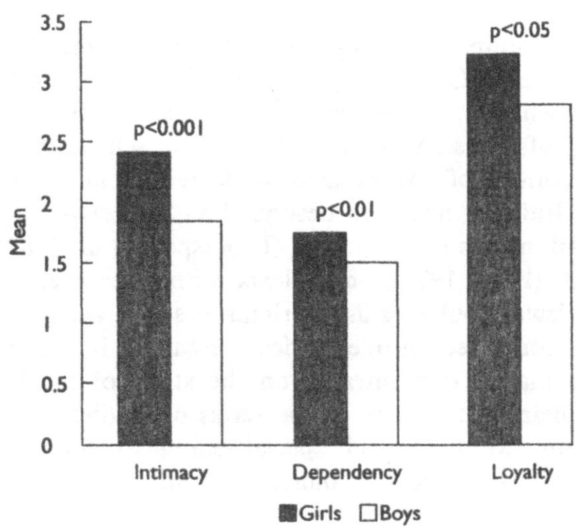

Figure 4.1 Gender differences in what 11-year-old children expect from a friend: intimacy, dependency and loyalty

What kind of aggression is bullying?

Bullying is a category of aggressive behaviour with some typical characteristics. One distinctive feature is that bullying is not occasional, but systematic aggression: purposefully harmful actions are repeatedly targeted at one and the same individual child. Another feature of bullying is that it does not take place between two equals: there is an imbalance of power. The victim is in some way or another incapable of defending him/herself against the aggressor; this may be due to physical weakness or for some other reason. This imbalance of power is often, of course, the reason why a particular individual is chosen as the target of harassment in the first place.

Furthermore, the bully is not necessarily in a state of aggression arousal – emotional or physiological – when he/she attacks the victim, but may act quite coolly. Bullying is rather like an institutionalized habit which is largely motivated by the bully's need to dominate others or to acquire status in the peer group. Following the distinction made by Dodge and Coie (1987), bullying can be seen as proactive, rather than reactive, aggression; it is usually not a reaction to some provocative act (although bullies may justify their actions by claiming so). Coie *et al.* (1991) have further divided proactive aggression into instrumental and bullying aggression. The distinction lies in that instrumental aggression has some external goal (such as getting a toy from another child), whereas no such goal can be observed to explain the bully's behaviour. However, it should also be pointed out that bullying may be instrumental in the sense that internal goals of status-seeking and dominating may be involved.

Yet another feature of bullying is that it usually takes place in a context of a group of peers. Often the group in question is a rather permanent social group where membership is involuntary – like a school class. Bullying may, of course, take place not only in schools but, for instance, in the social context of a workplace (Björkqvist *et al.* 1994) or any other social group. Bullying has been described as 'collective aggression based on social relationships in the group' (Lagerspetz *et al.* 1982), 'violence in group context' (Pikas 1975), or 'violence within the peer group' (Olweus 1972). This view of bullying as a primarily social activity has, however, seldom been converted into empirical research. In reality, studies on bullying have mainly concentrated on the study of the bullies and the victims and their relationship. In the series of studies conducted by our research group, we have laid special emphasis on, and empirically explored, the group aspects in bullying (Salmivalli *et al.* 1996a, 1996b, 1997, 1998).

Gender and bullying issues

At its initial stages, in the early 1970s, bullying research suffered, like aggression research in general, from lack of results generalizable to girls (as it still does, to some extent). Because female aggression was hard to tap with research tools planned to examine mainly physical and verbal forms of aggression, it was often ignored. Females were seen, if not as completely nonaggressive, as much less aggressive than males. In the early studies on bullying, this led to the fact that only boys were selected as research subjects (e.g., Olweus 1972), or bullying behaviour was defined and operationalized in a way which biased the results towards finding bullies and bullying only among boys, but not among girls.

Since then, concepts of indirect aggression and indirect bullying, as well as tools to measure them (e.g., DIAS), have been developed. In the field of bullying research, girls are now included in the samples studied and indirect aggression has been taken into account in many studies and included in the definition of bullying.

Including the item 'How often does it happen that other students don't want to spend recess with you and you end up being alone?' in his questionnaire, Olweus (1991) found girls to be more often exposed to this specific kind of indirect bullying – namely, social isolation – than to open, direct attacks.

In their questionnaire of bullying, Ahmad and Smith (1994a) included the following examples of indirect aggression: '[It is also bullying when a child is] . . . sent nasty notes, and when no one ever talks to them, and things like that.' They found that girls in the secondary school, rather than in the primary school, were exposed to these indirect forms of bullying more often than boys.

In the semistructured interviews of sixth-grade children, Salmivalli (1992) found indirect forms of bullying, such as spreading rumours and exclusion from the group, to be more frequent when the victim was a girl. When attacks were targeted at a boy, they more often consisted of pushing, hitting, kicking, taking his things, etc. For both sexes, however, the most typical way of bullying was name-calling and abusing.

The study by Rivers and Smith (1994) gives very similar results, and offers further evidence of the relatively high frequency of indirect bullying among girls. Using a definition of indirect bullying very similar to the one that has been developed and used in our research group, they found that more girls than boys were targets of it. Girls and boys did not differ in direct and verbal behaviours such as name calling or threatening. Both girls and boys had most often experienced verbal bullying.

All in all, it seems that the gender differences in aggressive styles are manifested also in bullying styles. When it comes to the amount of bullying, the results of many recent studies suggest that bullying occurs slightly more often among boys than among girls (Salmivalli *et al.* 1996b; Rigby 1995b; Whitney and Smith 1993). It seems that boys are usually more often identified as both bullies and victims than are girls – but the differences are not as large as had been thought earlier. It should be kept in mind that there is still room for improvement in the available questionnaires – too many of them still ignore indirect bullying or have scales with only one or two items measuring it. For this reason, there may still be a built-in 'male bias' in them.

A group view on bullying

Participant roles

In many studies concerning bullying, groups of 'bullies', 'victims' and 'controls' have been selected as subjects and then compared in some respects. The control group has been thought to represent non-involved (or, sometimes, prosocial) children. However, this group consists of pupils with very different attitudes and behavioural tendencies in regard to bullying – not so completely 'non-involved' after all.

We have developed a specific measure, the Participant Role Questionnaire (revised version, Salmivalli 1995), to explore how other children, in addition to bullies and victims, are involved in the bullying process; that is, what do the other children do when the victim is harassed by the bully. On the basis of the peer-evaluations of the pupils' typical behaviour in situations of bullying, participant roles of 'victim', 'bully', 'assistant of bully', 'reinforcer of bully', 'defender of victim', and 'outsider' can be assigned to them. The 22 items of the revised Participant Role Questionnaire constitute five subscales describing tendencies to act as bully, assistant, reinforcer, defender, or outsider, in bullying situations. For examples of the items of these scales, see Table 4.2. In addition to these scales, the questionnaire includes a separate peer nomination of victims.

Table 4.2 Examples of items in the participant role scales along with their reliabilities

Scale	*Alpha*	*Examples of items*
Bully	0.93	Starts bullying Makes others join in the bullying
Assistant of bully	0.81	Joins in the bullying Assists the bully
Reinforcer of bully	0.91	Comes around to watch the situation Laughs
Defender of victim	0.93	Tries to make the others stop bullying Says to the victim: 'Never mind'
Outsider	0.89	Is not usually present Does not even know about the bullying

Briefly, the criteria for classifying a child as having one or another participant role is that (a) his/her score on the corresponding peer-evaluation scale exceeds the mean of his/her same-sex classmates, and (b) he/she scores higher on that scale than on any of the other scales. The criterion for classifying a child as a victim of bullying is that 30 per cent or more of the classmates have nominated him/her as such. For details of the procedure, see Salmivalli *et al.* (1996b).

In Figures 4.2 and 4.3, the percentages of girls and boys having different participant roles in our sixth- and eighth-grade samples are presented. As shown by the figures, the number of victims is practically the same among girls and boys, while boys tend, more often than girls, to take the role of bully. However, the gender differences emerge even more clearly in other participant roles: girls mostly take outsider or defender roles, whereas it is typical of boys to act as reinforcers or assistants of the bully. The distribution of the roles is highly similar in both grades, although it is notable that there are fewer victims among the eighth graders than among the sixth graders.

When it comes to consistency in these participant roles, observations of our longitudinal data show that (1) the tendency to bully others is very stable in the case of boys, but not in the case of girls; (2) being victimized is highly consistent, even when a child changes class and has a 'fresh start' in a new social context; and (3) for other behaviours there is a significant consistency from sixth to eighth grade; however, this

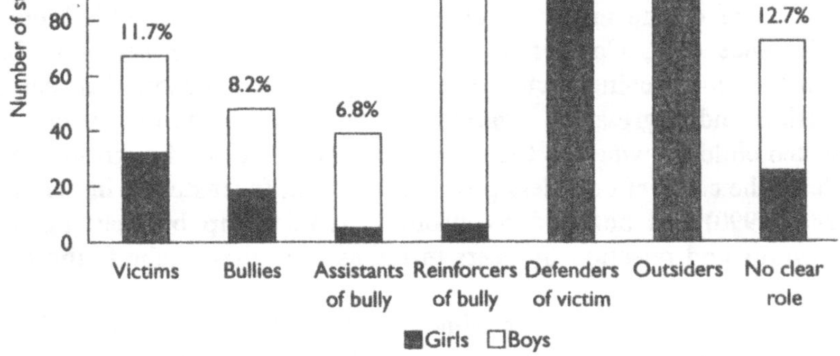

Figure 4.2 Percentual distribution of girls and boys in the different participant roles among the sixth-graders.

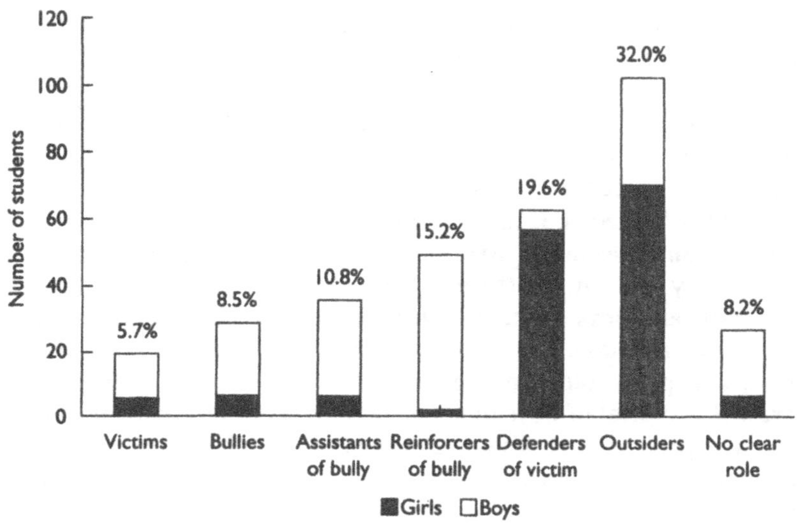

Figure 4.3 **Percentual distribution of girls and boys in the different participant roles among the eighth-graders.**

consistency is somewhat weaker in cases in which the child has moved into a new social context (a new class with no former sixth-grade classmates) (Salmivalli *et al.* 1998).

Participant roles and sociometric status

Bullies

Aggressive children and adolescents have often been reported to be rejected by their peers. Along with shy and withdrawn behaviour, aggression is one of the major correlates of peer rejection in childhood and adolescence (e.g., Coie *et al.* 1990). However, gender seems to be an important intervening factor determining the relationship between peer rejection and aggression. Aggressive boys are often found to be clearly rejected children, whereas the same is not always true of aggressive girls – at least the connection is less powerful. French, for instance, in her studies (1988, 1990) did not find as strong a relationship between aggressive behaviour and rejection by peers in the case of girls as she found among boys.

When it comes to bullying, similar findings have come up: while male bullies obviously are rejected children (although not as unpopular as the victims), the picture becomes more complicated in the case of girls. Lindman and Sinclair (1988), for instance, found girl bullies to be surprisingly popular, measured by questions like 'Whom would you like to sit next to in the classroom?' or 'Who would be the leader in the class if the teacher were absent?'

In our study with 573 Finnish sixth-grade children (Salmivalli *et al.* 1996b), male bullies turned out to be children rejected by their peers. However, female bullies scored high on *both* social rejection *and* social acceptance. They had a controversial status, being both highly liked and highly disliked by their peers. How could this be accounted for?

It is conceivable that the differences in the status of girl and boy bullies are due to qualitative differences in their ways of harassment. Boys harass their victims with direct and often physical aggression. Among the girls, the harassment is indirect, appears in a disguised form, and might possibly alternate with expressions of friendship or even affection.

Although this matter has not been much studied, there is some evidence that all kinds of aggression do not equally lead to rejection by peers. Coie *et al.* (1991), for instance, have shown that qualitatively different aggressive behaviours can have different consequences for children's sociometric status. Unfortunately, they had only boys as subjects. Furthermore, because of the categories of aggressive behaviour they compared in this regard (reactive, instrumental, bullying), the results do not shed light on the question of the consequences of indirect, compared to direct, aggression.

The question whether a practitioner of indirect bullying is spared from peer rejection remains, for now, unresolved. It can only be speculated that because these roundabout means of aggression are more hidden and more socially sophisticated than the disruptive, often physically aggressive behaviour of boys, they might also be better tolerated, and their usage may not always come to light.

Children in other participant roles

When it comes to children in other participant roles, the victims – both girls and boys – have the lowest status among their peers. Interestingly, although boy bullies are rejected, the same does not hold true for assistants and reinforcers, who join in the bullying behaviour too. It seems that it is acceptable, maybe even expected, among boys to engage in aggressive interactions to some extent. When a certain limit is exceeded, however, approval by peers comes to an end.

Both among boys and girls, children who tend to act as defenders of the victims have the highest status among their peers. This supports previous results about the high status of prosocially behaving children (Coie *et al.* 1990). Two interpretations are conceivable: (1) defenders have a high status just because they react to bullying in that particular way (defending the victim is appreciated by the peers), or (2) a high-status child does not have to be afraid of being victimized him/herself, even if he/she takes sides with the victim. Children who are high status are more able to defend victims.

Cliques in school classes

'Do adolescents behave aggressively because of their social affiliations', ask Cairns and Cairns (1991), 'or, alternatively, are they aggressive because they have been alienated and rejected by the social system?' Their answer is that both explanations may be right. Individuals are selectively allowed into social networks, and the network will gradually influence the values and behaviours of the newcomer. Similarity in aggression with other members of the group is one criterion which qualifies entry into a social group. It has been shown that, in school settings, children and adolescents who are similar with respect to aggression tend to affiliate with each other. Consequently, although rejected by their classmates at large, these aggressive individuals are supported by their own group of peers.

It has been found in our study that children and adolescents having similar – or complementary – participant roles, tend to associate with each other. They form pairs or groups within the class. What a pupil usually does in a bullying situation thus seems to be one feature around which the peer networks in a school class are organized. Hobbies, interests and other activities are often shared by friends; tragic as it is, harassing another child may also be an activity that unites (Salmivalli *et al.* 1997).

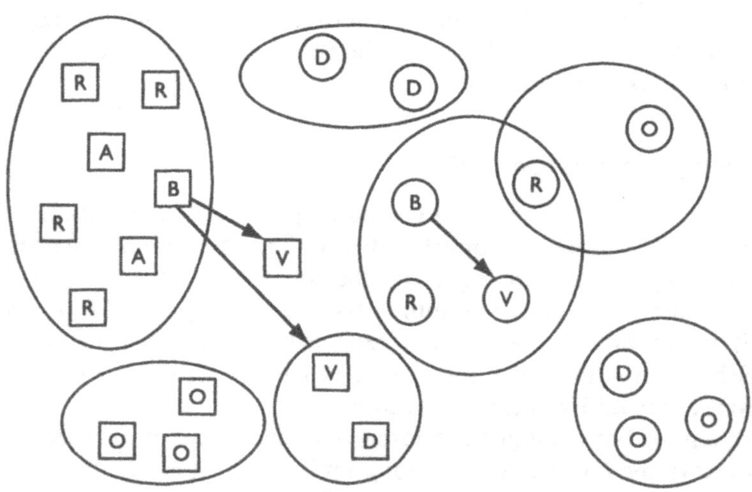

Figure 4.4 Illustration of a typical school class: peer networks, children's participant roles and bully/victim relationships.

Source: Salmivalli *et al.* 1997.

Note: Circles represent girls, squares represent boys, and letters (V, B, A, R, D and O) refer to the participant roles.

Bullies, although they are rejected by their classmates at large, are not rejected by all of them; they typically do have a group of friends in the class. Often these friends are other bullies, assistants, and reinforcers. Victims' defenders and outsiders, on the other hand, form networks with each other. Victims – especially boy victims – are the children most often found outside the networks, but when they belong to one, they often share it with other victims, outsiders or defenders.

Not only do the children who take part in bullying – that is, bullies, assistants, and reinforcers – belong to a network, but their networks usually have more members than those of victims, their defenders, and outsiders (Salmivalli *et al.* 1997). This is true among boys especially, although a similar but slighter tendency can be observed among girls as well. In general, the peer networks of the girls were smaller than those of the boys, the mean network size for girls being 2.98 and the mean network size for boys being 5.94 (sixth-grade children).

The differences in girls' and boys' participant roles, as well as the typical compositions and sizes of their peer networks are illustrated in Figure 4.4.

Conclusions

Aggression in the social relations of boys and girls differs in terms of styles and strategies. Girls more often use, and are targets of, indirect, manipulative means of aggression, whereas boys' aggression is more direct in nature. These differences can be seen also in bullying behaviour, which is one specific but unfortunately common manifestation of aggression among school-aged children. Until recently, aggression research has more or less underestimated, even neglected girls' aggression. Girls have been sometimes regarded as 'the gentle sex', but now that indirect aggression is taken into account, this picture has changed. In fact, the social life of girls can be regarded as rather cruel and aggressive. It can be questioned, however, whether it is meaningful at all to compare the sexes as to which is more aggressive than the other. Males' and females' aggression takes different forms, and different kinds of aggression can hardly be compared in intensity. Is writing malicious letters more or less aggressive than bumping someone on the head?

Girls and boys take on different participant roles when bullying goes on in a school class. These roles have to do with siding with either the bully or the victim. Siding with the bully by assisting or reinforcing him is quite typical for boys, while siding with the victim is much more common among girls. This seems to suggest, however, that boys adopt more aggressive roles in this process, compared to the prosocial activities of girls. Does this mean that boys are, after all, more aggressive? As was pointed out, aggression among boys is, to some degree, idealized and even expected, while the opposite is true in the social world of girls. This may explain something about the distribution of the participant roles. It should be noted, however, that the results could be different if indirect bullying had been addressed explicitly. Furthermore, admittedly there are items in the Participant Role Questionnaire's reinforcer and assistant-scales which cannot easily be applied in situations of indirect bullying (like 'comes around to watch the situation' – indirect bullying is hardly something that can be watched at all!).

The nature and quality of children's peer relations affect their aggression or nonaggression. Also the contrary is true: aggression certainly has certain effects on peer relations. In this chapter we have viewed these interactions both ways. First, we examined social relations as the soil in which not only friendly interactions but also hostility and aggression grow. For instance, the nature of girls' social networks may promote the use of social manipulation and other indirect, rather than direct, strategies of aggression. For instance, girls share more intimate personal information with each other than boys do. They also expect more from their friendships in terms of intimacy, loyalty, and dependency than boys do. These characteristics of girls' social networks create opportunities to hurt others quite easily, just by revealing their secrets or spreading malicious rumours. It seems that girls' social relations form a good training ground for practising indirect strategies of aggression, along with other types of social interaction, like prosocial behaviour.

Another example of the effects of peer relations on children's aggressive behaviour is obviously bullying, which is maintained and reinforced by peer group members' mutual interactions. It can be speculated whether there would be so many bullies without reinforcers or assistants. The peer networks in school classes seem to be organized around the different participant roles. Children with similar or complementary roles in regard to bullying, associate with each other. Not only do 'the birds of a feather flock together', but once an aggressive subgroup has formed, its members further socialize each other. The norms arising within a certain subgroup may demand that its members engage in bullying, if not as active initiators then as passive followers. From the victim's viewpoint, it must be much more frightening to be harassed by an aggressive group than by only a single bully. When the bullies and their siders are friends with each other, it is even more difficult for a victim to defend him/herself – a uniform group is hard to beat!

The way a child expresses his or her aggression or what he or she does in a bullying situation, has gender specific consequences for his/her social affiliations and his or her status in the school class. Aggressive boys are often found to be rejected by their classmates, whereas the same is not always true of girls. One explanation comes from the girls' 'sophisticated' ways of using aggression in their social relations. Unfortunately, aggressive behaviour is also a skill, which can be developed into greater perfection. Furthermore, perhaps social skills which are needed for indirect aggression are also used to maintain positive status.

The group nature of bullying also demands a different approach from the interventions to stop it. When interventions against bullying are traditionally targeted only at an individual child (identified as the bully, for instance), the changes in behaviour, if acquired at all, may not be permanent: the peer network exerts its old influence when the intervention is over. Targeting the interventions, based on an analysis of the children's roles, towards a school class or even a broader social context might help solve bullying problems, as well as other behavioural or social problems in school classes.

Acknowledgements

Our collaborators in the research project are Kaj Björkvist and Karin Österman from Åbo Akademi University, Vaasa, Finland. We are grateful for their indispensable contributions to our research project, and consequently to the present work. We also wish to thank Arja Huttunen and Roope Kankaanranta for their contributions. At its different stages, our research has been financially supported by the Academy of Finland, The Emil Aaltonen Foundation, The Konkordia Foundation, The Foundation of the University of Turku, and The Finnish Society of Sciences and Letters, all of which are gratefully acknowledged.

Chapter 5

The impact of race and ethnicity on children's peer relations

Julie Ann Robinson

Some research has shown that race and ethnicity dominate relations between children. Other research has shown that these have little importance. How can we make sense of this discrepancy? This chapter aims to provide a guide for the reader by outlining some of the concepts that underlie research in this field, providing a summary of relevant findings, highlighting methodological problems that inform the interpretation of these findings, and drawing attention to theories that may give coherence to apparently contradictory patterns of results.

Race and ethnicity

Despite their centrality, there is little consensus about the way the terms 'race' and 'ethnicity' should be defined, or whether these divisions represent 'natural categories' or are merely cultural constructions. In the present discussion, these terms are used to differentiate the types of cues peers provide. 'Race' is used to refer to differences in descent for which physical cues, such as skin colour and facial features, are usually available. Thus, Canadians of indigenous, European, Afro-Caribbean, and Asian descent show racial cues for group membership. In contrast 'ethnicity' is used to refer to differences in descent for which the primary cues are cultural (e.g., Flemish and Walloon groups in Belgium). This differentiation is consistent with dictionary definitions of 'race' and 'ethnicity' (e.g., *The Random House Dictionary* 1978). At least part of the current confusion in the research literature may result from studies relevant to the influence of ethnicity and studies relevant to the influence of race being pooled (e.g., Brown 1995).

Notwithstanding this, the boundaries of both ethnic and racial groups are usually unclear. A wide range of skin colour and other physical characteristics can be found within most racial groups, and a wide range of dialects, beliefs and customs can be found within most ethnic groups. Consequently, groups overlap in these respects. For example, if Nazi propaganda about the distinctiveness of Jewish Germans had been true, legislation requiring the wearing of an identifying yellow star would have been unnecessary.

Much of the research on the impact of race and ethnicity on children's peer relations has been framed in terms of majority or minority group membership. Rarely have possible differences between majorities been subject to empirical examination. For example, can the results of the white majority in the USA be pooled sensibly with those elsewhere when the composition of the majority, the size and identity of the minority groups, and the duration and nature (e.g., slavery, school segregation) of coexistence differ?

Minority groups also differ, for example in status and organization (Dreidger 1976), and this too influences the way group membership impacts on peer relations. In addition, there is heterogeneity within minority groups resulting, for example, from differences in distribution. Are peer relations the same for black Americans in Maine and Mississippi?

Moreover, it is important to use the ethnic distinctions current in the minority communities under investigation rather than in the wider population. A study of black children in London found: 'Jamaicans did not like Barbadians because they were Barbadians and vice versa. Both Jamaicans and Barbadians did not like Africans because they were Africans and vice versa' (Kawwa 1968: 179). What outsiders judged to be one group was judged by insiders to be many.

Despite this, several British studies have based analyses on an ethnically and racially heterogeneous 'coloured' group. Not surprisingly, results of such studies typically show that 'the in-group preferences of the majority white group of children is markedly stronger than the in-group preferences of the minority coloured group of children' (Durojaiye 1970: 199).

It should also be noted that the meaning of ethnic and racial categories changes with time. For example, the consequences of being Hutu or Tutsi in Rwanda have changed in the past decade. With one exception (discussed later) we have no information about the ways in which such historical change influences peer relations.

Peer relations

Following Burgess (1981), one can differentiate between three aspects of relations between children. 'Social behaviour' is evidenced whenever the behaviour of a child is influenced by the behaviour of one or more peers. The influence is unidirectional. (In the present context, it is useful to extend 'social behaviour' to include behaviour influenced by the ethnicity of peers.) 'Social interaction' occurs whenever two or more children exert a mutual influence on each other's behaviour. In 'social relationships', participants have interacted frequently over time with the result that their current behaviour is influenced by their previous history of interaction.

Most of the research on the influence of race and ethnicity on children's peer relations has focused on the first of these.

Social behaviour

Preferences among unknown peers

It is likely that the impact of race and ethnicity differs at different stages in the development of a relationship. One domain of social behaviour that may explain the initiation of acquaintanceship concerns children's preferences among unknown peers. This represents the largest body of data about the influence of race and ethnicity on children's peer relations, and almost all the data concerning the influence of ethnicity on social behaviour (cf. Banks and Rompff 1973; van Avermaet and McClintock 1988). However, it is difficult to provide a succinct summary of research findings because these vary with children's age, racial or ethnic group and cohort, and with situational variables such as instructions, stimulus materials and the race or ethnicity of the tester. The comprehensive summary of factors that influence preferences in adults and children provided by Brand *et al.* (1974) remains useful.

Most data on children's preferences for unknown peers were collected as an indirect measure of prejudice rather than for their own sake, and research designs reflect this. Children are typically shown an array of drawings or photographs[1] depicting peers from different racial or ethnic backgrounds and asked to nominate the peer who meets a certain criterion, e.g., 'Show me the one you like best' (Horowitz 1936) or 'Which person would you not like as a friend?' (George and Hoppe 1979), to answer the same question about each peer, e.g., 'Would you like to play with these children?' (Williams and Morland 1976), to rank order the array according to preference (e.g., Richardson and Green 1971), or to independently rate each member of the array on a scale, e.g., according to how close one would wish to sit near them (Aboud and Mitchell 1977). Because the information available to children is limited to cues of appearance, these techniques have usually been used to assess preferences for peers who provide racial cues of difference (Tajfel *et al.* 1972, Black 1987 and Maine 1996 are exceptions.)

Although the authors interpret their results in terms of preferences for ethnic or racial groups, this is unwarranted. Children are usually presented with only one or two exemplars of peers from each group. There is no empirical basis for the assumption that children prefer all peers from the same group equally, and instructions do not direct children to treat the peer as a representative of a group. Moreover, systematically collected data on children's reasons for preferences among unknown peers typically show references to inferred behaviours or personality characteristics, or to physical features (e.g., 'He has a nice smile') not closely linked with ethnicity or race (Aboud 1977; Maine 1996). Therefore, the most parsimonious position is that the results of individual studies reflect children's preferences for the particular peers they were shown, and that only consistency in findings for comparable samples would allow conclusions to be drawn about one group of children's general preference or dispreference for peers belonging to another group. Few studies involving similar measures or samples are available. Therefore the patterns in findings which are described below need to be viewed with caution.

Majority/minority status may influence bias in preferences for unknown peers. Many studies report an own-group bias[2] in preferences among children belonging to the majority group, but not children from minority or lower status groups. The latter children either favour peers from the majority, or, as a group,[3] show no consistent bias. This pattern is widespread. A bias in favour of the peer from their own group has been found among English but not Scottish children (Tajfel *et al.* 1972) and white but not West Indian children in Britain (Richardson and Green 1971); among white but not black (e.g., Horowitz 1936) or Hispanic children in the USA (e.g., Weiland and Coughlin 1979); among white but not Chinese children in Canada (Aboud 1977); among Pakeha (European descent) but not Maori (indigenous) children in New Zealand (Vaughan 1964); among Anglo-Australian but not children belonging to minority immigrant groups in Australia (Black 1987); and among children of European but not Oriental descent in Israel (Tajfel *et al.* 1972).

However, this pattern is not universal. For example, own-group preference or a bias against peers from the majority has been found in some minority groups, including Native Indians in Canada (e.g., Aboud and Mitchell 1977), Hispanic children in the USA (e.g., Newman *et al.* 1983) and the children of Indian immigrants to Australia (Maine 1996). In addition, own-group preference has not always been seen in children belonging to the majority group (e.g., Maine 1996).

Research has also examined the influence of several other sample characteristics. Own-group preference is not determined by whether one's society is racially homogeneous or racially heterogeneous, if race is not the basis for social stratification (Morland 1969; Morland and Hwang 1981). However, it is influenced by family composition and the age of the child. Marsh (1970) found that, unlike their peers, over 70 per cent of white British children with black adopted siblings preferred a black unknown peer. The direction of effect for age appears to differ across groups (e.g., Aboud 1988).

It has also been argued (e.g., Aboud 1988) that the sample cohort affects results. In particular, it has been argued that recent findings more often show an own-group bias for black children in the USA and Maori children in New Zealand than studies conducted prior to 1970.

These changes have been attributed to historical increases in racial consciousness (e.g., Vaughan 1987). However, it is unclear whether the change in results is real or illusory. Many samples of black children in the USA continue to show no bias in their preferences for unknown peers (e.g., Newman *et al.* 1983), and data from New Zealand are inconclusive.

In addition, the activity for which a partner is chosen influences whether an own-group bias is seen. Black (1987) found that while many Australian children 'didn't mind' who among an unknown Italian, Lebanese, Vietnamese and Anglo-Australian peer they played with, most did mind who was their neighbour or very good friend. Similarly, even though white children in the USA rarely nominate black unknown peers as the most preferred, most accept them as playmates (Williams and Morland 1976).

The form of sociometric questions may also influence results. Because many studies require children to nominate the single most preferred unknown peer, the degree of bias may be overstated. Studies using independent ratings of preference for each unknown peer have shown that children often like a peer from another ethnic group almost as much as one from their own group (Aboud and Mitchell 1977).

In summary, while many studies of children belonging to majority groups have found that the most preferred unknown peer for long-term or intimate relationships is a peer from the same group, this own-group preference is not always present for children belonging to minority groups. Although this pattern has been reported in many countries, it is sensitive to the composition of the child's family, task characteristics, and perhaps also to broad social and political changes.

Moreover, it is important to keep findings of bias in preferences for unknown peers in perspective. First, long-term, intimate relationships are likely to be influenced by characteristics other than appearance. For example, Maine (1996) found that preferences changed when children were told whether unknown peers shared their play interests. Second, an own-group bias in the most preferred peer may mask a high level of acceptance of children belonging to other groups. Finally, in most instances in which an own-group bias is seen, it is far from unanimous (e.g., Marsh 1970).

Drawing conclusions about the role race and ethnicity play in the development of acquaintanceship from these findings presents several difficulties. First, Brown's criticism of forced choice designs is valid for almost all preference studies involving unknown peers: 'the children were more or less obliged to differentiate between them on ethnic grounds if they were to discriminate at all' (Brown 1995: 136). It is unclear whether ethnic cues are normally attended to by children. For example, Davey (1983) reported that children often focused on small details of hairstyle and dress rather than on racial cues in deciding on their preferences. In addition, Richardson and Green (1971) found that disability exerts a greater influence than ethnicity on children's peer preferences. Clearly, further consideration of the salience of the ethnicity of peers is necessary.

In addition, because researchers determine the cues available in drawings and photographs, preferences for unknown peers reveal little about the types of ethnic and racial cues children typically attend to, or the purpose of this attention. Moreover, because systematic matching of photographs is rare, it is unclear whether it is ethnicity *per se* or specific features of appearance that account for children's preferences. However, it should be possible to exploit the overlap between groups on features such as eye, hair and skin colour, or to use computer manipulated images to determine this (see Maine 1996).

Salience of the ethnicity of unknown peers

Cues of ethnicity and race are not inherently perceptually salient differences between persons. Infants 5 to 6 months of age differentiate between photographs of unknown persons on the basis of age and gender but not race (Fagan and Singer 1979). After infancy, the salience of race and ethnicity relative to other characteristics of unknown peers appears to differ with differences in the wording of tasks (Davey 1983; Ramsey 1987), how peers are depicted (compare Ramsey 1983 with van Parys 1983), the group to which participants belong (Brown 1995), its size (e.g., Ramsey 1983), children's age (e.g., Aboud 1988; Davey 1983), and the wider sociopolitical context (compare studies using the same stimuli and instructions by Yee and Brown 1988 and Ferraresi 1988).

Given the large range of appearances, abilities, interests and personalities within each group, and the overlap between groups, the surprise is not that children are so inconsistent in the importance they accord ethnicity and race, but that these should ever be accorded importance. While this is also true for adults, several additional factors may be particularly relevant for children. First, many children do not know which ethnic group they belong to (e.g., Aboud 1977). (What do findings of own-group and other-group biases mean in such cases?) Second, children's understanding of the boundaries of other groups is often idiosyncratic. For example, Ramsey (1985) found that some young white children in the USA describe Chinese-American and black peers as being 'a little Chinese' and 'a lot Chinese', respectively. Third, young children rarely understand the racial or ethnic constancy of others. That is, they often indicate that skin colour is not permanent (Ramsey 1987), and that changes in costume alter the ethnic identity of peers (Aboud 1988). Fourth, children's own ethnic identity appears to be dynamic. For example, Rosenthal and Hrynevich (1985) found that adolescent children of immigrants to Australia identified as Italians or Greeks in some situations and as Australians in others.

The question then is whether, under normal circumstances, children make inferences about unknown peers on the basis of racial and ethnic cues, and if so, why these inferences are sometimes salient in peer relations. Very little systematically collected data are relevant. However, Aboud and Mitchell (1977) found that Canadian children inferred that peers would most prefer to play with another child from the same background. This raises the possibility that children choose unknown peers from their own group in order to minimize the risk of rejection. Would the pattern of past results be replicated if children were explicitly told that all the unfamiliar peers they were shown wanted to play with them?

Preferences for known peers

One means of assessing the salience of ethnicity relative to other characteristics of peers is to examine children's preferences among familiar peers. With familiar peers not only do children have access to cues to group membership that are not available in photographs or drawings, but also to information about the peer's individual personality, play interests, academic achievement, racial attitudes, and so on.

Once again it is difficult to provide a summary of findings. First, there is little overlap across studies in the ages of students, groups studied, or demographic composition of schools or communities. Second, many different measures have been used, relating to many different activities. Both factors influence results. For example, Shaw (1973) found an own-group bias for the most preferred peer, but no bias for the least preferred peer. In addition, as is the case for preferences for unknown peers, the intimacy of the partnership influences preferences (Carapetis and Robinson 1995; Whitley *et al.* 1984). Third, data have been presented and analysed in different ways.

Despite this, findings reveal several patterns. Whether or not biases in preferences are found is influenced by the ethnic composition of the classroom or school. In several different populations, own-group preferences have been found only in the group which comprises the minority in the school (Loomis 1943; Whitley *et al.* 1984; Carapetis and Robinson 1995). However, not all studies have found different patterns for the majority and minority groups in a class or school (e.g., Doyle 1982). The size of groups may be relevant to this inconsistency in findings. Durojaiye (1970) found that the majority group showed an own-group preference only when racial minorities comprised one-third or more of the class. The influence of class composition is a sufficiently consistent finding to raise concern over the interpretation of studies in which data were pooled from schools and classes that differed greatly in composition, but that have not included this factor in their analyses (e.g., Jelinek and Brittan 1975; Singleton and Asher 1979).

In summary, most studies have reported some evidence of own-group ethnic biases in preferences for known peers. However, these are sensitive to a number of characteristics of the child, the task and the context.

In addition, it is important to keep the evidence of biases in perspective. Three comments about the analysis of results are warranted. First, even when an ethnic bias is found for some activities, many children nominate a peer from another group as their preferred partner for at least one activity (Davey 1983). Because such patterns are common, the term 'ethnic cleavage' is not justified in most of the cases in which it has been used. Second, heavy reliance on sociometric questions requiring single nominations, and the use of conventional analysis of variance with ratings data, has resulted in little attention being paid to the variability in preferences for peers belonging to the same group. When round-robin analysis of variance is used, it is clear that children respond differentially to individual peers (Whitley *et al.* 1984). That is, the unique characteristics of the peer being rated are more important than his/her ethnicity in determining preferences for work and play partners. Third, few studies have examined effect size. In an exception, Singleton and Asher (1979) found that although there was a statistically significant own-race preference, race accounted for only about 1 per cent of the variance in children's peer preferences.

Social interaction

Most research investigating interactions between children from different racial and ethnic groups has focused only on the overall quantity of interaction. Much was triggered by the racial desegregation of schools in the USA following the Brown decision by the Supreme Court in 1954. Carithers (1970) provides a review of this research. She concluded that 'racial cleavage' increased with age. Subsequent research and research on other groups has not been consistent with this, or any other, simple pattern.

In summary, findings suggest that the particular groups under study (Doyle 1982; Carapetis and Robinson 1995) and whether a group is in a majority or minority in a class (Lederberg *et al.* 1986) may influence the quantity of inter-group interaction between preschool children. Among school-age children, such factors as the length of time in school (Finkelstein and Haskins 1983), present and past class organization (Schofield 1979), the size of the minority group (Shaw 1973; Silverman and Shaw 1973), and the activity for which the partner was chosen (Finkelstein and Haskins 1983) influence the quantity of peer interaction.

Other research concerns the frequency of particular types of interaction. For example, in Britain there appears to be no ethnic bias in bullying (e.g.,Whitney and Smith 1993).

Few studies have compared the quality of interactions between children from same and different ethnic and racial groups. Almost all have found differences. Hispanic, black and white preschool children show greatest interactive play with children belonging to the same group (Lederberg *et al.* 1986). Neither hearing status, children's age, nor time of the school year influence this pattern. Similarly, French- and English-speaking preschool children in Quebec have longer interactions, talk more, and engage in more pretend play with children from the same ethnolinguistic background (Doyle 1982).

Other studies suggest that differences in the quality of interaction between same-group and other-group play partners may be mediated by quantitative differences in the number of social acts directed to the same-race and other-race peers and in differences between groups in styles of interaction (Finkelstein and Haskins 1983).

The role of behavioural style and language

The behavioural styles of children belonging to different racial and ethnic groups may influence not only interactions but also peer preferences and peer relationships. Young children adopt patterns of behaviour, along with social rules and values, from their families and communities. When they encounter behaviour that contravenes these, they may become angry, confused or disgusted (e.g., Ramsey 1987). In addition, the awkwardness of interactions involving stylistic differences may lead to an own-group bias in preferences and relationships (Allport 1954). For example, both Swedish preschool children and teachers perceive Mediterranean children to be 'very wild' because of their higher activity level (Stockfelt-Hoatson 1979: 119).

Despite their relevance to all types of peer relations, most research on ethnic and racial differences in behaviour patterns has focused only on peer interactions or ethnic identity (e.g., Heller 1987).

Some stylistic differences in interactions between groups relate to language use. Corsaro (1994) found that Italian preschool children were distinguished by participation in intense and involved debates, 'discussione', black children in the USA by verbal jousting, and white children in the USA by use of language to regulate their partners' behaviour. He also found that these language styles were central to the formation and maintenance of peer relationships within each group. The potential for misunderstanding in inter-group interactions, and the consequences this might have for relationships, seems obvious.

Other differences in interactions appear to be related to linguistic ability. Stockfelt-Hoatson (1979) found that over 30 per cent of the variance in the popularity of immigrant children was accounted for by their ability to speak Swedish. The importance of language in relations between adults from different ethnic groups has been the subject of much research (e.g., Giles 1977). Much less attention has been paid to its influence on children.

Three Australian studies sharing similar designs and measures shed light on the way language proficiency can influence interactions between children from different ethnic and racial backgrounds. Target children were asked to play one-on-one using the same toys with two peers from their preschool class who differed in either ethnicity or language proficiency. The findings suggest that ethnic difference may influence the quality of inter-group interaction only when one of the peers has limited proficiency in the shared language. The quality of both play and speech during interactions between a target child from the majority and two minority group peers depended on the peers' proficiency in the shared language (Robinson 1994). When target children from the majority played with peers who were proficient in the shared language, ethnicity made no difference to the quality of play or speech (Carapetis and Robinson 1995). Target children from minority groups who were proficient in the shared language did not accommodate their speech when peers from the majority group had limited language proficiency (Ho 1995). This latter finding suggests that such interactions may be unsatisfactory for both partners.

Other aspects of linguistic behaviour may also influence interaction. Doyle (1982) reported that the quality of interaction between French-speaking and English-speaking children in Quebec depended not on fluency but on children's willingness to use the language of the preschool. Similarly, Brown (1973) attributed differences in the quality of same-group and other-group interactions between British primary school students to differences in the number of verbal contacts.

Several researchers have argued that what appears to be ethnic or racial bias in the quantity of interactions may really be a bias in favour of peers whose language (e.g., dialect, accent) is similar to one's own. However, Lederberg *et al.* (1986) found no evidence of this. This proposition has not been examined with respect to quality of interaction.

Social relationships

It is likely that ethnicity and race have a different impact on different types of relationships. However, ethnicity has been studied only with respect to friendships. Moreover, research on friendships has focused more on their frequency than their character. Studies of junior high school (Rosenberg and Simmons 1971) and high school students (Hallinan and Williams 1990) in the USA show a pronounced bias in favour of own-group peers when both black and white students nominate their best friends. This pattern has not always been observed among younger children in the USA. For example, Porter (1971) found no bias in friendships among nursery schoolchildren, and Hraba and Grant

(1970) found that over 60 per cent of both black and white 4- to 8-year-old children had other-race friends. It is unclear whether these different patterns reflect a developmental change related to racial awareness or friendship, or some other factor.

St. John and Lewis (1975) found that several factors influenced friendship patterns in multi-racial elementary classes. When there was a history of contact, no difference in academic achievement or social class, and no 'bussing' (of black students to schools in white neighbourhoods to meet desegregation requirements), there was no racial bias in the friendships of either black or white children. When the reverse was true, there were no inter-racial friendships. The presence of some but not all factors was associated with intermediate levels of bias.

Most other research has been conducted in Britain. It suggests that own-group bias is greatest for students in the minority in a school (e.g., Braha and Rutter 1980; Kawwa 1968). Kawwa's (1968) findings also highlight the importance of looking beyond the own-group/other-group distinction. For white, Cypriot and black children, a different pattern of friendships was observed for each of the other groups.

There has been little research on the qualitative differences between friendships with peers from the same and another group. However, these friendships may serve different functions (Hallinan and Williams 1990) and be associated with different levels of interpersonal acceptance (Damico *et al.* 1981).

There is very little research on the influence race and ethnicity exert on different aspects of friendships between children. First, we know little about whether race and ethnicity influence some facets (e.g., intimacy, competition) more than others, or influence some in different ways to others. Second, the interrelationships between developmental changes in children's understanding of ethnicity and race and children's inter-racial and inter-ethnic friendships are not understood. Third, there has been little attention to whether ethnicity influences changes within friendships, despite evidence that the factors that influence the initiation of relationships may differ from those that maintain them (e.g., Graziano and Musser 1982).

Theoretical contributions

The theories most frequently cited in this field are Allport's (1954) Theory of Prejudice, Attribution Theory (Heider 1958) and Social Exchange Theory (e.g., Burgess and Huston 1979). The potential of another, Self-categorization Theory (e.g., Oakes *et al.* 1994), has not been fully exploited.

This latter theory argues that the purpose of categorizing people into ethnic, racial or other groups is to bring together stored knowledge and the information currently available in a form that both makes sense of the world and facilitates the perceiver's goals. The process of social categorization selectively draws out aspects of similarity and difference between persons that are relevant to the perceiver's current requirements. Thus, a peer who is perceived to belong to another group in one context may be perceived to belong to one's own group in another, if either the aim or the set of comparison peers changes. Peers are more likely to be judged to belong to the same group if differences within the group are smaller than differences between it and others within that context (Oakes *et al.* 1994).

This has profound implications for the design of studies and the interpretation of results. It suggests that the composition of the stimulus array and the task in which the child is engaged are critical in determining who will be judged to be a member of the child's group and who will not, and therefore the basis for own-group biases. It also predicts that ethnicity will only be evoked as a social category in situations in which it has utility. This may explain the inconsistency in findings concerning the salience of ethnicity relative to other attributes of peers. In addition, the notion of changing frames of reference provides a possible explanation for apparent errors in young children's ethnic identity, and the dynamic nature of some adolescents' ethnic identity.

However, none of the above theories addresses developmental changes in the impact of ethnicity on children's peer relations. Age differences have not featured in the preceding review because too little research has used comparable measures and samples for a clear picture to emerge. However, Aboud (1988) has devised a three-stage developmental model based on changes in cognition. Many results concerning children from majority groups are consistent with this model, but it is unclear whether it can be applied to children from minority groups (e.g., Brown 1995).

Conclusions

Our understanding of the role race and ethnicity play in children's peer relations has a very narrow base: many ethnic groups in Western nations have not been subject to systematic study, and most of the world's multi-ethnic and multi-racial communities have not been studied at all. The drawing of general conclusions requires considerable caution since the impact of ethnicity on children's peer relations in the communities yet to be studied may be very different from the picture we currently have.

Nevertheless, does our present knowledge hold public policy implications? Are own-group biases in preferences, interactions and friendships a means by which the marginalization of minorities is perpetuated, and a forerunner of nationalist political movements and programmes of 'ethnic cleansing'? Or are they the inevitable consequence of a psychologically healthy identification with one's own group? Or both? The answers given by social scientists have changed over time. For example, the failure to find an own-group preference in black children in the USA was once interpreted as evidence of self-hatred, but this interpretation is now discredited (see Stephan and Rosenfield 1978). It is currently unclear whether the goals of peace and justice are best pursued by the elimination or the encouragement of own-group biases.

Similarly, whether patterns of bias have public policy implications depends on whether a society is pursuing a policy of apartheid, assimilation, integration or pluralism (Schofield 1986). For example, for those favouring assimilation, evidence of bias is evidence of failure. In contrast, pluralism values difference and tolerates the separateness that may be necessary for the preservation of culture.

One possible ground for concern, for those favouring assimilation, integration or pluralism, is the finding that some children would prefer to have more other-group friends than they do (Jelinek and Brittan 1975). Psychologists and educators have the techniques to overcome this discrepancy, regardless of whether it is caused by prejudice (e.g., Brown 1995; McGregor 1993; Rosenfield and Stephan 1981) or other factors (e.g., Johnson and Johnson 1995), and there seems little reason not to do so.

Notes

1 Data based on preferences for dolls or puppets will not be presented here. It is unclear whether children interpret these as toys, representations of peers, or representations of adults. Moreover, because these stimuli usually differ with respect to only a small number of physical features (often only skin colour) it is unclear either that the racial cue to which children typically attend is present, or that children interpret the stimuli as representations of real racial groups.
2 Also referred to as ingroup bias.
3 Group frequencies cannot be interpreted on an individual level (Aboud 1988). For example, a group that has preference scores that do not differ from chance may be comprised of two subsets of individuals with strong but opposite preferences.

Part III

Disability/illness/isolation

Chapter 6

The development of friendships and the puzzle of autism

Verity Bottroff

Autism and friendships may appear to some people as diametrically opposed or mutually exclusive concepts. This would not be surprising as the general perception of autism is still primarily the stereotype of individuals who prefer to be totally withdrawn from other human beings, and indeed Leo Kanner (1943), who was the first person to differentiate this syndrome, saw the extreme withdrawal of these individuals as a major aspect of the condition and hence utilized the term 'autistic' from the Greek word 'aphtotistis', meaning 'withdrawn into oneself'. All levels of intellectual functioning can occur in association with autism and it is recognized that significant intellectual disability occurs in approximately three-quarters of this population according to the *Diagnostic and Statistical Manual of Mental Disorders*, IV (DSM-IV) of the American Psychological Association (APA 1994). However, it is mainly those individuals with autism of normal and above intellectual functioning who have contributed in a significant way to our understanding of the disorder of autism in recent years and, in particular, have provided insights associated with their motivation and attempts at forming interpersonal relationships.

I am a member of a research team that works with individuals who have autism and are relatively able in intellectual functioning. Interactions with these individuals suggest that they not only have the desire for social interactions, but also some of the skills necessary for peer acceptance and social relating. Nevertheless, members of this team are also consistently struck by the persistent problems that confront students with autism in their attempts at reciprocal social relations. For example, there are individuals with autism who have graduated with various degrees from universities who report to members of this team that they experience difficulties understanding and developing friendships. What is striking and devastating is the discrepancy between specific areas of development. For example, the demonstration of real competencies in gaining tertiary qualifications on the one hand, with a genuine lack of understanding about what constitutes friendships on the other. Similar reports have been provided in writings from people with autism (Sinclair 1992; Williams 1994).

In addition, the research and clinical experience of members of the research team indicates that many adolescents with autism, particularly if they have developed relatively effective verbal and communication skills, often present with disturbed emotions of anxiety and depression (Tonge *et al.* 1993). It appears that during adolescence and young adulthood there is a realization of differences between themselves and others, including their difficulties in friendship development and peer relations generally. Such individuals have reported either personally (Miedzianik 1986; Sinclair 1992; Williams 1994) or through parental (Akerley 1992) and professional accounts (Mesibov 1992; Hartup and Sancilio 1986), of their desire to develop friendships during adolescence or young adulthood.

Hobson (1993: 8) provided a case vignette of a high functioning individual with autism who had a preoccupation with his inability to grasp the meaning of 'a friend'. He would continually ask people if they were a friend, and professional staff attempted to help him understand the concept of friend and even located someone to act as a 'befriender' to accompany him on outings, but he still appeared unable to understand the concept of a friend. Hobson raised the following thoughts about friendship upon reflection of the plight of this individual.

> What is so special, and in this case so elusive, about the concept of 'friend'? After all, this patient had little difficulty with other concepts that would have been far more problematic for young normal children. As children, most of us can be taught the meaning of the word 'friend' because we experience something of what it is like to engage with others in ways that are fitting between friends. We know what it is to have friends, to be a friend, to enjoy doing with friends those things that are the stuff of friendship.
>
> (Hobson 1993: 8)

Autism spectrum disorders

In addition to the personal insights from those with autism or people closely associated with them, attention has also been given to the higher functioning individuals with the recognition of the work of Hans Asperger, a Viennese Psychiatrist. Frith (1991) provided the first English translation of Asperger's original paper in which he described a very similar condition to that of Kanner's syndrome. However, it appears that those individuals identified by Asperger were of generally higher intellectual functioning. More recently, different variants of the condition have been referred to as 'Autistic Spectrum Disorders' (Bishop 1989; Gillberg 1991, 1995; Wing 1991) or 'Autism Spectrum Disorders' (Gillberg

1995), and include those individuals who experience the most extreme symptoms of Kanner's syndrome to those generally higher functioning individuals described as having Asperger's syndrome. Throughout this chapter the general term 'autism' will be utilized to refer to both high functioning autism and Asperger syndrome, as both groups were represented in the research carried out by the author.

Autism is a pervasive developmental disorder according to the widely accepted diagnostic classification, the DSM-IV (APA 1994). This classification system associates a diagnosis of autism with impaired functioning in social interactions (including emotions), communication (including pragmatics or communicative intention and function, and symbolic representations, including imaginative play), and restricted, repetitive behaviours (including difficulties in coping with changes to routines). In addition, the presence of this impaired development occurs before the age of 3 years. Gillberg (1995) highlighted that the prevalence of autism needs to take into account the various syndromes that comprise the Autism Spectrum Disorders, and the 'new' studies suggest a prevalence rate for autism of 10 in 10,000 children (Steffenburg and Gillberg 1989). The highest prevalence reported is in school-age children for whom the rate is 12–20 per 10,000 children born (Gillberg 1995). Gillberg (1995) indicated that this prevalence rate is likely to be closer to the true rate in the population than the rate for very young children, given the difficulties in diagnosing autism in the infancy and preschool periods. Males are four to five times more likely to have autism than females (APA 1994). The male:female ratio in Asperger syndrome is considered to be even higher (Gillberg 1995).

Research associated with the proposed primary deficits in autism

Since the time that Leo Kanner (1943) first described children with autism there has been considerable research and debate as to whether autism is primarily a disorder of affective and social functioning, or a disorder of cognitive and intellectual functioning (Fein *et al.* 1986). In order to provide context and a rationale for the major areas covered by the author's research, a brief overview will be presented of the major research positions associated with the possible primary deficits related to autism.

Hobson (1992, 1993) has been the strongest proponent for the role of affect or emotion, in the development of 'personal relatedness', as the primary deficit in individuals with autism. Although Hobson views affect as part of emotion, he does explain that affect is the expression or the sign of inner feelings, and it is the understanding of the signs that is the measurable component, and hence the focus of research. He considers that there is sufficient evidence to appreciate that reciprocal affect in early social interchange, such as facial, vocal and gestural expressions, poses particular difficulties for individuals with autism.

Baron-Cohen (1989a, 1989b, 1991, 1992, 1993) and Baron-Cohen *et al.* (1985, 1986) are the major researchers responsible for the focus on a 'theory of mind' impairment in individuals with autism. A theory of mind concept has arisen from the work of Premack and Woodruff (1978) who state that individuals possess a theory of mind if they impute mental states, such as intentions, beliefs, and thoughts, to themselves and others. Such mental states are not directly observable, they are inferred, and can be used to make predictions about the behaviour of self and others. Those researching theory of mind in individuals with autism (for example, those referenced above) view the difficulties associated with developing an understanding of mental states as the result of an impairment in the cognitive process of metarepresentation, where pretence is viewed as an early manifestation of the ability to understand mental states of self and others and to predict behaviour on the basis of such states.

Mundy and Sigman (1989), Mundy *et al.* (1993), and Yirmiya *et al.* (1992) proposed a model whereby the information source (shared affective exchanges) and the capacity to interpret this information (cognitive processes involved in the analysis) may be dysfunctional in individuals with autism. They propose that this may lead to specific joint attention deficits. Research highlights that children with autism understand adults as agents who can facilitate their acquisition of what they want in their environment, but they demonstrate real deficiencies in understanding a shared focus of attention. Unlike normal 1-year-olds, they rarely make gestures such as showing, giving, or pointing in order to share awareness of an object's existence or properties, or comprehend such gestures when these are made by others (Landry and Loveland 1988; Mundy *et al.* 1986; Wetherby and Prutting 1984). This apparent difficulty in shared communication appears to continue through development as even high functioning individuals with autism, when using language presumably to share experiences or topics, engage others in conversations that usually concern their specific interests rather than true social sharing (Akerley 1974). This model can be seen to incorporate aspects of the above two positions; namely, the importance of affect in personal relatedness and an understanding of concepts associated with theory of mind. This highlights the interaction of affect and cognition as a further possibility associated with a primary deficit in individuals with autism.

Development of friendships in individuals with autism

The area of friendship has not been the focus of research studies in the field of autism, despite the concerns expressed by individuals with autism about their difficulties in understanding and establishing friendships (Miedzianik 1986; Sinclair 1992; Williams 1994). In relation to the development of friendships and the puzzle of autism, the following questions are posed. How do proposed primary deficits relate to the difficulties experienced by individuals with autism in their understanding of friendships? What aspects appear most crucial to understanding and establishing peer friendships? In exploring these questions it is anticipated that what we may learn from the field of autism could provide further insights into the general field of peer relations. There is a further question that is of primary concern for people with autism and practitioners in the field. What can assist people with autism to establish and maintain peer friendships?

Although developmental levels associated with the definition and acquisition of friends have been a primary concern in the research report that follows, the definition of friendship by Hartup and Sancilio (1986: 61) that focuses on 'reciprocity and commitment within a relationship between individuals who see themselves as equals', is proposed as a general definition. It is recognized that this definition highlights a relatively mature level of development in acquiring and maintaining friends, including a high level of social-affective and cognitive skills. Such a concept of friendship involves aspects of development that individuals with autism find difficult, as discussed in association with the proposed primary deficits in autism. However, such an understanding of the concept provides a valuable reference point in an analysis of underlying skills. For example, the concept of reciprocity involves a sharing of interests, thoughts and feelings, incorporating a 'theory of mind'.

Recent research involving social cognition and friendships in individuals with autism

The author has recently conducted research with adolescents and young adults who have autism, to explore their understanding of concepts in the following areas of development: attributes of self and others, friendships, affects or emotions of self and others. A structured interview was designed to access this information and the content of this interview schedule took into account the research issues associated with the primary deficits of autism. Although it is only possible to summarize and discuss a small sample of the range of questions, those selected will address the major issues raised in the above discussion as well as represent the overall trend of the results.

The sample included 21 adolescents and young adults with autism (mean age 20.19 years) diagnosed either in early childhood or early teens by practitioners in the field, and they were receiving or had received services from centres for individuals with autism affiliated with the Autism

Associations of South Australia or Victoria. A comparison group consisted of 21 non-autistic adolescents and young adults with other developmental disabilities (mean age 18.33 years) assessed as having either significant learning difficulties, learning disabilities or mild intellectual disabilities. A third comparison group included 42 individuals with an age range of 4–18 years who were developing within the expected norms. For data comparison, this normative group was divided into the following sub-groups: 4–7 years, 8–11 years and 12–18 years. In terms of a Piagetian developmental profile these groups represent preoperational, concrete operational and operational thinking. Although the oldest group is the most appropriate group for comparison in respect to chronological age, it was anticipated that valuable information could be gained in having younger groups for comparison, particularly given the severity of difficulties reported in the area of social cognition for individuals with autism.

The two disability groups were matched on verbal ability and both groups divided into high and low functioning for additional comparisons. High functioning was defined with a score on the Peabody Picture Vocabulary Test (Form M), of 70 and above, and low functioning, below 70. The scores for non-verbal ability were significantly higher for the group with autism as is expected with this group (Wing 1989). Inter-rater reliability was carried out on the analyses of responses to the interview schedule and reliability was 0.85 and above (kappa statistic) for all ratings. The Kruskal Wallis statistic was utilized for the analyses of responses involving developmental levels, and a Chi-square test was employed for assessing qualitative differences in the nature of responses. The level of significance was set at 0.05.

Friends

The first area to be examined is that of 'friends', and the responses to the following two questions:

1 What is a friend?
2 How do you make friends with someone?

The responses to these questions were analysed utilizing a coding scheme based on the developmental trends demonstrated by researchers Selman (1980) and Z. Rubin (1980). Levels 1–5 included the following concepts: physical reality of proximity; knowledge of an individual's likes and dislikes; need to be liked and the importance of prosocial behaviour; need to know someone (interests, traits and values) over a period of time; awareness of phases in knowing someone. A score of 1–5 was awarded according to the developmental level reflected in the response. A score of 0 was given for 'don't know' or an irrelevant response.

Between-group comparisons in the analysis of the first question indicated that the difference in mean rank between the individuals with autism and those with developmental disabilities was not significant. However, a developmental trend could be seen in that the individuals with autism produced significantly lower levels of concept development in defining a friend, when compared with the normal 12–18 year group, and those with developmental disabilities were significantly more able than the normal 4–7 year group. Therefore, the group of individuals with autism presented responses which were more closely associated with the youngest normal group, and those with developmental disabilities responded more in-keeping with the oldest normal group.

When both disability groups were divided into high and low functioning, the major finding was the change in pattern for the sample of individuals with autism. The high functioning group did not demonstrate a significantly lower level of performance when compared with the normal 12–18 year group, but the low functioning group continued to do so. This pattern of difference was not evident for the group with developmental disabilities.

The second question focused on knowledge of skills associated with the acquisition of friends. The responses indicated increased difficulties for those with autism. The sample of individuals with autism scored a lower mean rank than the sample with developmental disabilities, but there was no significant difference between these two groups. Both these groups were significantly lower in performance when compared with the 12–18 year group. However, the individuals with autism were closer to the 4–7 year group in performance and those with developmental disabilities were functioning at the same level as the normal 8–11 year group.

When the disability groups were again divided into high and low functioning, both the high and low functioning individuals with autism were still clearly significant in their difference from the normal 12–18 year group. The low functioning autistic group was comparable to the youngest normal group in performance and the developmental trend for the high functioning autistic group was between the performance of the two youngest groups. However, the scores for both groups with developmental disabilities were comparable to those of the 8–12 year normal group, with marginal differences in terms of significance with the oldest normal group, whereby the low functioning group was significantly less able in performance and the high functioning group not significantly different. It was also apparent that it was somewhat easier for the high functioning individuals with autism to develop a concept of a friend than to understand how you make a friend.

Attributes of self and others

In the section 'Attributes of Self and Others', the focus of the analysis involved an understanding of an inner psychological self and theory of mind concepts, at the higher levels. The analysis of responses to the following question provides an example of the general trend in results for this section: How would you describe yourself?

The coding system for this question utilized the developmental progressions of self concept outlined by researchers Selman (1980) and Harter (1983). Levels 1–3 (allocated 1–3 points) included: physical appearance and possessions; the inner self, personal characteristics such as feelings, traits and motivations and the emergence of introspection including a second-person perspective, such as a parent's perspective of their behaviour; the psychological self, a third person perspective, including attitudes and beliefs reflecting a concept or theory of mind. The results provided evidence of cognitive processes reflecting theory of mind concepts for individuals with autism.

The group with autism was not significantly different from the normal 12–18 year group, whereas those with developmental disabilities marginally reached significance, demonstrating less ability. The other significant result to report involved the division into high and low functioning, whereby the mean rank for those classified as high functioning autism was comparable to the normal 12–18 year group and the low functioning group was significantly below that of the normal 12–18 year group. This pattern of contrasting results between high and low functioning individuals was less marked for the high and low groups with developmental disabilities than occurred between those with autism. Given these somewhat surprising results, particularly in view of most of the findings involving theory of mind concepts and autism, a further analysis was carried out to clarify further the number and percentage of responses associated with the three levels of development.

In comparing results with the normal samples, a developmental profile emerged which demonstrated that individuals with autism, particularly those high functioning individuals (verbal score of 70 and above), could produce cognitive responses associated with theory of mind concepts (Table 6.1). However, there was not a comparable level of cognitive ability evident in concepts associated with friends.

It is also relevant to note that only the high functioning group with developmental disabilities provided responses categorized as Level 3, theory of mind concepts. In addition, a developmental factor appears evident in that no Level 3 responses were indicated in the two youngest normal groups, whereas a relatively high number of such responses was recorded for the oldest normal group (72.22 per cent).

Given the social cognitive difficulties associated with autism, it was perhaps even more surprising that the high functioning autism group provided responses that conveyed either personal characteristics such as feelings, traits and motivations and the emergence of introspection including a second-person perspective (Level 2) or a third-person perspective,

Table 6.1 Comparison of levels of responses associated with descriptions of self (Level 3 representing the highest conceptualization) between the seven groups

	Level 1		*Level 2*		*Level 3*	
Group	*Number*	*%*	*Number*	*%*	*Number*	*%*
AUHF	0	0.00	5	45.45	6	54.55
AULF	5	50.00	5	50.00	0	0.00
DDHF	2	22.22	5	55.55	2	22.22
DDLF	5	41.66	7	58.33	0	0.00
1N	12	100.00	0	0.00	0	0.00
2N	8	66.66	4	33.33	0	0.00
3N	2	11.11	3	16.66	13	72.22
Total	34	40.48	29	34.52	21	25

Key
AUHF = Autistic High Functioning (score of 70 and above on the Peabody Picture Vocab Test).
AULF = Autistic Low Functioning (score of below 70 on the Peabody Picture Vocab Test).
DDHF = Developmental Disabilities High Functioning (score as above for AUHF).
DDLF = Developmental Disabilities Low Functioning (score as above for AULF).
1N = Normal 4–7 yrs.
2N = Normal 8–11 yrs.
3N = Normal 12–18 yrs.

including attitudes and beliefs reflecting a theory of mind (Level 3). No other group provided such a pattern of responses. Such results present somewhat of a puzzle when comparing responses to questions associated with friendship, as even the high functioning autism group, particularly in responses to the question about how you make friends, demonstrated a level of understanding that more closely resembled the youngest normal group.

Emotions

The third major category of questions involved concepts associated with affects or emotions. Respondents were asked questions such as:

1 What makes you happy?
2 What worries you?

Coding for these questions utilized the developmental findings of Harris *et al.* (1981) and Harris (1985). Level 1 (allocated 1 point) involved a situation-response, whereby the situation was linked to the emotional feeling, and Level 2 (allocated 2 points) involved the linking of the individual's emotions by reference to inner mental states. Across the results for perceptions about emotions a relatively consistent pattern was the unexpected high performance of the high functioning group with autism. This group was closer in performance to the 12–18 year group, which was not the trend hypothesized. The lower verbal ability in respondents with autism impacted negatively on their ability to process information associated with feelings about themselves. Although this trend was generally highlighted throughout the research, it was less marked in questions associated with friendship, where even the higher functioning group with autism experienced difficulties.

However, when a qualitative analysis (chi-square) was carried out on the nature of responses associated with emotions, a different picture emerged. For example, a significant difference was found in the degree to which people, in particular, friends and family, were associated with an individual's feeling of happiness. Happiness for individuals with autism was significantly less associated with people than for all other groups. There was no trend for the high functioning individuals with autism to be more people-oriented in their perceptions of what makes them happy than lower functioning individuals with autism.

In addition, individuals with autism cited rather unique, idiosyncratic activities in association with happiness. For example, the following response came from a member of the high functioning group:

> I'm happy doing something that I enjoy. Happiness is hard with me because unless I'm really doing something that I'm interested in . . . very specific things . . . such as Japanese cartoons, I'm not really happy.

Theoretical and personal issues arising from social cognition and friendship research

What do the above results suggest in relation to the questions about development that were posed at the beginning of this chapter and in the light of the current position regarding the primary deficits in autism?

With regard to social cognitive processing, individuals with autism, including those high functioning individuals, demonstrated particularly low developmental levels on concepts associated with friends. This was in contrast to the level of cognitive ability demonstrated in responses involving theory of mind concepts. Although theory of mind has been proposed as a possible primary deficit in individuals with autism, and a possible explanation for their difficulties in understanding and developing meaningful interactions with others, including peer relations, the results of this research do not appear to support this position. They do, however, provide some support to the likelihood of a developmental delay in theory of mind in autism rather than a specific primary deficit that underlies and can explain the condition of autism.

In addition, these results support the findings of Eisenmajor and Prior

(1991) and Leslie and Frith (1988) that verbal mental age is likely to be an important factor for theory of mind ability. There were 54.55 per cent of high functioning individuals with autism able to give responses categorized as Level 3, concept of mind, in describing self (Table 6.1). No such responses came from individuals with a verbal ability below 70. These results provide further support for the possibility of a developmental delay in theory of mind in autism rather than the likelihood of a specific deficit 'with pervasive explanatory power' (Eisenmajor and Prior 1991).

The area of affects and emotions indicated significant qualitative differences in the responses of individuals with autism. For those with autism, people were less associated with feelings of happiness, and the idiosyncratic interests in reference to happiness and activities that they enjoy or could enjoy doing with others would certainly limit their opportunities in developing peer friendships. The results of this research do highlight difficulties that could be associated with Hobson's proposal of the possible primacy of the social-affective impairment in autism. However, the interactive, joint attention model suggested by Mundy and Sigman (1989) also appears relevant to the search for an explanation of the real difficulties experienced by individuals with autism in their pursuit of peer relationships and friendships. The inability to share focus of attention in the early years of development may contribute towards difficulties in first understanding what friendships are really about and then knowing how to acquire and maintain them. This shared focus of attention would appear to have a primary function in the development of reciprocity that was highlighted in the definition of friendship proposed by Hartup and Sancilio (1986).

There is much to be learned about what happens to overall development when specific aspects of development are not synchronous. For example, if the reciprocity inherent in early social interchange has not developed during the primary years and individuals have a desire during teenage years to interact with others, and indeed develop what they perceive gives pleasure to others, namely friendships, will their future development be harmoniously integrated or will there be significant discrepancies or idiosyncrasies? How much time is required for individuals to practise, receive feedback and learn about the acquisition of friendships? How does this relate to individuals with autism who have great difficulties, particularly in their early years, in developing relationships with others that would provide the experiences for friendship development?

The findings from this research suggest that there would be value in pursuing Hobson's (1992: 177) postulation that we may need 'a more complex account of "cognitive" and "social-affective" impairments that may involve both developmental and nondevelopmental functional interdependencies'.

Personal implications

It is so easy to lose the individual human impact of situations with statistical group comparisons, therefore, the following comments from one of the high functioning individuals with autism have been selected to highlight the personal affect associated with difficulties in acquiring friends. The respondent's comments convey so vividly the desire and striving to improve peer relationships, to make friends, and the frustrations in not knowing what is really required, followed by the hurt and despondency. The risk of anxiety and depression would appear ever present.

'Why do you find it hard to make friends?'

For some reason I can't go much further than just saying, 'Hello . . . I'm [name] . . . and what are you doing?' . . . and all that sort of stuff. I can't go much further. I seem to be able to form a good first impression and get off to a good start but then somehow, for some reason, I can never get further than that. That's one of the things that I get worried about. I'm just not able to take things that extra step. I want to take things a bit closer, a bit . . . I want to be, like, with people more of the time and, you know, invite them around to my place and get invited around to theirs and share in their lives a bit more and have them share in my life and all the rest of it, but somehow that just never seems to materialize. I mean you can't make people like you but by the same token it makes life pretty awful.

'How do you feel about not having the sorts of friendships that you would like?'

I'm accepting of the situation. Sometimes I feel pretty lonely and yet I think I'll endure. I'm not . . . I'm not exactly, you know, over the moon about the way things are, but I'm not terribly, you know . . . I mean I've seen people that are a lot worse and I know there are worse things than . . . the way I am and I'm . . . I guess I accept it on the one level and on the other level I'm always trying to, trying to change it, and trying to get new friends and trying to get particularly, particularly good.

Other respondents from the high functioning group were able to elaborate somewhat on the above questions, expressing similar sentiments, although not as vividly as the above respondent.

'Why do you find it hard to make friends?'

It is hard to make friends because people often expect quite a lot of you. (Respondent 1)

Well most people are different to me, I suppose. Just say different personalities, different interests. (Respondent 2)

Oh, I just can't socialize very well. I hate sort of going out, going over to somebody else's house that I know. I just hate it. (Respondent 3)

'How do you feel about not having the sorts of friendships that you would like?'

Lonely. (Respondent 1)

Just feel empty, I suppose, and depressed. (Respondent 2)

Really lonely and depressed. (Respondent 3)

The acquisition of friends was viewed by research respondents as an important aspect to their quality of life. Romney *et al.* (1994) consider the ultimate determinant of a person's quality of life to be psychological well-being. Respondents have certainly highlighted negative psychological states associated with a lack of desired friendships.

Future research and practice

The above comments highlight the need for the development of programmes designed to teach a cognitive understanding and practical expression of friendship to individuals with autism. The development, implementation and evaluation of such a programme is an extension of this research (Bottroff and Duffield 1997). Although there have been programmes designed to teach social skills to individuals who have autism (Mesibov 1984; Williams 1989), and more recently attempts to analyse mental-state understanding (for example, theory of mind concepts) into simple principles to try and teach them through intensive training (Baron-Cohen and Howlin 1993), there have been no programmes located that focus specifically on the teaching of friendship skills. In addition, programmes that are intended to assist individuals develop positive peer relationships tend to rely upon basic social-cognitive skills that individuals with autism may lack.

A focus of the friendship programme (Bottroff and Duffield 1997) will include an analysis of the social cognitive skills that appear essential to the development of friendships, and have been highlighted as difficult concepts for individuals with autism to acquire. For example, concepts associated with a shared focus of attention (social-affective cognition) will be integrated into structured teaching activities including roleplaying, video feedback, and friendship games, incorporating the design of a computer game. Social activities will be included whereby teaching techniques such as coaching and modelling can be utilized to encourage practice of the cognitive concepts and facilitate generalization of skills. Developmental profiles, such as those utilized to analyse responses associated with concepts of friendship and knowledge of how friendships are acquired, will also be employed in assessing individuals' levels of understanding, as a guide for teaching sequential cognitive concepts, and in evaluation of cognitive outcomes. The teaching emphasis is on changing the individual's understanding and way of thinking, and not just changing behaviour. The overall aim of the project is an investigation of whether teaching key aspects of social cognition that appear associated with the ability to acquire friends, is possible, and if so, whether such teaching affects social behaviour.

It is anticipated that such a programme, designed to assist individuals with autism acquire peer friendships, will have relevance to other populations experiencing similar difficulties – for example, individuals with acquired brain injury. It is hoped that more knowledge can be gained about the stages or 'stepping stones' to successful peer relationships and peer friendships that may contribute to our knowledge of the field in general. In particular, knowledge of the cognitive and social-affective areas and their possible developmental and functional interdependencies as highlighted by Hobson (1992). For example, what role does emotion play in the development of a shared focus of attention? Is this an aspect of development that is crucial to reciprocity, and if so, can individuals with autism be taught skills associated with emotional cognition that may assist them in developing reciprocity associated with friendships? A personal experience reported by Sinclair suggests that individuals with autism can learn such skills if professionals are sufficiently aware of the difficulties that may be experienced:

> No one ever told me that they expected to **see** feelings on my face, or that it confused them when I used words without showing corresponding expressions. No one explained what the signals were or how to use them. They simply assumed that if **they** could not **see** my feelings, **I** could not **feel** them. I think this shows a serious lack of perspective taking!
>
> (Sinclair 1992: 297)

What is known about general human development suggests that shared focus of attention (for example, a young child giving a toy to the caregiver for the sole purpose of a shared experience) is an earlier stage than the development of a 'theory of mind'. However, a puzzle remains if individuals with autism can cognitively demonstrate a theory of mind, yet indicate difficulties in cognitively processing an understanding of reciprocity in association with friendships.

Finally, if individuals with autism can learn cognitive skills associated with the acquisition and maintenance of friends, can they learn how to utilize such skills and then actually put them into practice in order to achieve peer friendships? The following accounts by two people with autism suggest that such learning is possible. Williams (1994: 120), provides personal evidence of how she gained insights into social interactions, when in her adult life she learned that the primary function of words was putting them together to share back and forth 'as part of how people grow together'. Through her ability to speak with focus she 'learned to enjoy conversation and how friendship grows, not in spite of language but because of it'. Sinclair (1992: 296) also highlights how he was in his early teens before he realized that speech 'could be a way to exchange meaning with other minds'. Given the evidence from the research carried out by this author, that individuals with autism are likely to have very specific interests that may not be shared by the majority of their peers, it may be easier initially to facilitate friendships between individuals with autism as reciprocity could be more readily established. This may be a valuable 'stepping stone' to a wider choice of friendships in accordance with an individual's view of his or her quality of life.

Acknowledgements

The author wishes to acknowledge the support of the three other members of the research team, Dr Lawrence Bartak, Pam Langford and Professor Bruce Tonge.

Chapter 7

Social skills and peer relationships of siblings of children with disabilities

Parental and family linkages

Barbara L. Mandleco, Susanne Frost Olsen, Clyde C. Robinson, Elaine Sorensen Marshall and Mary Kay McNeilly-Choque

For a number of years researchers have studied families of children with disabilities and their impact on family relations and individual well-being. Early work in this area tended to be narrow in focus since it typically relied solely on the mother, who as an informant described her own perceptions of the experience (cf. Crowley and Taylor 1994; Powell and Gallagher 1993; Stoneman and Brody 1993). More recently, researchers have broadened their studies by using other family members (including siblings, fathers) as informants and assessing their well-being. This chapter extends this later strategy and has two purposes. First, we examine one aspect of children's well-being, i.e. the social skills and peer relationships of children who have a sibling with special needs. Second, we investigate the relationship between these children's social skills (rated by teachers) and parental and family variables, as measured by perceptions of both mothers and fathers.

The experience of living with a child with a disability is almost always an unanticipated event which may place additional stress on family members and create the potential for disrupting the family (Heaman 1995). A family systems perspective recognizes that stresses associated with living with a child with a disability may be linked not only to the adjustment of individual family members, but also to general family functioning, including marital, parent–child, and/or sibling relationships (Bristol and Gallagher 1986; Crowley and Taylor 1994; McHale and Gamble 1989).

Early research on the well-being of siblings of a child with special needs typically compared siblings of well children (non-disabled) with siblings of children with disabilities to examine differences in personal adjustment (psychological well-being) between the two groups (Gamble and McHale 1989; Gath 1972, 1973; Lobato *et al.* 1987). Individual differences between groups, if found, were assumed to be attributed to the presence of the child with special needs in the family. By only examining individual differences between sibling groups, researchers neglected the study of family relationships that may be related to sibling personal adjustment, leading to a failure to identify or explain family processes associated with individual adjustment (Stoneman 1989).

In this chapter, we examine children's social skills and peer relationships, and also identify linkages among perceptions of parental depression, family functioning (cohesion, conflict), and siblings' social skills in the school context. We begin by discussing social skills of children in families with well siblings and how they are linked to peer relationships. Next, we discuss the social skills and peer relations of children who have a special needs sibling. We then examine relationships among parental depression, family functioning, and children's social skills, integrating research on well children with studies of children who have a sibling with a disability or chronic illness. We also include some of our current research findings to enhance the discussion. Finally, we discuss implications for interventionists and suggest avenues for future research.

Children's social skills and peer relationships

The establishment of positive and effective peer relations in early childhood is important, since children who initially have peer problems are considered to be at risk for many social/psychological difficulties throughout their lives (DeRosier *et al.* 1994; Parker *et al.* 1995b). For example, Kuperschmidt and Coie (1990) followed children from fifth grade through high school and found aggressive behaviour in childhood was related to poor school performance, juvenile court appearance, and teenage truancy. Similarly, Eron (1987) found that a high level of aggression towards peers during childhood was related to adult criminal behaviour, spousal abuse, and harsh disciplinary practices towards their own children.

Because early experiences may be related to negative adult outcomes, researchers have sought to identify specific behaviours that have implications for social interactions occurring in relationships. Three prominent broad behavioural categories of social skills that impact children's social interactions have been identified in the literature: internalizing, externalizing, and sociable behaviours. Internalizing behaviours may be manifested as reticence, withdrawal (Rubin *et al.* 1995), solitary-passive, solitary-active or immature play (Hart *et al.* 1997). Children may seem anxious, sad, lonely, or have poor self-esteem. Depending on the child's age or other considerations, these behaviours may or may not be maladaptive in terms of isolation from or rejection by peers (e.g., Coplan *et al.* 1994). Externalizing behaviours typically include verbal or physical aggression towards others, poor control of temper, arguing, and impulsive/disruptive and non-conforming behaviours which are related to peer rejection

(Campbell 1995). Externalizing behaviours have been found to be quite stable across time and contexts (Campbell *et al.* 1994).

Internalizing and externalizing difficulties in preschoolers and elementary children reflect social skill deficits not conducive to normative social/emotional growth and well-being, which impact relations with others. Internalizing young children who demonstrate a consistent pattern of reticence or unassertive social and communicative strategies, and externalizing children, who tend to communicate their desires less skilfully, may be seen by others as less socially competent, and therefore may have difficulty establishing effective peer relationships (Rubin *et al.* 1995).

Sociable behaviour, on the other hand, refers to behaviours leading to positive psycho-social outcomes, such as peer acceptance and effective relationships with others. They may be manifest as impulse control, and conforming, friendly/amicable, helping, sharing, comforting, or co-operative behaviours. Young children displaying sociable behaviour are able to discern the emotional states of others, are more adept at regulating their own emotions (Eisenberg *et al.* 1995), and during social interactions, communicate appropriately and relevantly (Black and Logan 1995; Guralnick *et al.* 1996).

The ability to establish social skills used in relationships is hypothesized to be linked to three types of family and ecological factors: distal, proximal, and personal (Hart *et al.* 1997). Distal factors include extra-familial variables such as employment/role strain, intergenerational factors, socioeconomic status, stress and support, and culture. Proximal factors are described as intra-familial variables such as parenting practices, and interactions and relationships within and between family members, including the siblings and parents. Personal factors include innate personal/psychological characteristics of both the parent and child, such as gender, genetics, and developmental level.

One of the most important proximal factors thought to be related to child development and peer relationships is the sibling relationship (Dunn 1992). Sibling relationships are unique among family relationships because of their common cultural milieu, egalitarian nature, and duration. In many families sibling relationships provide physical and emotional contact at critical life stages, help children learn sociable and problem behaviours (Martin and Ross 1995; Stormshak *et al.* 1996), and are usually the first, most intense, and longest peer relation an individual will have (Powell and Gallagher 1993).

Social skills and peer relationships of siblings of a child with special needs

Because the presence of a special needs child in a family may have social, mental and emotional effects on siblings there may in turn be unique consequences for well-being, development, and relations with others (Brody and Stoneman 1986). Sibling reactions to a disabled brother or sister, however, may vary with the type of disability (Cicirelli 1995; Stoneman 1993). In addition, sibling adjustment also depends on the type and quantity of stress the disabled child may place on the family, the affective reactions to a potentially stressful event, and coping responses employed by parents and siblings (Cicirelli 1995; Gamble and McHale 1989).

The presence of a special needs child in a family may have both direct and indirect effects on siblings (Brody and Stoneman 1986; Simeonsson and Bailey 1986). Direct effects include day to day interactions, as when the well sibling is a caretaker, manager, teacher, or helper for the disabled child. Many of these roles influence interactions with peers, as children learn to develop understanding and compassion for others (Stoneman *et al.* 1989). Children with these experiences may realize it is important to have close social bonds with others, learn to value these bonds, and therefore work harder to keep their relationships satisfying (McHale and Gamble 1988).

Indirect effects refer to the influences of family circumstances and interactions on the well child. For example, often in families with children with disabilities, parents have less time and energy for the well siblings' needs and limited resources for recreation and leisure. Other challenges may include an unequal division of responsibility for physical care of the special needs child, or smaller social networks with fewer friends and neighbour contacts (Boyce *et al.* 1991; Lobato 1990; McHale and Harris 1992; Powell and Gallagher 1993; Simeonsson and Bailey 1986). These situations, as well as differential treatment by parents, loss of normal sibling interaction, increased family stress (Dyson *et al.* 1989; McHale and Harris 1992), frequent disruptions of family plans, and occasional absences of the disabled child and parents for special treatments, may influence a child's relationships with others, including their peers (Lobato 1990). Indirect influences also may impact empathy development, or, on the other hand, can result in feelings of guilt, resentment, or jealousy over less attention from other family members (McHale and Harris 1992; Simeonsson and Bailey 1986).

Recently researchers have focused on how children with a special needs sibling interact with others, especially in the peer group. Past work on sibling well-being in families with a child with special needs has yielded inconsistent results (Boyce and Barnett 1993; Gallo and Knafl 1993). For example, McHale and Gamble (1988) report school-aged children with disabled siblings do not differ in their social networks from children with well siblings. Some research indicates there are no differences between groups of school-aged siblings on measures reflecting sociable behaviours as perceived self-concept, social and self-competence, acceptance, and empathy (Lobato *et al.* 1987; Powell and Gallagher 1993).

In contrast to the research showing no differences between groups, other studies have found positive or negative outcomes. For example, positive effects for siblings of children with disabilities include sociable behaviours such as feeling warmth, compassion, and increased tolerance for differences in others, higher levels of empathy, affection and helpfulness, an increased sense of responsibility and maturity, happiness, and a well-adjusted outlook on life (McHale and Harris 1992; Powell and Gallagher 1993). Other investigators, however, found negative effects for siblings of children with special needs. These included internalizing and externalizing behaviours such as increased sibling conflict, anxiety, bitterness, resentment, loneliness, guilt, fear, role tension within the family, and decreased opportunity for peer contacts and activities outside the home (Abramovitch *et al.* 1987; Cadman *et al.* 1988; Dunn 1992; Frank 1996; Powell and Gallagher 1993; Howe 1993; LeClere and Kowalewski 1994; Stoneman *et al.* 1989; Tritt and Essess 1988).

Depression (Lobato *et al.* 1987; McHale and Gamble 1989; Treiber *et al.* 1987), aggression (Lobato *et al.* 1987), lower levels of perceived competence in social acceptance and conduct (McHale and Gamble 1989), irritability, social isolation, loneliness (Meyer and Vadasy 1994), poor peer relations (Cadman *et al.* 1988), withdrawal (Tritt and Esses 1988) and feelings of inferiority and guilt (Simeonsson and Bailey 1986) are other behaviours indicating negative effects.

Several reasons for these problems have been proposed. McHale and Gamble (1987) speculate adjustment problems, if they do exist, might be related to the extra burdens assumed by siblings when there is a child with special needs in the family. For example, sisters older than the child with disabilities are more likely to have behaviour problems, and generally are asked or expected to assume greater responsibility in the family (Frank 1996; McHale and Harris 1992). Alternatively, other factors influencing sibling adjustment include the age of the special needs child and the severity of the disability (Powell and Gallagher 1993). In addition, the more atypical and aggressive the behaviour of the special needs child (Frank 1996), and the closer in age the sibling with the disability is to the well child (Cicirelli 1995), the greater the adjustment problems. Well siblings may also feel left out or excluded from the parent–special child dyad, and assume parents expect more from them (Simeonsson and Bailey 1986). McHale and Harris (1992) report that children (ages 6–12 years) with disabled siblings give more than they receive from relationships which, in turn, is related to their adjustment. Adjustment does, however, seem to be better for children in large families, perhaps because of shared caregiving responsibilities (Dyson 1989; Lobato 1990). Finally, Cicirelli (1995) suggests sibling adjustment is related to age. School age and adolescent children seem to adjust better, probably due to their higher levels of cognitive ability which allows them to understand the nature of the disability and problems associated with the condition.

Current research project

In our own research, we studied two groups of children. The first group consisted of 39 siblings of children with special needs or disability. Special needs was defined as any condition that qualified a child for federally mandated early intervention programmes. The majority of children with special needs (85 per cent) had multiple disabilities, including speech disorders, visual and hearing impairments, Down's syndrome and other types of mental retardation, congenital heart anomalies, cerebral palsy, autistic disorders, and developmental delay. The second group was a sample of children with well siblings. The two groups were matched by age and gender. Each group included 26 boys and 13 girls. The mean age for siblings in the disability and non-disability groups was 7.36 and 7.43 years, respectively (range 4–11 years). Demographics for the matched sample and differences between variables of interest appear in Table 7.1. T-test results indicated no significant differences between the two groups of siblings on the variables age, number of children in the family, and parents' age and hours worked. In addition, chi-square tests (not shown) revealed no difference between parents in both groups in relation to parents' full-time employment and education. The majority of fathers were employed full time, and more mothers were employed part-time. Both mothers and fathers had completed at least one year of college. The only variable where significant differences existed was family income, which was higher in families where there was a child with special needs.

Because parental reports concerning their children may be positively biased (Cicirelli 1995), teachers were utilized in assessing children's social skills. Teachers who had known the children for at least six months completed a modification of the Social Skills Rating System (Gresham and Elliot 1990) which rated siblings' social skills and problem behaviours. Subscales in the measure included conformity, co-operation with peers/assertion, self-control, hyperactivity, internalizing, and externalizing behaviours in school settings. Ratings were 0 (never does behaviour), 1 (sometimes does behaviour), and 2 (very often does behaviour). Teachers also evaluated sibling's peer status with a scale that ranged from 1 (very well liked) to 5 (very disliked).

Mean scores for social skills and problem behaviours are presented in Table 7.2. No significant differences were found between groups on problem behaviours. For positive measures of social skills, findings show group differences. Siblings of children with disabilities scored significantly

Table 7.1 Demographic variables

	Mean well siblings	*Mean special needs siblings*	*t-test*
Age in years	7.43	7.36	0.86
Number of children in family	3.42	3.18	−0.76
Mother's age in years	31.26	32.97	1.52
Father's age in years	33.35	34.81	1.14
Father's hours worked	39.11	44.11	1.59
Mother's hours worked	24.53	24.50	−0.01

Table 7.2 Means, standard deviations and t-tests, social skills and problem behaviours

	Well sibling	*Special needs sibling*	*t*
Self-control	1.36	1.62	2.72*
Co-operative with peers/assertion	1.18	1.56	3.69†
Conformity	1.62	1.73	1.26
Externalizing	0.40	0.26	−1.52
Internalizing	0.55	0.40	−1.34
Hyperactivity	0.60	0.46	−1.13

Notes
*$p < 0.01$; †$p < 0.001$.

higher than siblings of well children on co-operation ($t = 3.69$; $p < 0.001$) and self-control ($t = 2.72$; $p < 0.008$).

To test the relationship between sibling social skills and peer status, correlations were calculated. Lower peer status for siblings of disabled children was associated only with externalizing ($r = 0.46$; $p < 0.001$) and internalizing ($r = 0.55$; $p < 0.001$) behaviours; children scoring higher on these behaviours were less well-liked by their peers.

Our project results support findings of previous research (McHale and Gamble 1988; McHale and Harris 1992; Powell and Gallagher 1993; Stoneman *et al.* 1989) that indicate in some cases siblings of children with disabilities demonstrate positive social skills necessary for effective peer relations. Also in support of prior work (Rubin *et al.* 1995), we found that sibling internalizing and externalizing was related to lower peer status.

Parental depression, marital conflict, and family functioning: linkages with children's social skills

As mentioned above, work on siblings of children with disabilities typically has neglected the empirical investigation of the relationship between siblings' social skills and parental and family functioning. These associations should be considered, however, because such studies provide insight into family processes that may underlie differences among families where there are children with disabilities and families with well children (Stoneman 1993). In this section the literature linking parental depression, marital conflict, and several dimensions of family functioning with children's social skills is reviewed. The limited research concerning these relationships in families with a child with special needs will also be highlighted, and then information from our research related to associations between these constructs will be presented.

Parental depression

Research on families with well children demonstrates a link between parental depression, family relationships, and children's social skills outcomes. Depression may be directly and indirectly related to children's social skills. A direct relationship has been shown in research by Zahn-Waxler *et al.* (1984), who found that children whose parents were more depressed also show lower levels of sociable behaviours in playmate interaction. Other direct effect research (Ladd 1992) indicates children of depressed parents also seem to be at risk for social withdrawal as well as adjustment problems at school. An indirect relationship between parental depression and children's social skills has also been documented. Parents who are depressed often experience difficulties in close, interpersonal relationships and have higher rates of marital conflict (Downey and Coyne 1990); they also are more likely to have an authoritarian or permissive parenting style. Thus, mothers scoring highly on depression are more likely to be ineffective in their parenting, resulting in their children exhibiting higher levels of externalizing and internalizing disorders (Dix 1991; Downey and Coyne 1990; Field 1995; Frank 1996).

Several explanations have been offered for the mechanisms linking parental depression and children's internalizing behaviours. One suggestion is that internalizing problems are inherited. Continual exposure and interaction with parental depression also may affect children. Other factors such as poverty and marital conflict may be linked to depression in both parents and children (Downey and Coyne 1990; Zahn-Waxler *et al.* 1984). Children's depression-related problems could also be related to dysfunctions within the child (i.e., negative attributional styles or self-concept), and other factors including the spousal relationship and/or family functioning. The extent of the influence, however, may depend on other protective/risk factors (Zahn-Waxler *et al.* 1992).

Research on families with a special needs child indicates that mothers' reports of their own physical and mental health are positively correlated with sibling adjustment (Lobato 1990; Lobato *et al.* 1988). Similarly, in families where a child has a chronic illness such as sickle cell anaemia, maternal depression and anxiety are related to sibling problems (Treiber *et al.* 1987). Frank (1996) also observed that parental depression may indirectly be related to sibling adjustment. For example, depression may drain parental internal resources, leaving them less available to support and attend to siblings' needs (Gamble and Woulbroun 1993). In these families, parental depression also may lead to inconsistent or punitive parenting which may induce unhealthy levels of guilt and anxiety in children (Frank 1996).

Howe (1993) suggests that a child's disability also may indirectly impact sibling adjustment by influencing both the parents' emotional health and marital relationship. Other findings (Breslau 1983) concur, indicating that maternal depression and family cohesion are linked to disability; however, this occurred more often when the family experienced economic loss as a result of the disability.

Current research project

In our own work, parents in both groups evaluated their own level of depression by completing the Center for Epidemiological Studies Depression Scale (CES-D), a measure developed for use with the general population (Radloff 1977). When we compared parents in the two groups, both mothers and fathers of children with disabilities scored higher on the depression scale than parents of well children (mothers: $t = 2.14$, $p < 0.037$; fathers: $t = 2.44$, $p < 0.022$). Our findings support earlier work which found that mothers of children with disabilities score higher on depression (Breslau and Davis 1986; Wilton and Renaut 1986). In addition, we add to the literature by showing that fathers of children with disabilities also rate themselves higher on depression than fathers of well children.

When parental depression scores were correlated with siblings' social skills ratings in families with special needs children, we found that as maternal depression scores increased, so did teacher ratings of sibling internalizing behaviour ($r = 0.44$, $p < 0.01$). An unusual finding was that in families with well children, higher maternal depression scores were related to lower teacher ratings of internalizing behaviours for the sibling ($r = -0.46$, $p < 0.006$). In families with well children, paternal depression scores were correlated with ratings of less co-operative behaviour of siblings ($r = -0.43$, $p < 0.04$).

In sum, findings indicate that depression scores of mothers and fathers in families of children with disabilities were higher than those of parents of well children. Additionally, maternal depression scores were related to teacher ratings of internalizing behaviours of siblings in both groups. Fathers' depression scores were linked to teacher ratings of less co-operative behaviour of siblings in well families only.

Marital conflict

Marital conflict has been linked to poor social skills outcomes in children (Cummings 1994a, 1994b). What is not well understood, however, is whether the same dynamics operate in families where there are children with disabilities. For families of well children, marital conflict seems to be a better predictor of children's internalizing and externalizing behaviours than are global measures of marital satisfaction (Cummings 1994a, 1994b). Marital conflict is associated with poor social competence and internalizing and externalizing behaviours (Katz and Gottman 1994). In addition, lower levels of marital satisfaction and increased spousal conflict have been found to negatively influence prosocial behaviour among siblings (Brody 1987).

The link between marital conflict and child outcomes for families with well children has been explained by a variety of interpretations (cf. Hart *et al.* 1997). First, children may model interparental conflict, believing it is acceptable (Cummings 1994a). Second, parental conflict may contribute to a context within the family that includes background anger as a family stressor. For example, angry and argumentative adult exchanges have been related to externalizing and internalizing childhood behaviours (Bryant and DeMorris 1992; Grych and Fincham 1993). Recent empirical research in Russia (Hart *et al.* 1998a) supports this explanation. Third, children who observe their parents fighting may develop 'hostile attributional biases', resulting in more aggressive behaviour (Rutter 1994). Finally, parenting may mediate marital relationships and children's social development outcomes (Belsky 1984), perhaps because parents involved in their own conflicts may be less effective or consistent in their disciplinary practices, or the conflict itself may drain emotional energy from the parent–child relationship (Wilson and Gottman 1995).

In families where there are children with disabilities, marital relationship quality also may play an important part in siblings' adjustment (Lobato 1990). Because of additional stressors, marital quality may be compromised in these families, resulting in marital relationships that are more dissatisfying and argumentative. Thus, in families where there is a child with special needs, sibling social maladjustment may reflect the child's responses to stressed or disharmonious marital relationships (Lobato *et al.* 1988).

Current research project

In our research, mothers' and fathers' reports were assessed because mother reports, though common, are but one perspective in the complex family system (Crowley and Taylor 1994). Therefore, each parent's perceptions of marital conflict in front of the children was assessed using the Porter–O'Leary Scale (1980).

When using reports from both parents, Furman (1993) notes that the magnitude of differences in perceptions between family members may be greater in families where there are children with disabilities. Contrary to this, in our sample, paired t-tests indicated there were no significant differences between mothers' and fathers' reports of marital conflict. We also found that mothers' and fathers' marital conflict scores were moderate to highly correlated ($r = 0.67$, $p < 0.001$). When no significant differences exist between mothers' and fathers' scores and correlations are higher than 0.30, it is deemed appropriate to sum the two scores to create a 'family variable' score (Larsen and Olson 1990). Therefore, we used this strategy in computing the variable of marital conflict and other variables of family functioning.

We then compared marital conflict scores for families with and without children with special needs. There were no significant differences between groups. Next, correlations were calculated using marital conflict scores and teacher ratings of children's social skills. Results showed, for both groups of families, marital conflict scores were related to teacher ratings of sibling social skills, but the type of social skills varied across groups. For example, in families with well children, we found the more the marital conflict, the less co-operative the behaviour of the sibling ($r = -0.42$, $p < 0.01$). However, in families with a child with special needs, marital conflict was related to increased amounts of sibling externalizing ($r = 0.65$, $p < 0.001$) and internalizing ($r = 0.34$, $p < 0.05$) behaviours and lower amounts of self-control ($r = -0.52$, $p < 0.001$). Thus, in both groups of siblings, the dynamics between marital conflict and children's behaviours were similar to those found in previous research with families of well children: marital conflict was related to less positive social skills in children; however, the specific social skills linked to marital conflict varied across groups.

Family functioning

In addition to marital conflict, family functioning is also considered to be linked to children's social skills (Campbell 1995), although these relationships have not been studied extensively in families of children with disabilities. Family functioning has been conceptualized as multi-dimensional, including family cohesion, idealization, conflict, and enmeshment (Bloom 1985; Bloom and Naar 1994). Every family has a characteristic manner of functioning (Slee 1996), which may be perceived uniquely by parents or other family members. In general, children showing adjustment problems come from families that are more dysfunctional (Campbell 1995).

Family cohesion is one dimension of family functioning where empirical findings with families of well children support a link with children's social skills, although research addressing this relationship is not extensive and comes from a variety of sources. For example, in research performed in Italy and England, lack of family cohesion is related to bullying in middle childhood (Berdondini and Smith 1996; Bowers *et al.* 1994). Associations also have been found between less cohesive family relationships and younger children's problem behaviours (Crnic and Greenberg 1990). In contrast, popular children are more likely to come from cohesive families (Bryant and DeMorris 1992). Research with clinical families also indicates that those with moderate amounts of cohesion have children with fewer behaviour problems (Smets and Hartup 1988).

Another dimension of family functioning associated with children's adjustment is family conflict. In families with well children, Campbell (1995) reports mothers of children with problem behaviours are more likely to have conflicted family relationships. Slee (1996) also indicates mothers of conduct-disordered children perceive their families as less cohesive and expressing more conflict than mothers of children without these problems.

Although the research on children with well siblings has found relationships between family functioning variables and siblings' social skills, studies of children with special needs have not focused on family functioning, instead this research typically has centred merely upon family demographic variables or disease characteristics and their association with siblings' social skills (Simeonsson and Bailey 1986). An explanation for this narrow focus is that such variables are more easily quantified and described than more complex family system variables; however, the 'functional patterns of the family may be the more essential ingredients to understanding sibling functioning' (Lobato *et al.* 1988: 403).

In support of the idea that family functioning is related to sibling outcomes, Frank (1996) has noted that styles of conflict resolution in families of children with disabilities can have an impact on the sibling relationship and also influence the dynamics of the family subsystem. Slee (1996) points out that there is empirical research showing that family functioning in families who have experienced a prolonged crisis, such as a child with a learning disability or conduct disorder, may be different than the family functioning in other families. For example, family cohesion, conflict, and expressiveness have been linked to social competence of siblings in families of children with disabilities (Dyson *et al.* 1989). Moreover, increased family cohesiveness, expressive family environment, and mother's health are related to fewer sibling adjustment problems in families where children had rheumatic disease (Daniels *et al.* 1986). Closeness and good communication in the family may be important buffers for siblings of children with disabilities (Lobato 1990).

Although the family environment for siblings in families with children with special needs may present unique challenges, in most cases the problems or stressors experienced may be surmountable, and long-term consequences are generally not negative. The evidence suggests that greater awareness of the needs of others and greater maturity may be fostered in these siblings (McHale and Gamble 1987).

Another body of research perhaps applicable to our understanding of families of children with disabilities comes from the work of McCubbin and McCubbin (1989, 1992). Their work examines families adapting to a wide variety of stressful situations, within and outside of the family. Included in the body of their work is a line of research addressing families who have children with chronic diseases or illnesses. In these families, positive family functioning is related to healthy family adaptation to the crisis situation (McCubbin and McCubbin 1992). Thus, positive family functioning is considered to be related to positive outcomes for individuals within the family as well as the family unit.

Current research project

In our research both fathers' and mothers' perceptions of family functioning were measured using four subscales from Bloom's family functioning measure: family cohesion, family idealization, family conflict, and family enmeshment (Bloom 1985; Bloom and Naar 1994). Because the family functioning variables met the criteria described by Larsen and Olson (1990), similar to the marital conflict scores, 'family scores' were computed for each family functioning variable by summing mothers' and fathers' scores and taking the average. We then compared scores on the family functioning variables for families with and without children with special needs. Our findings revealed no significant differences between the two groups on all family functioning variables. Therefore, for our sample, the presence of a child with a disability did not appear to alter family functioning. To understand why this apparent lack of group effect occurred is beyond the scope of our present analysis.

To determine if patterns of relationships between family functioning and siblings' social skills were similar in both groups, we next correlated the family functioning variable scores with teacher ratings of siblings' social skills. In families of a child with a disability, family conflict scores were positively related to teacher ratings of sibling externalizing ($r = 0.48$, $p < 0.01$) and internalizing ($r = 0.33$, $p < 0.05$) behaviours. Also, family enmeshment scores were related to sibling internalizing ($r = 0.33$, $p < 0.05$) ratings. However, in families with a well sibling, family conflict scores were linked with teacher ratings of externalizing ($r = 0.35$, $p < 0.05$) behaviours and self-control ($r = -0.31$, $p < 0.06$). On the other hand, family cohesion and idealization scores were not related to sibling social skills ratings for either group.

These results support previous research with well children which indicates that poor patterns of family functioning are linked to negative social outcomes in children (Campbell 1995). Similar patterns of relationships were found in both groups: negative types of family functioning were related to poorer sibling social skills; however, similar to marital conflict, subtle difference in the specific social skills linked with different types of family functioning became apparent.

Summary, and future research directions

Early studies on families of children with disabilities were conducted using a deficit perspective, assuming that the mere presence of the disabled child would have a negative impact on other individuals (parents and siblings) in the family. More recent work, however, has focused on a positive adaptation perspective in these families (Boyce and Barnett 1993). The results of our research seem to support the positive adaptation perspective.

Specifically, our research showed that siblings in families of children with disabilities did not score significantly higher on problem behaviours, but were rated higher on co-operation/assertion and self-control by their teachers. Apparently siblings of children with disabilities may develop sensitivity and tolerance for others, which facilitates acceptance of peer ideas, co-operation with peers, and making friends. In addition, because they may experience difficult sibling interactions more regularly than other children, they may develop social skills related to self-control, such as compromising and controlling their tempers.

Because of the mixed findings in past research, future studies examining the social skills of siblings of children with disabilities should include measures of both problem behaviours and positive social skills. More importantly, families of children with disabilities should not be considered a homogeneous group. Therefore, future work should not only study families with well and disabled children, but should also attempt to compare families of children with disabilities who are successfully coping and contrast them with those who are not. Such studies could inform interventionists as they develop programmes to help those children and families who may be experiencing more problem behaviours.

In contrast to our findings of group differences for sibling social skills, marital conflict and family functioning were not influenced by group status. Moreover, for families in both groups, positive family functioning was moderately linked to siblings' more positive social skills while marital conflict was related to siblings' poorer social skills. Future research might explore in which specific cases and circumstances family relationships of families of children with disabilities may or may not differ from families with well children.

Although in our research few differences were found when some family variables were compared, depression scores were higher for both mothers and fathers in families of children with disabilities. This may be due to a number of stressors related to having children who exhibit atypical behaviours or require extra amounts of care. Future research should address other dynamics operating among depression, family functioning, and social skills outcomes in families of children with disabilities.

Finally, longitudinal data sets are needed to help determine the long-term effects, if any, of having a child with disabilities in the family. Data collected from multiple family members through multiple methods may help provide a clearer picture of family dynamics and how they may be linked to siblings' social skills. Such research agendas also may provide data for developing intervention programmes tailored to better meet the needs of individual family members.

Acknowledgements

The authors would like to thank the Center for the Studies of the Family, College of Nursing, the College of Family, Home, and Social Sciences at Brigham Young University and Sigma Theta Tau International, Iota-Iota chapter at large, for financial support of this work. We are also grateful to the families who participated in this research.

Chapter 8

Aggression at school, post-traumatic stress disorder and peer relations

Peter Randall

This chapter examines the effects on children of severe aggression in or near schools within the context of childhood post-traumatic stress disorder (PTSD) and links it to subsequent dysfunctional peer relations that affect later adult functioning. In particular, it is argued from the basis of clinical studies that the aggression generally referred to as bullying may produce, in the long term, post-traumatic responses associated with later victim status in adulthood. It is already acknowledged that severe harassment at work can result in post-traumatic effects amongst adults who have had no previous difficulties of that type (e.g., Groeblinghoff and Becker 1996) but this chapter is concerned with an enduring PTSD effect which appears to degrade peer relations throughout the life course.

The chapter commences with a description of childhood PTSD and a brief review of some of the research and clinical evidence which differentiates it from that experienced by adults. It then examines aggressive incidents at schools associated with PTSD and relates this to the kind of peer relations formed subsequent to severe exposure to peer aggression. Clinical narratives suggest that the impact may so damage peer relations that individuals may become less able to develop normal skills of assertiveness and so, as adults, become susceptible to harassment in the workplace or community.

Childhood post-traumatic stress disorder

It has been a popular misconception that PTSD is only a problem for adults who have been traumatized. Although there is a recognition that children who have been neglected or emotionally abused may suffer long-term emotional difficulties (e.g., Iwaniec 1995), there is little formal awareness of the complex nature of childhood stress disorders. It is the case, however, that childhood post-traumatic stress disorder (PTSD), although less obvious, is as complex and harmful as the adult variation. Apart from the developmental difficulties that may ensue, serious behavioural and relationship problems may cause long-term difficulties (Ferguson *et al.* 1994; Robins 1966).

Clinical studies of children have persistently reported a number of individual post-trauma responses that are consistent with DSM-IV criteria for PTSD (American Psychiatric Association 1994). In response to an identified stressor or stressors, children are reported to show symptoms of re-experiencing the trauma (Newmann 1976; Terr 1979; Pynoos and Eth 1985), numbing of responsiveness or repressed involvement with external events (Green 1983) and heightened states of arousal (Burke *et al.* 1982). Although early reports were inconsistent in the selection of individual symptoms reported, there has been a significant demonstration over recent years of a similar relationship between the proximity or severity of exposure to life-threatening events or other trauma and subsequent intensity of symptoms or levels of impairment for children as for adults (Pynoos *et al.* 1987).

This similarity of relationship is borne out in that the diagnostic criteria for PTSD of children is hardly differentiated from the PTSD of adults. DSM-IV provides the following major symptom cluster:

1 There has been an exposure to an event which most people would find traumatic. The wide range of events associated with childhood PTSD is described below.
2 Intrusive re-experiencing of the trauma. In younger children this may take the form of night-terrors and re-enacting the behaviour that produced the trauma through doll play or other forms of play. Other subjects report intrusive recollections.
3 Numbing of responsiveness or reduced involvement in normal daily events across the child's environment in general. There may be avoidance of thoughts, feelings and situations associated with a traumatic event, reduced rates of peer interaction and play behaviour. The children's range of emotional expression may significantly reduce and memory impairment concerning the trauma is common. Immature behaviours may re-emerge, such as bedwetting or clinging to adults.
4 Persistent hyperarousal is demonstrated in sleep disorder, anger, poor attention control, reduction of academic standards, hypervigilance and exaggerated startled responses.

Unfortunately many of these symptoms overlap with other diagnostic categories. This is particularly so in respect of anxiety and depressive disorders and some conduct and adjustment disorders (Jones and Barlow 1990). As a result some diagnoses of childhood PTSD are not made with confidence. In certain situations there are suggestions that broader diagnostic categories should be employed, and, in the case of child sexual abuse, other explanatory models are preferable (see Finkelhor 1988). The author has argued elsewhere, however, that PTSD is important when conceptualizing the effects of child sexual abuse (Parker and Randall 1996).

Given these difficulties, the application of the PTSD criteria has been controversial and questions have been raised as to whether children show PTSD symptoms of the same type and range as adults (e.g., McNally 1991). One significant difference lies in the nature of traumatic re-experiencing in that adults report dissociative flashbacks which children do not (Nadar and Fairbanks 1994). The flashbacks that children experience often come in a different form, perhaps as nightmares, with attributes of the traumatic event (Lipovsky 1991). These nightmares are often terrifying interpretations of the trauma that serve to reinforce the distress and fear. The author was asked to work with a 7-year old who had experienced severe bullying from older children. The presenting problem was his challenging behaviour expressed as physical and verbal aggression. The child stated that his behaviour resulted from his dreams of being spat upon, hit and unable to get away. He thought that the only way to stop the dreams was to hit out at others; ultimately he became alienated from his age-peers.

Another significant difference between adult and childhood PTSD is concerned with the possibility that the child form may be of two types. On the basis of extensive clinical observation and casework experiences Terr (1989) proposes Type I and Type II childhood PTSD. The first type is thought to result from a single but severely traumatic event. Conversely Type II is the product of a series of traumatic events or prolonged exposure to a repeated set of specific stressors. In Terr's experience Type I PTSD does result in children showing the classic re-experiencing symptom, whereas the Type II variety is more often associated with dissociation, numbing and denial and with the possible later development of multiple or dissociative personality disorder. Obviously, if this typology is an accurate reflection of PTSD variation amongst child sufferers then it is of great relevance to clinicians who work with them therapeutically because particular attention has to be paid to the predominant symptom.

Stressors that provoke PTSD

A wide variety of stressors have been shown to be associated with PTSD amongst children and adolescents. These include road traffic accidents (Jones and Peterson 1993), shipping disasters (Yule 1992), murder of a parent (Black *et al.* 1992), sexual abuse (McLeer *et al.* 1992), separation from parents during warfare (Diehl *et al.* 1994), surviving severe illness and its treatment (Stuber and Nader 1995), severe weather conditions (Newman 1976) and natural disasters such as earthquakes (Pynoos *et al.* 1993).

In addition, children are traumatized by events occurring at school. As an example, Parker *et al.* (1995a) report on the long-term effects of the tragedy that occurred in 1981 when a gale blew the roof off a primary school killing a girl. Two years later nineteen of her classmates were interviewed. PTSD symptoms were found in these pupils and their parents. Close friends of the deceased girl suffered more symptoms than others. Parker *et al.* (1995a) suggest that experience of loss is much to do with symptom formation. The subjective perception, partly determined by cultural issues and societal approval, plays a large part in how the events are given meaning and, subsequently, how the symptoms develop (Hodgkinson and Stewart 1991; Strentz 1995).

Of particular importance to this chapter are the research studies that link the experience of aggression to childhood PTSD. For example, Elbedour *et al.* (1993) report a wide range of symptoms including fear, depression, anxiety, anger, phobia, restlessness and other difficulties. The researchers estimate that at least 21 per cent of the Gaza Strip children face the risk of severe adult problems in mental health in comparison with only 5 per cent of children in the United States randomly sampled using the same instruments. The Gaza children were exposed to both single- and sustained-event aggressive trauma. It is reasonable to predict, therefore, that they will show the presence of both Type I and Type II PTSD according to Terr's (1989) description, and this was borne out by the research findings.

The effects of long-term South African township aggression on very young children has been studied by Magwaza *et al.* (1993). This important study used crèche teachers, trained as field workers, to survey a random sample of children placed in their crèches. These workers completed a post-traumatic stress disorder questionnaire about these children who then drew pictures of events they had experienced. One significant finding was that preschool children exposed to prolonged aggression incurred PTSD, which was strongly revealed in their drawings.

Many children who witness serious incidents of aggression in their homes are also more likely to show symptoms of PTSD. This includes children as young as 2 as reported by Osofsky *et al.* (1995) in their description of twins who had witnessed the death of their mother, shot to death by their father. Taylor *et al.* (1994) investigated the effects of witnessing violence in 115 children, aged 1 to 5 years, and 115 mothers, aged 16 to 66 years. Of the children 10 per cent had witnessed a knifing or shooting, 10 per cent had witnessed shoving, kicking or punching incidents and 47 per cent had heard gunshots. Of the mothers, 36 per cent had witnessed knifing or shooting and 9 per cent had been victims of a knifing or shooting. PTSD symptoms were accompanied by severe limitations on children's movements and excessive concern for safety to an extent that was deleterious to their normal development.

Childhood PTSD and aggression in schools

It is tragic that children witness very severe violence at school and that these incidences appear to be on the increase. In the UK recently there have been tragic events at Dunblane leading to the deaths by shooting of 16 pupils and their teacher, and at Middlesborough a pupil was stabbed to death in her classroom. In America the US Department of Justice records that 25 children die every two years from gunshot wounds and 21 per cent of High School students know of someone who has died violently. Many countries have armed guards in some schools in order to deter the use of firearms, including France after an incident on the outskirts of Paris in 1993 when an armed hostage-taker was shot to death in front of pupils in a nursery school (Follain 1996). Armed guards are commonplace in American schools but, despite this, horrific incidents still occur. For example, a 16-year-old boy was shot to death outside his High School in front of hundreds of children making their way home (*Deseret News* 1994). This tragedy was quickly overtaken by the shooting of a teacher in the car park of her school by an ex-lover. Some of her pupils witnessed the slaying (*Deseret News* 1995).

Research literature covering similar events demonstrates the clear links between school-associated aggression and childhood PTSD. Thus Pynoos *et al.* (1987) studied 159 children who were subject to a short but intense trauma when a sniper opened fire on their school yard. Their results revealed that acute PTSD symptoms were incurred by the children with a significant correlation between the proximity of the violence witnessed and both the type and number of PTSD symptoms. In support of this, and following their investigation of a school shooting incident, Schwartz and Kowalski (1991) stated that post-disaster intervention should be offered to offset PTSD effects, not only to those who were close to the traumatic event but also to those with the greatest emotional reactivity to it, independent of their location at the time of the event. McNally (1993) estimates that PTSD is the result for 2–100 per cent of children who experience such major stressors. Pynoos (1990) suggests that these symptoms may last for several years and in recognition of this psychologists in many areas have established school-focused rapid response strategies to prevent the insidious build-up of PTSD effects (e.g., Cameron *et al.* 1995).

Peer aggression, PTSD and victim status

The incidents described above concern intensely dramatic events which have been vividly portrayed in the media. Yet, violent as these incidents have been, they are overshadowed by the huge frequency of aggressive events, generally referred to as bullying, occurring on a daily basis in or near schools everywhere.

Using Terr's (1989) dichotomy, it is reasonable to assume that the experience of bullying may provoke both Type I and Type II PTSD. A single but very severe encounter with a bully may be a sufficient single-impact trauma to provoke a Type I response but, alternatively, Type II responses may be provoked by regular and severe exposure to bullying. In both cases the children involved would require therapeutic intervention designed to alleviate the effects of PTSD in order to reduce the associated long-term difficulties; it is unlikely that simply treating them as the victims of bullying would have the same beneficial effect. The following case study describes one such child victim and the development of his PTSD symptoms.

Mark, a normally happy, friendly child, became known to the Education Welfare Service because of his sudden poor attendance at school. In addition, on those occasions when he did go he was often late home from school and claimed that he had gone for a walk 'the long way round'. Often his clothes were dirty from where 'I fell down' when in actuality he had been rolled in the mud. He was found to be stealing from his mother's purse in order to pay off the bullies and he had often had clothes, books and his packed lunch taken away from him.

At home he was bedwetting, eating little and frequently complaining of feeling sick. His busy parents did not correctly identify his problems until he was knocked down by a car, running blindly away from his tormentors.

For two years after the incident Mark showed significant signs of childhood PTSD; his dreams were frequently of being chased by the bullies and of being in front of the car screaming. His play became solitary and he frequently enacted stories of violence against a single person. In addition, he showed general reduction of his involvement with his family and peers and he became solitary and friendless.

The nocturnal enuresis continued and he sometimes attempted to hide soiled underwear. His teachers described attention control and significantly poor study habits and task organization. On moving up to secondary school, a prolonged period of school refusal began.

He was eventually treated by a clinical psychologist who diagnosed PTSD, but he remained a subdued and isolated youngster with poor peer relations both within the community and the school. He could not tolerate confrontations, and his parents were aware that he never asserted himself in order to protect his best interests.

Mark's continued presentation as an isolate with poor peer relations provides precursors for later adult harassment at work or in the community (Randall 1997). His situation is common to many adults with a similar history and there is growing evidence of the link between unresolved childhood PTSD and the development of a 'victim personality'. For example, as part of the author's continuing survey of child victims and bullies, children aged between 8 and 12 years were given a variety of diagnostic tests. The outcome of this survey will be published separately but one of the instruments completed by the parents already shows significant evidence of PTSD amongst the characteristic behaviours shown by young victims. This instrument, the Devereux Scales of Mental Disorders (DSMD), identifies psychopathological and behavioural problems in children by providing a measure of overt problem behaviours exhibited by them. The DSMD provides an overall score and separate scores for factorially derived scales of discrete psychopathological symptoms. Information is provided on three broad composite factors known as 'externalizing', 'internalizing' and 'critical pathology'. These are derived from the separate scores on scales of conduct, attention, anxiety, depression, autism, and acute problems. These composites and their separate scales are described as follows:

Externalizing Composite: Behaviours that involve conflict between the individual and his or her environment.
- Conduct Scale – Disruptive and hostile acts.
- Attention Scale – Problems with concentration, distractibility and motor excess (overactivity).

Internalizing Composite: Behaviours that reflect the individual's state of psychological well-being.
- Anxiety Scales – Problems with worries, fears, low self-concept and tension.
- Depression Scale – Problems with withdrawal, few emotional reactions, lowered mood and inability to experience pleasure.

Critical Pathology Composite: Behaviours that represent severe disturbances of childhood.
- Autism Scale – Problems of impaired social interactions and communication and unusual motor behaviours.
- Acute Problems Scale – Behaviours that are hallucinatory, primitive, bizarre, self-injurious, or dangerous.

The preliminary results of this unfinished survey suggest that regular bullies score heavily amongst the externalizing scales. Such children are rated as aggressive, annoying to others, disruptive, overactive or restless and inattentive. Frequently they score high on the conduct scale which rates disruptive and hostile behaviour characterized by the violation of the basic rights of other people and a disregard of the norms of age-appropriate social behaviour.

By contrast, the regular victims assessed on these scales fall within the internalizing range showing excessive worrying, social withdrawal, anxiety, and over-control. They score high on both the anxiety and depression scales with both generalized and specific fears (many of which are related to bullying), high levels of tension, low self-concept and frequent complaints of somatic problems. These are combined with withdrawal from social contacts, lowered mood and little or no interest in age-appropriate pleasurable activities. They show poor social comprehension and problems of self-assertion.

Specific examination of the items identified by parents as characteristic of their victimized children's behaviour (Randall 1997) include:

- appearing discouraged or depressed;
- not showing joy or gladness at a happy occasion;
- remaining alone or isolated from peers;
- failing to communicate effectively with peers;
- appearing uncomfortable or anxious with others;
- refusing to go to school;
- withdrawing from or avoidance of social contacts;
- becoming easily upset;
- telling lies;
- having difficulty sleeping;
- frequent nightmares, dreams of the bullying incidents or related dream material;
- showing a strong fear of rejection;
- showing an exaggerated fear of getting hurt;
- appearing sleepy or tired during the day;
- becoming distressed when separated from parent/guardian;
- demanding physical contact from others;
- getting startled or act jumpy;
- clinging to adults.

As may be seen, these behavioural items include several that are symptomatic of PTSD and others strongly indicative of a developing victim personality. It is noteworthy that the child, Mark, referred to above, scored highly on the internalizing composite scale.

PTSD, victims' status and poor interpersonal problem-solving

Given that unresolved PTSD appears to be strongly associated with victim status continued into adulthood, it is appropriate to seek the mechanism(s) which may account for this. A number of clinical narratives collected by the author provide some direction for further enquiry into these mechanisms; one of these is presented here:

Ray, a 29-year-old trading standards officer, referred himself to an Employee Assistance Programme directed by the author. He complained of harassment at work by three men and two women who were well-known socially to the line manager. They had not wanted Ray to be appointed over another colleague and used every opportunity to demean him, spoil his work and make fun of him generally. They arranged for his leave requests to be blocked and for him to do much of the most unsavoury investigatory work that came into their section.

Ray's main fears did not concern the fact of the harassment but were associated with his inability to find the strategies to do something about it. He recognized a personal characteristic that was essentially submissive and lacking assertiveness in his personal life. He did not feel that he was a coward because he frequently had to tackle very aggressive people during the course of his work; instead he felt unable to understand social contexts fully or relate successfully to people and win them over. Stress at work was compensated by limited alcohol abuse and he had begun a pattern of sick leave to avoid work. These and other signs led eventually to a diagnosis of PTSD.[1]

He recounted a history that was unremarkable until the age of 12 years when, on moving to a new school in the middle of a term, he was subjected to severe verbal and some physical bullying that persisted over a two-month period. He had been unable to stop this or attract much adult support. Although it had quickly faded out he had found himself to be unwilling to form peer relations for fear of being bullied again. Intense night terrors were accompanied by fear of school and separation anxiety. He described watching and listening to other children but not being able to understand the means by which they related to each other. On those occasions that he did attempt to engage with children, they seemed to find him 'different' and drifted away from him. Ray believed that after his short but intense history of childhood bullying, he had lost the ability to make age-appropriate use of social cues.

Children behave in their characteristic ways within the social world according to the outcomes of the processes through which they deal with and understand social cues. Those, like Ray above, who incur PTSD as a consequence of exposure to peer-aggression seem to fail to develop their social understanding normally and this has long-lasting effects most evident as social withdrawal. Our understanding of socially withdrawn children helps to provide the link between incursion of PTSD and the development of victim status.

Rubin and Krasnor (1986) provide a social information processing model based upon a five-part sequence. This model suggests that children start the first stage by selecting one or more *social goals* which requires the establishment of a cognitive representation of a desirable *end state*. The second stage is one of scanning and interpreting all the cues they consider to be relevant to their social goal, a process referred to as *examining the task environment*. Rubin and Krasnor (1986) found gender differences in the way that this is accomplished and note that boys and girls arrive at different solutions when faced with the same type of dilemma. In addition, social status, age and familiarity influence strongly individual children's goals and strategy selections. The third stage concerns *accessing* and *selecting strategies*, a process that involves the generation of plans of action for achieving the social goal(s) and making a judgement as to which are the most appropriate within the particular social context. During the course of the next stage children *implement the chosen strategy* and in the fifth and final stage they *evaluate the outcome*, a process which assesses the situation to determine the level of success in achieving the social goal(s). If the initial strategy has not been successful it may be repeated or a new one selected, but under certain circumstances the child may accept failure and abandon all strategies.

When the characteristics of socially withdrawn children are examined by this model, it is evident that preschool and infant children are more likely than their non-withdrawn peers to show adult dependency behaviours by attempting to engage adults to solve their interpersonal problems (Rubin *et al.* 1984). In addition, LeMare and Rubin (1987) found that non-withdrawn children of this age are more able to accept the social perspectives of others than those who were socially withdrawn. These findings indicate that the Piagetian-based assumption about the importance of peer group interaction for the development of social cognition is correct in that the socially withdrawn children show clear social cognitive deficits. As noted above one of the major impacts of PTSD is the development of social withdrawal. Older children, however, do not demonstrate the same difficulties as the preschool child. Instead their problems are to be found in the production stage of the social information processing model (Rubin 1985).

It is fairly simple to see how victimized children will attract the attention of potential aggressors. The younger ones can be easily singled out by their strong tendency to involve adults in getting their own way, a circumstance which even preschool children will object to strongly, and the older ones will behave in a way that draws attention to their *naïveté* and immaturity.

With regard to children of middle childhood, which is the age range during which regular victim status first becomes evident, then it is reasonable to speculate that production and enactment difficulties result in a social interaction style characterized by low assertiveness, submission and social immaturity. It is possible to find significant points of comparison here to Ray's narrative above. Rubin (1985) has shown that socially withdrawn children are less assertive then their non-withdrawn peers and that, when they do assert themselves, they are more likely to be rejected than their socially competent assertive peers. Conversely, however, they are more likely to accede to the wishes of their non-withdrawn peers. Over a period of time, therefore, their behaviour shows a steady trait of failed or low assertiveness and ready compliance such that they become recognized as easy-to-bully individuals. Their problems become more overt with increasing age (Stewart and Rubin 1995) and reveal the 'flattening' of active social behaviour associated with both submission (Randall 1996) and PTSD.

The increasing rejection and self-imposed isolation of these children inevitably leads to poor self-perception and low self-esteem (e.g., Rubin and Mills 1998). Not surprisingly, as childhood progresses they socially withdraw as a characteristic trait and express greater depression and loneliness than their more socially competent peers. Other research studies (e.g., Hymel *et al.* 1993) report that socially withdrawn children aged 10 to 12 years think of themselves as lacking social skills outside of social support networks and of not belonging to their peer group. Many report, in their own words, that being bullied is about the only form of attention they get from their peers. These beliefs have a profound impact on the long-term social development of such children and it is inevitable that adult socialization is affected. For this reason it is possible to trace, for many clients, a long history of victim status from their infant education through to the time of being a bullied adult at work or in the community with 'numbing' of social awareness as a major consistent symptom of PTSD.

A childhood legacy

Most of the victims of bullying in childhood are able to recover from their experiences and develop normal adult assertiveness. It is also clear, however, that many do not, although the relative proportions are not known at this stage. There may be many reasons why some childhood victims fail to develop normal social skills and later become adult victims. Severity and frequency of bullying during childhood are direct factors which strongly correlate with later submission to dominant and aggressive individuals during adulthood, but these variables do not explain the plight of those individuals, like Ray, whose experience of childhood bullying was brief but who still retain an inability to understand or assert themselves against harassing adults. Unresolved childhood PTSD is known to have a significant influence on adult social behaviour (e.g., Pynoos and Nadar 1988) and may well act to predispose individuals in adult life to block effective responses against would-be bullies and harassers.

The following case study reveals the variety of victim characteristics that one would expect to find if childhood PTSD was a key to later adult victim status.

Sally was a 29-year-old graphic design artist from Surrey who worked in a large advertising company with a branch in the North of England. She worked alongside four other women and one man. The line manager and another woman were often scathing to Sally; their harassment of her taking the form of immature jokes about 'poor Southerners'. She found their other jokey remarks about her distasteful as many of them were explicitly sexual.

Sally found that she was unable to assert herself against these two women but neither could she ignore them. Instead she found herself having 'flashbacks' to a time at school when she was badly physically bullied by older girls and the mother of one of them. Her recollections were both recurrent and intrusive. In addition her sleep was distorted by dreams in which both the mother and the two co-workers were present. She began to experience profound psychological distress to any kind of hostility, whether real or on the television, and her arousal levels became high causing her to sleep badly, lack concentration, and roam around her home aimlessly.

She was treated for PTSD and concurrently given some assertion training. Eventually she was able to take control of the situation and silenced her oppressors.

(Randall 1997)

Note

1 Ray responded well to cognitive-behavioural interventions and learned to use his job-related assertiveness within his personal life as well. He made successful use of his employer's personal harassment policy.

Chapter 9

Peer relationships of children with chronic illnesses

Rosalyn H. Shute

Introduction

This chapter introduces some of the main issues in an emerging field of study – peer relationships in children with chronic illnesses. It features, in particular, recent and current work carried out by the author and several of her students in the School of Psychology, The Flinders University of South Australia.

Chronic illnesses are those which cannot be cured, but which need to be managed on a long-term, often lifelong, basis. Typically, the child and family must be heavily involved in day-to-day management, for example, in administering medications and attending to special dietary needs. In 1972 the commonest childhood chronic conditions were reported to be asthma, epilepsy, cardiac conditions, cerebral palsy, orthopaedic conditions and diabetes mellitus (Mattson 1972). By the 1980s cancer, cystic fibrosis and end-stage renal failure were also being considered in the paediatric psychology literature as conditions being survived by increasing numbers of children as a result of improving medical treatments (Johnson 1985). Other conditions addressed by paediatric psychology researchers include haemophilia and sickle cell anaemia (La Greca 1990).

It is not easy to determine the incidence of childhood chronic illness as the available statistics are influenced by a range of factors, including how conditions are classified, the level of severity that is included (and how this is measured) and by diagnostic criteria for some conditions, which may differ between practitioners and over time (e.g., Desguin *et al.* 1994; Mrazek 1986). An incidence of up to 10 per cent of children with serious chronic illnesses has typically been quoted over the past 20 years (e.g., Magrab and Calcagno 1978), rising to 20 per cent if milder cases are included (Gortmaker and Sappenfeld 1984, cited in Desguin *et al.* 1994). However, more recent estimates are higher, with Newacheck and Taylor (1992, cited in Desguin *et al.* 1994) giving a figure as high as 35 per cent for children in the USA, and with the incidence of asthma alone in South Australian rural primary schoolchildren reported to be 25 per cent

(Crockett *et al.* 1986). Despite the difficulty of establishing incidence precisely, it is quite clear that there are substantial numbers of children with chronic illnesses living in industrialized nations today.

Research on the peer relationships of children with chronic illnesses is a relatively new enterprise. Psychosocial research with these children initially focused upon the family, driven in part out of a concern for family factors which might interfere with adherence to a prescribed treatment regimen and thus impact on the child's physical health. The importance of social contexts other than the family for a child's adaptation (such as the school and health care system), and the interactions between such contexts (such as parent–doctor interactions), has become recognized more recently. Furthermore, earlier views of the ill child as being passively affected by a medical condition have been replaced with dynamic, coping models, and a recognition that chronic illness does not inevitably lead to psychosocial maladjustment (La Greca 1990). Today, chronic childhood illness is frequently viewed from a systems perspective, which considers the dynamic interactions between the biological, psychological and social levels of analysis, taking account of the various social contexts within which the child exists (e.g., Hanson 1992; Shute and Paton 1990). This broad framework gives peers, whether siblings, schoolfriends or other ill children, an explicit place in the life of the child with a chronic illness.

The relationship between peers and child health

Research on children's peer relationships is now so commonplace that it is easy to forget just how recently peers have been recognized by psychologists as having an important place in children's lives. For example, in 1971 it was possible for a book on socialization (Danziger 1971) to be almost entirely concerned with how children develop under the influence of adults, peers being considered mainly within the context of determining how they undermine adult influence. It is only during the last quarter of the twentieth century that we have gradually come to appreciate the importance of the role that children play in one another's lives, and that their influence can be positive as well as negative. As readers of this volume will be well aware, there is now much evidence to indicate that satisfactory peer relationships in children are strongly associated with good socio-emotional functioning, both concurrently and later in life (e.g., Bayer 1996). There is also considerable literature on children's prosocial and helping behaviour (e.g., Foot *et al.* 1990). Nevertheless, negative bias sometimes persists, as exemplified by a 1993 article on creating safe schools; the listed influences on student well-being include on the one hand 'supportive adults' but on the other 'peer pressure' (Petersen and Petersen 1993).

The early tendency to consider negative, rather than positive, aspects of peer relationships has been somewhat apparent in the child health area.

For example, it is often assumed that young people take up smoking because of peer pressure, whereas it is equally plausible to suggest that children learn smoking behaviour from their parents initially, and later associate with peers who have similar attitudes and behaviours (Eiser and Van der Pligt 1984). The negative role of peers in chronic illness management has also been addressed. For example, Kaplan *et al.* (1985) found that those adolescents with diabetes who were most satisfied with their peer relationships also tended to have poorer metabolic control. One possible explanation is that they were heavily involved with non-diabetic friends in a way which made it difficult to adopt healthy behaviours, such as eating the right foods at the right times and taking their insulin regularly (Kaplan and Toshima 1990). There are also reports in the literature of children with diabetes being directly tempted by friends to eat inappropriate foods (e.g., Sullivan 1979).

Alongside these suggestions that peers are bad for children's health were studies suggesting that chronic illness is bad for children's peer relationships (this will be discussed further below). This was part of a wider research thrust examining 'maladjustment' in children with chronic illness, an approach which has been challenged in recent years. For example, Bennett (1994), reviewing 60 studies of depressive symptoms amongst children and adolescents with chronic medical problems, found that although as a group they were at slightly increased risk for depressive symptoms, the majority were not clinically depressed.

With specific reference to peer relationships, it is certainly not being proposed here that any negative aspects should be ignored or denied. Rather, what is needed is a balanced and detailed approach. Garbarino (1982) has commented that the contexts within which children develop offer both developmental risks and opportunities, and there is no reason to suppose that peer-defined contexts are any exception. Kazac (1992: 268), with specific reference to chronic childhood illness, has said that in the peer group, as well as the family environment, 'children learn about interpersonal relationships and social strengths and weaknesses, and establish templates for personal and work relationships'. In the same vein, La Greca, discussing the lack of research on peer relationships in chronic illness, has noted that 'by neglecting to consider youngsters' peer status and daily social milieu, we are missing significant pieces of the overall adaptation picture' (1990: 288). A consideration of both positive and negative aspects of peer relationships is in line with approaches to chronic illness adaptation currently being taken, in terms of identifying both risk and resistance factors (e.g., Wallander *et al.* 1989).

The question of whether or not peer relationships are normal in children with chronic conditions has become a matter of some debate. As La Greca (1990) has discussed, early reviews were suggestive of psychosocial vulnerability in children with chronic conditions (e.g., Drotar 1981), while various studies during the 1980s noted peer adjustment problems amongst some children (e.g., Hurtig and White 1986). La Greca (1990) has suggested that peer relationships are more likely to be affected if the illness interferes with opportunities for social interaction, such as by placing restrictions on physical and other everyday activities or by changing a child's physical appearance.

Many of the early studies which indicated peer relationship problems relied on parental reports. More recent research has used the children themselves and their peers as reporters of peer relationships. An example of such a study is that by Noll *et al.* (1991), examining the peer relationships of children with cancer. They found that children with cancer were not different from their 'healthy' peers in terms of their general acceptance by peers, their self-concept and their feelings of loneliness, but they were perceived by peers as more ill and more socially isolated.

Graetz and Shute (1995) used similar methodology in a study of Australian children aged 8 to 13 years with moderate to severe asthma (all were taking daily inhaled corticosteroids). Overall, the children were not found to have poorer peer relationships than their 'healthy' matched controls in that they were not found to be less popular, nor more rejected; they did not have fewer friendships and they did not feel lonelier. Furthermore, while they were perceived to have greater levels of illness, they were not considered to be more socially isolated, more aggressive nor less sociable than other children. These findings are broadly similar to Noll *et al.*'s (1991) study with children with cancer in that they were just as well accepted and liked by their peers despite being seen to be more ill. However, whereas the children with cancer were seen as more socially isolated, the children with asthma were not.

Graetz and Shute's (1995) study demonstrated the problems that can occur in research on chronic illness in terms of measuring severity. Three uncorrelated aspects of asthma severity were found; namely, medication, frequency of asthma attacks and frequency of hospitalization. Only the latter was found to be related to peer relationships, in that children who were hospitalized more frequently were less preferred as playmates, were perceived by their peers as more sensitive-isolated and felt more lonely. So the general finding that children with moderate to severe asthma have no peer relationship problems has to be modified somewhat, as those hospitalized more often do seem to be at some risk. This may be related to school absenteeism. Although the children with asthma were, as a group, perceived by their peers to be absent from school more often than other children, presumably those who were hospitalized most frequently had the highest levels of absenteeism of all. Their situation may be similar to the perceived isolation of the children with cancer in Noll *et al.*'s (1991) study, who would also have experienced frequent school absences for medical interventions. In the Australian study, although frequent hospitalization with asthma did not impede the formation of mutual friendships, it was associated with being a less-preferred playmate. The children's associated feelings of loneliness and reputation for being isolated may therefore stem not just from the separations themselves but from being less preferred as playmates on their return to school. It is not clear at present whether these children experience brief periods of loneliness and isolation following hospitalization, from which they recover, or whether they are at risk of entering a self-perpetuating cycle of loneliness and social difficulties, a process which Renshaw and Brown (1993) have suggested might happen in the case of some children with peer relationship problems. Although further research is needed in this area, the available evidence suggests that there may be a place for interventions targeted specifically at children who are hospitalized frequently with their chronic illness, with the aim of maintaining peer relationships during and after periods in hospital.

In the light of La Greca's suggestion that peer relationships may be more affected if a child's condition interferes with physical activity, we can note in passing that the children in Graetz and Shute's (1995) study were predominantly boys, for whom sporting ability may play a more important social status role than for girls (Lever 1978). They may therefore suffer socially more than girls if they have a condition which interferes with their sporting ability. However, in that study, the children with asthma were perceived as just as able in sport as their peers, even though they were perceived as being more sick.

These recent, more sophisticated studies (Noll *et al.* 1991; Graetz and Shute 1995) represent a move away from asking the very broad question of whether children with a chronic illness are less well-adjusted socially than their peers, to investigating in more depth any specific areas of difficulty which may occur, and/or identifying which particular children are likely to be at risk. Research of this nature paves the way for the development of interventions which are appropriately targeted.

Peer helping and social support in chronic childhood illness

Not only has there been a shift away from the assumption that chronic illness necessarily has a negative influence on children's peer relationships, but there are the beginnings of a recognition that children may even be able to have a positive influence on one another's health and psychosocial adjustment. For example, although as we've already noted, some research suggests that peers can negatively affect the health of a young person with diabetes (Kaplan and Toshima 1990), other workers have suggested that peers with diabetes may provide the best models for young people with regard to managing their condition effectively (e.g., Simonds 1979); and some peer-based health education programmes have been devised, for example, in the areas of smoking and dental health (Morgan and Eiser 1990).

Shute and Paton (1990) identified a wide range of issues which can arise in some cases of childhood chronic illness and which may be amenable to peer-based interventions. Issues which may need addressing include: learning self-management techniques; compensating for missed academic and social opportunities because of frequent school absences; educating schoolmates about a child's condition, such as when a child with cancer loses their hair; intervening with those children and families who are having difficulty in coping with the demands of the child's condition. Shute and Paton (1990) drew up a list of suggested ways in which co-operative learning methods might be applied to these issues within various social contexts, as follows:

Within the school context:

- co-operative learning between child with illness and classmates, both on general educational and health-related matters.

Within the family context:

- siblings provide valuable peer interactions for isolated child with chronic illness;
- family therapy including siblings;
- siblings assisting with disease management;
- tutoring by sibling for child who has missed school through illness;
- tutoring of younger sibling by the child with illness – may benefit both;
- siblings performing a bridging role between family and peer culture.

Within the health-care context:

- group discussion between children with illness to enable carers to tap concerns and misunderstandings;
- peer tutoring in disease management;
- peer tutoring within hospital school;
- self-help groups for children with chronic illnesses;
- group therapy.

Anecdotal accounts are sometimes given of such interventions being utilized, but empirical evaluations remain rare. One such evaluation, a study of the effectiveness of group relaxation therapy for children with asthma, was carried out in South Australia (Simpson 1994). Results were mixed: although peak expiratory flow rate was not improved by the programme, those who received group relaxation therapy rather than group asthma education developed more positive coping strategies and reported fewer fears. As part of a current research project, Gannoni, with the present author, will be evaluating group-based social skills training (Petersen and Gannoni 1992) as a means of promoting adaptation in children with diabetes, renal failure and cancer, identified as being psychosocially at risk. This research programme is also consonant with a call by La Greca (1992) for more within-group research which examines factors which predict psychosocial adaptation in children with chronic illnesses.

Whereas Shute and Paton (1990) relied heavily on the co-operative learning literature to provide a theoretical basis for understanding helpful peer relationships in children with chronic illnesses, the present author has more recently also drawn upon the social support literature as a framework for understanding how children can help one another within the context of chronic illness. Social support can be conceptualized as a resistance factor in adaptation to chronic illness (Wallander *et al.* 1989). It has been known for some time that good social support networks generally promote the health of adults (e.g., Wortman and Dunkelshetter 1987), but examining social support in children, both in the context of chronic illness and more generally, is a recent undertaking.

Research on social support in children began, as it did in adults, by focusing on the size of the child's social support networks, often with adults as informants. This approach has two drawbacks. First, sheer numbers of people is a very gross measure of social support – what really matters is the nature of the interactions with those people (Kaplan and Toshima 1990). Second, using adults as informants has the same drawback as in the early research on peer relationships discussed above: it bypasses the child's own perspective on the nature of the social support they receive. It has been suggested by Cauce and colleagues that the effect of support on development may be mediated by the individual's subjective appraisal of that support (Cauce *et al.* 1990). This is also consonant with Shute and Paton's (1990) systems approach to the development of a child with a chronic illness, which incorporates a social cognitive element. If it is indeed the case that the effects of social support are filtered through the child's cognitive system, then obtaining the child's own perspective is clearly vital.

Recently, a new reliable and valid instrument for measuring social support in children, called 'My Family and Friends', has been developed in the USA (Cauce *et al.* 1990). It was conceived within a systems framework, which fits well with current approaches to chronic childhood illness, and permits the examination of the social support a child receives within different social contexts, such as the family and school. It also meets the requirements discussed above in that support is evaluated from the child's point of view and it also provides a detailed breakdown of supportive relationships, in terms of who provides the support, the nature of the support and the child's satisfaction with it.

Several types of social support have been identified in both the adult and child literature, and the instrument addresses these, using an interview format. One type of support (instrumental support) concerns practical help, such as assistance with homework. The other types are informational support, emotional support (concerned with discussing feelings) and companionship support (having fun together).

The information gained from the interview enables profiles of social support satisfaction to be built up. Cauce and associates' work showed, for example, that some support providers, such as parents, have high, 'flat' profiles, indicating that they function as support generalists, providing high levels of all four types of support. Others, such as friends and teachers, have 'jagged' profiles, indicating that they are support specialists. Cauce suggests that a mixture of both types is probably the best way of both expanding developmental opportunities and acting as a safety net against developmental risks.

I have been using 'My Family and Friends' with children with diabetes aged from 7 to 16 years. Although the instrument measures perceived social support in a general sense it can be adapted for specific research or clinical contexts and, for the present research project, several diabetes-related items were added.

Preliminary results indicate some differences between the present Australian sample of children with diabetes and the US ('healthy') children with whom the instrument was developed. In particular, companionship is overwhelmingly provided by friends in the Australian children, whereas the US children also reported high levels of companionship from parents (the Australian parents were thus not so markedly 'generalist' in their support in comparison with the US parents). One possible explanation, of course, is that children with diabetes have a different kind of support network from 'healthy' children. This explanation does not seem likely, however, given the findings of a study by De Blasio (1994) with 'healthy' Australian children (the first in-depth study of the social support networks of Australian children); the support profiles he found are closely matched by those of the current study with children with diabetes. It seems to be, therefore, that Australian children make a sharper differentiation than do US children between their parents and their 'mates'.

Friends also appear to play a different role in Australia in terms of support specifically for diabetes. In a study with adolescents in the US, discussed further below, La Greca and colleagues (1995) found that friends provide emotional support for teenagers with diabetes in the sense of making them feel good about their diabetes. The author's present research in Australia suggests that although any support given by friends for diabetes is of the emotional type, this is at a very low level. In fact, health care workers appear to be giving more emotional support than do friends. Post-assessment interviews indicated that most of the children do not want their friends to know about their diabetes for fear of being stigmatized. Even those adolescents who attend a diabetes youth support group perceive this as a social group where one can have fun, and where one could receive help in the event of a hypoglycaemic episode, but where it is inappropriate to discuss diabetes with other youngsters. This research indicates the importance of taking cultural differences into account in considering the peer relationships of children with chronic illnesses: research findings and peer-based interventions developed in the US may not be directly applicable within Australia.

'My Family and Friends' examines social support in a broad sense. Another approach which has been taken is to consider support given for quite specific aspects of a chronic illness management regimen, which will differ from condition to condition. La Greca *et al.* (1995) have devised a structured interview schedule to examine how adolescents with diabetes perceive support for aspects of their daily management such as insulin injections, blood glucose testing and exercise. They identified this as an important issue since mid-adolescence is a time when it is not unusual for non-adherence to self-management routines to emerge. This is not a trivial matter given recent evidence that poor diabetic control has serious implications for future health, with an increased risk of complications such as renal and visual problems (Diabetes Control and Complications Trial Research Group 1993). La Greca *et al.* (1995) found, not surprisingly, that families gave most support for such instrumental activities as insulin administration, monitoring of blood glucose and the purchase of exercise equipment. However, friends were an important source of emotional support for diabetics, and friends' companionship support was evident for lifestyle aspects of diabetes management such as exercising together and sharing healthy snacks.

A similar research methodology is currently being used by Graetz in Australia, using an interview schedule to examine the social support received by adolescents with cystic fibrosis. This represents an important piece of research as the support needs of young people with cystic fibrosis have been little researched, despite the fact that they have not only to cope with the day-by-day management of their illness, but face severe stressors such as heart–lung transplants and the prospect of an early death.

Conclusions

This chapter has provided an overview of research on peer relationships in chronic childhood illness. Although this has been a relatively neglected area of research, it is clearly of importance given the large numbers of children living with chronic illnesses and the importance of peer relationships in children's lives. Research on peer relationships, as on psychosocial adjustment in general, has moved away from the premise that chronic illness implies maladjustment, to examining in more detail the ways in which peer relationships act as both risk and resistance factors in adaptation to a chronic condition. The recent use of co-operative learning and social support frameworks acknowledges the fact that peer relationships can have positive, and not just negative, features. Although more is gradually being learned about peer relationships in childhood chronic illness, and peer-based interventions for those at risk have been proposed and practised, there is very little evaluative research in this area.

This overview has highlighted recent and ongoing Australian research which is running parallel to similar research in the USA. For example, while La Greca *et al.* (1995) observed that their research on support for adolescents' diabetes management was, to their knowledge, the first of its kind to be published, the present author was already undertaking similar research in Australia (Shute 1994). Findings to date suggest that Australian children's perceptions of the social support received from family and friends may differ in some respects from the perceptions of children in the USA. This underlines the importance of undertaking culturally specific research in this area, and of ensuring that interventions are sensitive to the Australian context.

Chapter 10

Isolated children, bullying and peer group relations

Keith Sullivan

Introduction

> [Isolated children are] actually almost hidden, aren't they? If you have a list of priorities, then you can't not be with the disruptive child because they will throw your whole classroom out of kilter unless you actually deal with them, whereas [an isolated child] . . . will be put on the backburner and they just sit their life away. And gradually they just fail more and more.[1]

This New Zealand primary school teacher observes that in the classroom, teachers are likely to be drawn to where the noise is loudest, to where disruptive behaviour is most visible, and to where the greatest potential for disruption is located. In this setting, it is likely that the teacher will not have the time or energy to devote to children who do not demand their attention, who are alone and who are excluded by their peer group both inside and outside of the classroom.[2]

This chapter examines the notion of isolated children and argues that such children are in fact the victims of bullying. Rigby (1994: 1) defines bullying as 'repeated oppression, psychological or physical, of a less powerful person by a more powerful person or group of persons'. When children are isolated, humiliated and teased, they are being subjected to a barrage of exclusionary behaviour which is orchestrated at whim by members of their peer group as an expression of power, status and approbation.

Rubin *et al.* (1994) argue that when children are isolated and excluded they miss out on the social and cognitive development that they would normally get in a peer group situation, and are also the victims of antisocial behaviour and academic deprivation. The immediate effect is that they lack confidence and self-esteem, and the long-term effect is that they may have difficulty forming good relationships and lead less successful lives.

Rubin and Coplan (1992) state that isolated children may appear to be incompetent and as a result suffer academically even though they may be very capable. This is similar to Besag's observation that not only are they the children most at risk of being bullied at school but also the ones most likely to be misunderstood by their teachers: 'The shyness or confusion of such children can lead to them being thought of as stupid or, in some cases, disobedient' (1989:117). If this happens, then the isolated child has nowhere to turn.

These children are the victims of two sets of dynamics: in the social world both inside and outside the classroom they are marked by their peer group as in some way inadequate, and within the classroom their behaviour and social standing may also detrimentally affect their teachers' attitude towards them.

If teachers ignore isolated children or treat them as stupid or disobedient, and thereby inadvertently reinforce the behaviour of the other children, then it can be argued that the teacher is condoning the bullying of that child and allowing that child to sit 'on the backburner'. It is crucial therefore that teachers should have tools in their professional arsenal to deal with social dynamics in the classroom, so that they have a better understanding of what is going on and can then take steps to prevent or remedy problems. This may in turn alter the dynamics that are at play whenever the child is surrounded by their peer group.

In this chapter, I will provide my observations of the processes and characteristics of peer group interactions and the isolation of some children. I will then discuss a case study of one isolated child's unhappy school experiences and of how the teacher, the school and the parents responded as the situation developed over time, the dilemmas that arose and the conclusions reached.[3] The next stage is quasi-action research[4] in that an expert teacher is asked to reflect on her own recent experiences in order both to identify characteristics of isolated children and how she addresses the needs of such children. The final section deals with a comparison of the case study school and the expert teacher's responses to isolated children, bullying and peer group interaction.

Although research of this nature does not claim to provide conclusions with statistical significance, ethnographic approaches – in this instance, combining scholarship with classroom observations, a case study and an interview with an expert teacher – can provide interesting and deep illuminations of human experience which can be very useful, particularly for practitioners (that is, teachers, principals, teacher trainees and guidance counsellors) in understanding the experiences of the isolated child and in suggesting some possible solutions.

I first became interested in the difficulties faced by isolated children when I was carrying out fieldwork in a New Zealand primary school. I was making observations in the combined standard 3 and 4 classroom of a well-established and experienced older teacher, who was regarded as being excellent at her job. It struck me therefore as odd that in her classroom there appeared to be examples of unacceptable peer group behaviour of which she seemed unaware. There was one particular girl who was the butt of much class ridicule and aggression. This girl was plain, wore glasses and was dressed in a slightly old-fashioned way. On one occasion I saw two of the most dominant children in the class,[5] a boy and a girl, take her pencil case and throw it around the room. She tried to be assertive in getting it back (i.e., she demanded it back firmly but not aggressively), but this had little effect. They just laughed at her. Several other children observed this and they either giggled or ignored what was happening. The girl's behaviour was such that she did not 'make a lot of noise' and made no attempts to draw the teacher's attention to herself. Although there was some distance (15 feet or so), there were no physical barriers between the teacher and this interaction. She did not intervene or seem to be aware of what was going on. In this particular interaction, several inferences can be made:

1 The child was being bullied to varying degrees by the group as a whole.
2 No one took her part in it (i.e., she had no support).
3 The teacher did not intervene, and in fact did not seem to notice.
4 The dominant children had power and control.
5 The bullied child had no power.
6 This child did not have the teacher's sympathy.
7 This was a repetition of other similar events.

This child was at the bottom of the pecking order. She was also low in self-esteem and not a particularly good academic performer. To avoid drawing too much attention to herself and as a form of protection, she often withdrew and became 'invisible' in the classroom. While this may have offered her immunity in some circumstances, it also meant that when the power dynamics in the classroom demanded a scapegoat, she was invariably chosen. She also seemed to lack any skills which would have helped her obtain the teacher's attention in the way that other children do, either positive attention-seeking skills or the negative skills of the disruptive child. So, as well as being isolated by her peer group, for much of the time this child was also ignored by her teacher.

Isolated children are very vulnerable. They lack allies and are therefore at risk – notably in the classroom but also in the playground. There is no one there to support or defend them. They are an easy target. In the classroom situation where the teachers are caught up in the hurly-burly of incessant demands, they are not always able to support the child in learning the social skills necessary to develop and maintain a more positive role or to be able to avoid being bullied, as was the case with the above scenario. The world is a frightening place if you are alone.

I have also observed that when peer group interactions are being established or adjusted, either at the beginning of the year or when new children have joined the class, it is the dominant children who can set the tone for a peer group or for the entire class as they test what is and is not acceptable. Others then tend to follow in their footsteps. If, for instance, one of these dominant children decides to ridicule or otherwise mistreat a child who is vulnerable, as in the classroom example cited above, this type of interaction sets the trend for who is in and who is out, and a child on the outside can gradually travel down the pecking order and social isolation can be the outcome. This process also clearly gives the message to the less powerful children that they should emulate or support the dominant children's act of acceptance or rejection of a child or they too will be rejected. It also means that once a child has been pushed outside, it is extremely difficult to get back in.

The case study

The 'problem'

In order to provide an understanding of the experience of isolated children I will present a case study of one child, whom I will call Sarah, who was attending a New Zealand state primary school.[6] For Sarah, life at school was very difficult. Sarah is the youngest of three children and her parents are both professionals and are caring and supportive. They describe Sarah as being creative and happy at home and say that her way of interpreting the world is interesting and imaginative, but also quite unusual. As a toddler, she was described as a dreamy child who was largely self-contained and by preference enjoyed the company of adults or of children a little younger than herself. At the time of this study, she had a long-time friend who was half a year younger than her who went to a different school. Sarah was tall and mature looking for her age, seeming to be at least a year older than she was. This created problems for her because she sometimes acted younger than her age.

In the early childhood setting, Sarah played with the other children but did not form strong attachments within her peer group. She also tended to prefer the company of the care-givers to the other children. When she started primary school, she had difficulty forming friendships and was reported to have been sexually abused by two of the boys in her class who felt they could take advantage of her because 'she was so little' (their words as reported by Sarah's parents), even though she was a head taller than they were. Her next years of schooling were passable, but Sarah continued to have few friendships or friendships that started off strongly but did not last. Her parents thought that any friendships she did form were being undermined by her peer group.

When Sarah was 8 and finishing off her standard 2 year, her parents approached the school to try to arrange for her to be placed in a standard 3 class where she would be happy. None the less, this year proved to be a difficult one for Sarah. A pattern seemed to have developed whereby Sarah made friends with new girls as they intermittently arrived in the school and they initially reciprocated. However, each of these new girls was soon given a very clear message that Sarah was not 'in', and each time the new girl quickly withdrew her friendship as the peer group took her over. In one incident, Sarah's peers told the new girl that Sarah was 'retarded'. In addition, each of Sarah's teachers adopted the same negative attitude to her and approached her initially as a 'problem child'.

Sarah's parents said that at the beginning of the school year they had spoken with the woman who was to be Sarah's standard 3 teacher about their concerns and had agreed to support the teacher in developing strategies for dealing with Sarah's difficulties. On one occasion, when the parents became worried about Sarah's unhappiness, the teacher used the strategy of talking to the class (in front of Sarah) to explain that she was having difficulties and that they should all be nicer to her. This had the effect of everyone being nice to Sarah for two or three days in a patronizing fashion (i.e., Sarah was presented as a child with problems who needed taking care of rather than as a child with interesting qualities that needed to be acknowledged). Some girls offered to give her 'smiling' lessons and 'making friends' lessons. The kind and supportive immediate responses of the children did not last. In the long term, this had the effect of embarrassing and exposing Sarah to humiliation rather than providing a solution. On another occasion the teacher made Sarah sing solo in a school assembly, believing that if Sarah succeeded, all her problems would disappear. Sarah sang quietly and sweetly while feeling very fearful, but her difficulties persisted.

It became obvious in observing this classroom and in talking with the teacher that she believed Sarah's work to be inferior to that of her peers, and the teacher made this generally and publicly clear. On one occasion when the children had to give an oral presentation of a project, Sarah was clearly very frightened and was unable to get very far with her presentation. She said afterwards that she felt sick and her knees were shaking. What she did present, however, was interesting, although her teacher told her it was inadequate and that she should sit down. She dismissed Sarah's presentation, and did not encourage her to go on. This sort of treatment was not uncommon, especially when Sarah had difficulty finishing work on time, which she often did. The teacher's treatment of Sarah was picked up by the children in the class, although the teacher seemed entirely unaware of the negative effects of her reactions, and that these reactions seemed to shape the attitude of the class towards Sarah.

The child

On pupil aptitude tests, which are standardized in New Zealand, Sarah scored very well in her listening skills and average elsewhere. Her school is largely middle class, and an average score in this particular school and especially in Sarah's class tends to be considered inadequate rather than good. About herself, Sarah said: 'I'm the dumbest at reading, the dumbest at maths and the dumbest at friends.'

In her peer group, Sarah was not accepted. Although a pleasant and attractive child, she was labelled as dumb and ugly. She was also criticized for the way she dressed and the clothes she wore: she was certainly a non-conformist, and liked colourful scarves and hats. To me, however, she dressed in an interesting and creative way.

Amongst the girls in this class there were a few who were dominant and most of the others were 'in', but in order to stay 'in' they had to follow the directions of these peer group leaders. Then there were a few children such as Sarah who were outside of the group completely. Sarah was once invited to play at the house of a child who was 'in' but not a leader. She told Sarah that she could not tell the other children she had invited Sarah home. Although the two children appeared to play well together (as reported by both mothers), Sarah was not invited back and all invitations for this child to come to Sarah's home to play were turned down.

It was decided between the parents and the school to call in an educational psychologist to try to find some solutions.[7] He described Sarah as seeing the world as a frightening place. He suggested that she was more than normally sensitive, was a child who was easily set back, had fragile defences, and was unable to cope with the snubs and rejections that were part of the normal learning processes for this age group. He concluded that essentially it would be impossible for her to retrieve her social networks. He advised that Sarah should work with a female therapist in order to help build her self-esteem and develop strategies on 'how to win friends and influence people'.

The parents' perspective

The parents initially trusted the standard 3 teacher when she explained to them that her strategy was to be very hard on Sarah in order to bring her work 'up to scratch' academically. She said that if Sarah's work improved, the other children would probably like her more. The parents agreed not to intervene if Sarah appeared unhappy about school, but to support the teacher in maintaining her 'being tough and consistent' programme. The teacher said that Sarah was manipulative and would try to get her parents to stop this hard strategy by saying that the teacher was being 'mean' to her. The parents agreed to step back, to support the teacher and not interfere. However, after only two phone calls from the teacher in the first six months, Sarah's parents felt that they were not receiving enough feedback, and when faced by Sarah's misery about school on at least a weekly basis they became increasingly concerned. Instead of her work, her self-esteem and her social standing improving, Sarah's parents saw her getting unhappier and unhappier, with poorer and poorer posture, and more and more reluctance to get up in the mornings, until she told them that she could not 'stand it any more', that she had had enough.

Her parents ended up being very dissatisfied with the teacher and her interventions or lack thereof on behalf of Sarah. They felt that they had brought their concerns to the school on several occasions, and although the school and the teacher had appeared both to share their concerns and to be willing to seek solutions, nothing lasting had been achieved. They felt that the teacher's hard treatment of Sarah had been counterproductive and she had continued to treat Sarah as if she was 'dumb', clearly giving this message to the children of the class.

The school's perspective

The school is a state school in an affluent inner-city suburb. Many of the pupils' parents are middle-class professionals, business people, medical practitioners and academics. Material possessions are highly valued and there is a lot of emphasis on academic success.

The school's principal felt that the school had done all that it could for Sarah. He believed that she needed psychological help to sort out her problems. He stated that he had observed her alone in the playground and generally not interacting with the other children. He used this observation to support his view that the problem was solely hers.

The assistant principal also thought Sarah's behaviour both inside and outside the classroom accounted for all of her difficulties. At a meeting between the school and the parents, she cited instances when Sarah's poor maths performances or her inability to complete work on time had attracted ridicule from the other children. She shrugged her shoulders, looked skywards, and said in a hopeless voice, 'So you see?'

In a group discussion between three staff members and the parents, the principal stated that all of the teachers who had had contact with Sarah were of the same mind. The school therefore closed ranks against a child whom they had not been able to integrate. There was also a sense that the school was starting to find the parents unreasonable and blind to the real problem, which was their child.

The teacher's perspective

Sarah's teacher described her as difficult to deal with and worrying, and as demanding more of her time than she was either able or prepared to give. She felt that she had tried to give Sarah support. She had been tough on her to get her to improve her work. She had tried to make her smile more and to develop behaviour that would help her to be liked more by the other children in the class. She told Sarah's parents that she considered Sarah 'unintelligent', and when they argued that her homework was good and that she was clearly intelligent, the teacher told them that her homework was satisfactory only because they helped Sarah to do it. At school, the teacher felt that the child was unfocused and did not get her work done quickly enough. She did not complete her projects and was lacking in basic maths skills (i.e., the times tables), and was performing below the level of the class generally.

The teacher said that she had a very clever standard 3 class and that Sarah's performance was just not up to their level. She felt that Sarah's work was so poor that she attracted ridicule. She believed that her strategy of trying to get Sarah to improve her work and thus to be more acceptable to the other children was a correct and appropriate one. She did not believe that the little cluster of girls which excluded Sarah and made her a subject for class rejection was in any way to blame.

The solution

The parents removed Sarah from the school and enrolled her in another school where the class rolls are smaller, and where Sarah is one of the older children in her class. The parents hoped that in this new setting, where the philosophy of the school is geared towards recognizing different personality types and developing children's creative skills, Sarah would have a better chance of being valued, nurtured and educated. They still feel very angry about what they see as the original school's lack of effective handling of Sarah's educational experience and its possible long-term harm to their child.

The principal of the original school said that he wished the child well at her new school but that he had his doubts about whether it would make a difference. He believed that she would take her problems with her.

'The child is the one with the problem'

When I discussed what to do with situations like Sarah's with a group of teacher trainees, they came up with a variety of ideas. For instance, one popular suggestion was that the child be put in a leadership role so that the other children would see her in a positive light and accept her into their peer group. What was common between the trainees' suggestions and the viewpoint of Sarah's school was that both assumed that it was the child who was the one with the problem rather than the dynamics of the peer group and the school culture.[8] In Sarah's case, the victim was blamed and the school presented itself as blameless.

In defence of this position (i.e., that it is the child who has the problem), it is true that if the child is going at least to live safely in the world then he or she needs to develop appropriate survival skills. The suggestion of the educational psychologist that Sarah should work with a therapist in order to develop both her self-esteem and more effective communication skills so as to be able to encourage her peers to like and play with her, also reflects this belief.

Essentially, in taking a stance of blaming the child, the school denies any responsibility for allowing the existence of a situation which is surely destructive to at least one of the children entrusted to it. In Sarah's case, the school and her teacher were completely unsuccessful in creating a safe environment for her, and then blamed her for this outcome.

An alternative approach: making the classroom a safe place

A solution to Sarah's isolation had been reached. Sarah's parents had transferred her to another school and hoped she would fare better there. Her original school considered it had done the best job it could have done under the circumstances. I found this conclusion unsatisfactory and decided to pursue the issue of Sarah's isolation. In order to try to find some creative solutions for children like Sarah I pondered what to do further and decided to interview an acknowledged and successful teacher from another school to discuss how she identifies and deals with Sarah's type of isolation. This teacher has developed an understanding of school and classroom culture and peer group relations from her participation and observations over 15 years as both a full-time and part-time teacher, and also as a mother taking part in the school experiences of her own children.

Identifying the problem

The essence of this expert teacher's perspective is that she believes it is the teacher and the school who are responsible for making the classroom a safe place for the children entrusted to them. From her recent experience in the classroom, she identified three children as isolated from their peer groups. What she perceived as the common thread for all three was what she terms a high level of sensitivity. She sees it as being her job to provide some stability and consistency for these children when they are at school:

> Well, these three children . . . one of them came from a very abusive family so her boundaries were totally confused because she was quite frequently physically abused. So that caused total chaos. She just needed that time and space and to feel secure with someone, to trust someone. That was what her time was for. Another one was a diabetic child who obviously had enormous emotional difficulties because of the strict [timetable] her illness required which caused lots of conflict in the family, and so she needed the emotional security of that. And the other one was just from a very free gentle family that I think had [more liberal] attitudes that don't actually fit in with a lot of the authoritarian strict attitudes of our society generally and the school culture in particular . . . He couldn't quite cope with the conflict between the freedom that his family gave him in his emotional development and the lack of support that the school gave him that way.

She also identifies that in being isolated from their peer group such children are traumatized and therefore cannot work effectively in the classroom. She feels that dealing with a child's trauma is basic and needs to be done as a prerequisite for effective learning:

> I found that they actually got lost in the system. [They were emotionally so] spun-out that they actually found it very difficult to make any gains academically . . . They weren't actually academically not able, it's just that they were so focused on coping with the emotions of the situation, they didn't have the energy to focus on the work. And then that was a self-perpetuating thing because they got behind, then they felt inadequate, then they got treated badly. That's how I found it.

Five strategies in relation to isolated children

This expert teacher identifies five interrelated strategies for both meeting the needs of the isolated child and addressing the pressures of the peer group. These are: spending quality time with the isolated child, role modelling for the class, putting the child into successful situations, having a reasonable number of children in her class, and effective classroom management.

Quality time

> I found that actually spending short but clear times with them each day, getting them to talk about their emotional situations, not directly but making them feel supported [was useful. I was] then able to work

> on one of the barriers they had difficulty with academically. And even for just that short time [this] made an enormous difference.

The teacher suggests that having quality time with these children is essential. With the teacher's busy schedule, this may be only for five minutes a day but it is important that this should be both daily and at the same time. In other words, the child knows that she will have this regular contact with her teacher and can discuss any difficulties experienced during that day. The teacher stated that when she initiates this quality time, initially the time is used just to talk to the child, to deal with the trauma at the child's own speed. Gradually, as trust is established and the child's trauma is worked through, the teacher can also work on academic difficulties such as missing links in learning due to the child's having fallen behind with his/her work.

Role modelling

This teacher also feels that it is important to change the peer group dynamics. She sees the peer group as tremendously powerful, but that if she tries to impose her sense of what was right on the peer group they might do what she asks them to her face in terms of treating the child with kindness but act differently behind her back. This would obviously be self-defeating. So she sees it as more important to teach by example, in other words, to role model appropriate behaviour:

> I think the tone of the teacher's voice is important. And the things that she says or he says can influence enormously the attitudes of acceptance. When teachers accept a child then children model that. They accept each other and that affects the atmosphere. I found that if . . . the rest of the children were aware . . . then they tended to support the child too when they saw that I was supporting that child.
>
> I think it is part of that nurturing [principle] if you create or do your best in the classroom to create a positive environment. Not just for those children [who are isolated] but for everyone. That people don't generally put each other down. That that's not acceptable behaviour. Then you can create a nurturing situation where people do accept others who are different and accept each other too.

Putting the child into successful situations

Part of nurturing the child is to put her into what this teacher describes as successful situations. For the teacher, this means being aware of the child's strengths and weaknesses and creating situations where the child can be successful, can be seen to be successful and can be supported and acknowledged by the teacher as being successful:

TEACHER: Probably I would verbally support the child a lot. Probably put the child in successful situations where she's going to feel good about herself.

KEITH SULLIVAN: So what happens in successful situations?

TEACHER: Well, if you have some sort of creative thing you were doing in the classroom, give them a situation where you know they would be happy and confident about taking a part in it. Start to make them feel good about themselves so that they are then brave enough to deal with what's happening to them. And also verbally [to] support them.

Sarah's teacher suggested something similar with her strategy of being tough on Sarah so that she would do well academically and as a result would receive approval from the rejecting peer group. In contrast to the expert teacher's approach, this is flawed for at least four reasons:

1 the expert teacher would address the issue of Sarah's trauma before she put her in a situation where she was 'in the spotlight';
2 she would put Sarah in a situation of strength rather than one where she was struggling, as Sarah was;
3 she would role model to the class an acceptance of Sarah;
4 she would do this within a classroom setting where Sarah knew she was 'safe'.

Sarah's teacher thought her unintelligent and was prepared to treat Sarah more positively only if and when her academic work improved. This turned out to be a no-win situation for Sarah.

Having a reasonable number of children per class

Another basic consideration for this teacher is based on her past experiences with large and small classes:

> I find that usually with between 20–25 [pupils] you start to get beyond your ability to [act effectively]. I think [that with] 20 [pupils] or below you are able to do that successfully, but once you get over 25, I think it gets increasingly hard to keep your finger on where everybody is. I would see up to 20 as an optimum number that you are able to do it with, but after that I think you lose it.[9]

Effective classroom management

Going by the sort of objections raised by Sarah's school, the suggestions made by this expert teacher could be seen as unreasonable. For instance, it could be asked, how in the often unpredictable classroom setting can you possibly set aside five minutes every day exclusively for perhaps three isolated children? The teacher's reply indicates a sensible central and unifying tenet behind her philosophy which is her belief in the need to run an effective and efficient classroom. She states that a well-thought-out approach and an organized classroom enable the teacher to know what is going on and assist in making sure that the needs of *all* of her children are being met. It also means that routines can be established which provide structure for the isolated child and the rest of the class:

> And I think for young children and maybe for older children too I find that routines establish security. [It helps] if they can predict what they are going to do. And also that they are actively engaged in what they see as succeeding in what they are doing. That they know what they are learning, they're involved in knowing what they're trying to learn, they feel safe about where they are and that they are going to [be able to] make the next step. I think all those sorts of things are important.

The healthy peer group

In relation to children's peer groups, the teacher suggests that if these children feel a need to exclude and pick on a child, then the group and its members must feel insecure:

> You've sort of got to think about what's happening to the whole group that's making that group react like that. That they feel that insecure that they've got to keep pushing people out to make themselves feel safe. That's just symptomatic of all of them feeling insecure really . . . in the whole environment of the classroom. It's not accepting of everyone, that they're feeling that they have to cling very tightly to a group to feel secure, to feel safe. In this case the classroom is not a safe place to be.

The teacher suggests that in her classroom when things get out of hand, she gives the children something peaceful to do where she feels in control and able to provide the children with a more secure and comfortable environment:

> I suppose I feel comfortable teaching art, I always found providing quite a bit of art work at certain times allows you to switch into a

> different mode, to calm down, and create and be at peace with ourselves when those sort of [stressful] situations develop. And then through the art I found that a lot of language work would come out. It was a very soothing sort of thing . . . developing in that way in the classroom. Like using clay, you have that sort of tactile security of pleasure that you can get from some art forms. You can start to feel at peace and comfortable and pleasant in what you are doing and then you can just gradually but slowly develop on that. And then support everyone in that situation and then gradually you can build up securities again. But it does take a while. But I think it has to slow down and it has to become quite simple.

Support for teachers

An important issue for this teacher is one that relates to the school as a whole. In order to be effective, she says that the teacher needs to feel supported. If a principal and staff provide a safe and supportive environment for each other, then teachers are more likely to be able to function effectively – not only in developing a useful approach to isolated children, for instance, but also in the various other roles that are demanded of them:

> I think perhaps a lot of teachers feel too frightened to deal with situations early so they put them off. And then things can build up. You know, like anything. And maybe they don't feel supported enough or clear enough about their own [aims] . . . it's got very complicated.
>
> Well, I don't suppose anybody wants to feel that they're failing in the work they're doing. And then therefore the teachers have to feel secure as well, don't they? And they have to be supported and doing appropriate things that make them feel comfortable in the environment, so they then pass it on to the classroom.
>
> I think teachers basically, like anyone, need to be supported in what they're doing and they need to be clear about what they're doing and it shouldn't be too complicated for them.

Teachers, power and prejudice

In a setting of positive support, negative stereotyping is less likely to occur for both disruptive and isolated children. This teacher and others I have spoken to identify that within the culture of the staffroom there can be a conspiracy mentality developed whereby when teachers discuss their students they can create a persona for a child that stays with that child and indeed can stretch to other members of the child's family. It also helps to make teachers feel that if they hear their opinions echoed back at them a few times, then they are justified in treating the child in a particular way:

> When I started teaching him, he was very much not accepted by the other teachers . . . They found that irritating because he couldn't respond quickly or move quickly, or work quickly . . . So the attitude within the culture of the teachers was such that they would actually not acknowledge the child. Kids actually pick up on that . . . The teachers put him down and so then the children started putting him down. The children were modelling what the teachers were doing. The teachers are saying this is right, this is wrong, we want to be in, we'll accept this child, we'll reject that one, and that will make me more in.

If what this teacher is suggesting is true, that the attitude children have towards isolated children can in some situations be largely dependent upon the judgement of the teacher, then a teacher must be aware of this potential and act with responsibility. Within the safety of a positive and supportive school they are more likely to do this.

A teacher's intuition

A final and important theme relates to teachers having the confidence to trust their intuitive understanding of situations and encounters. This teacher places a lot of value on her own intuition and that of her colleagues. This means that she feels competent to call upon her own experiential knowledge to solve problems rather than finding them too difficult or requiring 'expert' intervention:

> The thing is, I'm very intuitive and I think I'm good at observing children so I find it very easy to notice children who are having emotional difficulties and are likely to be in a bullied situation. But I think perhaps some people only react to children who are outwardly naughty, being disruptive and sometimes teachers don't pick up on those children who are quiet because they're not disruptive. You could just say to them 'go and read a book in the corner' and they do. I think sometimes they are not actually picked up on in the classroom.

A final note

This teacher's central tenet in dealing with isolated children is that she avoids blame.[10] In relation to the children who could be accused of victimizing and isolating vulnerable children, she finds ways of supporting a positive sense of self-worth in all of her pupils, valuing and tolerating difference, and modelling behaviour that shows the children how to act with responsibility in a group. She creates situations with the victimized child that help her to integrate into the group or at least to cope better. In other words, she does not act as the 'rescuer' of a victim – in popular terms, she develops win/win situations.

Conclusions

This study has considered two very different ways of approaching the problem of bullying, isolation and the peer group. In the first instance, Sarah's school states that the child is the one with the problem, that it is not the job of teachers and schools to look after the psychological well-being of a difficult child, and that teachers are not trained to deal with such situations. They have neither the expertise nor the time to do so. They feel that the school can help to sort out problems as they arise but that the job of teachers is to teach and not to be involved in the solving of psychological problems. It is also probably the case that if Sarah's parents had not been assertive, Sarah's case would probably have been ignored and 'put on the backburner'.

The second perspective, that of the expert teacher, is based on the conviction that the job of the teacher and the school is to make a classroom and school environment a place where the needs of the various children are met and where each child can feel safe. I personally favour the latter perspective. I believe that it is essential to create a safe environment where each child feels grounded.

An essential characteristic of the way that the teacher who represents this perspective chose to handle the situation was that she was willing to take on the responsibility herself. She had not developed the institutional 'yes but' approach that Sarah's first school obviously had. Yes, we would like to help Sarah but she needs to help herself; yes, we would like to sort out this difficulty but we are not psychologists, we are not trained to deal with this sort of problem; yes, we would like to help Sarah but the teacher already has too many things to do.

The second perspective is not only positive and proactive and of benefit to the child, it is also empowering for the teacher. The types of strategies and the answers this teacher has come up with are not presented here as the only way or even the preferred way of dealing with an incidence of peer group isolation of a child. It is an illustration of what can be done with a positive problem-solving and professional approach to teaching.[11] This teacher perceives good teachers as having the means and the experience effectively to handle the day-to-day dynamics of her classroom, and she also regards this particular problem as a learning problem rather than as a psychological one, which puts it clearly within her professional frame of reference. She also realizes that for isolated children it is necessary first to deal with the emotional trauma of the situation before learning can take place. The teacher is also seen as having an obligation to the rest of the class to show them that there are many different ways of being in the world which are acceptable, and that within a nurturing and tolerant setting there is no value in bullying those children who are perceived as being weaker than others or who do not 'fit the norm'.

Two years after the case study material was gathered, I revisited Sarah in her new school and with her family. Her new teacher and peer group are accepting of her and she is now functioning as a normal and socially healthy adolescent. She has friends at school for the first time, and socialises frequently after school and at the weekends. Her body language has changed and she talks ruefully and sometimes with anger about her earlier school experiences, sure now that she could handle any situation.

Notes

1 All unattributed statements were made by a New Zealand primary school teacher with excellent communications skills and fine-tuned empathic understanding in relation to children she worked with. She was interviewed in January 1994. Her contributions to this chapter are enormously appreciated. She is not identified to protect confidentiality.

2 In Hargreaves's sociometric terminology (1973), he calls these children isolates; Besag (1989) refers to children alone; Rubin and Coplan (1992) refer to them as rejected children; and Rubin *et al.* (1994) as withdrawn children. 'Withdrawn' suggests an act by the child, whereas 'rejected' suggests an act towards the child by the peer group. The term that for me encapsulates all of these intersections and which I will use in this chapter is 'isolated children'.

3 The case study was recorded between 1991 and 1994, with a follow-up in 1996.

4 Action research is based on problem-solving in a particular situation and it includes all participants as co-researchers. In this particular fieldwork situation it was not appropriate to develop an action-based research response but rather it was essential to focus on the situation and its context. However, the addition of some *post-hoc* problem-solving could be described as quasi-action research.

5 Hargreaves (1973) refers to these children as 'stars'.

6 Since four out of five examples of isolated children cited in this chapter are female, it may appear that girls are more prone to this type of bullying than boys. Although bullying researchers have found that for girls bullying tends to be indirect and psychological rather than physical (Björkqvist *et al.* 1992a; Frost 1992; Elliott 1992; Ahmad and Smith 1994b; Smith *et al.* 1994), Olweus (1993a) suggests that a large proportion of bullying among boys is also of this nature (although overall boys do indulge in much more physical bullying than girls).

7 In New Zealand, psychologists from the Special Education Services can be hired by schools to help sort out various problems. They tend, however, to be used as a final recourse. Unlike in secondary schools, there is no equivalent to a trained guidance counsellor, and teachers' training does not specifically provide skills to deal with isolated children or peer group dynamics.

8 This is not to say that putting the child in a leadership role is not a good idea.

It may be a useful strategy if it is well considered before being implemented, and is monitored and reinforced. It is useful to develop a child's skills, but the main issues in Sarah's case are that (a) the child was being bullied by her peer group and (b) that no one was prepared to say that this was what was actually happening. It is useful to help the child find solutions as long as the victim is not blamed for the problems. The main criticism of Sarah's teacher and her school is not that they did not make attempts to find solutions, rather that they based their efforts on a belief that Sarah was to 'blame', and their efforts were piecemeal and prescriptive rather than planned and preventative.

9 This is a contentious issue and one that needs further investigation. At the 1994 Children's Peer Relations Conference in Adelaide, Dan Olweus, a leading authority on bullying research, argued vigorously that reducing class size did not make a difference to the incidence of bullying. See Olweus 1973, 1978 and 1993a.

10 Focusing on finding solutions rather than finding out who is to blame is also the central philosophy of Barbara Maines and George Robinson's (1992) anti-bullying programme, the No Blame Approach.

11 Over recent years there have been several useful programmes developed to counter bullying at school. Rigby (1994) provides a useful overview of the best strategies, as do Smith and Sharp (1994). Of particular usefulness are the Pikas method of shared concern (Pikas 1989a), the No Blame Approach of Maines and Robinson (1992), and for older children Peer Counselling (see, for instance, Sharp and Cowie in Smith and Sharp 1994). However, the real value of the expert teacher's approach in this study is that rather than immediately calling on the experts she is prepared to use her own developed skills in the first instance.

Part IV

Peer status

Chapter 11

The location and arrangement of peer contacts

Links with friendship initiation knowledge in 4- to 7-year-olds

Kym Irving

Friendship formation entails the co-ordination of a range of complex social and psychological processes. As adults, we may take for granted our relationships with close friends, giving little thought to how these relationships came about. The processes involved in forming adult friendships are largely learned during childhood and are a function of our history of relating to others, including parents and peers, our temperaments or social dispositions, and our social and cultural environments which give rise to the patterns and norms of our social conduct. In this chapter, I would like to examine three features of children's learning about friendships: the nature and location of children's peer contacts, the roles of children and adults in the arrangement and supervision of contacts, and children's knowledge of strategies to initiate friendship. Research on these three themes has found variations in children's experiences which are linked with the development of social competence. For example, children who have more extensive peer networks are more likely to achieve peer approval and acceptance than those with limited networks (e.g., Bost 1995). Children who are active in arranging peer experiences and have parents who provide appropriate advice and supervision are also more likely to display a range of socially competent behaviours (Kennedy 1992; Ladd and Golter 1988; Russell and Finnie 1990). Finally, knowing what to say or do to make friends is a key ingredient in friendship formation and is associated with children's capacity to enter into close relationships with others (Rubin and Rose-Krasnor 1992).

While previous research has addressed the links between the location, organization and supervision of peer experiences, and various measures of peer acceptance and social behaviour, less is known of how, or indeed, whether, the context and management of peer experiences relate to social cognitive development. Contextual approaches to the development of social cognition emphasize the role of experience in the formation of knowledge and scripts for social interaction (Cohen and Siegel 1991; Costanzo 1991). The salience of individual social strategies may vary from context to context depending on the social and physical features of the context, the social tasks and demands of the situation, and the likely success of the strategy in achieving social goals (Harkness and Super 1995; Rubin and Rose-Krasnor 1992; Weisner 1984). To what extent, then, do the nature and context of children's peer experiences have bearing on the strategies children identify as pertinent to friendship formation?

In this chapter, findings from a study of Brisbane children and their families (Irving 1994) are used to highlight some of the changes which take place from preschool (4- to 5-year-olds) to the early primary years (6- to 7-year-olds) in the contextual, organizational and social cognitive elements of peer relationship development. The research is presented in three sections corresponding to the three areas just described (Social Networks and Peer Contacts, Arranging and Supervising Peer Contacts, and Friendship Initiation Strategies) and culminates in a discussion of the ways in which the context and structure of peer experiences may influence the development of friendship knowledge. The chapter ends with a consideration of issues for future research.

Social networks and peer contacts

The development of social networks and peer relationships occupy a prominent place in the research literature on social development because supportive and extensive networks are generally seen as a balm to psychological distress and trauma across the lifespan. Social networks generally include all individuals known to a child and the relationships they encompass (Cochran and Brassard 1979; Howes *et al.* 1992). For young children, social networks and peer contacts provide children with opportunities for relationship learning and are associated with social competence development. Where children experience larger and more varied networks, peer acceptance and social competence tend to be higher, at least in Western cultures (North American research predominates in this field). Children who fail to develop such networks and who have limited or unsatisfactory peer contacts may therefore be buffeted to a larger degree by life's uncertainties or may be at risk for peer difficulties such as rejection and neglect.

According to Belle (1989), few sex differences exist in the composition and size of social networks of school age children with similar numbers of kin, adults and children appearing for both sexes. A preference for same-sex peers, however, has been documented from age 3 and appears to gain strength during the late preschool and early school years (Ramsey 1995). A number of authors argue that same-sex preference may be strongly influenced by cultural and social expectations (Belle 1989), while others see mutual avoidance as resulting from the widening gap between boys and girls in their play styles (Erwin 1993) and differential maturation rates (Howes *et al.* 1992). Additionally, as children show preferences for their same-sex playmates, peer group size diminishes for girls and increases for boys (Hartup 1992).

A number of factors influence the frequency, location and structure of peer contacts and these include environmental setting (including social density and the location of neighbours and parks), parental control over contacts (e.g., arranging and supervising), and the individual characteristics of the child (e.g., temperament). Parents may create family climates where friendships with others are valued, modelled and discussed. They may also choose neighbourhoods and extracurricular activities which expose their children to a range of friendship possibilities. Often, parents who set the stage in this manner spend time finding out about their children's friends at child care and school, discuss how friends can be a source of pleasure, and offer advice on how to overcome peer difficulties. They may also manage the social calendar of children through various invitations to visit, stay over, or share in outings and gatherings. Possibly, where children have immediate access to other children, perhaps in terms of a large family of siblings or safe opportunities for extensive peer-play over the back fence, there is less need for organized activities.

Gathering information about children's social networks and peer contacts is achieved in several ways. Children may be observed for the nature and conduct of peer interactions, while parent and teacher reports provide more global perceptions of children's activities. Diary reports and telephone logs offer an effective methodology for tracking peer contacts over time and place. Where children are able, self-reports of networks may be elicited, although these may not always correspond with adult reports, with preschool children reporting smaller social networks than their mothers, for example (Bost 1995).

While research concerning preschool children's peer contacts has grown steadily in recent years, less is known of contacts during the early school years and the changes which may take place as children move into formal schooling. Several questions guided the first phase of data gathering in the Brisbane study: what are the characteristics of peer contacts for 4- to 7-year-olds, where do they take place and who do they involve, and to what extent do peer contacts vary according to the sex and age of the child?

Method

Sample

The participants were 279 preschool and early primary (grades 1 and 2) children and their mothers. The mean age of the preschool children was 4 yrs 11 mths (SD = 7 mths), while the mean age of the primary children (grades 1 and 2) was 7 yrs 2 mths (SD = 10 mths). In Queensland, the preschool year is a non-compulsory year of education prior to formal schooling, during which children typically turn 5 years of age. The preschool group comprised 80 males and 62 females, while the older group consisted of 64 males and 73 females. Forty-one per cent of the children were first-born. Number of siblings ranged from none to five with an average of 1.5.

Mothers ranged in age from 23 to 48 yrs (mean age = 34 yrs, SD = 5 yrs), with 62 per cent having completed high school (to year 12) and 36 per cent tertiary education. Half of the mothers were in full- (14 per cent) or part-time (36 per cent) employment. Ninety per cent of mothers were in relationships with an average length of 11 yrs (SD = 5 yrs). Partners ranged in age from 23 to 55 yrs (mean age = 37 yrs, SD = 5 yrs), with 41 per cent being tertiary educated and 97 per cent in full-time employment. Families were contacted through undergraduate students completing a course in early childhood education.

Diaries

Mothers were asked to keep a diary of their children's peer contacts outside of preschool or school hours over a two-week period (14 continuous days). Parents were provided with a pro forma requesting information about the location of the activity, the age and sex of the children involved, the activities engaged in, how the activity was organized and the level of supervision provided by the parent. Pro formas were based on Ladd and Golter's (1988) telephone interview format. At the completion of the 14-day period, parents were asked to comment on whether the activities were typical of a usual two-week period. Diaries which were incomplete or included holiday periods or atypical events (e.g., illness or long stays by relatives) were removed, resulting in a final sample of 199 families (104 preschool, 95 primary).

Results

Where were the contacts?

Over the 14-day period, peer contacts most often occurred in the home (42 per cent). Next came structured classes and activities (26 per cent) (e.g., sport or art classes), then friends' or relatives' homes (21 per cent) and, finally, neighbours' homes or yards (11 per cent). The location of peer contacts showed a similar pattern for preschool and primary children and for boys and girls. While children aged 4 to 7 entertained peers to a large extent in the family home, a substantial percentage of contacts involved structured events. Given the characteristics of the families who participated in this study, in terms of education and employment, the prominence of organized events in the children's lives possibly reflects the tendency for middle-class families to encourage extracurricular activities (Berg and Medrich 1980; Rubin and Sloman 1984).

Who were they with?

The number of children's nonschool contacts ranged from 2 to 39 with a mean of 12.1. There were no significant variations due to age or sex. On average, for each peer contact, there were 1.42 peers, 0.46 siblings, 0.18 relatives and 0.15 large groups present. Not surprisingly, the presence of siblings in peer contacts was associated with the proportion of contacts occurring at home ($r = 0.31$, $p < 0.001$). The presence of relatives was associated with contacts at friends and relatives ($r = 0.33$, $p < 0.001$), and the presence of groups associated with structured activities ($r = 0.61$, $p < 0.001$). The presence of same and opposite sex peers was not linked to particular locations, suggesting a spread of peers across contexts. Clearly then, children's peer experiences were varied, involving not only peers but siblings and relatives, with the composition of each contact depending to some extent on location. While the number of peer contacts for the 14-day period did not vary with age, it is important to note that older children maintained their level of peer activities despite their longer attendance at school. While the number of hours spent by preschoolers in their programmes was not elicited in this study, on average, preschool children spend fewer hours in programme attendance than primary school children. When Ladd and Golter (1988) controlled for programme duration they found an increase in peer activities with age.

In regard to same-sex preference, the average number of male and female peers present across the fortnight did vary according to the age and sex of the child. Both sexes showed a preference for same-sex playmates over opposite-sex peers, and this was most marked for primary aged children. There was a clear increase in male peer contacts for boys from preschool to primary and a decrease in male peer contacts for girls from preschool to primary, indicating the divergence, found in other studies, in preferred playmates as children entered primary school.

What were they doing?

Children's activities were classified as free play or structured. Structured activities included events away from home and routine (e.g., Wednesday music class) or special arrangements. In comparison to primary children (mean = 0.77, range 0.07–1.00), preschool children (mean = 0.82, range 0.00–1.00) engaged in a higher percentage of free play, while there were no age or sex differences for structured activities (mean = 0.21, range

0.00–0.93). While 53 per cent of children did not view television during peer contacts, for 10 per cent of children viewing ranged from 0.25 to 0.65 of contacts. On average, nearly twice as many contacts involved TV or video viewing for boys (mean 0.10, range 0.00–0.65) than for girls (mean = 0.05, range 0.00–0.35). For boys, the proportion of contacts involving television was positively correlated with sibling presence ($r = 0.30$, $p < 0.01$) and the proportion of contacts in the home ($r = 0.25$, $p < 0.05$).

Discussion

Both preschool and primary children experienced a range of peer contacts in terms of composition and location. Peer contacts often involved the presence of siblings and relatives and included opportunities for free play as well as structured, large group activities. The relatively large proportion of structured activities suggests that studies exploring relationships between frequency of peer contacts and various indicators of social competence development may need to examine more carefully the nature of peer activities in facilitating such development. For example, how do experiences in large groups differ from free play experiences in their contribution to social competence? Do children who experience higher rates of structured activities develop different skills to those for whom free play predominates? While television viewing was not a common feature of children's peer contacts, the finding that, on average, around 10 per cent of boys' interactions with peers involved television viewing raises the question of the significance of such viewing for the nature of peer exchanges.

Arranging and supervising peer contacts

Along with the 'Who?', 'What?' and 'Where?' of children's peer contacts, the involvement of parents in arranging and supervising contacts has been linked to teacher and peer ratings of popularity and social competence in the classroom (Bhavnagri and Parke 1991; Finnie and Russell 1988; Ladd and Golter 1988; MacDonald and Parke 1984; Pettit *et al.* 1991). Parents have been variously described as gate-keepers, stage-setters, managers, scaffolders, supervisors and coaches of children's peer relationships. Where parents are involved in arranging frequent peer contacts preschoolers show more prosocial behaviour with peers and greater peer acceptance (Ladd and Golter 1988; Ladd and Hart 1992), and mothers view their children as more sociable (Profilet and Ladd 1994). Additionally, maternal beliefs about the value of peer activities are associated with their involvement in arranging peer experiences for children (Kennedy 1992; Ladd and Hart 1992).

While data on the parental role in facilitating children's peer contacts prior to school entry continues to expand, little research has been directed towards children of school age. Comparisons have been made of children aged 2 to 3 yrs and 3 to 5 yrs, as well as younger (3 to 4 yrs) and older preschoolers (4 to 5 yrs) (Bhavnagri and Parke 1991; Ladd and Hart 1992). Bhavnagri and Parke (1991) found that 3- to 6-year-olds were more likely to initiate peer activities than 2- to 3-year-olds, and their parents were less active in arranging and maintaining contacts than for younger children. Returning to the Brisbane study, it was expected that parental involvement in arranging and supervising peer contacts would decline further as children enter school and develop more sophisticated social cognitive and behavioural repertoires for peer interactions.

There is some debate as to the influence of parental supervision on children's developing social competence. Ladd and Golter (1988) for example, found that mothers who undertook higher levels of direct supervision, by being present during peer activities, had children who experienced higher levels of peer rejection. One possibility is that more directive parents are more interfering parents who hinder their children's interactions with peers. Alternatively, a parental response to children's rejection, because of high levels of aggression, for example, may involve more direct supervision. Direct supervision has been found to enhance children's peer acceptance when mothers suggest or model appropriate interactional strategies (Finnie and Russell 1988; Kennedy 1992; Russell and Finnie 1990). While it appears that the nature of direct supervision, which may be influenced by parenting style and perceptions of child competence (Mize *et al.* 1995), is the key to the likelihood of positive or negative consequences for children, little is known about the context of parental supervision. Forms of supervision may vary as a function of the location and organization of peer contacts, with, for example, parents being more likely to intervene in children's activities when they occur in the home as opposed to other venues. In the Brisbane study, the nature of supervision and the degree of adult and child involvement in organizing peer contacts was predicted to vary according to the location and composition of peer contacts.

Results

Arranging and supervising peer activities

From the diary reports, the percentages of contacts arranged by children, peers, mothers and other adults were calculated. The percentages were not mutually exclusive as more than one individual could be involved in organizing a contact – for example, child and peer or child and mother. School aged children were found to arrange a higher proportion of their peer activities than younger children, while mothers and other adults were more often involved in organizing contacts for younger children than for older children (see Table 11.1). For younger children, there was roughly equal involvement of children, peers, parents and other adults in arranging contacts, suggesting a higher level of scaffolding of experiences by adults for this age group. On the other hand, older children and their peers were more involved than adults in arranging contacts ($p < 0.01$, follow-ups at $p < 0.05$).

Supervision during peer contacts was categorized as 'present/watching', 'participating', 'checking on', 'absent', or 'other adult supervising'. Multivariate analyses revealed that mothers were more often present and watching during younger children's peer activities than they were for older children. Mothers also participated more often in the activities of younger children, while they were more often absent for school aged children's contacts.

Associations among location, nature, arrangement and supervision of contacts

There were clear associations between the location of the contact, the nature of the activity, child and parental involvement in arranging the event, and parental supervision (see Table 11.2). For both preschool and primary children, higher levels of peer activity in the home were associated with greater use of checking by parents and greater organization by children. Parental presence and participation in children's activities (preschool) and the involvement of other adults in organization and supervision were less likely in the home.

Table 11.1 Arrangement and supervision of contacts (proportion of total contacts)

	Preschool		*Primary*		
	Mean (SD)	*Range*	*Mean (SD)*	*Range*	*Difference*
Arranger					
Child	0.35 (0.27)	0.00–1.00	0.46 (0.24)	0.00–1.00	$p < 0.01$
Peer	0.39 (0.27)	0.00–1.00	0.43 (0.25)	0.00–1.00	n.s.
Parent	0.37 (0.22)	0.00–1.00	0.25 (0.21)	0.00–0.91	$p < 0.001$
Other adult	0.32 (0.22)	0.00–0.92	0.26 (0.21)	0.00–0.93	$p < 0.05$
Supervision					
Present/watching	0.40 (0.25)	0.00–1.00	0.27 (0.17)	0.00–0.80	$p < 0.001$
Participating	0.18 (0.19)	0.00–0.73	0.11 (0.13)	0.00–0.50	$p < 0.01$
Checking	0.38 (0.25)	0.00–1.00	0.41 (0.21)	0.00–1.00	n.s.
Absent	0.21 (0.18)	0.00–0.88	0.29 (0.20)	0.00–0.93	$p < 0.01$
Other adult	0.13 (0.17)	0.00–0.88	0.18 (0.20)	0.00–0.92	$p < 0.05$

Table 11.2 Correlations among location, activity, organization and supervision of contacts

		Supervision					*Arranger*			
		Present/ watching	*Participating*	*Checking*	*Absent*	*Other adult*	*Child*	*Peer*	*Parent*	*Other adult*
Location:										
Home	Preschool	−0.21*	−0.20*	0.43†	−0.23*	−0.17	0.19	0.19	−0.11	−0.36†
	Primary	−0.05	0.12	0.42†	−0.29‡	−0.47†	0.43†	0.29‡	−0.02	−0.51†
Organized	Preschool	0.18	0.14	−0.33‡	0.16	0.15	−0.20*	−0.23*	0.18	0.31‡
Class or activity	Primary	−0.02	−0.10	−0.31‡	0.27‡	0.33‡	−0.28‡	−0.20	−0.06	0.42†
Neighbour	Preschool	−0.01	−0.14	−0.13	0.12	−0.01	0.11	0.12	−0.18	0.09
	Primary	−0.00	−0.08	−0.04	−0.05	0.06	0.22*	0.18	0.01	−0.22*
Friend/	Preschool	−0.06	0.09	0.08	−0.04	−0.01	−0.03	0.01	−0.05	0.09
relative	Primary	0.07	0.03	−0.08	−0.01	0.11	−0.24*	−0.14	0.05	0.16
Activity										
Free play	Preschool	−0.06	−0.10	0.25*	−0.14	−0.03	0.30‡	0.33‡	−0.18	−0.23*
	Primary	−0.07	−0.23*	0.36†	−0.09	−0.22*	0.23*	0.19	−0.01	−0.39†
Structured	Preschool	0.10	0.22*	−0.21*	0.11	0.01	−0.33‡	−0.37†	0.31‡	0.33‡
activity	Primary	0.11	0.19	−0.40†	0.12	0.25*	−0.27‡	−0.29‡	0.05	0.45†
Number of	Preschool	−0.24*	−0.20*	0.08	−0.04	−0.00	−0.08	−0.06	0.03	0.04
siblings	Primary	−0.05	−0.09	0.15	−0.21*	−0.03	−0.07	−0.10	0.04	−0.00
Arranger										
Child	Preschool	−0.25*	−0.17	0.25*	0.05	0.01	1.00			
	Primary	−0.04	0.05	0.19	−0.19	−0.28‡	1.00			
Peer	Preschool	−0.24*	−0.21*	0.30‡	−0.01	−0.04	0.86†	1.00		
	Primary	−0.02	0.01	0.27‡	−0.15	−0.21*	0.72†	1.00		
Parent	Preschool	0.17	0.37†	−0.09	−0.08	0.07	−0.51†	−0.58†	1.00	
	Primary	0.09	0.21*	−0.09	0.01	0.17	−0.51†	−0.50†	1.00	
Other	Preschool	0.19	0.17	−0.23*	0.14	0.14	−0.55†	−0.61†	0.24*	1.00
adult	Primary	0.11	−0.11	−0.36†	0.19	0.32†	−0.61†	−0.49†	0.04	1.00

Notes
*$p < 0.05$, †$p < 0.001$, ‡$p < 0.01$.

For preschool and primary children, higher rates of organized events were linked to lower rates of parental checking and child arrangement and higher rates of other adult supervision. For primary children, this also corresponded with higher parental absence. Higher rates of free play were associated with higher child (preschool and primary) and peer (preschool) involvement in arranging contacts and higher rates of parental checking (preschool and primary). Other adults were less likely to be involved in arranging peer contacts which involved free play (both age groups).

For preschool children, when children arranged higher proportions of peer contacts, parents were less likely to be present and more likely to be checking on the play. Where there were higher proportions of peer organized contacts, parents were less likely to be present or participating and, again, more likely to be checking. For preschool and primary children, parental involvement in arranging contacts was positively associated with parent participation in activities. For preschool children, parental participation and arrangement were associated with the proportion of structured activities.

Arrangers of peer contacts and the nature of contacts

Using a median split, children within each age group were grouped according to their level of involvement in arranging their peer contacts. Grouping within age was undertaken because of age related differences in the organization of peer contacts. For the younger children, high arrangers were involved in the organization of an average of 57 per cent of peer contacts, while low arrangers were involved in an average of 13 per cent ($p < 0.001$). For older children, high arrangers helped organize an average of 66 per cent of peer contacts, while low arrangers organized an average of 25 per cent ($p < 0.001$). Similarly, mothers were grouped according to their involvement in arranging peer contacts. For younger children, high maternal arrangers organized an average of 53 per cent of contacts while low arrangers were involved in an average of 18 per cent ($p < 0.001$). For older children, high maternal arrangers organized an average of 41 per cent of contacts while low arrangers were involved in an average of 8 per cent of contacts ($p < 0.001$).

A series of analyses, aimed at identifying whether children who were high arrangers of activities differed from low arrangers in the nature of their peer contacts (number, type, location and supervision), were conducted. Regardless of age and sex, children who were high arrangers had significantly more contacts over the fortnight than low arrangers (high mean = 12.93, SD = 4.97; low mean = 11.17, SD = 4.14, $p < 0.05$). They also experienced a higher proportion of contacts at home (0.48 vs 0.36, $p < 0.001$) and with neighbours (0.14 vs 0.08, $p < 0.005$). High organizers also had more siblings involved in their peer activities (0.53 vs 0.39 per contact, $p < 0.05$), possibly as a consequence of having a higher proportion of home and neighbourhood contacts. On the other hand low arrangers, had a higher proportion of contacts which were structured (0.33 vs 0.20, $p < 0.001$) and involved groups of children (0.21 vs 0.09, $p < 0.001$).

Level of parental involvement in arranging nonschool contacts was unrelated to the number and location of contacts, and the activities engaged in. High maternal arrangers, however, were more likely to participate in children's activities than low arrangers (0.22 vs 0.09, $p < 0.001$).

Discussion

These results show a clear developmental change from preschool to the early primary years in children's experiences with peers. Children became more involved in arranging their own peer contacts while adults became less involved. During this time, direct forms of parental supervision also decreased. Younger children were more often supervised and joined in their play by mothers and had more of their peer activities organized by mothers. Older children, on the other hand, displayed greater independence by organizing a higher proportion of their contacts with peers and by having mothers who were less likely to be present during activities, although they were still likely to be checking. These findings suggest two possibilities. One, that as children further develop their social skills and their ability to initiate and organize peer contacts, parents respond by reducing their levels of direct support. In other words, parents respond to what they see as their children's increasing ability to do it themselves. Another possibility is that, based on developmental expectations, parents withdraw their help, thereby encouraging their children to take a more assertive role in organizing their friendships. No doubt both mechanisms are at work, with parents encouraging independence and children taking a more active role. While parents may initially help their children develop networks of friends, they also identify when children are able to take on the role of 'manager' themselves. These results, in comparison with previous findings, illustrate the further waning of parental and other adult involvement in the arrangement of children's peer contacts into the early primary years. Accompanying this clear decline is the growth of child and peer initiations.

The results also indicate a number of important links between location, activity, supervision and organization of peer experiences. Where children were more highly involved in arranging their own activities, contacts were more likely to take place in the home, involved higher rates of free play and included siblings. In the home, parental supervision was more likely to consist of checking than being present or participating. Parental presence and participation also decreased with the number of siblings in the family, suggesting that parents felt less need for direct forms of supervision when other family members were involved. When children met with peers in structured activities, they were more likely to engage with groups of children which were organized and supervised by other adults. Greater involvement in structured activities was linked with lower rates of child and peer organization of peer contacts and higher rates of parent and other adult organization. While emphasis has been placed on the roles of parents in facilitating young children's social competence, less is known of the significance of other adults in this role. Given the relatively high rates of other adult involvement in peer contact organization and supervision, particularly for children aged 4 to 7, more research into the nature of such contacts and the role of organized activities in social competence development is highly warranted.

Previous studies have emphasized the importance of maternal arrangement of contacts to the frequency and nature of peer contacts (Ladd and Golter 1988). These results were not replicated in this study. Instead, high levels of organization by children were associated with the frequency of peer contacts and the location of contacts in the home. In contrast to the findings of Ladd and Golter (1988) where no significant associations were found between organization and supervision, maternal organization was related to the practice of participating in children's activities. In the present study, child and peer organized events were less likely to involve parental participation, while parent organized events were more likely to. One possible explanation for the discrepancy between the studies lies in the differentiation of direct forms of supervision. For Ladd and Golter, direct supervision was an aggregate of participation and presence. In the present study, these two forms were analysed separately because of expected age variation in the frequency of types of supervision. The present results suggest that the nature of direct supervision may require further elaboration in terms of context and the 'etiquette' of participation. In past research, direct supervision has been suggested to impede children's peer acceptance. Perhaps direct forms of supervision which impose upon children's initiations are more likely to influence peer acceptance than those which are related to parental initiation.

Friendship initiation strategies

Social cognition, in its broadest terms, refers to children's thinking about and understanding of the social world. In regard to peer relations, a key area of research has been that of children's social problem-solving and strategy knowledge. Social problem-solving interviews target a number of cognitive skills including the abilities to generate solutions to solve a problem, recognize interpersonal dilemmas, consider the means by which a social goal is achieved, consider the consequences of actions, and identify motives and behaviours (Dodge 1986; Rubin and Rose-Krasnor 1986; Shure and Spivack 1978). In the first of these, generation or retrieval of strategies, children are asked questions about how they might seek entry to a group situation, make a new friend, or resolve a conflict with a peer. Typical methodologies utilize the presentation of hypothetical stories either in a picture format (e.g., Rubin 1988) or through enactments of social scenarios using puppets or dolls (for younger children). Strategy knowledge reflects children's social competence to the extent that children who have difficulties forming peer relationships or entering play situations may have limited repertoires of appropriate strategies. For example, children who spend excessive time on the perimeter of group play may not know what to do or say to enter the play situation without being rebuffed. With age and experience, children's repertoires become more complex and decentred (Rubin and Rose-Krasnor 1992).

In the Brisbane study, age differences in children's use of strategies to initiate friendship were anticipated to reflect social cognitive gains as well as experiential influences. Associations between children's social experiences and their strategy knowledge were investigated to identify the ways in which the nature of peer experiences may influence the scripts that children develop for friendship initiation. For example, strategies nominated by children who experience a wide range of child-initiated contacts located in the family neighbourhood and home might be expected to differ in salience from those nominated by children who experience high levels of adult-arranged, structured activities.

Method

Social problem-solving interviews

Children's social problem-solving skills were assessed with Rubin's (1988) *Social Problem Solving Test – Revised* which identifies strategy knowledge in two domains – object acquisition and friendship initiation. Only the data pertaining to friendship initiation will be discussed here. Children were interviewed at home by the early childhood student who had initially contacted the family regarding participation. The students were provided with a set of stimulus cards for the hypothetical situations, an interview protocol and instruction on administration. Administration of the test is straightforward, requiring a story to be told with stimulus cards, followed by a question such as 'What can [the child in the story] do or say to make friends with [other story child]?' Following the first response, children are asked what else they might do or say. All students had experience of working with children in the 4- to 7-year range in educational settings and were known to the participating families and their children. The home setting and context of familiarity were considered valuable in eliciting typical and relaxed responses from the children. Following the coding format provided by Rubin (1988), responses were coded for flexibility, relevance and category: conversation openers (e.g., introductions and sharing of information), invitations (e.g., to visit or engage in an activity), indirect (e.g., proximity seeking) and direct attempts at friendship (e.g., engaging in play), prosocial suggestions (e.g., compliments), seeking adult help (e.g., asking an adult to introduce them) and non-normative responses. All response sheets were coded by two independent coders who reached 96 per cent agreement. In the small number of cases where there was lack of agreement, the two coders jointly determined the appropriate category.

Results

Friendship initiation strategies by age, gender and level of involvement in arranging contacts

Multivariate analyses of variance were used to examine the relationship of age, gender and involvement in arranging contacts to children's friendship initiation strategies. Where appropriate, arc sine transformations were employed (Winer 1971).

Older children were found to use more *prosocial suggestions* and *invitations* than younger children (see Table 11.3). Of the preschool children, girls with mothers who arranged fewer contacts suggested a higher proportion of *adult help* strategies (mean = 0.07) than all other groups of children. Similarly, preschool girls who were low organizers themselves, also suggested the highest proportion of *adult help* strategies (mean = 0.06). While these groups were significantly higher in their use of *adult help* in general, this strategy was the least often referred to.

For girls, the use of *conversation openers* was more often reported by preschoolers than primary aged children. Highest use (mean = 0.52 of responses) occurred amongst preschool girls who were high arrangers of their peer contacts. For boys, there was an increase in the reports of *conversation openers* by high arrangers from preschool to primary (from 0.33 to 0.49) and a decrease in reports by low arrangers from preschool to primary (from 0.33 to 0.23).

Associations between location and supervision of contacts and friendship initiation strategies

Age

For preschool children, the use of *adult help strategies* was negatively associated with free play ($r = -0.21$, $p < 0.05$) and positively associated

Table 11.3 Friendship initiation strategies

	Preschool		*Primary*		
Strategy	*Mean (SD)*	*Range*	*Mean (SD)*	*Range*	*Difference*
Adult help	0.03 (0.08)	0.00–0.38	0.02 (0.06)	0.00–0.38	n.s.
Conversation opener	0.38 (0.35)	0.00–1.00	0.32 (0.28)	0.00–1.00	n.s.
Direct	0.12 (0.18)	0.00–1.00	0.11 (0.16)	0.00–0.83	n.s.
Indirect	0.18 (0.23)	0.00–1.00	0.20 (0.22)	0.00–0.83	n.s.
Invitation	0.14 (0.19)	0.00–1.00	0.20 (0.20)	0.00–0.80	$p < 0.01$
Prosocial	0.09 (0.18)	0.00–1.00	0.14 (0.17)	0.00–0.80	$p < 0.001$
Relevance score	4.63 (1.44)		5.44 (0.98)		$p < 0.001$
Flexibility score	4.07 (2.77)		5.64 (2.57)		$p < 0.001$

Note
Mean proportion scores except for 'relevance' and 'flexibility'.

with group experiences ($r = 0.34$, $p < 0.01$). The lower the proportion of free play and the higher the level of group activities, the more the use of *adult help.* The use of invitations was positively correlated with peer contacts at neighbours ($r = 0.22$, $p < 0.05$).

For primary children, the use of conversation openers was negatively correlated with parental checking ($r = -0.24$, $p < 0.05$); that is, children whose mothers used a higher percentage of checking used fewer conversation openers. Use of direct strategies was positively associated with maternal absence ($r = 0.25$, $p < 0.05$).The use of invitations was negatively associated with maternal absence during peer contacts ($r = -0.26$, $p < 0.05$) and supervision by other adults ($r = -0.26$, $p < 0.05$). That is, children suggested a higher proportion of invitations when mothers were absent less and other adults supervised less.

Gender

For females, the use of invitations was positively correlated with contacts at neighbours ($r = 0.29$, $p < 0.01$) and the proportion of free play ($r = 0.25$, $p < 0.01$), and negatively correlated with structured activities ($r = -0.27$, $p < 0.05$). The use of adult help was positively correlated with maternal presence ($r = 0.22$, $p < 0.5$) and with the proportion of activities organized by other adults ($r = 0.31$, $p < 0.01$).

For males, the use of invitations negatively correlated with number of siblings ($r = -0.21$, $p < 0.05$) and birth order ($r = -0.22$, $p < 0.05$). Males with fewer siblings and closer to being first-born suggested higher proportions of invitations. The use of adult help was positively associated with contacts at friends and relatives ($r = 0.29$, $p < 0.01$), and with the number of child relatives present during activities ($r = 0.30$, $p < 0.01$). The use of indirect strategies correlated with the proportion of contacts organized by parents ($r = 0.21$, $p < 0.05$) and negatively with maternal absence ($r = -0.21$, $p < 0.05$).

Discussion

The cross-sectional data indicates that, from preschool to primary school, children showed advances in their social cognitive repertoires, particularly in relation to the increased use of invitations and prosocial suggestions for friendship initiation. Increases in the use of invitations and prosocial suggestions parallel increases in the proportion of child arranged peer contacts with age, suggesting that as children take more control for their peer interactions they increase their use of particular strategies for initiating peer contacts. While social-cognitive gains may enable children to take a more active role in initiating their friendships, it is equally plausible that increasing experience of peers encourages the use of more complex strategies.

The location and context of peer experiences also played a role in children's strategy use and varied according to age and gender. The use of conversation openers (sharing and requesting information) was more prominent among children who were involved in arranging a high proportion of their contacts, suggesting that either the experience of organizing peer contacts led to more awareness of this interpersonal strategy or that children with good conversation-initiating skills were more likely to be active participants in their social arrangements. Amongst the high arrangers there was an effect for gender and age, with girls making most use of the strategy during preschool and boys during primary school. The earlier use by girls possibly reflects differential maturation rates (Howes *et al.* 1992) or the more verbal nature of female interchanges at preschool.

Strategy use was also related to the location, nature and management of contacts. The use of invitations by preschool children was associated with the proportion of contacts with neighbours, suggesting that participation in a neighbourhood based network encourages the use of invitations to play. For girls, the use of invitations was less frequent when they had greater exposure to structured activities. For primary children, greater use of invitations occurred when mothers were less absent from peer contacts and other adults were less involved in supervision, suggesting that mothers may be more likely to encourage invitations than other adults. For boys, family structure was important in that males with fewer siblings and lower in birth order responded with higher proportions of invitations, indicating that where boys have fewer opportunities for sibling interaction they may be more likely to invite others to play.

Although the use of adult intervention strategies was less frequent on average than for all other strategies, their use was also linked to the nature of peer activities and their organization and supervision. Where girls experienced lower levels of organization of peer contacts both by themselves and their mothers, more activities organized by other adults, and higher levels of parental presence during peer contacts, they were more likely to suggest adult help strategies. Preschool-aged children also used a higher rate of adult help when they experienced higher rates of group activities.

In summary, these results suggest that the experience of structured large group activities which involve adult supervision and presence may encourage children to develop strategies which rely on adult assistance for friendship initiation, particularly for preschoolers. Where children's experiences are less structured and neighbourhood based, child initiated strategies, such as invitations to play, may be more likely to arise. Ecocultural theory is useful in interpreting the role of context in such strategy development (Howes *et al.* 1992; Weisner 1984). According to this framework, activity settings differ in composition, the values and goals underlying behaviour, the behaviours which are performed, and the scripts which guide interaction (Weisner and Gallimore 1985, cited in Howes *et al.* 1992). These varying characteristics may help to explain the differences which arise in children's peer behaviour and cognition. In this study, differences between structured activities and neighbourhood play settings in composition, goals, behaviour and scripts may be associated with differential influences on the development and use of strategies for friendship initiation. The extent to which these contextual features may be related to other areas of social cognition or social problem-solving may be a fruitful area for further research.

Conclusions and future directions

Links between problem-solving and behaviour

The results reported in this chapter highlight the importance of context to the nature of children's peer contacts. Additionally, the nature and context of peer experiences appear relevant to the use of particular friendship initiation strategies as elicited in hypothetical scenarios. It is unclear, however, to what extent these features are related to the actual strategies used by children with peers. Further research in this regard would shed light on the link between problem-solving and children's behaviour with peers, as well as the characteristics of settings (e.g., structured activities) which are influential in the development and use of particular social problem-solving strategies.

The role of other adults in the organization and supervision of contacts

Mothers have been seen to play a central role in the arrangement of young children's peer contacts because of their availability and presence in young children's lives. However, the research reported in this chapter suggests a significant role is also played by other adults. Further research might investigate the identities of these other adults and the roles they play in facilitating social competence and peer acceptance. It is anticipated that such adults include family friends, relatives and parental network members. With increasing availability of alternate care arrangements, it is probable that care providers feature in this group, along with adults who provide expertise through routine classes and activities.

Cultural variations

The contexts of children's peer experiences vary not only structurally and geographically but also in terms of social and cultural values. Recent research suggests that there are cultural variations in the facilitation, location and extent of children's peer contacts (Balda and Irving 1997; Irving and Balda 1996; see Hart *et al.* this volume), the correlates of peer acceptance (Chen and Rubin 1992; Chen *et al.* 1995b) and the use of social problem-solving strategies (Balda and Irving 1997). This research suggests that, although it may be important for parents to provide their children with appropriate instruction and guidance in forming peer friendships, it is also important to examine the social and cultural contexts in which families live and the ways in which those contexts enhance children's knowledge of and opportunities for friendship.

Chapter 12

Who says? Associations among peer relations and behaviour problems as a function of source of information, sex of child and analytic strategy

Ann Sanson, Sue Finch, Elizabeth Matjacic and Gregor Kennedy

Introduction

In this chapter we examine the associations among measures of peer relations and of internalizing and externalizing behaviour problems in preadolescent children. Links have been found between peer relations (PRs), especially acceptance/rejection, and a range of indices of concurrent and future social and academic competence (for review see Rubin *et al.* 1998; Parker *et al.* 1995b). While such links make conceptual sense, the literature reveals that they are far from uniform. Correlations between peer rejection and other concurrent indices of social adjustment usually range between 0.3 and 0.6 (Cilleson *et al.* 1992), and only about a third of children with poor PRs experience maladjustment beyond adolescence (Parker and Asher 1987).

The studies in this area are nearly all based on classmates' reports which are analysed using sociometric classification techniques, resulting in five peer status groups: popular, rejected, neglected, controversial and average (e.g., Asher and Dodge 1986; Coie *et al.* 1990). There is considerable instability of classification, with only 40–50 per cent remaining rejected over a one year period, and a smaller proportion over longer periods (Coie and Dodge 1983; Newcomb and Bukowski 1984). The neglected and controversial categories are particularly unstable (Rubin *et al.* 1998). It has also become clear that there is considerable heterogeneity within the groups (e.g., French 1988, 1990; Parker *et al.* 1995b), leading researchers to investigate subdivisions within groups, for example between rejected children with and without accompanying aggression (e.g., Zabriski and Coie 1996). Another response to the heterogeneity within sociometric groups is to look closely at the nature of the information being collected. Peers are clearly key informants on children's PRs, but sociometric classification techniques may not be the best way to summarize that information, and there are other potentially valuable sources of information which may add to our understanding of the nature and significance of children's PRs. These issues are among the questions addressed in this chapter.

Between-informant agreement

Parents, teachers, peers, independent observers and the children themselves can each sample different domains of peer-relevant behaviour within different contexts. These raters vary in cognitive competence and verbal skills, in the nature of their relationships to the child being rated, and in the range of contexts in which they can observe relevant behaviour (Coie *et al.* 1990; Newcomb *et al.* 1993). There has been considerable research on between-informant agreement on children's behaviour problems (BPs). Only moderate agreement between sources of information is typically found (Achenbach *et al.* 1987; Lancelotta and Vaughn 1989). Agreement tends to be higher for externalizing (acting out, aggressive) BPs than for internalizing (anxious, depressed) BPs (e.g., Lambert *et al.* 1993), and some studies have found that agreement is higher for ratings of boys than girls (e.g., Lancelotta and Vaughn 1989). Teachers' and peers' ratings have often been found to converge more with each other than with self-ratings (Newcomb *et al.* 1993; Bierman and McCauley 1987). On the other hand, Lancelotta and Vaughn (1989) reported that clinical diagnostic ratings correlated with children's self-ratings of depression but not with parent or teacher ratings. Again, Stanger and Lewis (1993), in comparing mother, father, teacher and self-ratings, found the lowest agreement on internalizing ratings for pairs of raters which included teachers. In general, it seems that on highly visible disruptive and negative behaviours, peers, teachers and parents agree better with each other than with self-ratings, but less visible internalizing problems may be better assessed via self-ratings and perhaps parent ratings. It is apparent that no single source can simply substitute for the others.

Very few studies have compared different informants' judgements of children's PRs, for which school peers are by far the most common source of information (Parker *et al.* 1995b). More often, peer-rated PRs have been linked to other sources' ratings of other constructs (e.g., parent, teacher or self-ratings of BPs), thus addressing predictive validity rather than between-informant agreement (e.g., Cantrell and Prinz 1985). The one report we could locate comparing self- and teacher-ratings of peer status failed to find any relationships between them (Adams *et al.* 1982).

In recognition of the particular strengths of different informants, there has been a growing trend to form composite measures from data from several sources. The argument is that such scores can provide more unbiased and stable estimates than any single measurement. However, this may mask the specific usefulness of individual sources. Recent findings from the Australian Temperament Project, a large-scale longitudinal study of Victorian children (Prior *et al.* 1989), suggest that sensitivity may be lost by using composite measures. Only around half of the children identified to be at risk for a psychiatric diagnosis by scoring in the top 16 per cent of the sample on BP scales according to at least two of three sources (parent, teacher, self) were identified to be at risk according to a composite score criterion. However, around 40 per cent of those meeting the two-source criterion but not the composite score criterion, received a diagnosis through a clinical diagnostic interview (Prior *et al.* 1997). This sizeable group of children would have been missed by use of a composite score alone. Thus, both the unique and shared information provided by different sources is likely to complement our understanding of children's psychosocial status.

Gender

There is evidence that the nature of PRs differs for boys and girls, with boys relating more to extensive peer groups and girls more focused on intimate dyads (Belle 1989; Benenson 1990). Sociometric classification procedures, however, use the same algorithms to determine peer status for both genders. There are some suggestions that lack of peer acceptance is more closely related to adjustment problems for boys than for girls (Coie 1985; Dodge 1983). Girls' adjustment problems may be linked more closely to the intimacy of their close friendships or family relationships (Sanson *et al.* 1994; Prior *et al.* 1993). Further, behavioural characteristics like aggression seem to have differential impact on boys' and girls' PRs (Bukowski *et al.* 1993). Gender differences in source agreement have been little examined. Some research has indicated that teachers are especially poor at picking up on the problems of girls, perhaps due to the lower incidence of disruptive externalizing problems among girls (Rolf 1972).

Potential problems with sociometric classification

As noted, sociometric procedures (e.g., Asher and Dodge 1986) have been the principal method employed in research on children's PRs. Peer nominations of liked and disliked classmates have been shown to be reliable and valid indicators of children's actual interactions with classmates (Bukowski and Hoza 1989). However, they disregard out-of-school peer relationships. Sociometric classification systems, by categorizing children into one of a small number of groups, are limited in the information they provide on each child. A large proportion of children are typically classified as 'average', 'controversial' or 'other' and disregarded in subsequent analyses. More fundamentally, these techniques are based on the assumption that some standard social typologies apply in every school class, every age group and both genders, and that there is comparability among children categorized into a particular peer status group (e.g., rejected) in different school classes and different studies. These assumptions deserve examination. Social network analysis (e.g., Arabie *et al.* 1978; Pattison 1993; Wasserman and Faust 1994) has been used extensively to characterize social relationships in the adult literature but has been used very little in the childhood literature (Belle 1989). It offers a range of methods which avoid imposing a preconceived structure on the data, and thus allows us to address issues raised about sociometric systems.

Aims

The principal aims of this chapter, then, are to address the questions of the measurement and significance of preadolescent children's PRs, by examining how measures of PRs from three different sources relate to each other and to measures of BPs, also from three sources, and to illustrate an alternative way to conceptualize PRs and to examine its usefulness in comparison to sociometric classification.

Method

The participants were 117 children drawn from four Grade 6 primary school classes in Melbourne (54 girls, 63 boys, aged 10–11 years) and their teachers. The children came from ethnically varied and principally lower-middle-class backgrounds. After obtaining school and parent consent, the researchers visited the schools, distributed questionnaires to teachers, and supervised the completion of the questionnaires by the children.

Measures of peer relations

Peer ratings

Children were classified into the five status categories of popular, rejected, neglected, average and controversial, using the classification scheme of Asher and Dodge (1986). In brief, children were asked to nominate three children whom they liked the most; the sum of same-sex nominations was used to derive Liking (L) scores. Children also rated every child in their class on a five-point scale on how much they liked to play with them, where a score of '1' meant 'never' and '5' meant 'almost always'. The total number of '1' ratings received from same-sex peers was used as an index of disliking (D). (This question was chosen over directly requesting 'dislike' nominations, about which ethical questions have been raised.) Social Impact (SI) scores (sum of L and D scores) and Social Preference (SP) scores (L minus D) were calculated. The L, D, SI and SP scores were then used to categorize children into the five status categories using cut-offs modified slightly from those used by Asher and Dodge (1986) (see Sanson *et al.* 1994, for further details).

Continuous scores were also created for peers' ratings of popularity, rejection and neglect. The L score was used to reflect popularity, the D score to reflect rejection, and the SI score, reversed, to reflect neglect. For the social network analyses, the 'like to play with' ratings were scored to indicate positive and negative ties; ratings of 1 and 2 indicated 'not like' or negative ties (reflecting a negative relation from rater to ratee), and scores of 4 and 5 indicated 'like' or positive ties (reflecting a positive relation).

Teacher ratings

Teachers were asked three questions about each child's peer status, adapted from Patterson *et al.* (1992): the proportion of each child's classmates who accepted them (popularity), rejected them (rejection) and ignored or were neutral about them (neglect). A score of 1 signified 'very few, less than 25 per cent', whereas a score of 5 meant 'almost all, over 75 per cent'.

Self-ratings

The children answered five questions adapted from Marsh *et al.* (1983) on self-rated peer status, on a five-point scale from 'true' to 'false'. Two questions reflected popularity ('I have lots of friends' and 'I am popular with kids of my own age'), two reflected neglect ('Other kids often ignore me' and 'Most kids have more friends than I do') and one (reverse scored) reflected rejection ('Other kids want me to be their friend'). All three scales were scored so that high scores indicated high popularity, rejection and neglect respectively.

Measures of behaviour problems

Peer ratings

Children rated each classmate on four questions which are key items in commonly used behaviour problem scales (e.g., Gresham and Elliott 1990; Rutter *et al.* 1970) to represent externalizing and internalizing problems, using a five-point frequency scale. The two questions relating to externalizing problems were 'fights and picks on other kids, teases them' and 'gets angry and loses temper easily'; the two questions relating to internalizing problems were 'seems unhappy, looks sad' and 'gets worried, feelings get hurt easily'.

Self-ratings

Self-ratings were obtained using the same questions and response scales as the peer ratings. When the child encountered their own name on the class list, they simply rated themselves as they did the other children.

Teacher ratings

For each child in their class, teachers answered eight questions on a five-point scale. Four items assessed externalizing problems, two of which were identical to the peer items; the additional two were 'talks back to adults when corrected' and 'threatens or bullies others'. The four items assessing internalizing problems were 'appears lonely'; 'shows anxiety about being with other children'; 'acts sad or depressed'; and 'is easily embarrassed'.

Results

Agreement between sources on peer relations

The first question addressed was the degree of agreement among the three sources on the children's PRs, separately for boys and girls. Small group numbers meant statistical testing was inappropriate, but examination of the ranked mean scores for teacher- and self-ratings of popularity, rejection and neglect for the five peer-rated sociometric groups suggested a limited degree of agreement. The most clearcut agreement with sociometric groupings was for boys' self-ratings of popularity – the popular group had the highest mean self-ratings of popularity, the rejected group had the lowest, and the neglected group was second lowest. The rejected group was rated highest on both self- and teacher rejection and neglect for boys. Other findings were more surprising; for example, the popular group was second lowest on teacher-rated popularity, whereas the neglected group was rated most popular and least neglected according to teachers. The sociometric controversial and average groups had quite high self- and teacher ratings of popularity and low ratings of rejection, suggesting little discriminability.

Among girls, even less agreement between self- and teacher ratings and sociometric classification was evident. Both self- and teacher ratings of popularity in the sociometric popular group were at the median of scores, and similarly self- and teacher ratings of rejection in the rejected group were at the median, while the sociometric neglected group members gave themselves the lowest neglect ratings, and teachers gave them the second lowest scores. Teachers rated the popular group as the most rejected. These findings reinforce previous concerns about the meaning of the sociometrically defined neglected group (Rubin *et al.* 1998), and also raise questions about whether the classification system is as applicable to girls as boys.

Agreement between self- and teacher ratings of PRs is shown in Table 12.1. For both sexes there was a moderate cross-source negative correlation between popularity and neglect. Two other findings are notable. First, for boys there was moderately strong agreement on popularity ratings but little on neglect whereas for girls there was agreement on neglect, but little on popularity. Second, for neither sex was there agreement about rejection; in fact for girls there was a significant *positive* correlation between self-rated popularity and teacher-rated rejection.

Associations between peer relations and concurrent adjustment

Table 12.2 shows some quite strong relationships between teacher ratings of PRs and both teacher and peer ratings of BPs, and some modest relationships with self-ratings of BPs. There were striking differences in the size of associations for boys and girls, especially for teacher PR ratings where correlations were almost always higher for boys than for girls. Peer ratings of popularity and rejection had some relationship to peer ratings of internalizing BPs, but few other regular patterns among the correlations are apparent. A tendency for higher correlations when the same source rated both BPs and PRs is evident for teacher and peer but not self-ratings. Table 12.3 indicates that rejected boys were consistently rated highest on externalizing and internalizing BPs, and rejected girls also had the highest scores by peer and teacher but not self-report. However, for both sexes, no other patterns are discernible in the relationships of BP ratings to sociometric groups.

Overall, then, a high level of heterogeneity in the relationships found, between raters and between sexes, was evident in these data, with generally weaker levels of between source agreement and associations

Table 12.1 Correlations between self- and teacher-ratings of popularity, rejection and neglect, separately for boys and girls

Teacher	*Popularity*		*Rejection*		*Neglect*	
Self	*Boys*	*Girls*	*Boys*	*Girls*	*Boys*	*Girls*
Popularity	0.44*	0.17	−0.15	0.29*	−0.39**	−0.28*
Rejection	−0.1	−0.23	−0.03	−0.06	0.14	0.09
Neglect	−0.36**	−0.35**	0.18	0.03	0.22	0.46**

Notes
(* $p < 0.05$; ** $p < 0.001$).

Table 12.2 Correlations between peer, teacher, and self-ratings of externalizing and internalizing behaviour problems and of popularity, rejection and neglect for boys and girls (peer PR ratings are treated as continua here)

Rater		*Externalizing*			*Internalizing*		
		Peer	*Teacher*	*Self*	*Peer*	*Teacher*	*Self*
Teacher							
Popular	M	−0.23	−0.30	−0.43**	−0.46**	−0.42**	−0.34**
	F	−0.21	−0.32**	0.04	−0.36**	−0.41**	−0.05
Rejected	M	0.53**	0.64**	0.28*	0.54**	0.50**	0.34**
	F	0.42*	0.51**	−0.15	0.41**	0.34*	0.04
Neglect	M	0.03	0.15	0.25	0.24	0.31	0.36**
	F	0.02	0.02	−0.25	0.35**	0.29**	−0.19
Peer							
Popular	M	−0.07	0.01	−0.27*	−0.35**	−0.20	−0.12
	F	−0.23	−0.01	0.16	−0.14	0.05	0.19
Rejected	M	0.12	0.16	0.24	0.28*	0.23	0.12
	F	0.29	0.09	−0.20	0.39**	0.19	−0.24
Neglect	M	0.04	0.14	−0.03	−0.06	0.02	0.00
	F	0.05	0.07	−0.04	0.20	0.20	−0.05
Self							
Popular	M	0.08	0.01	−0.19	−0.40**	−0.09	−0.32*
	F	0.31*	0.31*	−0.04	0.11	−0.10	−0.08
Rejected	M	−0.04	−0.02	−0.05	0.18	−0.10	−0.01
	F	−0.04	−0.04	0.16	0.14	0.25	−0.01
Neglect	M	0.04	0.21	0.38**	0.33*	0.24	0.38**
	F	0.27	0.27	0.07	0.41**	0.27	−0.06

Notes
* $p < 0.05$; ** $p < 0.001$.

with BPs for girls than for boys. The weak associations with the sociometric groups may be partly due to the use of a standard classification scheme where many different forms of social relationships are possible, the essence or significance of which may not be fully captured by the groups. There was marked variation between the four school classes and between the sexes in the proportions assigned to each sociometric category; for example, 8 per cent of boys in Class 1 but 35 per cent of boys in Class 2 were classified as popular, and 8 per cent of Class 4 girls versus 42 per cent of Class 3 girls were classed as neglected. This reinforces the question of how well the sociometric groups represent PRs within each and every class, leading us to explore alternative ways of conceptualizing PRs within classes, using a form of social network analysis.

Table 12.3 Mean peer, teacher, and self-ratings of externalizing and internalizing behaviour problems (and ranks in parentheses) across the five sociometric groups for boys and girls

		Externalizing			*Internalizing*		
		Peer	*Teacher*	*Self*	*Peer*	*Teacher*	*Self*
Popular	M	2.10 (5)	2.07 (2)	2.14 (4)	1.75 (3)	2.36 (3)	1.82 (2)
	F	1.69 (4)	1.61 (2)	2.21 (1)	1.96 (4)	2.57 (2)	2.63 (2)
Rejected	M	2.36 (1)	2.27 (1)	2.92 (1)	2.21 (1)	3.13 (1)	2.46 (1)
	F	2.02 (1)	1.64 (1)	1.90 (2)	2.21 (1)	2.80 (1)	2.00 (4)
Neglected	M	2.24 (3)	1.90 (3)	2.29 (3)	1.79 (2)	2.25 (4)	1.54 (3)
	F	1.72 (3)	1.50 (5)	1.73 (4)	1.79 (5)	2.04 (4)	2.19 (3)
Controversial	M	2.30 (2)	1.80 (5)	2.30 (2)	1.42 (5)	1.40 (5)	1.50 (4)
	F	1.52 (5)	1.54 (4)	1.50 (5)	2.00 (3)	2.50 (3)	1.83 (5)
Average	M	2.18 (4)	1.86 (4)	2.07 (5)	1.68 (4)	2.39 (2)	1.36 (5)
	F	1.81 (2)	1.61 (2)	1.81 (3)	2.01 (2)	1.97 (5)	2.78 (1)

Social network analysis

Social network analysis does not rely on assumptions about the network structure or social roles present in any social grouping. It therefore requires separate analysis of each social grouping, in this case, each class, and because boys and girls interact little at this age, also by sex. One simple form of social network analysis is block modelling (Arabie *et al.* 1978), in which a matrix of ties between members of a social group is used to identify clusters or 'blocks' of children with similar patterns of ties. As noted in the Method section, positive and negative ties were coded from ratings on the 'liking to be with' question. Each was coded 1 if present, 0 if absent. Ties are directional (Child A's liking of Child B may not be reciprocated). Complete matrices include the ties among all same-sex students in a class. Block modelling procedures provide a reorganization of matrices to identify homogeneous blocks of children (if such blocks exist in the data), so that children in the same block have similar patterns of ties to other block members and to other blocks. Thus it is simply a redescription of the original data. Block models for two classes of boys are presented in order to examine the structure of ties across classes, and for girls from one of these classes in order to examine sex differences. Some typologies are suggested from these patterns of ties, and these are then compared to the sociometric groupings and the BP measures.

Block modelling is a hierarchical, divisive procedure, with the possible number of blocks ranging from two to the total number of subjects. While there is no single criterion for choosing between solutions, the 'fit' of the block model improves as the densities converge to 0 per cent or 100 per cent. The density of a block is the number of ties observed as a percentage of the total possible number of ties. Thus an 'ideal' block model would have densities close to 0 per cent or 100 per cent, in which case members of the same block would have identical patterns of ties, but this is unlikely to be found in PR data based on school classes. For each class, a range of solutions was examined; the model chosen in each case was one in which densities converged towards 0 per cent and 100 per cent and where there were few blocks comprised of single individuals.

Block model for boys from Class 1

A six-block solution was selected to represent the structure for the 18 boys in Class 1. Table 12.4 shows the density of both positive and negative ties for the six blocks, which had from one to five members each. Figures on the diagonal represent ties *within* the block; that is, for Block 1, 95 per cent of the possible positive ties among members of the block were present. Density of ties *from* a block are read across the table, for example, the density of positive ties *from* Block 1 to Block 2 is 85. This means that 85 per cent of the 20 possible positive ties from the five boys in

Table 12.4 Density of positive and negative ties for six blocks of boys in Class 1

	1 (n = 5)	2 (n = 4)	3 (n = 3)	4 (n = 3)	5 (n = 2)	6 (n = 1)
Density of positive ties						
1	95	85	87	80	30	40
2	35	58	82	67	0	50
3	80	92	100	100	17	67
4	40	67	100	33	17	33
5	0	13	20	17	50	0
6	20	100	67	100	0	—
Density of negative ties						
1	0	5	7	7	50	20
2	20	0	0	8	75	50
3	13	0	0	0	33	33
4	20	8	0	50	83	67
5	30	38	20	17	0	0
6	60	0	33	0	100	—

Block 1 to the four boys in Block 2 were observed in the data. The ties received *by* a block are found by reading down the columns. Thus only 35 per cent of the possible positive ties were received *by* Block 1 from Block 2.

Figure 12.1 provides a simplification of the data in Table 12.4 and shows strong ties (present for more than two-thirds of possible ties) as solid lines, and weaker ties (present for between one-third and two-thirds of possible ties) as broken lines; the weakest ties are not pictured. The weaker ties indicate potentially greater individual variation in the ties.

Table 12.4 and Figure 12.1 suggest two friendship groups within this class of boys. Block 3 can be characterized as a popular and sociable friendship group. The three boys liked to be together, had strong reciprocal positive ties to three other blocks and relatively few negative ties. Block 1 also had strong within-block positive ties. They were friendly (giving out strong positive ties), but not popular in the same way as Block 3 (they did not receive as many strong positive ties).

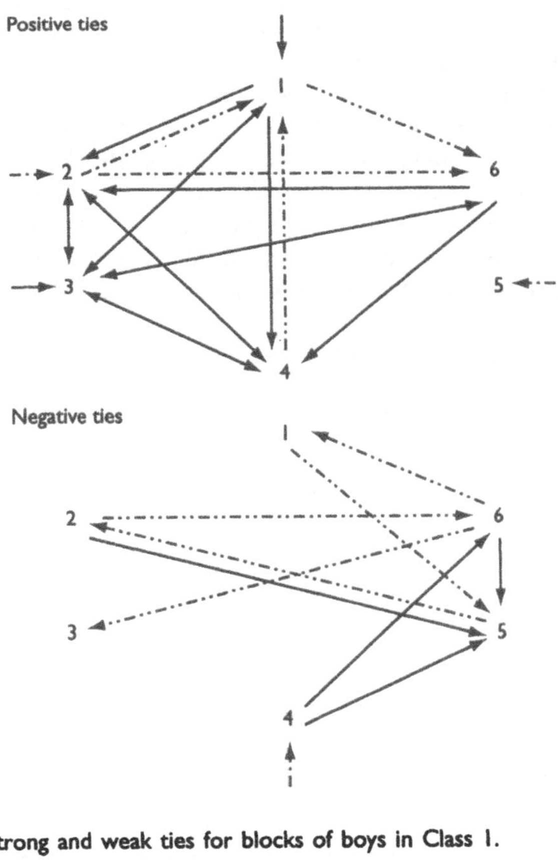

Figure 12.1 Strong and weak ties for blocks of boys in Class 1.

Boys in Blocks 2 and 4 can be described as friends of the popular boys. These blocks did not reflect social groups (because the within-block positive ties were relatively weak), but rather were individuals with similar social roles. However, boys in Blocks 1, 2, 3 and 4 all appeared to be positively positioned considering the relatively large number of positive ties and small number of negative ties.

In contrast, the boys in Blocks 5 and 6 received only weak positive ties, but were the predominant givers and receivers of negative ties. The two boys in Block 5 could be characterized as relatively unpopular or rejected; they received negative ties from all other blocks and few positive ones. The role of the single boy in Block 6 is more ambiguous – he was neither strongly liked nor not liked, but appeared isolated or neglected.

Block model for boys in Class 2

For the 17 boys from Class 2, a six-block solution again best fitted our criteria for choosing solutions (Table 12.5, Figure 12.2). Block 2 was a friendship group, which was relatively popular, receiving positive ties from all other blocks, and few negative ties. Block 1 could be described a friendship faction, with strong internal ties but few between block ties. Blocks 5 and 6 received many negative ties and few positive ties, and thus occupied unpopular social roles. Block 6, like Block 4, tended to be unfriendly, with negative ties to all but the most popular groups (and giving only weak positive ties). Block 6's unpopularity and unfriendliness together suggest isolation. Blocks 3 and 4 reflected mixed social roles. Members of both groups gave and received both positive and negative ties.

Table 12.5 Density of positive and negative ties for six blocks of boys in Class 2

	1 (n = 2)	*2 (n = 4)*	*3 (n = 3)*	*4 (n = 2)*	*5 (n = 3)*	*6 (n = 3)*
Density of positive ties						
1	100	63	17	75	17	0
2	38	83	67	25	9	8
3	50	67	67	67	22	0
4	0	50	50	50	0	17
5	33	58	33	17	0	44
6	33	50	33	33	11	0
Density of negative ties						
1	0	13	50	25	0	83
2	25	0	17	0	82	92
3	33	17	0	17	67	89
4	0	25	50	50	100	83
5	33	25	11	50	83	56
6	17	17	44	50	78	80

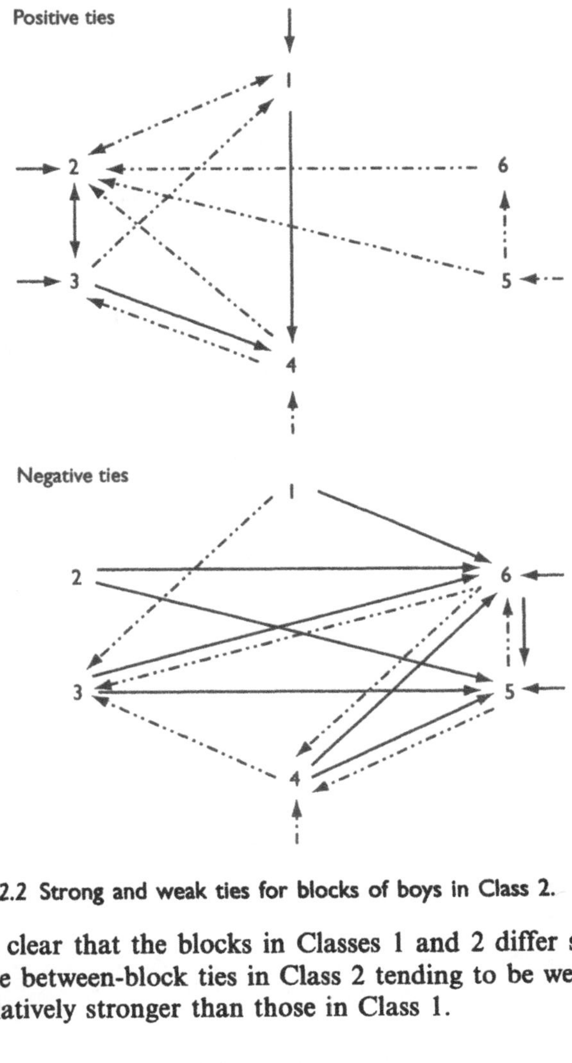

Figure 12.2 Strong and weak ties for blocks of boys in Class 2.

It is clear that the blocks in Classes 1 and 2 differ substantially, with positive between-block ties in Class 2 tending to be weaker and negative ties relatively stronger than those in Class 1.

Block model for girls in Class 2

For the 15 girls in Class 2 a parsimonious description was based on four blocks (Table 12.6, Figure 12.3). Densities for positive ties were generally stronger for the girls than densities for negative ties. A strong social coherence can be identified for the girls in Blocks 1 and 2. They liked most members within their blocks; there were no negative ties between or within these two blocks. Together these friendship groups were faction-like as they tended not to have positive ties with the other two blocks, but had weak (and differing) negative ties with them.

Table 12.6 Density of positive and negative ties for four blocks of girls in Class 2

	1 (n = 4)	*2 (n = 4)*	*3 (n = 2)*	*4 (n = 5)*
Density of positive ties				
1	83	94	38	30
2	100	92	0	5
3	25	25	50	80
4	32	5	80	26
Density of negative ties				
1	0	0	25	35
2	0	0	38	45
3	38	50	50	0
4	5	53	0	37

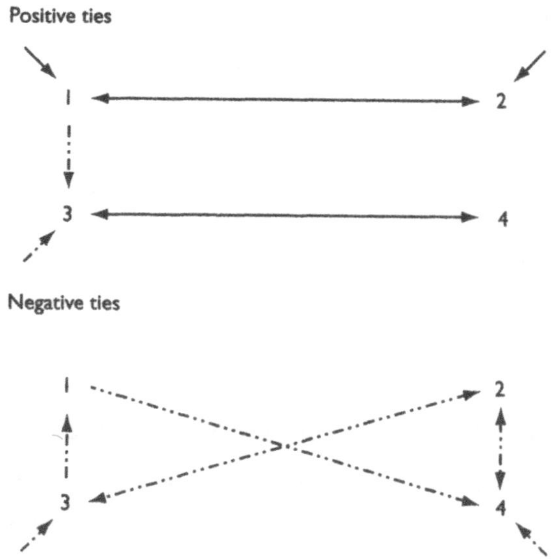

Figure 12.3 Strong and weak ties for blocks of girls in Class 2.

The positioning of Blocks 3 and 4 was somewhat different. They had strong mutual positive ties, but there were mixed positive and negative ties within the blocks, and moderate to weak negative ties to other blocks.

The data on Class 1 girls were not analysed since there were some missing data. However, Class 3 girls' data revealed a similar pattern of friendship and mixed groups as for Class 2 girls; these results are not reported in detail due to space limits.

Comparison of blocks with sociometric classification

The sociometric classification of children within each of the blocks for the two classes of boys and Class 2 girls was examined. Many anomalies between the block models and sociometric classification emerged. For example, for Class 1 boys, Block 1 appeared to be a strong friendship group, but the sociometric classification labelled one boy in this block as neglected, and only one as popular. Similarly, in Class 2 boys, both friendship groups (Blocks 1 and 2) included a sociometrically neglected boy. In both classes of boys, Blocks 5 and 6 referred to unpopular and isolated boys respectively, and the blocks had characteristically different patterns of ties; however, these boys were all classified as rejected, obscuring these differences. Girls in Block 2 in Class 2 appeared to be a strong friendship faction; the four girls in this block each had different sociometric classifications. All girls in Block 4 had sociometric classifications of neglected or rejected, whereas the block model shows an exchange of strong positive ties between Blocks 4 and 3, and the girls in Block 4 did not appear as clearly unpopular or isolated as boys characterized as such by block model results.

Block models and popularity

The ranked means for teacher- and self-rated popularity ratings for each of the blocks were then examined. Among Class 1 boys, both teacher- and self-rated popularity accorded well with block model characterizations; friendship groups were ranked highest, friends of these groups ranked next, and unpopular and isolated boys ranked lowest. For Class 2 boys, the results were less consistent. The teacher ratings tended to relate more closely to the block model characterizations than did self-ratings. There was a marked disparity between teacher- and self-rated popularity for Block 4 (Class 2), this being least popular by teacher report and most popular by self-report. Among Class 2 girls, the girls in friendship groups ranked highest on self-rated popularity (although there were only marginal differences in means across three of the four blocks). Teacher-rated popularity of girls did not show consistent ranking between blocks.

Block models and behaviour problems

Ratings of internalizing and externalizing BPs from the three informants were examined next. On internalizing BPs, there was reasonable consistency between sources in ranking unpopular and isolated blocks of boys highest. There was less consistency in the ranking of the other four blocks in each class, where in many cases the means were very similar. For externalizing BPs, the patterns of rankings between sources and between classes showed little consistency. The isolated boy in Class 1 was ranked highest on externalizing BPs by all sources, but isolated boys in Class 2 were ranked differently according to source. For girls, patterns in the rankings of both internalizing and externalizing BPs were difficult to discern.

Discussion

The analyses reported here lead to several conclusions about the nature, significance and measurement of children's PRs. Agreement between sources was moderate at best, and typically lower for girls than boys. The results support and extend previous findings that the relationships which emerge between PRs and BPs depend to an important extent on informant and sex of child. The relationships between PRs and BPs were consistently weaker for girls than boys. Finally, the findings provided striking evidence of the heterogeneity within sociometric groups, of differences in the nature and patterning of PRs in different social groupings (classes) and between sexes, and of divergency between the sociometric classification technique and the block modelling which summarized the liking relationships within classes. Each of these findings is discussed below.

Informant agreement on children's peer relations

Agreement between raters of children's PRs was never high, but varied from weak to moderate depending on the raters considered, sex of child, and the analytic technique used for the peers' ratings. For boys, both teacher and self-ratings of PR showed some agreement with peer sociometric groups on popularity and rejection, but rejected groups were also characterized as neglected, and controversial and average groups were not differentiated from the other groups. For girls, there was little agreement between either teacher or self-ratings and sociometric group. On the other hand, when teacher and self-ratings were compared with each other (Table 12.1), it was apparent that they agreed, for both sexes, that popularity and neglect were negatively related, and the two sources agreed on boys' popularity and girls' neglect. The teachers and the children themselves thus seem to be characterizing neglect in a different way from the sociometric classification. Teacher and self agreement for girls was again low, especially in relation to rejection. However, there was perhaps slightly stronger agreement overall between teacher and self-ratings than between either of these with sociometric groupings, although the need to use different statistical techniques for the analyses (based on categorical and continuous data respectively) precludes direct comparison.

When peer ratings were analysed using block modelling, blocks of boys identified as friendship groups were indeed rated as the most popular by teacher and self-ratings, isolated boys had very low teacher and self popularity ratings, and unpopular groups' ratings were also low but above those for isolated boys. For girls, peer, teacher and self data again agreed less well: self-ratings of popularity accorded reasonably well with the block models, but there was less consistency for teacher popularity ratings, and for 'mixed' groups. (Space limits precluded investigation of self- and teacher rejection and neglect ratings.) Friendship blocks of both boys and girls contained children with very mixed sociometric classifications, including some classified as neglected and rejected. Sociometric classification did not differentiate between unpopular and isolated groups of boys, all of whom were classed as rejected. In general, then, teacher and self-ratings of popularity appeared to agree better with peer ratings of PRs when these were analysed using a social networks approach rather than sociometric classification.

It is also clear that there was better agreement for children with clearly defined (positive or negative) social roles than for children with more intermediate and less well-defined placement. These children appear to be fairly easily identifiable using any source, and thus higher between-source agreement is apparent for them. As argued below, one reason for the lower agreement for girls than for boys may be because there were fewer girls in clear and extreme positions.

The associations between peer relations and behaviour problems

As in previous studies, some linkages between PRs and BPs emerged; for example, in general, rejection was linked to higher levels of BPs, and popularity to lower levels (although, as discussed below, these relationships also varied by source and by sex). In interpreting such findings, causal directions are uncertain. It is possible to regard peer status variously as an *index* of psychosocial adjustment (arguing, for example, that children without positive and reasonably extensive peer interactions are *ipso facto* less well adjusted than popular children); as an *outcome* of psychosocial adjustment (e.g., aggression and withdrawal lead to peer rejection and isolation); and as an *influence* on adjustment (e.g., healthy peer relationships promote social and cognitive development). There is indeed evidence of all three causal pathways (see Rubin *et al.* 1998, and Parker *et al.* 1995b, for review). Much work remains to be done, however, to identify the developmental processes involved. The findings reported here are not intended to address the causal links, but rather to shed light on the complex nature of the relationships between the two domains and on some of the methodological issues involved.

The strongest relationships between PRs and BPs emerged in teachers' ratings. Their ratings of PRs (especially of rejection) were related to their own and peers' ratings of internalizing and externalizing BPs, and more strongly for boys than girls. Some relationships between self-ratings of BPs and teacher PR ratings were also suggested. However, relationships between peer and self-ratings of PRs and ratings of BPs were weaker and patchy. While the rejected sociometric group was regarded as having more BPs than other groups by all three sources (except girls' self-ratings), no other BP relationships with sociometric groups were apparent. The sociometric classification did not seem to result in appreciably stronger relationships with BPs in comparison to continuous peer ratings of popularity, rejection and neglect, despite the fact that each of these was based on only one question. When associations between block model groups and BPs were examined, some tendency for isolated and unpopular boys to have more BPs, and for boys' friendship groups to have least, was evident. Again, little pattern was evident for girls.

It is clear that the relationships found between PRs and BPs depend on the source of the data. The clear source effects in teacher and peer ratings, where relationships between PR and BP ratings were stronger when the same source rated both constructs, suggest 'eye of the beholder' effects and reinforce the caution required in interpreting single source data. Interestingly, self-ratings did not show this pattern as clearly. Forming composite scores of different sources' ratings may be a simple response to the problems of source differences, but doing so may simply avoid confronting the complexity illustrated here.

Gender differences in relationships between peer relations and behaviour problems

Relationships between PRs and BPs were weaker for girls than boys, irrespective of how PRs were assessed. Rubin *et al.* (1998) have suggested that peer rejection may have less deleterious consequences for girls than boys. Alternatively, it may be that behavioural status has less impact on girls' peer acceptance than on boys', especially if peers are not particularly good at observing girls' problem behaviours. Or again, our instruments may be better tuned to detect the BPs typical of boys than those typical of girls. For example, teachers (and others) may give more attention to boys' problems than girls' (Pepler and Slaby 1995).

While all the above factors may have some explanatory power, another aspect of the girls' data deserves consideration. In this sample, as in many others, girls tended to have lower levels of BPs than boys (Sanson *et al.* 1994), and the block models showed that girls did not emerge as having problematic (isolated, unpopular) PRs as some boys did. The generally positive PRs among almost all the girls contrasts with the stereotype of 'bitchiness' among preadolescent girls (although of course a girl may like someone but still behave in a character defaming and alienating way towards them from time to time). A contrasting stereotypic belief, that girls should be 'nice' to each other, might translate into greater social desirability bias in completing peer ratings; that is, girls may respond to the rating task differently to boys. However, teachers also gave lower BP ratings to girls, suggesting any such bias is likely to be slight.

Nevertheless, an alternative explanation for the weaker associations for girls is that there was in fact little strong differentiation within the groupings of girls in these classes. While the sociometric algorithms guarantee that a proportion of any social grouping will fall into each category, the meaning of being classed as (e.g.) rejected may differ in different social contexts. The block models certainly suggested that even those girls classified as rejected had a number of positive ties with other girls. It may be that only extreme PRs and extreme BPs have an impact upon each other, and these extremes were largely absent among the girls assessed here. No doubt in other classes or social groups such extremes might emerge among girls.

It may also be that out-of-class social relationships have more salience for girls. In the longitudinal Australian Temperament Project, we found that girls' behavioural adjustment was more determined by parental and family variables than was boys' (Prior *et al.* 1993). Further, social exchanges before and after school, at the weekend and during holidays may be equally significant peer interactions as those occurring with classmates for children of this age. Of course, this then raises the challenge of finding a satisfactory way of assessing the multiplicity of children's social relationships with peers. Techniques such as asking the subject to nominate their friendship and social networks, both in and out of class, and incorporating others' (e.g., parents') ratings of family based relationships, may offer potential here, and may result in more valid assessments of preadolescent children's PRs.

Class and sex differences in peer relations

The proportions of children in each sociometric group differed substantially from class to class and between boys and girls. It seems highly likely that the psychological meaning of being 'rejected' when a child is one of 35 per cent of his same-sex classmates receiving that classification (such as boys in Class 2) differs from the meaning when only 13 per cent of boys in the class are so classified (which was the case for boys in Class 3). However, these differences between classes and sexes tend to be obscured by the classification method, which imposes a standard algorithm across classes. On the other hand, differences in the structure of PRs across classes and between sexes were highly visible using block modelling. While six blocks best described the boys in both Classes 1 and 2, the pattern of across- and within-block ties differed substantially. Girls' PRs fell best into four blocks, and simpler patterns of ties were evident.

In general, fewer children were characterized in negative social roles by the block modelling procedure compared with sociometric classification. In particular, block modelling differentially characterized sociometrically neglected children, and identified separate blocks of unpopular and isolated boys, all of whom were classed as rejected by sociometric classification.

While blocks do not necessarily reflect social groups, the block models provided little evidence of girls' PRs consisting predominantly of exclusive dyadic relationships while boys' were more extensive, as has been suggested in previous literature (e.g., Belle 1989). The block models showed both boys and girls had PRs which were group based at the same time as having more extensive ties. Girls' blocks tended to have positive ties to other blocks, suggesting positive interaction across much of the class. The friendship groups identified were larger than two (i.e., not dyadic). It is quite possible that 'best' (dyadic) friendships also existed within these classes, but without ruling out more extensive liking ties. One of the advantages of social networks analysis is that it can be used to examine co-existing tendencies for dyadic and extensive relations within any network structure.

Heterogeneity in sociometric classification groups

Sociometric measurement has become the almost unquestioned method for ascertaining peer status, and although theoretically meaningful links to both concurrent and later adjustment are regularly found, they are generally relatively weak. Such relationships as are found may be largely driven by children with extreme social placements. The more fine grained analyses currently being undertaken by some researchers (e.g., Zabriski and Coie 1996) who are examining groups with different behavioural characteristics (e.g., aggressive and non-aggressive rejected children) is undoubtedly a worthwhile approach for coping with within-group heterogeneity. However, the more radical step of exploring alternative analytic strategies such as illustrated here may also deserve consideration. It is notable that such approaches were not mentioned in two major recent reviews of the field (Parker *et al.* 1995b; Rubin *et al.* 1998), confirming the extent of acceptance of the sociometric classification method. The method we have presented here provides simple redescription of a data set. An extensive array of more sophisticated social networks analyses exist for identifying structural characteristics and social roles and positions, including stochastic models (e.g., Pattison 1993; Wasserman and Faust 1994).

A comparison of the classification based on the sociometric status approach and the block models indicated minimal concordance between them. Since the block models were simply a redescription of the raw peer rating data, this suggests substantial variations in the types of social relations (positive and negative ties) present for children within any one sociometric group. Thus imposing the preset categories onto social network data may entail a loss of valuable information and in the worst case lead to misleading conclusions. These data illustrate the dangers of treating placement in a sociometric group as a label or descriptor of an individual. At best, such placement represents one form of description, based on one data source, of a group of children within one particular social grouping. The use of uniform labels across social groups, ages and sexes, misleadingly implies comparability and homogeneity among children classed into one group. Continuous scores formed from peer ratings seemed to operate about as well in terms of agreement with other sources and relationships with BPs, and avoided such categorizing and labelling, without obscuring the variability among children. The block models provided another alternative description.

A notable feature of the research in this area has been the focus on problems rather than competence, both in terms of peer relationships and overall psychosocial adjustment. Morison and Masten (1991) noted that the predictive power of positive aspects of peer relationships may have been obscured by the relative emphasis in the literature on the negative dimensions of peer relations and negative outcome measures. Sociometry has only one 'positive' category, popular, whereas the block models showed several different forms of generally positive forms of PRs – friendship groups, friendship cliques, sociable groups, and combinations of these.

Conclusions

Overall, we hope these data highlight several dangers which need to be avoided in research in this area, and in its interpretation. First, there is the danger of becoming 'locked in' to using peers as the sole informants on children's PRs. The perspectives of teachers and the children themselves, and probably of other informants who can report on children's out-of-class PRs, are necessary to build a comprehensive picture of a child's PRs. If PRs affect current and future psychosocial adjustment at all, it is this broader level of peer functioning which is likely to have most impact. Simply forming summary composite scores is unlikely to be the best way to handle these multiple informants' contributions. Second, recognition of the heterogeneity within sociometric groups as currently defined implies a need to assess even class-based PRs in a more specific and sensitive way. Third, the substantial sex differences in the nature of PRs, BPs and their interrelationships demonstrate that combined sex analyses are likely to cloud important distinctions and to introduce much 'noise' into results.

The nature and implications of peer relations appear to differ for boys and girls, and observers have different sensitivity to different types of problem and to boys' and girls' problems. It seems probable that, to increase our understanding of children's PRs, research will need to consider these complexities.

Acknowledgements

The authors would like to acknowledge the contributions of Kate Reid and Diana Smart to data collection and analysis for this chapter.

Chapter 13

Bullying amongst Australian primary school students

Some barriers to help-seeking and links with sociometric status

Phillip T. Slee

Introduction

The school peer group and, in particular, the nature and quality of the relationships within such groups are presently attracting considerable research interest. The peer group is a vital source of nurturance and support affecting students' physical and psychological well-being and the nature of their learning experience (Bennett and Derevensky 1995). A factor associated with the quality of peer relations is bullying. In the present chapter preliminary findings regarding several aspects of the bully/victim problem amongst Australian primary schoolchildren are reported, including the frequency with which it occurs, the barriers to help seeking and the relationship between peer bullying and social status.

Research into the topic of bullying stimulated by the pioneering work of Dan Olweus in Norway (1993a) and the substantial British research of Peter Smith and colleagues (Smith and Sharp 1994) has encouraged research in other countries such as Ireland (O'Moore and Hillery 1989); United States of America (Perry *et al.* 1988); Canada (Pepler *et al.* 1993) and Australia (Rigby 1996a). The corpus of this research has highlighted bullying as a physically harmful, psychologically damaging and socially isolating aspect of student's peer relations. Bullying is a reliably identifiable subtype of children's aggressive behaviour (Dodge *et al.* 1990; McNeilly-Choque *et al.* 1996). As generally described, bullying behaviour is characterized by a deliberate intention to inflict hurt by repeatedly, over time, taking advantage of being superior in strength, either physically or psychologically (Olweus 1989). Australian research suggests that approximately one in five students are bullied at 'least once a week' (Rigby 1996a).

An important question arising from the findings regarding the frequency and effects of bullying concerns factors that prevent victims seeking help (as many do not), and bystanders providing help although they are sympathetic to the plight of victims (Rigby and Slee 1991, 1993b). Tisak and Tisak (1996) have found developmental trends in bystander behaviour, with primary school students more likely than secondary students to seek help from an authority. One aspect of peer relations that might provide some insight into the issue of help-seeking associated with bullying concerns the link between peer status and bullying. As Tisak and Tisak (1996: 325) note, bystanders' response to aggression may be mediated by 'the relation of the bystander to the aggressor'.

Various methods have been developed to assess children's peer status, and the advantages and disadvantages of a number of these have been referred to and discussed by several authors in the present text. Briefly, sociometric techniques are essentially measures of interpersonal liking. The nomination method used in the present study has been previously described by Coie *et al.* (1982) who combined positive and negative nominations into 'social preferences' ('like most' votes minus 'like least' votes); and social impact ('like most' votes plus 'like least' votes). Using this schemata 'popular' children receive a high number of liked nominations and a low number of disliked nominations. The children who receive a low number of disliked nominations are identified as 'neglected'. 'Rejected' children receive a high number of disliked nominations and few liked nominations. Finally, 'controversial' children receive a high number of liked and disliked nominations. Studies comparing the behaviour of students of differing social status have resulted in a range of findings.

One commonly reported finding as reported by Coie *et al.* (1990) is that rejected children at primary school level are perceived as more aggressive, disruptive, likely to violate rules and as more inconsiderate generally of their peers. However, some researchers have reported little or no relationship between aggressive behaviour and social status (Hazen *et al.* 1984; Olweus 1989; Cairns and Cairns 1994). As Cairns and Cairns (1994) note, aggressive children are frequently solid members of a like-minded peer group. One aspect of peer relations that has received little research attention concerns the link between sociometric status and aggressive behaviour as reflected in peer bullying.

Perry *et al.* (1988: 812) noted in a study of primary school children that 'victimised as well as aggressive children were disliked by their peers'. Boulton and Smith (1994) reported that both primary school bullies and victims have high levels of rejected peer status scores compared with popular children. They also reported a tendency for bullies and victims to be over-represented in the controversial group.

To date, few attempts have been made to understand the relationship between the quality of children's interpersonal peer relations and sociometric status. Such research has important implications for better understanding the health and well-being of children and the viability of school-based intervention such as peer mediation (Tisak and Tisak 1996; Smith and Sharp 1994; Slee 1997).

In the present chapter findings from ongoing research are presented in the form of two studies. A question addressed in the first study includes the extent to which bullying occurs amongst a sample of Australian primary school students. Other questions concern why students do not help victims and why students think victims do not ask for help. The second study considers the question of the nature of the link between sociometric status (especially, popularity, rejection and neglect) and bullying and victimization.

Study one

A total of 936 children from year levels 3 to 7 from three primary schools participated in the first study. The schools were all located in lower- to middle-class metropolitan Adelaide, a major urban centre in Australia. There were 434 girls and 512 boys with an average age of 10.8 years. Students indicated their self-reported experience of bullying on a six-point scale ranging from 'every day' to 'never'. Other questions were developed to understand why students would not help victims of bullying and what prevents victims from asking for help. Previous research (e.g., Slee 1994) had piloted these questions.

Prior to completing the survey teachers read students a definition of bullying adapted from Olweus (1989), as follows:

> Students sometimes bully students at school by deliberately and repeatedly hurting or upsetting them in some way, for example, by hitting or pushing them around, teasing or leaving them out of things on purpose. But it is not bullying when two young people of about the same strength have the odd fight or quarrel.

Teachers monitored students to ascertain if there were any adverse reactions to completing the survey but none were noted.

Results and discussion

Taking Boulton and Underwood's (1992) definition of 'serious' bullying as that which occurs several times a week or more, then across the three schools an average of 17.7 per cent of students (range 14.3 to 21.3 per cent) reported such an incidence (Table 13.1). More males on average (18.6 per cent) compared to females (16.6 per cent) reported experiencing 'serious' bullying.

The present findings concerning the extent of bullying amongst Australian primary school students around 11 years of age are similar to that reported through application of the Peer Relations Questionnaire to students in large scale studies in Australia where approximately 23 per

Table 13.1 Percentages of students (n = 947) reporting their experience of bullying for three schools (A, B, C)

	Every day		*Most days*		*1–2 days a week*		*Weekly*		*Less than weekly*		*Never*	
Schools	*M*	*F*	*M*	*F*	*M*	*F*	*M*	*F*	*M*	*F*	*M*	*F*
A (n = 540)	6.8	1.3	8.9	8.1	8.2	8.1	7.5	3.8	23.2	24.7	45.4	54.0
B (n = 139)	5.6	3.1	4.2	6.3	4.2	12.5	5.6	9.4	18.3	12.5	62.0	56.3
C (n = 257)	4.5	0.9	4.5	3.4	9.0	6.0	11.7	7.8	41.0	34.5	29.9	47.4

Table 13.2 What students say prevents them from helping a victim (n = 947, expressed as a percentage)

	Fear of retaliation		*It's none of my business*		*It's the other child's problem*		*Teachers should intervene*		*Another child should*	
Schools	*M*	*F*	*M*	*F*	*M*	*F*	*M*	*F*	*M*	*F*
A (n = 540)	19.7	23.4	31.5	35.1	10.0	7.4	28.0	28.6	10.4	5.6
B (n = 139)	8.7	22.6	23.2	22.6	11.6	9.7	30.4	40.3	24.6	4.8
C (n = 257)	18.8	29.4	30.5	37.6	11.7	5.5	32.8	24.8	6.3	2.8

cent of primary students this age report being bullied at least once a week or more (Rigby 1996b). The figure of 17.7 per cent is considerably higher than the mean of 9 per cent of North American primary school students being seriously victimized as reported by Perry *et al.* (1988). The high level of bullying reported by students in the present study is supported by the findings from an Australia-wide Federal Parliamentary inquiry (*Sticks and Stones* 1994) into violence in schools which concluded that, similar to other countries, bullying is a major problem in Australian schools.

The data pertaining to the frequency of bullying raises important questions regarding the social relations of all those involved in the bully/victim cycle. For the victim causal links with school maladjustment are now being identified (e.g., Kochenderfer and Ladd 1996). For the bully the adverse effects have been well documented in relation to outcomes such as delinquency (e.g., Olweus 1989).

Australian research has clarified that the majority of students are sympathetic to the plight of victims and do not endorse bullying behaviour (Rigby and Slee 1993b). In Table 13.2 information is presented from a question regarding what stops students from helping a child who is being victimized.

Some respondents (30.1 per cent) thought that students did not try to prevent victimization because they believed it was none of their business. Does this mean that as bystanders they do not wish to be involved or that something holds them back from intervening (e.g., fear)? Tisak and Tisak (1996), in a study of bystander behaviour, have drawn attention to the need to distinguish between what bystanders say they would do compared to what they believe they should do. Rigby (1996b) in research involving 8- to 12-year-old students notes that 66 per cent of boys and 70 per cent of girls believe that students should help stop bullying. However, only 43 per cent of boys and 44 per cent of girls reported that they 'always' or 'usually' tried to stop it when it occurred. As such there is a gap between what primary students know they should do and what they actually do. The possible implications for school-based intervention programmes include equipping students with some 'knowledge' regarding how to intervene and/or creating a safer environment in which students feel more empowered to intervene on behalf of the victim. This type of response needs further examination to understand what underlies it.

Over one-quarter of the students endorsed the idea that 'the teachers should intervene' (30.8 per cent). Tisak and Tisak's (1996) research has identified a developmental component to bystander assistance with younger primary school children more likely to defer to an authority than secondary school students. The idea that teachers were responsible for helping a victim was also understandable in as much as one-fifth (20 per cent) of students also reported that they would not intervene to help a victim for fear of personal harm to themselves. This explanation would also make sense if the bully had at least some level of support from other members of the peer group and this issue is examined in Study Two (p. 210). Research conducted by McGovern (1976) indicates that threat to one's physical safety or threat of physical attack upon oneself deters helping behaviour.

Only a few students (9.0 per cent) indicated they would not help a victim because they believed it was the victim's problem. One interpretation of this finding supported by existing research is that there is a small subset of victims who are provocative and irritating in their behaviour (Olweus 1978; Boulton and Smith 1994; Schwartz *et al.* in press). This issue is further examined in Study Two.

Overall, though, while previous research indicates that students are sympathetic to the plight of victims (Rigby and Slee 1993b), the present findings suggest there are barriers to providing help to victims in terms of students' attitudes and beliefs. The findings presented in Table 13.3 regarding student's opinions about what prevents victims asking for help highlight further possible barriers and strongly support the idea that bullying engenders a climate of fear as the majority of students (57.7 per cent) endorsed the idea that victims would be 'too scared' to ask for help. As referred to earlier in Table 13.2, some 20 per cent of students fear retaliation for helping victims, which perhaps refers to the

Table 13.3 Student's opinions regarding what prevents victims from asking for help (n = 937, expressed as a percentage)

	Victims are too scared		*Nothing will be done to stop it*		*Victims don't want to make trouble*		*Other reasons*	
Schools	*M*	*F*	*M*	*F*	*M*	*F*	*M*	*F*
A (n = 540)	56.5	55.5	12.0	11.9	21.2	23.7	9.3	8.9
B (n = 140)	54.2	70.3	8.3	6.3	31.9	15.6	5.6	7.8
C (n = 257)	54.3	55.5	17.1	16.4	20.2	17.3	8.5	10.9

physical/psychological strength of bullies or to the possibility that they enjoy some support from other peers. Finally, 21.6 per cent believed that victims would 'not want to make trouble', reinforcing the idea of a code of silence around the issue.

Considered together, then, the findings from Study One strongly support existing research that bullying is a not uncommon aspect of Australian primary school children's peer relations. The climate engendered by bullying could be understood to shape and influence the quality of peer relations rendering powerless the potential samaritans and threatening most victims into quiet and isolated submission. The findings in Study One have implications for the type of school-based intervention programmes used to address the issue of school bullying. For example, the fear associated with bullying highlights the need for schools to address the issue of creating a safe environment for all students. To further understand the relation between peer bullying and peer relations a sociometric analysis of students in one of the schools was undertaken; these findings are presented and discussed in Study Two.

Study two

Students in one of the schools (n = 301 males and 239 females) who completed the questionnaire in Study One also completed two other questionnaires:

1 *Measures of interpersonal relations with peers.* Three measures, each consisting of four items, tapped different aspects of relating including (a) the tendency to bully other children, or Bully Scale; (b) the tendency to be victimized by other children, or Victim Scale; and (c) the tendency to act in a prosocial manner, or Prosocial Scale. The items consisted of descriptions of behaviour, such as 'I like to get into fights with someone I can easily beat' (Bully Scale); 'I get picked on by other kids' (Victim Scale) and 'I enjoy helping others' (Prosocial Scale). Respondents indicated how often each statement was

true of themselves, using a scale ranging from 'never' to 'very often'. The sets of items have been shown to be both factorially distinct from each other and to have adequate levels of internal consistency, with alpha coefficients exceeding 0.7 (Rigby and Slee 1993a).

2 *Sociometric nominations.* Standardized instructions were given to teachers to ask all children to write down, privately, the names of three children they liked the least (the liked least nominations) and the names of three children they liked the most (liked most nominations). To minimize the salience of the peer nomination procedure and hopefully minimize subsequent discussion about who nominated whom, this exercise was embedded in the context of the general questionnaire where students were responding to a series of other questions regarding peer relations.

Like most (LM) and like least (LL) nominations were adjusted for class size by dividing the raw number of nominations by the number of participating children. To express the quotients in numbers of nominations each quotient was then multiplied by the average number of participants in each class (28.3). Adjusted LM and LL nominations were combined to assess two dimensions of sociometric status (a) social impact and (b) social preference (Coie *et al.* 1982). Social impact was calculated by adding the adjusted number of positive nominations plus the adjusted number of negative nominations (SI = LM + LL). Social preference was the adjusted number of positive nominations minus the adjusted number of negative nominations (SP = LM − LL). Using these dimensions students could be classified into the social status categories of 'popular' (high social impact, positive social preference); 'rejected' (high social impact, negative social preference) and 'neglected' (low social impact, negative social preference) according to Peery (1979).

Specific criteria were used to form each sociometric status category based on the number of nominations adjusted for class size where 'popular' = LM > 4.5; 'rejected' = LM < 1.5; LL > 4.5 and 'neglected' = LM < 1.5; LL < 1.5. These cut-off scores are based on those commonly reported in the literature (e.g., Strauss *et al.* 1988). Students' mean scores for the various sociometric status categories (derived from nominations by their peers) were then compared with students' mean scores (using self-ratings) on the interpersonal relations with peers measures (Bully, Victim and Prosocial Scales). Cut-off scores for these three scales were based on those originally reported by Slee and Rigby (1993).

Results and discussion

Altogether 60 bullies, 145 victims and 121 prosocial children were identified using the three interpersonal relations with peers scales. The issue addressed in Study Two concerned the relationships among the specific categories of sociometric status (popular, rejected, neglected, undifferentiated) and the specific interpersonal peer relations measures of bully, victim and prosocial. The relationship between sociometric status and peer interpersonal relations was first assessed in terms of group status, and each independent variable using four one-way ANOVA's. *Post hoc* tests (Scheffe) were performed to determine whether differences in scores for the four subscales were significant (Table 13.4). The results showed that the prosocial children received significantly more like most (LM) nominations than victims. Bullies and victims both received significantly more like least (LL) nominations than prosocial children. Prosocial children had significantly higher social preference (SP) scores than victims.

Table 13.4 also shows the number of students in each group who met the criteria for 'popular', 'rejected', 'neglected' and 'undifferentiated' sociometric categories. A four by three chi square showed a significant relationship between sociometric status and the interpersonal relations with peers measures, (χ^2 = 22.51, 6 d.f., $p < 0.001$). Further analysis indicated that this association was due to there being more prosocial students in the popular category than would be expected if sociometric status and interpersonal peer relations were independent, along with more victim students in the rejected category if independence was assumed. Subsequent exploration for each sociometric status classification was carried out using a goodness-of-fit test statistic, assuming equal expected number of observations in each personal relations category. Significant deviations from the null hypothesis were found for each of the four

Table 13.4 **Adjusted peer nomination measures (means) and sociometric status of bully, victim and prosocial groups**

	Bully (1) *(n = 60)*	*Victim (2)* *(n = 145)*	*Prosocial (3)* *(n = 121)*	
Adjusted number of peer nominations				
Like most (LM)	2.45	2.32	3.21	3 > 2
Like least (LL)	2.88	2.71	1.26	2 > 3 1 > 3
Social Impact (SI) (LM + LL)	5.33	5.10	4.47	NS
Social preference (SP) (LM – LL)	0.12	−0.13	0.34	3 > 2
Sociometric status (% in parentheses)	6 (15)	9 (22)	25 (63)*	
Popular				
Rejected	5 (19)	18 (69)	3 (12)*	
Neglected	8 (18)	25 (55)	12 (27)*	
Undifferentiated	41 (19)	92 (44)	79 (37)*	

Notes
χ^2 = 22.51, 6 d.f., $p < 0.001$; *$p < 0.001$.

sociometric status classifications (Table 13.4) as assessed by the difference between the observed and expected row values.

Overall, bullies and victims were less liked than prosocial children. Prosocial tendencies were also most strongly linked with popular social status, while being victimized was associated with rejected social status; the latter finding largely accords with the research of Perry *et al.* (1988) and Boulton and Smith (1994). Analysis of the data by gender could not be completed because of small cell sizes in the four by three table, but there was enough evidence for a difference in the patterns for males and females to warrant further study. In all, the present findings strongly suggest that being caught up in the bully/victim cycle is damaging for both bullies and victims in terms of the quality of their peer relations.

Explanations for why bullies, and more particularly victims, suffer poorer peer relations than prosocial children need to take account of intrapersonal and interpersonal factors and the qualities of the larger school system in which the relationships are embedded. In relation to a minority of victims one possible explanation is that children dislike and reject them because 'they just ask for it', which accords with the finding in Study One that 9 per cent of students would not help a victim because it is the other child's (victim's) problem. Peers are generally more accepting of children who are helpful, friendly, co-operative, and prosocial, while peer rejection is usually associated with aggression, disruption and fighting (Coie *et al.* 1982; Cantrell and Prinz 1985; McNeilly-Choque *et al.* 1996). Research suggests that some victims are not passive recipients of aggression from others but in some way either knowingly or unknowingly draw negative attention to themselves (Olweus 1978; Boulton and Smith 1994; Schwartz *et al.* in press). Kochenderfer and Ladd's (1996: 280) research has also clarified that physically victimized children were 'viewed by their teachers as more aggressive and hyperactive, and less cooperative and prosocial than nonvictimised peers'. Such children then, engage in irritating and provocative behaviour, the end result of which is likely to be peer rejection.

From a slightly different intrapersonal perspective the research of Hazen *et al.* (1984) is relevant as they have argued that aggressive behaviour is not a general characteristic of rejected children. They suggest that children who are rejected have deficits in attentional skills, which means that they fail to attend to the social setting or context and as a result have problems with social skills such as group entry or, as noted by other researchers, with co-operativeness (Rigby *et al.* 1997). In this way children are often perceived as intruders when they are attempting to join in an activity and are subsequently rejected or rebuffed for their efforts. Limitations in social skills means that rejected children often respond in social interactive situations in inflexible and stereotyped ways (Slee 1993).

A third possible explanation for why bullies and victims are more disliked (and, in the case of victims, more rejected) than prosocial children, needs to take account of the quality of interpersonal relations in the peer group. Bullies are certainly not isolated individuals. They appear to enjoy a certain level of support (even admiration!) from at least a small coterie of peers (Rigby 1997b), and as indicated are 'feared' (Study One) and disliked by at least some other children. Boulton and Smith's thoughtful analysis of sociometric standing and bullying reached a similar conclusion. As they note:

> Being well liked by some classmates could help explain why bullies continue in their negative behaviour; it may not matter to the bullies that they are (probably) disliked by their victims and the friends of their victims (if they have any), since they have their own friends.
>
> (Boulton and Smith 1994: 327)

Victims are disliked and rejected, suggesting that children do not wish to be associated with 'wimps' or 'losers' emphasizing their estrangement from the peer group. The present findings are a strong argument for early intervention programmes to assist both bullies and victims to enjoy better peer relations.

Finally, it is worth considering the findings from Study One where there was considerable variation among the three schools in factors such as the frequency of bullying and in the nature of the barriers to help-seeking. Children's school peer relations are enacted against the backdrop of differential quality in school policies and practice (e.g., peer mediation programmes) that help or hinder the development of good student peer relations (Slee 1997).

In summary, the findings from this preliminary study would encourage further research to overcome its limitations. A critical consideration is needed of the sociometric classification system used, in view of the large number of undifferentiated students. The broad categories of 'bullies' and 'victims' need to be further refined to allow for a more fine grained analysis of peer relations. A significant limitation in interpreting the present findings concerns the need to examine the issue of gender. While research at this individual level is important, attention could also be given to the interpersonal nature of peer interactions where bullying and victimization are embedded in the larger peer group. A better understanding is warranted of how the larger school system (reflected in its policy and practices regarding peer relations) adds to, or detracts from, the quality of peer relations. Intervention programmes would be wise to acknowledge the systemic nature and inherent interrelatedness of the various elements of peer relations in addressing the bully/victim cycle.

Chapter 14

Australian schoolchildren's perceptions of television representations of bullying and victimization

Marian Tulloch

The use of video to present dramatic vignettes has been a strategy in many anti-bullying intervention programmes (Cowie and Sharp 1994; New Zealand Police 1992; Olweus 1991; Rigby and Slee 1992). Video resources for use in schools need not be confined, however, to purpose-written material. Television drama can play a powerful role in educational programmes because of its potential to reveal attitudes, raise issues and shift perspectives. Fictional narratives can be both concrete (painting characters and situations that portray a context for bullying incidents), yet distant (providing classroom viewers an opportunity for critical discussion in which a fictional world can be compared and contrasted with the students' own school environment). Yet, using television drama in the classroom requires teachers to consider the different ways in which children may respond to the same programme. This chapter presents a study of students' varied responses to a story about school bullying and discusses how this research can inform attempts to promote anti-violence strategies through the use of videos in the classroom.

The power of television to foster attitudes that are deemed socially desirable has been examined in a number of areas. Although in an experimental study Durkin (1985) was successful in modifying the sex-role stereotypes of primary school students' particularly in relation to domestic roles, he was less successful in changing adolescent stereotyped views of occupations. Gunter and McAleer (1990) concluded that rather than producing any dramatic change in the racial beliefs of white audiences, the effects of television portrayal of other racial groups simply reinforced prior dispositions. Thus, while less prejudiced members of the audience interpreted the racial slurs of a bigoted character as satire, the comic critique was ignored by authoritarian viewers who shared the prejudiced attitudes. Responses to programmes designed to challenge social attitudes are varied and complex, and the process needs to be more fully understood if video is to become a useful classroom tool.

Too often the role of television in relation to problems of social violence is presented solely in terms of the traditional question, 'Does viewing violence on television increase children's violent behaviour?' Instead this chapter asks how school students' experiences of and attitudes to school violence influence their interpretation of a video drama portraying school bullying. Interventions that make use of video material have rarely theorized about the way children respond to media texts. Implicitly they appear to adopt a model of receptive viewers absorbing anti-violence messages. This rather passive view of the child audience has been adopted from a range of theoretical perspectives. Psychologists have focused on the direct effects of televised violence, or on children's information processing skills in the comprehension of television narratives, while media theorists have been concerned with detailed textual analysis. More recently, however, there has been a convergence of interest in the role of audience interpretation. Psychologists have recognized the importance of children's identification with programme characters in any attempt to influence their attitudes to televised violence (e.g., Huesmann *et al.* 1983), while recent work in the fields of media and cultural studies has been concerned with how young people use the media in making sense of their experiences, in relating to others and in organizing their daily lives (Buckingham 1993).

If we understand meaning not as a property of a programme but as constructed by each viewer, we must recognize that students may interpret and evaluate the same programme in quite different ways. A constructivist perspective (Livingstone 1990), therefore, has important implications for those who wish to use television to foster particular attitudes (including anti-violence). Rather than simply selecting a prosocial text to offer models of socially desirable behaviour, it is necessary to examine the meanings that a text has for the target audience. Evaluation of aggression is particularly influenced by cultural and even subcultural values. At the heart of the interpretation of conflict are issues of appropriateness, blame and responsibility.

The way viewers interpret a narrative and attribute responsibility for events will relate to their perceptions of particular characters (Livingstone 1990; Rule and Ferguson 1986). Children's response to aggression on television may be influenced by their perceived likeness to the aggressor or victim and the similarity of the situation to their own experience (Huesmann 1986). Livingstone (1990) found that identification with particular characters was associated with quite different narrative interpretations of a television serial. If identification is a critical variable in interpreting a narrative about school bullying, then it would be expected that the different narrative perspectives of bully and victim should be directly linked to students' identification with particular characters. Students' personal experiences of school violence could be expected to relate to this identification process. Noble (1975), however, argues that viewers need not identify with characters to adopt their perspective. An alternative possibility is that perspective-taking depends on evaluating characters in terms of a viewer's social norms and value systems. At the emotional level, creating empathetic responses to victims of violence is important to increasing students' prosocial responses (Feshbach 1988).

An active view of audience interpretation does not deny the importance of the text in structuring meaning. In selecting an appropriate narrative for the present study, the structural and psychological characteristics typical of bully/victim relations were seen as key elements. The chosen video narrative portrays many of the characteristics of bullies and victims identified by research (Besag 1989). Bullies have been characterized as tough, socially confident and fairly popular. Victims tend, however, to be socially isolated, often having not even one good friend in their class. Boy victims tend to be physically weaker than their attackers. They often have a close relationship with their mother who may be seen by teachers as overprotective.

The video selected incorporates many of these features in the characters of its main protagonists. The video *Top Kid*, produced by the Australian Children's Television Foundation, is set in Sydney in the 1940s. It tells the story of a studious boy with an exceptional memory who is selected to participate in a radio quiz programme. While supported by his mother and held up to other students by his teachers as a model pupil, Gary Doyle is teased, ridiculed and assaulted by his peers. His main bully, Sean Finnegan makes fun of him in class, abuses him for sporting failure, harasses him returning home from school and finally beats him up severely in a fight. Although the setting of the story, in post-Second World War Sydney, presents a critical distance from the viewers' own experiences, its location in an Australian context provides an element of familiarity.

Definitions of bullying include psychological as well as physical harm in a situation of differential power (Besag 1989). The chosen drama portrays various facets of bullying: ridicule, abuse, damage to property, physical harassment, as well as injury-causing physical assault. Such a series of incidents enables an exploration of students' systems of values and behavioural expectations. Selected for the potential to elicit multiple viewpoints, they reflect the ambiguities that surround children's peer relations. Although the story is told from the perspective of the victim, who is supported by the adults in the narrative, his deviation from the norms of his peer group may encourage an oppositional reading by some students. A series of questions is posed by the story. What do students expect of other pupils and teachers? What is an appropriate response to bullying? Should children involve adults, especially teachers, and if so how should they intervene? Are bullying and harassment seen as inevitable? How do students react to the characters of bully and victim?

The research process and participants

Two stages were involved in this research. Initially small groups of students in their first or second year of high school were shown the video excerpt and their discussion was taped. The role of the discussion leader (a person with teaching experience but not currently a teacher) was to elicit students' views but not to influence the debate. The aim of this part of the study therefore was to draw out students' views in a nonevaluative setting; there was no attempt to mirror the kind of follow-up discussion that might occur in a classroom.

Over 300 students (114 boys and 187 girls drawn from the first year classes of five rural New South Wales high schools) participated in the main part of the study. While all the schools were outside the metropolitan area, they varied considerably in size and student population. Two were small high schools centred in agricultural communities, one was a large high school in an industrial town, and the other two schools served a country town with a mixture of tertiary educational and service sectors as well as some light industry.

Measuring students' experiences and attitudes to peer relations at school

In order to tap students' experiences of bullying and their attitudes to peer relations at school, each student completed a simple questionnaire. Students were first presented with a broad definition of bullying which emphasized that bullying is not an occasional fight or quarrel between students of equal strength. Rather, bullying occurs when students are picked on or teased either physically or verbally. Students were then asked about the frequency with which they had been bullied in the last month and given a set of questions about their general experience of being picked on and teased. A similar pair of measures assessed the extent to which the student bullied others. Pupils' approaches to social relations were measured by a pair of scales assessing their tendency to act in a prosocial manner towards other students and their sense of themselves as socially competent and confident. Finally students' attitudes to bullying and co-operation were measured by two scales (Rigby and Slee 1993a), one assessing their acceptance of bullying and a belief that weak kids deserved to be bullied (e.g., 'Nobody likes a wimp', 'It's funny to see kids get upset when they are teased', 'It is OK to call some kids nasty names'); the other the extent to which they viewed a school as an interdependent community where teachers and pupils should work together to support weaker pupils (e.g., 'I would tell teachers if someone were picking on me', 'I like school', 'I like it when someone sticks up for kids who get bullied', 'It makes me angry when a kid gets picked on without reason').[1]

Such measurement of student attitudes and behaviours is not new and provides an overview only in general terms. The aim of the present study was to see if and how these experiences and beliefs affect students' interpretations of a specific television drama about school bullying. Is the way students interpret and evaluate such a programme dependent primarily on the programme content or on the preconceptions students bring to viewing? Video could be a way of opening students' minds to other viewpoints, but it could also serve only to reinforce existing prejudices.

In seeking a methodology to explore this question, I turned to the work of Sonia Livingstone (1990), who has contrasted alternative audience reactions to a particular episode of the British soap opera, *Coronation Street*. Using a set of questions about the story, Livingstone demonstrated that groups of viewers saw key events in quite different ways. She used a statistical technique called cluster analysis to develop a typology of viewers from the 'romantics' through to the 'cynics'. These audience groups differed, not only in the characters with whom they empathized but in their evaluations of particular actions and their underlying view of human nature.

In developing a narrative questionnaire, items were derived from several sources. Statements made by students during the discussion groups were a basis for items (e.g., 'Gary was a teacher's pet', 'I felt sorry for Gary when the kids made fun of him', ' It was funny when the boy tipped the garbage on Gary'). The second source of items was statements made by characters in the narrative (e.g., 'Gary should have gone to the gym and learned to fight as his father suggested'). Third, items asked students to evaluate alternative actions in the story (e.g., 'Gary should have told the principal who it was that beat him up', 'Kids are bound to tease kids who act smart like Gary').

To identify the key dimensions of different responses to the television drama, student ratings of these narrative statements were grouped together using the statistical technique of factor analysis. This enables responses to a large number of items to be reduced to a small number of dimensions linked by a common factor. The most central factor of students' reactions to the narrative was whether they responded seriously to the bullying incidents. Those with high scores on this dimension saw the harassment episodes as somewhat amusing and had little sympathy for the victim (e.g., 'It was funny when Sean poked Gary and made him shout out in class'). At the other end of this scale were students who had a sympathetic, serious attitude to the violence. A second factor, which can be termed the inevitability of bullying, was the extent to which students saw bullying as a natural reaction to Gary's academic success, his sporting failures and his favoured treatment by the teachers (e.g., 'Gary was asking for trouble by trying so hard to do well at school'). The third factor measured the degree to which students favoured adult intervention by teachers, parents and community members in disputes between students (e.g., 'Teachers shouldn't get involved when kids fight').

Attitudes to the two protagonists, the bully Sean and the victim Gary, were measured more directly by asking students to rate them on a series of contrasting adjectives such as weak/strong, good/ bad, funny/not funny, clever/stupid, pleasant/unpleasant. Subsequent analysis of student responses found ratings of seven adjective pairs tended to go together in contributing to the extent to which the bully was seen negatively (bad, stupid, not funny, unpleasant, violent, aggressor and unfair). Five items were indicative of a positive evaluation of Gary (good, clever, pleasant, nonviolent, victim). A combination of three adjectives formed an overall rating of the programme as interesting, exciting and realistic.[2] Statements of identification ('I am like Gary Doyle') and liking ('I like Gary Doyle') were also presented for both characters, with students responding from strong agreement to strong disagreement on a five-point scale.

Were there systematic differences in the way students interpreted the story?

To explore whether it was possible to identify groups of students who had quite different meanings and evaluations of the story, cluster analysis was employed. Students with a similar profile of responses to the narrative and character measures were placed together in a group. Five distinct groups were identified. The responses of each group will be considered in some detail as they represent the range of student views that may be found in any classroom.

The views of the two most extreme groups who can be seen as taking an anti-bullying and a pro-bullying stance are contrasted in Table 14.1. The differences between these two groups are very dramatic. Watching the same video, they respond in quite different ways. Contrasting perceptions of the victim Gary and the bully Sean seem very central to this difference, with the anti-bullying group liking Gary and the pro-bullying group liking Sean. Comments on Gary in the discussion groups flesh out this divergence.

> I thought Gary also deserves a bit of credit because he actually got up in the middle of the night just to do his homework, cos he knew something might have been wrong. He actually worked to be at the top.
>
> (Male)
>
> I think Sean was pretty good. I think it was Gary's fault, like he's a midget, he should of, like if he'd stood up for himself . . . they wouldn't bash him up.
>
> (Male)

Table 14.1 Group composition and responses to the video by the most extreme anti-bullying and pro-bullying groups

Anti-bullying group	*Pro-bullying group*
Viewed bullying very seriously	Bullying not taken seriously
Strong rejection of the view that Gary was a show off	Gary seen as a show off, asking for trouble by acting smart
None of the scenes where Gary was humiliated or Sean fooled around were seen as at all funny	Found scene where garbage tipped on Gary amusing
Very sorry for Gary	Not sorry for Gary
Somewhat accepting of adult intervention	Strongly rejected adult intervention
Saw bullying as somewhat inevitable	Strongly agreed bullying natural
Very positive evaluation of victim's character combined with strong liking	Positive evaluation of victim (as clever, good, etc.), but quite strongly disliked
Strong dislike of bully	Strong liking for bully
Saw selves as unlike victim but even less like bully	Saw selves as very unlike victim but quite similar to bully

Note
The extreme anti-bullying group was comprised of 41 per cent of female students and 24 per cent of male students. The pro-bullying group was comprised of 4 per cent of female students and 12 per cent of male students.

While the extreme pro-bully group is relatively small, a larger group including 29 per cent boys and 12 per cent girls held somewhat similar attitudes. These students took bullying more seriously than the pro-bully group, but they showed some amusement at the garbage incident, did not favour adult involvement and saw bullying as natural. Although they saw a clear dichotomy of bad bully and good victim, they did not like Gary much and saw themselves as more like Sean Finnegan. As such this group (of over fifty students and including nearly a third of the boys in the sample) provides a bridge with the more extreme group. They were less inclined to blame the victim but did not feel particularly sorry for him. Similarly, at the other end of the scale, there was a group of students with attitudes rather similar but less extreme than the anti-bully group. These students took bullying seriously, but not very seriously, seeing it as rather inevitable.

A final, middle-of-the-road group held a set of attitudes most similar to the anti-bully group in their belief in adult intervention and rejection of the inevitability of bullying. Yet they did not polarize Gary and Sean. While they liked Gary better than Sean, and saw little similarity to themselves in either of them, they rated both in more neutral terms than other groups. In particular, they were less willing than other groups to label Sean as a violent aggressor, a contrast even with the pro-bully group who rated Sean good, clever and funny despite seeing him as the aggressor. A possible explanation of this reluctance to polarize aggressor and victim emerged in one discussion group. Some students saw Sean himself as spurred on to antisocial behaviour by his classmates who stood by and let him get into trouble. They believed that all his classmates, not just a single bully, held negative attitudes to Gary, although they disagreed among themselves as to whether Gary was 'hated' or just thought to be 'too clever, and didn't belong'. An alternative view of the power dynamics was presented by students who took a very negative view of Sean. They believed that other pupils were scared to speak out, 'they had to agree or he'd bash them up'.

One clear difference between the groups was in the proportion of boys and girls holding particular perspectives. Over 70 per cent of girls but only 40 per cent of boys were found in the two groups most hostile to bullying, while over 40 per cent boys and only 16 per cent girls were in the two groups most accepting of bullying. Thus boys were under-represented in the groups sympathetic to the victim's position and over-represented in the groups that were tolerant of the bully's behaviour.

Relationships between programme meaning and general attitudes to peer relations

Having successfully identified a range of programme perspectives, the next step was to examine whether the patterns of programme meaning could be predicted from the peer relation measures and the students' gender. Discriminant function analysis was used as a tool for identifying the best combination of variables for predicting programme interpretation groupings.[3] The best predictors of a student's interpretation of the programme were the supportive interdependence scale, and the pro-bullying and the tendency to bully scales. Prosocial attitudes, self-reported bullying behaviour and students' gender were significant but weaker predictors.[4] Students in the most strongly anti-bully group saw the school as a supportive interdependent community. They strongly rejected bullying and reported that they rarely bullied others. By contrast, the group who were most supportive of the bully in their programme analysis had a generally positive attitude to bullying and tended to reject interdependence. While their prosocial scores were lower than other groups, they still showed some tendency to endorse prosocial items. They did not report a strong tendency to bully other students although their scores were higher than other groups. Acceptance of bullying and endorsement of a tough independent position, unsupportive of weaker peers, emerged more strongly in their reported attitudes than in their reported behaviours.

Although these students may not all have been involved in bullying other students, such attitudes make for a climate in which bullying is tolerated and victims are ignored or even blamed for their victimization.

It is interesting to note that the measures of victimization and social confidence did not significantly predict how students would view the programme. Given the expectation that victims of bullying would identify with Gary, the incidence of students who reported frequent victimization was examined over the five groups. About half of these victims (22 out of 43) were found in the most strongly anti-bullying group, while the remaining victims were spread evenly among the other groupings. It appears that the degree of acceptance of bullying (which is not significantly related to victimization) is a stronger predictor of how the programme is evaluated, particularly the extent to which harassment is taken seriously or considered amusing. Not surprisingly, however, among the relatively small group of students who reported frequent victimization there was a significantly higher proportion who were members of the group that most strongly identified with the victim's position.

Implications

Despite the historical context of the narrative, the majority of students found the story fairly realistic; it 'showed how it really is'. Importantly, however, the students who took the harassment least seriously, who identified more with the bully and rejected the victim, were also the least involved with the story. Because the bullying theme was intertwined with the story of Gary's selection and his moral dilemma as a member of a radio quiz team, the narrative focused on Gary, presenting the interaction of bully and victim very much from the victim's perspective. Yet the students whose general social attitudes and behaviours were tolerant of bullying were least likely to become involved in the narrative and did not identify with the victim's position.

It is noteworthy that gender-related differences occurred in the interpretation and evaluation of the narrative. Although membership of the two groups most tolerant of bullying was not confined to boys, a much higher proportion of boys than girls were members of these groups. However, while boys were predominant in the groups that held a 'tough minded', non-interventionist position, males and females were represented in each group, and gender was a less powerful predictor of group membership than the attitudinal and behavioural variables related to bullying.

Given this strong tendency for prior social attitudes to shape viewers' readings of narratives, what are the implications for using television drama as a way of exploring and influencing students' social values? The initial conclusion could be discouraging. The students we would most like to influence are the most dismissive of a story designed to provoke their sympathy. It is, however, important to recognize two features of the questionnaire part of the study. First, a spectrum of opinions emerged among students. The number of students who showed a high tolerance of bullying and little sympathy for the victim was fairly small, although the process of gaining agreement to participate in the study may have led to them being proportionally under-represented. A larger group, however, held somewhat similar if less extreme attitudes, providing the potential to bridge this attitude gap and to open up the possibility of communication and discussion.

Second, the questionnaire study measured only the individual reactions of students to the programme unmediated by any classroom discussion. Students were encouraged to express their honest opinions, which were not challenged in any way. Extracts from the discussion groups, however, indicate how the programme raised issues that could have been further debated and negotiated within a classroom setting. Several students in the Year 8 discussion group suggested the video would be more appropriate for younger children, probably primary age students, yet the discussion that it provoked indicated the power of drama to raise issues in a meaningful way.

One question canvassed in discussion groups was that of the similarities and differences between the 1940s and the 1990s. Although there was a feeling that in many ways the issues were the same, 'it showed bullying pretty well', two differences were highlighted. On the one hand, some students felt there was currently a greater awareness of the problem, 'more people doing something about it'. Teachers in the story were criticized for their lack of insight which made Gary's problems worse; now teachers are 'going through bullying seminars'. On the down side, however, some students saw the problem as getting worse because of the lack of adequate sanctions for bullying behaviour. While bullies used to be scared of the cane, 'now they just get one detention, it's over, and the other person is still hurt'. This group of students did not advocate a return to meeting violence with violence but argued that more severe penalties (e.g., suspension) were needed if there was to be an adequate deterrent. A perception that smoking was seen as a serious offence while violence was not, challenged schools to consider their priorities. Rigby (1996d) discusses the problems of a sanction-based approach to bullying, arguing that the potentially covert nature of bullying makes it hard to stamp out through a punishment regime. He recognizes, however, that the humanistic approach he favours will not work with all bullies and that in some cases sanctions such as suspension may be necessary.

An important dilemma facing students who are bullied is whether to report the incident to teachers or other adults. Even the most anti-bullying group of students were at best ambivalent on this issue. Two girls in a discussion group put it this way,

> I'm glad Gary didn't tell. I really don't like people who dob in other people. If people have done something they should have owned up.
>
> (Female)
>
> If Gary told, everyone would have thought he was a real wimp and thought he was just a loser.
>
> (Female)

Both these girls found the bully's behaviour unacceptable and saw his failure to own up as evidence of cowardice. Yet the ethos of 'not dobbing' was still strong, further supported by the view that if Gary had identified his attackers he would have been 'bashed up more'. Such discussions of responses to bullying by pupils and teachers provide an opportunity to debate these real dilemmas and develop policies and strategies that are acceptable to staff and students. This range of responses to a television drama can produce a powerful stimulus to classroom discussion and debate. A television drama supplies both a concrete context to discuss feelings, behaviours and strategies, and also the critical distance provided by the fictional narrative to avoid a personalizing of the debate. As such it can be a valuable tool in encouraging pupils and teachers to look together at issues of violence in schools.

Used in isolation, videos cannot solve the problem of bullying in schools. To be effective they need to be part of an integrated whole-school policy (Sharp and Thompson 1994). An evaluation of video activities used by a group of schools involved in the Sheffield Project stressed the importance of follow-up work by the teacher. One form of follow-up is dramatic role play where students actively explore the experience of victimization and strategies of assertion and intervention. Cowie and Sharp (1994) provide data indicating that over half the students felt a video had made them more aware of bullying and more likely to intervene to prevent it, and two-thirds felt it had made them more careful of their behaviour towards others. The present study suggests that the students who were part of the minority who did not respond positively may well have been those whose behaviour and attitudes are of most concern. Some teachers in the Sheffield study expressed concern that video and drama need to be very carefully handled or they could serve to provide models for bullying behaviour. Children are not short, however, of media models of violent power assertion. The value of presenting video drama within the classroom is that it provides an opportunity to engage with the attitudes, stereotypes and assumptions that support and justify abusive behaviour.

A sustained approach over time is necessary in any attempt to address issues of violence through the curriculum. Although a single video may be a useful part of developing an anti-bullying strategy, teachers need to draw on a range of video, drama and literary materials if these are to be part of a sustained anti-violence strategy aimed at creating long-term changes in school climate. The challenge for teachers is to recognize the range of interpretations that their students can make of video material and to use these differences constructively to engage with those who tolerate or justify violence. The process may also encourage teachers to reflect on their own attitudes and prejudices and the messages that their responses and interventions convey to their pupils about power, attribution and blame.

Notes

1 Reliability for the subscales were (alphas): Endorsement of bullying = 0.85, Co-operative interdependence = 0.77, Social confidence = 0.75, Tendency to bully others = 0.85, Tendency to be victimized = 0.85, Prosocial tendency = 0.62.
2 Reliability of narrative subscales were: Nonseriousness of bullying = 0.85, Naturalness of bullying = 0.59, Pro-Adult intervention = 0.51, Programme involvement = 0.63, Evaluation of victim = 0.62, Evaluation of bully = 0.77.
3 A single significant discriminant function, $\chi^2 = 179.14$, $p < 0.001$ accounted for 85.9 per cent of the variance. The group centroids on the discriminant function (−0.87, −0.21, 0.5, 0.8, 2.11) indicated a continuum of responses from Cluster 1 to Cluster 5, with this small latter group identified by extreme attitudes.
4 Significant correlations of predictor variables with the discriminant function were: Interdependence (0.79), Pro-bullying (0.78), Tendency to bully (0.72), Prosocial tendency (−0.54), Self-reported bullying (0.40), Sex (0.35).

Part V

Intervention

Chapter 15

An overview of prevention and treatment programmes for developing positive peer relations

Helen McGrath

There is a large body of research which suggests that children who experience poor peer relations at school are 'at risk' for short-term and long-term negative outcomes associated with school difficulties, delinquency, lower occupational success and mental health problems, and in general with a less satisfactory and unhappier life (e.g., Weissberg *et al.* 1981a; Roff and Wirt 1984; Blechman *et al.* 1986; Gresham 1986a; Hymel *et al.* 1988; Kupersmidt and Coie 1990; Kupersmidt *et al.* 1990). Social skills training is one of the most well-studied preventive and treatment approaches to childhood behaviour disorder available (La Greca 1993). The assumption underlying such programmes is that an adequate level of social competence is the most important factor enabling a student to form satisfactory relationships with peers and interact effectively with classmates.

What kinds of social skills programmes are most effective?

All reviewers of research studies published in the last 20 years which have investigated the effectiveness of social skills intervention programmes with children have concluded that there is much empirical support for the positive impact of social skills training programmes (Gresham 1981; Schneider and Byrne 1985; Gresham 1986a; Mastropieri and Scruggs 1985–1986; Weissberg and Allen 1986). Schneider and Byrne (1985), using a meta-analysis of research studies, concluded that social skills training is at least as effective as most other forms of psychotherapy over short periods of time.

Two main ways of assessing the social importance of an intervention have been suggested by Gresham (1988). The first way is to use subjective evaluation, whereby significant people such as teachers and peers are asked to judge the importance of the effects from a social skills intervention. The second way is to use social comparison, whereby comparisons are made between the level of social behaviour of referred children after intervention with the social behaviour of non-referred peers (e.g., through sociometric assessment). However, judgements and empirical comparisons do not always produce the same result, leading Gottman *et al.* (1976) to assert that if social skills training programmes are to be considered effective they need to demonstrate that they have taught specific social skills, and that these skills make a difference on social criterion variables. Other researchers (e.g., Witt and Elliott 1985; Gresham 1988) have also stressed the need to focus on the social validity of interventions (i.e., using programmes which are acceptable to teachers, children and parents, and which make a difference to children's everyday lives).

Types of intervention programmes

Many earlier studies of social skills programmes were conducted in clinical settings by nonschool personnel, and this may in part explain the failure of many of them to record generalization of the behaviours taught to naturalistic settings (Schneider and Byrne 1985). Hops and Greenwood (1988) have argued that the most effective approach would be to direct training and resources towards teachers. Schools are the most significant places in which students develop social skills, and in particular those skills which are essential for peer acceptance (Gresham 1988). There are many powerful arguments for the idea that social skills intervention programmes are best implemented by teachers in the school setting, preferably in a non-withdrawal context. Walker *et al.* (1995) argue that the 'selected' model of social skills training, in which children are trained in small withdrawal groups, inhibits generalization and does not address the issue of reputation. Hawkins and Weiss (1983) believe that three conditions are critical if children are to become socially competent. First, they must have the cognitive and behavioural social skills. Second, they must have many naturalistic or semi-naturalistic opportunities where they can practise these skills. Third, those with whom children interact on a regular basis must consistently reinforce socially appropriate behaviour. A classroom-based, whole-class, intervention offers a greater likelihood of producing generalization and maintenance of treatment effects through the provision of naturalistic opportunities to practise and receive naturalistic reinforcement from real-life peers and a wide range of teachers (Hops 1982; Hawkins and Weiss 1983; Weissberg and Allen 1986; Maag 1990). Another argument for teacher delivery of social skills programmes is that teachers already have considerable expertise and familiarity with many of the basic principles of learning and instruction used in social skills training procedures (Ladd and Asher 1985). Classroom-based programmes are more attractive to children than infrequent interactions on a withdrawal basis with an unfamiliar counsellor or specialist, and the stigmatization which is often associated with outside referral is avoided

(Weissberg and Allen 1986). A school-based programme is more cost-effective, in that, once trained, teachers can continue to use newly acquired skills with other students.

The acceptability of an intervention to teachers is also an important consideration. Witt and Elliott (1985) defined acceptability of an intervention as encompassing its appropriateness for a given problem, its fairness, its reasonableness, its intrusiveness, and whether or not it is consistent with conventional notions of what an intervention should be. Unacceptable interventions are less likely to be implemented or implemented correctly (Witt and Elliott 1985). Variables that relate to the acceptability of interventions are the amount of teacher time and effort required and the resources provided. Gresham (1988) hypothesizes that the type of problem may interact with the type of intervention, producing differences in what teachers see as acceptable in terms of time, effort and resources. For example a large time investment may be considered acceptable for an academic intervention, or for an intervention to manage classroom behaviour, but not for a social skills intervention. Another aspect of teacher acceptability is whether or not teachers agree with the selection of social skills to be taught. In a study by Gresham and Elliott (1990), teachers were asked to rate, using a checklist, the behaviours which they considered to be the most socially significant in their classroom. The ten they selected dealt primarily with classroom order and control rather than those which reflected peer interaction.

There are three main types of programmes used to develop social skills in children and adolescents which could be used as whole-class prevention and treatment programmes. These are direct social skills training (DSST) programmes in which students are taught specific social skills using a structured procedure; social cognitive training (SCT) programmes which focus on teaching the cognitive aspects of social encounters; and social ecological programmes which attempt to change the wider social context of the classroom.

Overall, most researchers have found that a DSST model produces the most socially valid changes (e.g., Oden and Asher 1977; La Greca and Santogrossi 1980; Bierman and Furman 1984; Ladd and Asher 1985; McGrath and Francey 1988), and that an SCT intervention is the least likely to produce such changes (e.g., Weissberg *et al.* 1981a; Nelson and Carson 1988; Elliott and Busse 1991). Schneider and Byrne (1985) reviewed 51 studies using a meta-analysis technique and concluded that, in general, direct social skills training programmes were more effective in producing successful social outcomes than SCT interventions. Gresham (1986b), in his review of studies, also found that direct social skills training procedures led to more successful outcomes than SCT programmes, and were the most cost effective. Nelson and Carson (1988) and Elliott and Busse (1991) also concluded that SCT approaches were the least effective overall. Weissberg and Allen (1986) similarly found that a direct social skills training approach was the most effective, but argued that there was also a place for social cognitive training programmes in school contexts.

Direct social skills training (DSST) programmes

In most DSST intervention programmes, social skills are taught by a process which usually involves discussion of the skill, verbal rehearsal of the steps of the skill, and practice of the skill. There is usually some role playing of scenarios where children practise the skill with corrective feedback. Reinforcement of correct use of the skill in naturalistic settings is also a feature. Schneider and Byrne (1985) used the term 'coaching' to describe this process, and others have used the terms 'direct instruction' or 'behaviour rehearsal'. McGrath and Francey (1991) outlined four basic steps in their *Friendly Kids, Friendly Classrooms* version of the DSST model: discussion of the skill to motivate students to learn it, identification of the correct ('do's') and incorrect ('dont's') aspects of the behaviour sequence, simulated practice of the social skill with feedback and real-life practice of the skill with reinforcement.

Oden and Asher's (1977) study is the one regarded as the most influential in this paradigm. They directly taught social behaviours to several poorly accepted 9- and 10-year-old students. These were behaviours which had been shown to be correlated with peer acceptance: participation (e.g., getting started, paying attention), co-operation (e.g., taking turns, sharing materials), communication (e.g., talking, listening), and validation/support (e.g., offering help and encouragement). The results suggested significant short-term gains in peer acceptance, but only minimal efficacy for changing peer status in the long run (Hops 1982). Hymel and Asher's (1977) attempt to replicate Oden and Asher's study was less successful. They found changes in sociometric status in the group who had received the DSST programme, but these were not significantly different from gains made by a group who had received just peer-pairing.

The first small group DSST intervention was implemented by La Greca and Santogrossi (1980). A sample of third, fourth and fifth graders were directly taught specific skills such as smiling/laughing, joining ongoing activities, extending invitations, conversational skills, sharing and co-operating, and complimenting verbally. However, there were no group effects for either total positive behaviour or sociometric acceptance. The group met for only a total of two hours and it seems unlikely that this length of intervention would have much power to influence peer ratings.

Gresham and Nagle (1980) also used poorly accepted third and fourth grade students in their study, and the skills taught were those identified as correlates of popularity in previous research. Children were also encouraged to practise their newly learned skills in the classroom after each session, but no steps were taken to maximize the likelihood of this actually occurring. The DSST group decreased significantly in negative responses given and received pre-treatment to follow-up. Although there were no pre-/post-treatment effects on either sociometric or observational data, there were changes on follow-up data.

In a well-designed study by Ladd (1981), DSST procedures were used to teach conversational skills to 18 boys and 18 girls, who were ranked lowest on peer acceptance in their six Grade 3 classrooms. The skills taught over eight sessions were: offering suggestions or directions, asking positive questions, and offering supportive statements. In two extra sessions, attempts were made to foster skill maintenance and generalization by encouraging children to initiate using the skills independently in a semi-naturalistic situation, and by reviewing instances where the children had used the skill well. Children who had received the DSST intervention showed increases in two of the taught skills and decreases in non-social behaviour during post-treatment playground observations. They also were chosen more as a playmate and these changes were still present at a four-week follow-up. However, those students who only received a 'peer-pairing' treatment also showed increases in this way.

Bierman and Furman's 1984 study was the first to show the benefits of a DSST in the context of the larger group. They found in their study of poorly accepted fifth and sixth grade boys that a DSST intervention had positive and sustained effects on small group interactions, dyadic conversations, and lunchroom interactions, but not on sociometric ratings of friendship. A study by Siperstein and Gale (1983), targeted rejected children compared to a control group of children who received adult attention only. The subjects who received the DSST intervention increased in 'work with' and 'play with' ratings, while they decreased in 'not a friend' nominations. Trained children also demonstrated decreased amounts of self-isolated and onlooker behaviour in the classroom. DSST techniques have also been successfully used to teach the specific social skill of assertiveness to children (Bornstein *et al.* 1977).

McGrath and Francey (1988) found increases in peer acceptance for poorly accepted primary-aged students who received a DSST intervention in a small group context which included classmates with fairly high levels of peer acceptance. McGrath (1996b), in a study of 16 primary level classrooms across two schools, compared a whole-class teacher-delivered DSST intervention, an SCT intervention, and an intervention which combined the two. The DSST programme was the only one of the three to significantly increase peer acceptance, reduce rejections, and decrease negative reputation in 'at-risk' students.

There are several limitations in the research studies which have experimented with a DSST intervention. The skills selected were often not based on empirical evidence that these skills are important in social interaction, the children selected for training were often not deficient in the skill in which they were trained, and many of the interventions were very brief. The main criterion used in most studies was an increase in peer acceptance, and this may not change easily as it appears to be closely related to reputation. Most studies did not include follow-ups, nor address the issue of generalization across settings. Most studies did not monitor whether the intervention was being accurately implemented. None the less, there appear to be good reasons to agree with Ladd and Asher's (1985) and Weissberg and Allen's (1986) conclusion that there is mounting evidence concerning the beneficial effects of DSST interventions on children's social behaviour and peer acceptance. Despite the research limitations, studies of DSST are among the most rigorously designed intervention studies in terms of using optimal control groups and multiple measures (Weissberg and Allen 1986).

Social cognitive training (SCT) interventions

The social cognitive approach to social skills training focuses on changing how children think about social situations, and how they solve hypothetical social problems. Some of the social-cognitive processes which have been suggested as important in the process of peer interaction are: the generation of alternative solutions to social problems, the thinking through of the consequences of social responses, perspective taking, the identification of emotions, the identification of cause and effect in social behaviour, intention detection (i.e., identification of others' motivations), the selection of social goals (specific types, short-term vs long-term), and accuracy of social perception of interpersonal features of a social context (e.g., status differences, relationship history).

The rationale for a social-cognitive approach stemmed from studies which suggested that less socially competent students tended to respond impulsively in social situations, and did not consider more successful alternatives (e.g., Camp 1977). Most early work in this area (e.g., Elardo and Caldwell 1979; Weissberg *et al.* 1981b; Ridley and Vaughn 1982) was based on studies by Shure and Spivack (1972), who developed an interpersonal problem-solving training programme in which teachers trained preschool aged children to recognize emotions, to take another's perspective, to generate alternative solutions and to anticipate the consequences of actions. Results were obtained (Shure and Spivack 1972) which indicated that the children used an increased number of alternative solutions to interpersonal situations, and a decreased number of aggressive solutions. An indirect effect was seen in significant improvements over the next two years in behavioural adjustment for the experimental children. However the work of Shure and Spivack (1972) has been criticized on several points relating to inadequacy and lack of validity of the measures used and failure to control for confounding variables such as teacher attention (Hops 1982; Furman 1984). Several researchers attempted to replicate the findings of the Spivack and Shure studies (e.g., Urbain 1980; Weissberg *et al.* 1981b; Rickel and Burgio 1982), but with very limited success.

Nelson and Carson (1988) have expressed doubt about the effectiveness of a social problem-solving intervention. In their study, they compared the effects of a SCT training programme with a peer-pairing programme, an SCT programme plus teacher–student conferencing and a student monitoring programme. These programmes had been given to third and fourth grade classes as a whole-class primary prevention programme. Their SCT programme was delivered for one hour per week over 18 weeks, using a whole-class approach. Consistent with previous research (e.g., Weissberg *et al.* 1981a, 1981b), they found that students given an SCT programme improved in terms of social problem-solving skills using hypothetical social situations but did not improve in peer acceptance or decrease problem behaviour.

One of the reasons for the relatively low level of effectiveness of SCT training may be the underlying assumption that less socially competent children differ from their normal peers in the kinds of social problem-solving strategies they use. Many researchers have obtained results which suggest that the way in which children respond on paper-and-pencil tests of social problem-solving, which allow time for reflective cognition, may be very different from the ways in which they actually respond in real-life or semi-naturalistic situations when emotional factors are more likely to be present such as affect, arousal and self-interest (e.g., Weissberg *et al.* 1981a, 1981b; Richard and Dodge 1982; Rubin *et al.* 1988). Langer (1978) has argued that most social behaviour is 'unthinking' in nature, and proceeds according to over-learned 'social scripts'. Rubin and Rose-Krasnor (1986) refer to this automatic responding as 'reasoning in action' and have argued that social situations which require or even allow reflective cognition may be relatively uncommon.

In their review of social cognitive interventions with children, Pellegrini and Urbain (1985) note that this process itself may be constant across all types of children, but may have different implications and repercussions for different kinds of children. They point out that, while most children may not brainstorm spontaneously in most social situations, the failure to do so may generally be of little significance for the well-adjusted child, whose natural recourse is to a relatively mature and effective problem-solving strategy. The same failure in an aggressive child may lead to peer conflict or goal frustration, due to the type of problem solution typically relied upon.

Caplan *et al.* (1991) have suggested that one major flaw of the hypothetical-reflective tasks typically used in most research is the failure of the researchers to provide contextual information in the scenarios presented. They had noted that adolescents involved in social problem-solving programmes frequently asked for more contextual information such as 'Is he a friend?' Is he bigger than me?' Yeats and Selman (1989) point out that solving problems with a higher-status peer may require a more deferential strategy than with a lower-status peer. Caplan *et al.* (1991) propose that, for older students in particular, social-cognitive programmes need to consider giving more contextual information in the problems used. In their own study (Caplan *et al.* 1991), students between the ages of 11 and 14 demonstrated a greater degree of skilfulness when generating alternative solutions to problems with friends than with acquaintances.

Dodge *et al.* (1984), and other researchers, have proposed that one kind of social cognition which differentiates aggressive children from non-aggressive children is intention detection. Intention detection is the ability to discriminate well-intentioned behaviour and ill-intentioned behaviour and to respond accordingly. They have argued that aggressive children fail to make this differentiation, and have an attributional bias towards assigning hostile motivations to the social behaviour of others, especially when the behaviour is somewhat ambiguous. However, other studies have demonstrated that differences in intention detection are not enough to explain the differences in behaviour of the aggressive children, because withdrawn children also showed deficits in intention detection and were also more inclined than other children to attribute hostile intentions to other children's behaviour (Dodge *et al.* 1984; Sancilio *et al.* 1989). Karniol (1978) had earlier demonstrated that the evaluation of ill-intentioned acts develops at an earlier age than the evaluation of well-intentioned acts, and thus studies using younger children may have been affected by the developmental stages of the subjects.

There are many other limitations in the research on the effectiveness of SCT interventions. The most frequent criticism relates to the limited nature and lack of validity of the outcome measures used. Another frequent criticism of the research into SCT interventions is the failure of researchers to specify precise details of the interventions, and thus clarify what particular elements of the interventions may mediate positive outcomes in real-life settings (Pellegrini and Urbain 1985; Weissberg and Allen 1986). Another limitation is that long-term follow-up data has not often been collected (Pellegrini and Urbain 1985). Therefore there is very little known about whether or not the gains made as a result of SCT programmes, however tenuous, in fact maintain over time.

Weissberg and Allen (1986) claim that the quality of SCT interventions has been so varied that it is not possible to offer a simple yes–no verdict on the value of SCT training overall. Some reviews of studies of the effectiveness of social cognitive interventions are very optimistic (e.g., Urbain and Kendall 1980). Others are quite pessimistic (e.g., Durlak 1983; Michelson and Mannarino 1986). Weissberg and Gesten (1982) concluded that most SCT interventions generally had positive effects on children's ability to generate alternative solutions to hypothetical-reflective situations, but none demonstrated that acquisition of these skills alone affected the behaviour of aggressive children in naturally occurring social interactions which usually do not allow 'reflection'. The lack of evidence confirming that SCT interventions foster greater acceptance by peers has also been noted by Schneider (1993) and Gresham (1985).

Although SCT programmes appear to have only inconsistently produced gains overall, they still show potential for benefiting large numbers of children (Weissberg and Allen 1986) as they are much easier for teachers to implement in a classroom (Pellegrini and Urbain 1985). Weissberg and Gersten (1982) point out that social problem-solving training can serve as a useful bridge between the educational model in which teachers function, and the counselling/assessment model of most mental health support staff. Hops (1982) argues that social cognitive skills, even if they do not automatically predict more effective social behaviour, may be the key to ensuring that specific behavioural skills learned in other kinds of programmes generalize across settings and over time.

Social ecological interventions

La Greca (1993) argues that schools need intervention models which view low peer acceptance as a function of the interaction of the child and the social system. Schneider (1993) talks about the social ecology of the school, classroom and playground (i.e., the environment in which the child interacts socially). Social ecology can involve, for example, whether or not work is assessed competitively or co-operatively, the use of classroom meetings, and planned seating arrangements. Many previous studies have identified aspects of the social ecology of a school or classroom which could potentially inform social skills interventions. Open classroom structure appears to foster more peer interactions than more traditional formats. Epstein (1986) studied secondary classrooms, and found that in classrooms where students participated more in their learning sessions (as opposed to being more passive listeners) more students were selected as best friends, fewer were left out and there was also less evidence of small social cliques. Wright and Cowen (1982) found that in upper primary classrooms where students perceived higher order and organization and greater socialization, there were higher overall levels of acceptance of each other. On the other hand, classes where students perceived high levels of teacher control were characterized by lower levels of peer acceptance.

Programmes which attempt to change social ecology are fairly recent, and there are only a few research studies in this area, none of which has yet demonstrated that changing the social ecology of a classroom affects more direct measures of social behaviour or peer acceptance. But, as Schneider (1993) notes, it's probably a waste of time to attempt to teach children social behaviour which is not encouraged by the social ecology of the classroom and school. Many researchers (e.g., Slavin 1983) have proposed adding co-operative learning to other kinds of social skills interventions. Sapon-Shevin (1994) notes that co-operative games are particularly useful ways of fostering co-operative relationships because they represent activities with high appeal for children, and they structure the environment with specific social rules.

The use of co-operative tasks and learning experiences has probably been the most active and most well-received effort so far to restructure social ecology (Schneider 1993). De Vries and Slavin (1978) demonstrated in their study of a primary school classroom that participation in academic teams increased the number of friendships. Increased peer interactions was the outcome of the study by Bierman and Furman (1984) which focused on poorly accepted grade 5 and 6 students who participated in a series of co-operative activities such as making a video film. However, these changes had disappeared at the six-week follow-up. Strain (1981) conducted a study using socially withdrawn intellectually disabled children in an integrated grade 4 classroom. The children were involved as part of a team which tried to win prizes in a beanbag toss game. When the at-risk children were made captains, when the scores were manipulated so that their teams won prizes as a result of the at-risk child's toss, and when the at-risk child distributed the prizes, there were positive changes evident during free play observations. Negative interactions decreased, positive interactions increased, and there were positive gains in sociometric status which were still present at a four-week follow-up. It would seem that being responsible for a group's success is more potent than just being part of a successful group.

Hill (1989) has noted that structured co-operative games and tasks provide a reason for more popular children to interact with low status peers they may choose to avoid in other situations. These more popular children often discover new reasons for liking the more poorly accepted children, and become more likely to integrate them into other peer group activities. Johnson and Johnson (1986) conducted a study in which grade 4 students worked co-operatively with peers who were either learning disabled or had behaviour problems and found that as a result there were markedly increased interactions between regular students and students with disabilities during free play periods. Tryon and Keane (1991) found that rejected students were less successful in 'joining' classmates in competitive class work, suggesting that competitive situations may exacerbate the social difficulties faced by socially rejected children.

Mesch *et al.* (1986) studied the impact of co-operative academic learning over six months on five year 8 students who were identified by teacher ratings and sociometric scores as learning-disabled and socially isolated. The programme also included some direct teaching of co-operative social skills and reinforcement for using them. The researchers concluded that the programme produced high rates of appropriate social interaction with peers, and increased acceptance and liking by peers as well as higher achievement.

It is evident that social ecological interventions may be a useful addition to other interventions, but as yet the evidence is not strong, as most studies have used less than rigorous research methods. Weissberg and Allen (1986) claim that future research should attempt to determine if a classroom-based DSST intervention combined with co-operative learning would be even more effective, given Bierman and Furman's (1984) findings about the benefits of DSST in the context of group co-operation.

Combining DSST and SCT interventions

Combining various components may ultimately prove to be the most effective way of improving social competence. Marchione *et al.* (1983), believe that combining SCT and DSST approaches should lead to the most effective way. Hops (1982) argued that social cognitive skills may be the key to ensuring that specific learned behavioural skills generalize across settings and over time. Weissberg and Allen (1986) have also argued that the approaches of DSST and SCT can be merged, and on the surface it is an appealing idea. DSST interventions can provide training of the skills needed to implement the most effective kind of cognitive solutions generated with SCT procedures. They suggest teaching students how to generate solutions and consequential thinking first, then training them in how to implement the best solutions. Both DSST and SCT programmes can be packaged in highly structured and clearly outlined curricula, and this makes them attractive to teachers (Weissberg and Allen 1986).

However Gresham (1985), in his review of studies, expressed reservations about such a merger. There is some evidence to support his call for caution in regard to combining DSST and SCT components. McGrath (1996b) investigated the relative effectiveness of three different whole-class social skills programmes with all students and also with students already identified as 'at-risk' (i.e., either low in peer acceptance and/or showing social difficulties). The first programme was a DSST intervention; the second was an SCT intervention; the third was a combination of DSST and SCT components. The programmes were implemented by teachers working in consultation with a psychologist. Subjects were students in 16 grade 3 to 6 classrooms across two schools and the programmes were implemented for a whole school year. Results suggested that the most effective programme was the DSST programme, not the combined programme. The DSST programme was the only one which was effective in producing gains for all students, as well as specifically for at-risk students, on the more critical measures such as peer acceptance, rejections and peer perceptions of behaviour. It was also the only programme to produce improved teacher ratings of at-risk students' specific social behaviour.

There are two possible explanations as to why the combined programme was less effective than predicted. First, the multi-component nature of combined programmes may make them too complex for effective teacher implementation. Second, the multiple components may make the programme less focused in that it involves less direct social skills training and this may, as previous research has suggested, be the most powerful component in any social skills training programme. As well, it may be unrealistic to assume that only social cognitive training programmes focus on social cognition. Even DSST programmes indirectly teach some aspects of social cognition and so there may be some indirect development of social problem-solving.

Conclusions

Research so far suggests that significant positive changes in social behaviour and peer relationships can be made if an effective social skills intervention is used. Schneider (1993) suggests that it is probably not realistic to expect that a single given environmental variable, such as an intervention programme designed to teach social skills, will by itself have an enormous impact on a specific child's overall social experiences. He argues that 'along with the emergence of statistical procedures for meta-analysis has come a reappraisal of the importance of small effects' (1993: 11), and he includes the effects one often encounters in psychological research such as the evaluation of social skills interventions. Therefore, an effective social skills intervention may have quite a profound impact on children's well-being and behaviour, even when the documented gains are in the moderate range.

Research so far has given teachers and consultants reasons to feel cautiously optimistic about identifying the kind of social skills programme which has the greatest likelihood of producing positive changes in peer relationships and in the skill development of individual students. It is most likely to be a programme which:

- is presented to the whole class as both prevention and treatment (although some students may need more intensive small-group work as well);
- uses a focused DSST approach in which specific skills are taught one at a time in a structured way;

- includes some aspects of social cognition but does not make them the main focus. SCT interventions appear to be less effective in general and, although they improve performance in hypothetical problem-solving, they do not appear to produce corresponding changes in real-life behaviour or social reputation (Elliott and Busse 1991; Gresham 1988);
- uses co-operative learning as a context in which students can safely practise skills learned through DSST procedures.

Chapter 16

Developing a social skills programme for use in school

Colin MacMullin

Although it has been long argued that the peer group is the primary source of social learning for students, and that children learn fundamental ideas and skills such as mutuality, interpersonal sensitivity, intimacy and trust from one another (Hartup 1983), there are, none the less, a number of compelling reasons why educators should become involved in children's social learning and teach interpersonal skills in schools. Foremost among these are:

1 a belief that skills for social living deserve a central place in a modern school curriculum;
2 a view that teaching prosocial skills is a valuable proactive approach to behaviour management;
3 the greater inclusion of students with disabilities in mainstream classrooms requires that all students learn skills for working, playing and generally socializing with a wider range of peers;
4 a realization that up to 10 per cent of school aged children are without friends or, at best, have poor quality peer relationships, and that many of these students lack the skills needed for successful relationships with their peers.

For some time, there has been agreement among educators, certainly in English-speaking countries, that skills for social living have a place in the primary or elementary school curriculum.

Similarly, there is increasing recognition that teaching students social skills can make a proactive contribution to behaviour management, for an analysis of the behaviour management problems that face teachers reveals that many of these problems have at their root students with poor social skills. For example, failure to share, poorly developed skills for resolving conflicts, an inability to be assertive and inadequate listening skills can all contribute to quarrels between students that present themselves as behaviour problems for the teacher. While most schools have developed clear contingencies, or consequences for typical breeches of acceptable behaviour, a proactive approach would have us ask the question, 'what skills do these students lack?' An investment of time and effort in teaching students a range of social skills could well return dividends in time and effort saved in refereeing conflicts and administering contingencies. This is nicely illustrated in an early book by Mick Rivers (1978) *Manipulating Freedom in Groups: Two Months Hell, Ten Months Heaven,* where the efforts of teaching students co-operative work and play skills during an intensive eight-week programme at the beginning of the school year resulted in a particularly satisfying year for the teacher as he observed the success that his students experienced in their relations with one another, and with himself. The idea of teaching social skills as a proactive approach to behaviour management is also finding its way into the behaviour management textbooks (e.g., Charles 1996 and Porter 1996).

These first two reasons given above for teaching social skills at school affect all students. The third and fourth reasons are concerned with two particular groups of students: those with disabilities and those who lack friends. Whilst there is a certain measure of overlap between these two groups of students with special needs, we will look at them separately. The inclusion of students with disabilities into mainstream classes has increased substantially in recent times. This is reflected in a new generation of textbooks such as *Integration and Inclusion in Action* (Foreman 1996) and *Inclusion: A Guide for Educators* (Stainback and Stainback 1996). Central to the idea of successful inclusion are successful relationships between students, disabled and non-disabled alike. Indeed, the warning advanced by Gresham (1982), that without carefully teaching social skills to all students we are in danger of turning mainstreaming into maindumping, continues to have contemporary relevance. We cannot assume that students with disabilities and their less disabled peers will accept one another and develop relationships by just being in the same classroom. However, we can increase the likelihood of social success by helping our students develop the skills that are needed to establish and maintain these relationships. The notion of inclusion, can, of course, be broadened to encompass students in other marginalized groups such as those who may be newly arrived from abroad or members of other minority ethnic groups.

The final reason for including social skills in the school curriculum is in response to a particular group of students that transcends ethnicity, ability, or socioeconomic status. This group is comprised of the 5 to 10 per cent of our school population who are without friends (Williams and Asher 1987). For some time now, teachers and others have been concerned about these students, for they are thought to be missing out on important social learning that takes place primarily within the peer group. This includes the development of co-operation, mutual respect and interpersonal sensitivity (Hartup 1976), companionship, intimacy and affection (Furman and Buhrmester 1985), and norms, values and other information pertinent to child or adolescent life (Fine 1981). We are concerned particularly about those students who are rejected by their peers, for the literature suggests that they are at greater risk than others for social and emotional difficulties later in life (Cowen *et al.* 1973). Students without friends have also been found to be disruptive of their own learning (Kohn 1977) and the learning of others (Coie *et al.* 1982). Furthermore, and as one would expect, these students are very often lonely and unhappy with their lot (Asher *et al.* 1984).

The dominant view concerning children without friends is that of the skills deficit hypothesis (Ladd 1985) which suggests that children lack friends because they lack skills – the corollary to this being that when children are taught social skills their peer relationships improve (Bierman and Furman 1984).

Whether our desire to teach social skills stems from a belief that social skills deserve a place in the curriculum for all children, a proactive approach to behaviour management, a commitment to include students with disabilities into the mainstream, a concern for students who do not have friends, a combination of these or any other reasons, we are still left trying to answer the questions: what do we teach and how do we teach it?

The importance of the distinction between content and method in curriculum varies from writer to writer. In my own case, it was not until I made this distinction clear that I began to make real progress towards translating well-meaning aims into measurable gains in skills for my students. It is the act of explicitly stating the outcomes that are desired for students that leads one to the various methodologies available to achieve these objectives.

What do we want students to achieve?

There are a number of ways of framing this question. What should a social skills programme for a group of students set out to teach? What is it that socially skilful students do, that less skilful students fail to do? What is it that makes a difference? Posing these questions begs a further question: what do we mean by the terms 'social skills' or 'social skilfulness'? The issue of definitions of social competence will be addressed later. It is important at this stage to point out that students relate to a number of different groups of people, and while there are many generic social skills, the skills that are necessary for children to have successful relationships with their peers are often quite different to the skills necessary for successful relationships with the adults in their world. This distinction becomes important as we consider the question of curriculum content. If we are not careful, we tend to think of the kinds of skills we would like children to use in their relationships with adults, the skills that we hope they will employ in their adult lives. Such an approach would see manners and courtesies high on our lists. However, if our focus was more towards the kinds of skills students need in order to conduct successful relationships with one another, we might place less emphasis on manners *per se* and more on knowledge and use of the particular norms of the peer group.

Given the importance of peer relationships in the development of children's interpersonal sensitivity, capacity to share with and respect others and capacity for intimacy, one could think of these relationships as being the 'classroom' for social development, the principal environment for social learning. This being the case, it is even more important that teachers help the 5 to 10 per cent of school-aged children who do not have access to this 'classroom' and the important lessons that are learned in it. What are the skills that children need to employ in order to have successful relationships with one another?

Four ways of deciding on the content of a social skills programme

Common and professional sense

In the first and, I believe, final analysis teachers work from their own personal theories. They trust their common sense. Writing out a list of the skills that students need to learn in order to improve their social relationships provides a very good starting point for a curriculum. Teachers and others who work with children and youth have a great deal of knowledge about child and adolescent development, how students learn, and the social worlds in which students live. When teachers and other professionals pool their ideas, as they do in training workshops, programme planning exercises or individual student planning meetings, they are able to generate comprehensive lists of skills for students to learn.

Often, however, more work is needed with such lists in order to translate them into learning objectives and to identify appropriate teaching activities. A common challenge is to be able to operationalize general aims such as *to be co-operative or to resolve conflicts.* Here, we may need to ask questions like 'what do children (this age) do when they are being co-operative?' or 'what are the component skills that children use when they successfully resolve conflicts with one another?' A further challenge requires us to sort objectives into those that are essentially skill-based and amenable to structured teaching such as *improving listening skills,* and those such as *developing self-esteem* which are more likely to be achieved by less direct methods. Typically, the lists of curriculum content that we generate by applying our common sense to the question contain both student skills and student attitudes. Of course, most, if not all, social behaviours contain both. Take *sharing* for example. We can identify the particular skills involved in sharing, which may include one-to-one correspondence, dividing a resource into equal portions or turn taking. Further, we know many activities to teach these concepts. However, having learned the skills, how do we teach our children to *want* to share? This is possible, as we will see later.

Consulting the literature

Whilst personal theories are crucial in making decisions about teaching, it would be short-sighted of us to rely solely on our own ideas, for much has been written about the teaching of social skills. Of particular interest in answering the question '*what* should I teach?' are books that list groups of skills for inclusion in class programmes. Skills identified in the literature generally include beginning conversations, solving conflicts, group work skills and leadership skills.

Using local research

A third method to generate content for a social skills programme could involve the development of an inventory of social situations that are typically problematic for a given group of students. Here the intention is to identify the particular social situations that are problematic for a given class, group or individual and then to determine the skills that are necessary to overcome those particular challenges. This is based on the notion that social competence is situation specific (Goldfried and d'Zurilla 1969). Early work in this area was undertaken by Dodge *et al.* (1985). Later work by MacMullin (1988, 1996) saw the development of the IPSIC (Inventory of Problematic Situations for Children). This procedure has two parts: first, constructing a local inventory; second, using the inventory with a particular group or individual in order to identify the situations that challenge these students.

To construct an IPSIC it is first necessary to identify the groups that will be sampled. This is necessary because although there are many social challenges common to most groups of children, for example, teasing or coping with exclusion, the particular expressions of these problems vary according to age and setting. For example, for one group of students teasing may concern brand names of clothing; for another teasing may involve taunts about parents' employment status.

In a typical primary (or elementary) school, three versions of the instrument may be constructed: a junior version (kindergarten to year 2, or second grade), a middle school version (year 3 to 5, or third to fifth grade), and a senior school version (year 6 and 7, or sixth and seventh grade). In other schools, a version may be developed for the children in each of the particular grade levels. This is often the case in secondary schools.

Having identified the particular focus of the instrument, a decision then needs to be made whether to select a sample of that population or survey all the members of the group. A class teacher may survey the whole class, whereas a person interested in developing an IPSIC for use by all the junior classes of a large school may choose to survey one or two classes or a group of students drawn randomly from a number of classes in the school. Many schools opt to have each teacher survey all the students in his/her class. This leads to the development of highly reliable instruments as well as providing teachers with direct involvement in the process and more immediate knowledge about their own students.

In this first stage, teachers provide their students with an understanding of the terms 'social situation' and 'problem', and then ask them to help draw up a list of social situations that lead students (in this class, or grade level) to experience problems with one another. In the junior years of school, for example, a social situation may be defined as 'something that happens between people', a social problem might be 'something that happens between people and gives some upset feelings', and upset feelings may be amplified to include 'causing someone to feel angry, hurt, tearful, cross, wanting to tell the teacher or a brother or sister'. The process is made easier if teachers ask students to start each suggestion with the word 'when' – for example, 'when other kids push in front of you when you line up at the school canteen'. After enough classroom discussion to ensure that children understand the task, they may then be asked to write out their own lists, starting each new idea on a new line and remembering to start each new idea with the word 'when'. It is often helpful to tape-record or have an adult write down the suggestions of younger children and others who may have difficulty writing.

When completed, the suggestions of all of the participants are then coded for gender and grade (in the case of a sample drawn from multiple grade levels), and then pooled and sorted. The intention is to identify between 20 and 40 different situations that represent the range suggested by the children. It is important that the instrument includes situations that have been suggested by both boys and girls, and children from each year level, if applicable.

The resulting inventory would provide children with a stem question such as: When the following things happen to you, how much of a problem are they? Each situation would then be followed by a Likert scale as in the following example:

Example of items in an IPSIC

How likely would it be that this situation would lead to you having a problem with other students?

I = never, 2 = hardly ever, 3 = sometimes, 4 = usually, 5 = almost always

When people tease you because of the way you look	I	2	3	4	5
When you get blamed for something you didn't do	I	2	3	4	5
When others talk about you behind your back	I	2	3	4	5
When friends play with someone else	I	2	3	4	5

Inventories of this kind may be administered to the whole class in order to identify the kinds of situations that are typically problematic for all of the children, or for particular subgroups of children. Similarly, such an inventory may be administered to an individual child as a diagnostic instrument for individual programming purposes. Other uses include administering the IPSIC to children in a setting in order to anticipate the kinds of difficulties that newcomers are likely to experience in this particular setting. Such was the case when teachers developed and administered a version of the instrument in the first class of a senior secondary school in order to identify the kinds of social challenges that were likely to confront students who were about to enter the school from the surrounding junior high schools. This information formed the basis of a transition social skills programme. Similarly, a support teacher surveyed the tenth grade classes in a particular school in order to prepare a ninth grade student with a hearing impairment for life as a tenth grader. This led to considerable rehearsal of the skills thought to be needed for success in the new environment.

The IPSIC approach to identifying curriculum content can be used in conjunction with other approaches. This is particularly the case with social problem-solving programmes. Rather than provide students with generic problems to solve, the IPSIC may be used to identify very specific examples of problems that could then be subject to a problem-solving model such as those suggested in the next section.

A theoretical approach to content

A fourth approach to deciding what is taught in social skills programmes could derive from a theoretical perspective on social competence. One would wish students to be more socially competent, not just as a result of maturation, but as a result of being taught. If one's goal is social competence, then one needs to know what constitutes social competence. There are about as many definitions of social competence as there are writers on the subject. Dodge *et al.* (1986) cited a number of definitions in building a rationale for their model of social exchange in children. In this model, which describes a cyclical relationship between social behaviour and social information processing, Dodge and colleagues theorize that responding to specific social problems, social information processing, skilful performance of social behaviours and the judgements of others are key components of all social interactions.

A model such as Dodge's can provide guidance for curriculum design. The use of local research as outlined in the IPSIC procedure provides a focus on specific social situations that may be problematic for individual students. The skilful performance of social behaviours may be fostered through rehearsal and feedback, both features of coaching (Oden and Asher 1977), as considered in a later section. An appreciation that social competence may be 'a judgment by others that an individual has behaved competently' (McFall and Dodge 1982), leads us to seek an understanding of the other people with whom our students share their social lives and the norms that prevail in those contexts. Importantly, this approach forces us to confront the adult versus peer perspective on curriculum design.

The final feature of Dodge's model involves social information processing. An early proponent of teaching social information processing to children was Weissberg (1985). The Rochester Social Problem Solving Program (Weissberg *et al.* 1980) presented children with activities that focused on the typical steps of such models: (a) identifying feelings in self and others, (b) identifying interpersonal problems, (c) articulating feelings associated with interpersonal conflicts, (d) determining appropriate goals for problem resolution, (e) generating alternative solutions, (f) considering consequences of possible actions, (g) developing action plans and executing them.

More recent programmes that have built on the same theoretical model include 'Stop Think Do' (Petersen and Gannoni 1989) and the Sheidow Park Social Problem Solving Program (MacMullin *et al.* 1992).

In summary, four ways of answering the question of what students should be taught have been considered. These have involved (1) calling upon common sense, (2) consulting the literature, (3) conducting local research with students, (4) examining theoretical models that can guide the development of a social skills curriculum. These approaches could provide us with an extensive list of skills to teach. The next task is to address the question, how do we teach these skills? How do we teach children to share, to be assertive, to read body language, to respect each other, and to resolve conflicts? This leads to a model for teaching and learning social skills.

A model for teaching and learning social skills

A four-tier approach to teaching and learning is advocated (see Figure 16.1). The model begins with a whole-school perspective; it is argued that the values and attitudes of the school staff, the explicitly stated policies of the school and the overall tone of the school have a marked effect on the nature of the relationships between all members of the school community, including those of the students. This is powerfully supported by the work of Olweus (1993a), who reported a 50 per cent reduction of incidents of schoolyard bullying in schools that developed policies to combat this behaviour.

Helen McGrath (1996a) suggested that the socially successful school is characterized by: a separate discipline and welfare policy to deal with bullying, a commitment to the development of students' prosocial behaviour, use of a supportive discipline with a focus on the teaching of alternative behaviours and encouragement of student participation in decision-making. To this one might add: a whole-school approach to social skills curriculum, modelling and the school explicitly valuing quality interpersonal skills through policy documents and the messages that are sent to members of the school community through assemblies, newsletters and other public documents.

The second tier is the teacher/classroom level. Like the whole-school

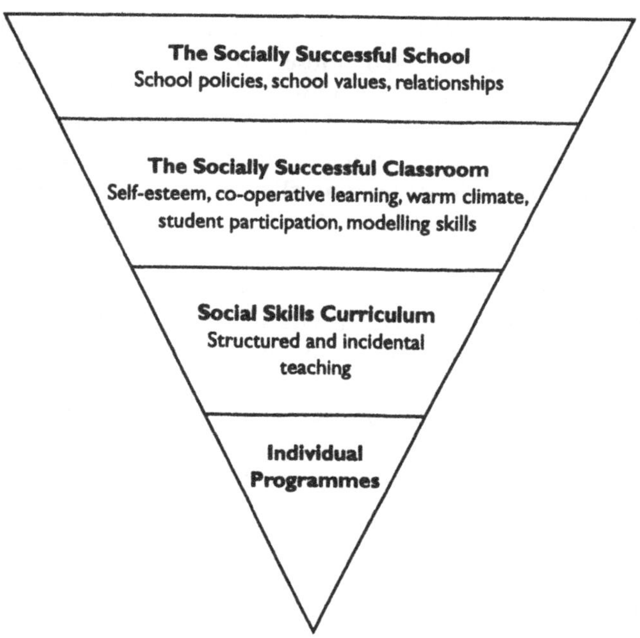

Figure 16.1 A model for developing social competence in children.
Source: Adapted from Brodie-Tyrell and Ahang (1991) and McGrath (1996a).

perspective, this is again important, for teacher attitudes and behaviour have been found to predict levels of prosocial behaviour (Wilson *et al.* 1979) and levels of acceptance and rejection amongst students in class (MacMullin 1988). This view suggests that children's social skilfulness is developed in an environment where teacher acceptance and modelling occur throughout the school day. In this environment children learn social skills by being educated in a social way. Children learn to respect one another by experiencing respect from the teacher, by observing people respecting one another, and by being made aware of the importance of respectful behaviour by a teacher who explicitly values such behaviour. In this classroom too, children learn to cooperate with one another by being taught skills for working together in groups and by being given plenty of opportunities to practise these skills.

Charles (1996) suggests that the prosocial classroom is characterized by teachers' efforts to enhance student self-esteem, a positive sense of group purpose, the use of co-operative learning, and a style of teaching that produces good results both academically and socially. In her list, McGrath (1996a) adds that prosocial teachers acknowledge the significance of prosocial competencies in students' lives, look for opportunities to teach prosocial skills incidentally, merge prosocial skills with the rest of their teaching, and analyse their own social behaviour and endeavour to improve it in the interests of acting as a role model. Further, McGrath suggests that the socially successful classroom is characterized by co-operative learning, the presence of prosocial rules, an emphasis on discussions so that respecting and expressing opinions appropriately is practised, the encouragement of risk taking, and an emphasis on the expression of warmth and affection.

The third tier of the teaching model involves the explicit curriculum. Here it is suggested that many of the skills identified in the first part of this chapter can be taught through lessons and structured activities. These lessons could well be integrated with other parts of the curriculum and included within subjects such as language arts, drama or health education. Alternatively, students may be provided with blocks of teaching under the heading of social skills, interpersonal relationships or the like. Here students may follow a set curriculum such as the Sheidow Park Social Problem Solving Program (MacMullin *et al.* 1992) or Stop, Think, Do (Petersen and Gannoni 1989) or progress through a curriculum developed at the school or class level. Whatever the case, the important features of this particular tier involve explicit teaching over a period of time, the pursuit of specific skill objectives, and opportunities for rehearsal and feedback. An amalgamation of cognitive problem-solving and coaching methods is suggested. The components of typical cognitive problem-solving curricula are listed above. To these may be added some of the features of the coaching approach of Oden and Asher (1977). These include the provision of general instructions about social interactions, having children generate specific examples, getting children to practise skills and monitor their own behaviour, and, finally, having children and teachers review progress after play or interaction sessions.

The fourth tier of the teaching and learning model involves specific teaching with individual students. Even with the most supportive of schools, classrooms and teachers, and the best use of a whole-class curriculum, there are still going to be individual students who will, from time to time, need more specific help in the development of their particular social skills. Individual programmes in social skills would involve identifying the particular situations that challenge the individual and the skills that are necessary for success in those situations. It is assumed that the student would contribute to the goal-setting process, for it is likely that a number of skills may need developing, and the student's preferences would be important.

While objectives may be devised for individual students and pursued with a teacher or counsellor, it is not always necessary to think of such teaching as being conducted on a one-to-one basis. Often programmes for individuals are best delivered within a whole-class format or by using a small group. One particular programme which set out to help a student learn how to cope with the disappointments inherent in a game of hand tennis at play-time involved a support worker initiating a new game with the student and inviting nearby children to join the game if they wished. Soon, there were four children on the hand tennis court and another three or four waiting in line for their turn in the game. The support worker was able to quietly point out to the student in question the ways in which each child accepted the inevitable disappointment of being dismissed from the court when declared 'out' by the other children. The programme involved the teacher assisting the children rehearse aloud self-talk to accompany the acceptance of being declared 'out'. She also modelled ways in which the children could extend condolences to one another and praise each other for accepting defeat in good grace. Soon this behaviour was being adopted by the children themselves. Over a number of play-times, the targeted child gradually achieved the objectives of the programme. Of course, the aim of any intervention of this kind is to help the individual student without drawing undue attention to him or her.

As can be seen from Figure 16.1, the bias in this model is to move towards the whole school and whole class tiers as much as possible. However, it is clear that action needs to be taken at each level.

Summary

This chapter has proposed that we address three questions in developing social skills programmes for school. We must first be clear about why we want to teach social skills in order to strengthen our personal resolve and marshal our arguments for use with others who may affect our success. Second, we need to be quite clear about what it is we want students to learn. What will be the learning outcomes for them? Finally, armed with strong reasons for wanting to teach social skills and a list of skills that we want our students to develop, we need to ask ourselves what are the best methods to bring about the development of these skills. The key to this can be seen in the term 'teaching and learning'. Some of the skills on the list are likely to be developed as a result of what we teach and how we do it, others are likely to be developed by the ways we construct the environment and relationships at school. We can *teach* skills such as those involved in active listening and we can provide the kind of environment in which children *learn* to respect themselves and others. In the end, however, the greatest gains in the acquisition of children's social skills will come from their participation in relationships with their peers. The role that adults play is important, but it's only part of the picture.

Chapter 17

Pride, shame and empathy among peers

Community conferencing as transformative justice in education

David B. Moore

Introduction

An earlier version of this chapter was presented to the Adelaide Children's Peer Relations conference in January 1994. At the time I was evaluating a juvenile justice reform programme in the Australian state of New South Wales. That programme centred on a process called the 'family group conference'. It was suggested to the Adelaide conference that this process might also be used in programmes of school behaviour management, particularly as a response to bullying. Within a year, that suggestion had been put into practice, and a large pilot programme was under way. The first training programme in North America was begun in 1995. By the end of 1996, many hundreds of educators had been trained to convene the process described in this chapter.

Accordingly, this revised version of the paper includes new information on the practice of what we now prefer to call 'community conferencing'. Some of the more general theoretical issues have been dealt with less extensively. However, the basic structure of the original paper has been retained. The contemporary police response when young people victimize others is compared to the response of schools. Community conferencing is then presented as an alternative response. This raises institutional questions. But it also raises deeper questions concerning social theory, questions such as whether there is an innate moral sense, and how sympathy and empathy are best explained. Some interdisciplinary answers are proposed. This theoretical debate ultimately returns to the practical question of how interventions seeking to engage both the head and the heart – whether in schools, justice systems or elsewhere – can be effective and appropriate in fair and democratic societies. More practically yet, in the school setting, the question can be posed in this way: when there is conflict between peers, how can we deal with that conflict in such a way that it is neither simply amplified, nor simply ignored, but is instead transformed?

Institutional questions

The development of compulsory school education and separate juvenile justice systems during the nineteenth century increased state responsibility for the social and moral development of children. These responsibilities of police and educators continue to overlap. Policing extends to education and welfare, while educators are involved in a form of 'social regulation'. The overlap is illustrated by school-based programmes in which police attempt to foster 'awareness' of one sort or another. Nevertheless, there is a fairly clear formal division of labour: schools deal with much of the good side of childhood and adolescence; police tend to deal with some of the bad sides.

How do police currently deal with victimization by young people?

Police have a range of options for dealing with young people whose actions have victimized others. Police attract criticism regardless of which option they choose, since the diversity of options reflects unresolved tension within juvenile justice between philosophies of welfare and of just deserts (Seymour 1988). The police approach is invariably seen as too soft by some, too harsh by others. Generally, the safest option is to pass the problem on to another department as quickly as possible. This strategy has the advantage of minimizing individual and collective exposure to criticism. Minor infringements of the law continue to be dealt with by way of the traditional police caution or some variation on that theme. The seriousness of the offence is determined largely on technical or procedural grounds; matters deemed more serious are dealt with by way of summons, court attendance notice, or charge. If the victims of offending behaviour are dissatisfied with a subsequent children's court judgment, police can reply that they have done all they can and that victims' anger should be directed at the courts. It often is. When that anger is given media exposure, schools tend to be criticized for their approach to behaviour management and ethics.

How do schools currently deal with victimization?

'Bullying' is used as a generic term for victimization in schools, and it is a significant problem. It harms individuals and it harms school communities generally. Definitions of bullying emphasize a consistent pattern of behaviour and an imbalance of power. Bullying may include verbal or psychological harm in addition to physical harm (Besag 1989; Roland and Munthe 1989; Smith and Thompson 1991; Olweus 1993b). It can involve school staff (as perpetrators and as victims).

Where a problem of bullying appears insoluble, one school may pass the problem on to another by excluding the offending student. In severe cases, schools delegate the problem to police and have offenders charged. In most cases, however, bullying needs to be addressed within the school environment. The traditional in-school response to bullying behaviour by students has been similar to the broader societal response: individual aggression is met with the institutional aggression of official punishment. But growing unease with institutional aggression in schools has prompted the search for alternatives.

Teaching staff are now exhorted to take a 'whole-school' or systemic approach to behaviour management. More formal teaching of ethical values in schools has been suggested, including targeting and reinforcing appropriate social behaviour (Glynn 1992). Effective techniques for responding to school bullying have in common that they attempt to provoke 'hot cognitions', so that an offender not only 'sees' but also 'feels' things from the other's point of view (Pikas 1989b). These approaches all seek to move away from traditional methods of punishment towards enforced self-regulation.

What do these approaches have in common?

In the final analysis, regardless of what environmental factors have been brought to bear, young people who bully their peers at school or victimize their fellow citizens with illegal acts all have one thing in common: their behaviour indicates a lack of empathy for another person's plight. Lack of empathy does not explain the *motivation to* victimize, but it is the common factor behind the *failure not to* victimize another person. The argument that young offenders are themselves victims under other circumstances, as is indeed frequently the case, is an argument that often confuses explanation with justification or condonation. It often has the effect of denying young people status as members of a moral community. Young people need to be encouraged to understand and adhere to basic rules of reciprocity and justice, not simply excused for failing to understand and adhere to them.

If a lack of empathy is the common factor in diverse acts of victimization, practical responses to victimizing behaviour likewise all have one factor in common. All are predicated – consciously or otherwise – on an answer to this question: what promotes or inhibits the development of empathy and an understanding of justice, whether in the family, school, peer group or justice system? Practical responses to this question often seek to send a message to other potential offenders. The idea is that present punishment should deter future offending. But the immediate aim of punishment is to make an impression on the offender in question. This consequentialist approach looks to the past and the future. It looks backward to the offence, believing punishment must be applied on behalf of the victim. And it looks forward, believing that the offender can learn from the experience. But this is not enough. In a genuinely just and democratic society, responses to harmful behaviour should also encourage community control, self-regulation and self-discipline over institutional control and the imposition of official punishment. Community conferencing offers one effective alternative to official control and punishment.

An alternative process

A community conference involves the perpetrator(s) of an offence and the victim(s) of that offence, together with families and friends of victims and offenders. The convener encourages participants to achieve several aims. One aim is that victims of offending behaviour participate in the official response to that behaviour. Another aim is that offenders understand the consequences of their actions. Yet another is that the broader community of people who have been adversely affected contribute to any final agreement. In practice, these aims cannot be separated. Involving a broader community encourages and supports the involvement of victims; both of these factors help young offenders to understand the ramifications of their actions. The ultimate goal is to repair the damage caused by victimizing behaviour, and to minimize (ongoing) individual and collective harm. Agreements usually involve appropriate restitution and reparation. Though formally agreed to, these agreements are not legally binding.

Community conferencing was adopted and adapted from New Zealand, where it is still called the 'family group conference'. The Maori term 'whanau', from which the English language title of the process is derived, has a much broader meaning than the English word 'family'. Furthermore, the process encourages communities to take responsibility for their own regulation. In making communities accountable, it appears to strengthen them. For these reasons, we prefer the phrase 'community conference'.

Community conferences increase the likelihood that victims will receive reparation for material damage. More importantly, participating in the response to the offending behaviour helps victims deal with their own anger, shame and resentment, and thus helps achieve symbolic or psychological reparation. The emotional dynamics of this process are complex and yet remarkably consistent. In essence, the negative emotions generated by the incident in question are openly expressed in the conference but are then gradually transformed into something positive.

Conference dynamics have been described in detail elsewhere (see Moore 1993; Braithwaite and Mugford 1994; Moore and Forsythe 1995). It is important to recognize that this approach exemplifies a third approach to conflict. Conflict is not simply being amplified, as occurs in authoritarian approaches to behaviour management. But nor is conflict being avoided, as occurs in permissive approaches. Rather, conflict is being acknowledged and transformed.

Such claims may seem implausible. Critics have, from the outset, insisted that conferencing simply won't work with some individuals. The evidence suggests otherwise. But this is the point at which institutional questions of where and how to employ community conferences give way to deeper questions about why the process does work with all-too-human participants.

Theoretical questions

Why are most people not selfishly exploitative most of the time?

When the family group conference was first considered in New South Wales for application in juvenile justice, proponents linked it with the 'theory of reintegrative shaming'. The theory was contained in John Braithwaite's book, *Crime, Shame, and Reintegration* (1989), which appeared around the same time as a number of other general theories of crime and legal compliance (e.g., Gottfredson and Hirschi 1990; Tyler 1990). Braithwaite sought to explain why most people obey the law most of the time. This formula inverts the traditional concerns of criminology. The so-called 'classical school' of criminology sought to explain why some people break the law. Their answer was that offenders generally weighed the advantages and disadvantages of committing an offence. If the advantages of offending – such as pleasure or wealth – outweighed the disadvantages – such as pain or loss of liberty – then the decision was taken to offend. The logical official response was to devise tougher sanctions.

Critics of classical criminology also asked why some people break the law, but they arrived at different answers. One school suggested that some people were born into criminality, predestined by their genetic inheritance. Variations included psychological or social determinism: people were driven to criminality by their psychological profile or by socio-economic circumstances. These theories likewise had policy implications: if the ultimate cause of criminal behaviour was beyond the control of the individual, punishment as an end-in-itself was inappropriate (see Torrey 1992: ch. 7).

Modern criminal justice practices have been influenced by all of these theories. But recent attempts to deal with some of their more obvious flaws have reversed the basic question about victimization and law-breaking. The focus has shifted from transgression to compliance. A better understanding of why most people abide by the law, why most people have some empathy for their fellows most of the time, may lead to better ways of responding to those who do victimize others. *Crime, Shame, and Reintegration* suggests that most people obey the law less because they fear formal penalties, and more for two reasons of greater personal significance. They obey the law, first, because their own conscience tells them to; to break a just law would violate their idea of themselves as moral agents. Second, most people obey the law because they fear disgrace in the eyes of the people who matter to them.

The phenomenon that links these two factors of private conscience and public disgrace is the feeling of shame, which is an important regulator of social life. The person whose inappropriate behaviour is subject to public exposure may be said to have experienced 'disgrace shame' (Schneider 1977). Conversely, a person deterred by the threat of disgrace from completing an action they had been contemplating has shown discretion. They may be said to have experienced 'discretion shame'. Thus, disgrace shame and discretion shame can be distinguished as two conscious experiences of shame. The public experience of disgrace shame is clearly unpleasant. The feeling of discretion shame is generally less unpleasant. It is a private means of intuiting what is publicly appropriate, an internal reminder of one's bonds with others that works to 'negate the spurious attraction of the immanent material reward' for committing an offence (Frank 1988: 82). People who are regularly reminded of their bonds with relatives, friends and colleagues should be able to avoid the more painful feeling of disgrace shame that is evoked by inappropriate behaviour. In short, discretion shame helps people to avoid disgrace.

Contemporary criminal justice systems have few mechanisms by which to foster an offender's ability to feel discretion shame, few mechanisms to strengthen bonds between offenders and their supporters. Instead, modern criminal justice systems seek to punish offenders by means of a 'ceremony of degradation', stigmatizing them, setting them apart from the community (Garfinkel 1956). Offenders may be set apart symbolically, through public denunciation, and quite literally, in detention centres and prisons. This public rejection is part of the punishment. Where an offender represents an immediate physical threat to other citizens, the physical removal of the offender serves to ensure the safety of others. But severing an offender's links with the community otherwise makes little sense. Social links need to be strengthened, not severed. New links need to be nurtured. These processes can begin in a 'ceremony of reintegration'.

A ceremony of reintegration makes a clear distinction between unacceptable behaviour, on the one hand, and the person responsible for that behaviour, on the other. The offender should feel guilt for the violation of rules, but shame for lowering their own moral status and that of the people close to them. This is an important distinction: shame is vicarious, guilt is not. Thus, people associated with the offender feel ashamed, though they are in no way culpable. A politico-legal system that assumes atomistic individuals as its subjects will focus solely on guilt (Moore 1993). A more mature polity will recognize the reality and importance of bonds between people, while guaranteeing individual rights. The community conference offers to do both. Dealing with both individual guilt and collective shame, it is an holistic approach that values individuals (Pettit 1993).

Having expressed remorse, and having accepted responsibility for their offending actions, a person may be forgiven and gradually accepted back into the community. They are offered a chance to regain the trust lost as a result of their actions. This is the basic pattern of a ceremony of reintegration: shame and remorse for the act are followed by reacceptance or social reintegration of the person who committed the act.

Of course, such ceremonies occur daily in informal settings. Children are shamed by their parents for inappropriate behaviour, and then accepted again moments later with some appropriate gesture. Relatives, friends, and colleagues offer apologies and forgiveness on a small scale and on a daily basis. Social life is regulated in this way. Having made mistakes and misjudgements, people are given an opportunity to learn from these. The boundaries between acceptable and unacceptable behaviour are drawn and redrawn, and are made explicit in cases where they had been misjudged. And yet, formal responses to offending behaviour use the opposite strategy, valuing stigmatizing punishment for its own sake and administering it according to a utilitarian formula of just deserts.

If ceremonies of reintegration succeed daily in informal settings, might they not also be formally adopted by officials of educational and justice systems? This is precisely how the family group conference came to be adopted in New Zealand, and this is the way it was interpreted in Wagga and then in other parts of Australia. But before the process of reintegrative shaming came to be applied in schools and other institutions, more needed to be said about the psychological mechanisms at work in the process. In particular, more needed to be said about what shame *is*, rather than what it does. And this has touched on a fundamental debate of modern humanities and social sciences: the relation of nature to nurture.

Is there an innate moral sense?

We have distinguished discretion shame from disgrace shame. The sort of incidents that invoke disgrace and warrant discretion vary over time, and differ from one culture to another (Elias 1982 [1939]; Schwartz *et al.* 1992). So it is clear that the expression of shame is determined in part by culture. But is shame entirely determined by culture, all nurture rather than nature?

Debates about the relative influence of inherited and acquired characteristics tend to be strongly influenced by ideological conviction. For much of this century, the Standard Social Science Model of psychology, sociology, and anthropology has argued for the dominance of nurture over nature, at times virtually banishing innate capacities from the picture. The key political reason for this is that misinterpretations of evolutionary theory have been used to justify eugenics, racism and reaction (Alexander 1987; Richards 1987; Degler 1991).

Unlike 'Social Darwinists', however, modern researchers are not looking for differences between members of different ethnic groups. Rather, they are concerned with fundamental similarities between all people (Brown 1991). And one of their central questions is of great relevance to ethics: how to account for sympathy, empathy and altruism. Theories that explain behaviour in terms of reason alone, and which assume crude self-interest, cannot account for selfless sentiments and 'irrational' altruism. And yet a better explanation for selflessness would be of great value by helping us to understand its opposite: selfish, antisocial behaviour.

The eighteenth-century British moralists addressed these questions, and produced answers very close to those proposed by contemporary social theorists (Pritchard 1991; Wilson 1993). All were concerned with the extent to which innate passions or sentiments provided the basis for morality. Hume's account is the best known (Wispé 1991). Hume remained convinced that sympathy for others was innate. Adam Smith (cited in Wispé 1991) followed this line in his theory of morality, which informed his better known economic theory. Smith called an inborn concern for others 'extensive sympathy'. He considered it to be based in passion rather than reason, and thus independent of any ethical system designed by philosophers. But sympathy was of itself not sufficiently powerful to act as the 'cement of society'. Something more was required: an adequate ethical system would combine subjective passion with the objective judgement of an impartial observer. Smith's resultant picture of the social self explained how 'self-awareness and self-control were systematically transformed into social awareness and societal control' (Wispé 1991: 18). A learned understanding of justice would complement inborn sympathy.

Darwin took these ideas further, approaching the 'great question' of the origins of morality 'exclusively from the side of natural history' (Darwin 1871: 71). He disputed an increasingly popular utilitarian assumption that people were motivated according to a rational calculus of pleasure and pain. The 'social instincts', according to Darwin, predispose a person to seek approbation and to avoid disapproval. Social instincts, more than rational calculations of pleasure and pain, explain basic human motivation.

This sounds similar to Braithwaite's more recently proposed theory of reintegrative shaming, and indeed it is – though reached by a quite different path. And other disciplines are reaching similar conclusions. Political scientists, economists, and anthropologists have followed the lead of cognitive theory and ethology and are looking to biology to help provide explanations for social phenomena such as sympathy and altruism (e.g., Axelrod 1984; Frank 1988; Schwartz et al. 1992; Barkow *et al.* 1992; Wilson 1993; Wright 1994). The resulting interdisciplinary model should give a more accurate picture of social interaction than is provided by a model of crude self-interest.

A general consensus in much of this interdisciplinary work is that people are born with a set of innate capacities which are then drawn out by learning and experience. The environment operates on a set of capacities and specialist sub-systems, some of which are remarkably flexible, others of which are firmly fixed (Konner 1982; Donald 1991; Gazzaniga 1992). With regard to questions concerning sympathy and empathy, interdisciplinary approaches have found that apparently selfless behaviour can confer long-term advantages. A reputation for trustworthiness and generosity brings advantages in repeated interactions, advantages that may not be evident in the short term. Sympathy and empathy enable us to assess another person's trustworthiness and generosity. This model understands people as 'opportunistic seekers of cooperation' (*Economist* 1994: 93). Where purely rational calculations of short-term interest would not produce sympathy or altruism, 'specific emotions act as commitment devices', helping resolve those 'important problems that simply cannot be solved by rational action' (Frank 1988: 5). Though socialization and education influence the expression of sympathy, empathy, and other such 'commitment devices', the capacity to experience these is innate. A ceremony of reintegrative shaming draws attention to 'commitment devices' and the bonds between people that are regulated by these. Thus, explaining what is really happening in such a ceremony requires a persuasive account of 'commitment devices'. But that, in turn, requires a substantive psychology of emotions.

Affect theory

A psychological theory that complements Braithwaite's theory of reintegrative shaming was first proposed some four decades ago. 'Affect Theory' was developed by philosopher and psychologist Silvan Tomkins in response to obvious flaws in major modern schools of psychological thought. Each school overemphasized one aspect of human psychology: psychoanalysis emphasized motivation at the expense of cognition and motor learning; behaviourism emphasized motor learning at the expense of cognition and motivation; Piaget and his followers emphasized cognition at the expense of motivation, and so on (Tomkins 1991: ch. 2).

This is not just a theoretical dispute. Practice in both educational and justice systems develops on the basis of reigning theories of human psychology. Utilitarian and behaviourist views remain influential, as does Freud's psychology, in which a person's libidinal drives struggle against cultural constraints. Piaget's psychology, which has significantly influenced educationalists, follows a major stream of Western philosophy in accepting that reason tames emotional demands as children become adults. In this model, motivation becomes subordinate to cognition in accordance with the Cartesian creed: 'I think, therefore I am.'

As Tomkins saw it, however, emotion continues to play an important, often dominant, role through adult life. Thus, in the first instance: 'I feel therefore I am.' Though hardly new, this position was academically unfashionable when Tomkins proposed it in psychology. However, modern neurological evidence supported Darwin's hypothesis of an innate human emotional repertoire. At the risk of obfuscation through oversimplification, the theory can be summarized as follows (see Nathanson 1987, 1992).

Affects are preprogrammed experiences that amplify changes in the internal or external environment. They register, in particular, as the facial and bodily gestures readily observable in infants. These are not secondary phenomena arising from the motor, drive or cognitive systems. Rather, they are the primary phenomena of an autonomous system that provides blueprints for all of these other systems. Affects are defined by a single principle: the density of neural firing. Three affects are associated with an increase in the density of neural firing: interest-excitement is triggered by a gradual increase in stimulus density; fear-terror is triggered by a rapid increase; and surprise-startle is triggered by a sudden increase. Hence the familiar liminal experiences in which excitement verges on fear, or the facial expression of terror verges on the blank mask of the startle.

Two affects are associated with a constant level of stimulus density: distress-anxiety is triggered by low level constant density and anger-rage by high level. Hence, the association between stress and quickness to anger. Enjoyment, or contentment, in its various forms is the only affect associated with decrease in stimulus density. It is evoked regardless of whether the previous stimulus was negative or positive, whether it was pain, fear, distress, anger or excitement. This is why 'relaxation' and 'enjoyment' are almost synonymous.

In addition to interest, fear, surprise, distress, anger and enjoyment, Tomkins counted a further three affects, making a total of nine. However, these last three are more accurately described as auxiliaries to the drive and affect systems. Disgust and 'dissmell' (a negative response to the bad-smelling) act as brakes on the drives to ingest food, imbibe fluid and inhale air. Hence they are classed as 'drive auxiliaries'. They protect the organism from the biologically poisonous. However, disgust and 'dissmell' are also used by primates for symbolic, affective display. The most significant example of this is the phenomenon of contempt, which affect theory defines as a learned combination of anger (the most toxic affect) and 'dissmell' (the most toxic drive auxiliary). The object of contempt does not necessarily literally smell bad, but the corresponding expression, in combination with the expression of anger, is used to convey individuation and hatred.

Whereas disgust and 'dissmell' act as brakes on the drives to ingest, inhale and imbibe, shame acts as a brake on the positive affects. Shame is associated with any sudden impediment to interest and joy (Tomkins 1963: 123). Hence shame is classed as an 'affect auxiliary'. The evolution of shame as a protection against the *socially* poisonous is analogous to the much earlier evolution of disgust and dissmell as a protection against the *biologically* poisonous.

To remedy the lack of general agreement about the terminology concerning affects and related states, psychologists such as Basch (1988) have proposed the following definitions: *Affects* are 'hard-wired' physiological experiences. *Feelings* occur as one becomes conscious of the experiencing of any affect. Feelings may be reasonably complex, combining various affects registered with varying intensity. *Emotions* are generated when feelings evoke memories of related experiences from the past. Emotions place feelings in biographical context, and so are yet more powerful and complex than feelings. If the process by which present feelings evoke past feelings continues over hours, or even days, then the original affect is no longer registered as a simple feeling, nor just as the combination of past and present feelings that we are calling emotion. The original affect has been transformed into a *mood*. Thus, a single incident or series of incidents prompting the affect and feeling of enjoyment might, in turn, gradually bring on an enduring mood of happiness.

In the complex transition from affects to feelings to emotions to moods, a person generates 'scripts' about who they are and how they should feel about, think of and act in the world. (Significant interdisciplinary contributions to this complex field include: Tomkins 1987; Conway 1990; Edelman 1992; Middleton and Edwards 1990; Modell 1990; Shank 1990; Singer and Salovey 1993). Whether scripts are (re)written consciously or not, the physical sensation is an essential component. Again: 'I feel, therefore I am' is closer to the essence of the process than 'I think, therefore I am.'

According to Tomkins (1963: 5), motivation appears subordinate to cognition in adulthood only because 'a substantial quantity of the affect we experience as adults is pseudo, backed-up affect'. But the parameters within which our various goals are pursued as adults tend to be delineated by habits formed much earlier. The formation of habits, preferences and beliefs involves committing emotionally significant events to memory in the process of long-term potentiation (Winson 1985). So 'there is nothing in long-term memory that was not first in the emotions' (Fox 1989: 182). And there is nothing in the emotions that was not first affect.

Far from transcending affect and emotion then, people work within a set of habits, preferences and beliefs that are built on affective experience. Furthermore, although 'pseudo-affect' becomes more common than the real thing as one matures, raw affect can still rule adult, and certainly adolescent, life under certain circumstances. People sometimes become so 'emotional' that they no longer appear 'rational'. Ingested chemicals can produce this result, but so can any event that recalls powerful feelings, triggering the affects experienced at the time of the original incident. Whatever the source, a person engulfed by affects such as anger, fear or distress, may 'lose control'. Their subsequent actions may bring them into contact with disciplinary systems that cannot account well for, or respond effectively to, such behaviour. As a theorist of the psychology of justice has lamented, 'the psychological study of the powerful emotions, and the impulsive actions unleashed by them, [has been] much neglected so far' (Scherer 1992: 14). Powerful negative emotions certainly appear to override sympathy and empathy for others. Feelings that normally encourage people to see things from another's point of view seem to be blocked by affects of anger-rage or disgust.

How, then, are sympathy and empathy described in terms of this model of the affect system? Sympathy is defined as feeling another person's distress, and can thus be understood as transferred affect. Empathy is the mechanism by which this transfer occurs. Empathy enables a person to share the distress, anger, or excitement of another. It is the mechanism by which affects are communicated. Nathanson describes how infants 'broadcast' affect such that all those around them are influenced (Nathanson 1992). Basch calls this observers' response 'empathic resonance' (Basch 1988). And there is certainly no mistaking unmediated affect. It is contagious. Observers feel themselves compelled, for instance, to share an infant's distress or joy.

The concept of empathic resonance seems to capture precisely the powerful experience of shared emotions that has been regularly observed in community conferences. It also helps explain why conferences are such powerful learning experiences. This is learning that takes place with the heart as well as the head. People are experiencing real affects, not pseudo-affect, nor the 'sober rationality' of castigation delivered to offenders under current arrangements in criminal justice and other regulatory systems.

But can this theory account for those few people who display little affect and emotion, and who seem incapable of empathy? Why do they apparently feel no shame for the trauma they have caused others? Such appearances may be deceptive. The impulsive, apparently irrational actions of school bullies or recidivist offenders appear best explained not in terms of the absence of shame but, rather, in terms of scripts learned in response to an excess of shame. This distinction requires further examination of the function of shame.

The affect auxiliary of shame

As Darwin (1969 [1872]) observed, shame appears to be expressed only by the higher mammals. Affect theory understands shame as a brake on the two positive affects of interest and enjoyment. Shame is activated whenever physical or social limits are reached or exceeded, when desire has outrun fulfilment, suddenly impeding interest and/or enjoyment (Tomkins 1963: 123). The associated sudden negative evaluation of the self helps to define personal limits. Shame thus has an important protective or restraining function, and plays a key role in developing a sense of self.

Developmental psychology recognizes that children develop a sense of self much earlier than was once thought, and so it is now easier to accept Tomkins's claim that the infant trying and failing to walk displays a basic shame response (see Donaldson 1992: ch. 3). The physiological experience is essentially the same as that felt by the adolescent who has breached some code of social etiquette. Feelings and emotions experienced in these circumstances will vary because of differences in context and experience, but the essential physiology, the affect of shame, is the same.

Feelings of shame are normally counterbalanced, if not exceeded by, feelings of pride. Personal development proceeds as a dialectic between shame and pride, between experiences of failure and of success. During the general emotional turbulence of late childhood and adolescence, however, there is a danger that temporary but regular shameful experiences, if not counter-balanced by sources of pride, may develop from feelings into emotions and thence into a lasting mood of shame. (Hence the concern of educators to foster what is most commonly called 'self-esteem'.)

Excessive exposure to shame may prompt counteraction, in posture, facial expression, and behaviour. Chronic shame may manifest in impulsive, initially inexplicable, irrational actions and in subtler physical expressions. Indeed, there are several classes of scripted responses to shame. Nathanson (1992) identifies these as four points on a 'compass of shame'. First, a person may withdraw from threatening situations and relationships. Second, they may avoid shame through aggressive acquisition of trophies (such as cars or cash), or competencies (such as bigger biceps or qualifications). (Shame avoidance in moderation is not necessarily problematic. Shame may be avoided by any process that involves setting and achieving goals: interest in the pursuit of goals is followed by enjoyment at their achievement. Multiple sequences of interest and enjoyment produce pride, which counteracts shame.)

The third response to shame is to attack oneself, a noted example of which is anorexia. The fourth response is to attack others. Thus, a person may defend against shame by learning to trigger rage. This learning process involves brutalization over a long period, at the end of which the victim of brutalization has become an unpredictable and dangerous offender who may take pride in violence (Athens 1989). This only occurs in extreme cases. Even among those few young offenders who apparently seem driven to offend again, virulent aggression is rare. But in nearly all of these cases of repeat offending, shame seems to be at the core of the problem.

Surely, then, a process that evokes shame can only do further harm? Critics might readily concede that shaming followed by reintegration can work for most offenders, whose actions may have been motivated by interest, enjoyment, anger or distress, which in turn overrode any sympathy for their victim(s). For this majority of offenders, who make a serious mistake and who deserve an opportunity to learn from that mistake, the process of reintegrative shaming should be beneficial. It should foster enough discretion shame to thwart further victimization. But for those suffering chronic shame, things must be different.

Yes, things *are* different for people suffering chronic shame. But in those cases where a victim has eventually 'got through' to an initially impassive or defiant young offender, the community conference appears not to be harmful. Indeed, it may offer the best hope to that minority of offenders whose demeanour and behaviour indicate chronic shame. If personal development and successful interaction with others are indeed only possible through the dialectic of pride and shame, then a person in a state of chronic shame is closed to relational and personal development, cut off not only from their own emotions but also from those of others. Only when chronic shame is made manifest can the 'psychic numbing' be undone. Some process is required to restore the emotional link of empathy, to move beyond the blank stare and the look of contempt generated as the chin is thrust forward in defence against chronic shame. When prompted in a community conference to give their version of events, people fitting this description are often unable to explain their motivation. Yet, when questioned further, they describe a trigger for their shame and rage, some incident which everyone present but themselves recognizes as a trigger. They then describe their actions with a curious tinge of pride. This need reflect no particular contempt for the victim, since shame and rage need no object.

Nathanson describes the revelatory experience of patients in psychotherapy being 'pulled out of humiliation' through the forging of emotional links with another person. Community conferences achieve a similar outcome through different means. In a climate of unusually strong empathic resonance, where a clear distinction has been made between the offending behaviour and the person who committed it, where family and other community members are present, and where shame is displayed by the other participants, shame becomes conscious. Affect becomes feeling, and participants experience a superficially paradoxical lesson: one need not be ashamed of shame.

This lesson is not only valuable for offenders. Victims, humiliated by their experience of victimization, regularly experience relief from excessive shame only moments after they become most conscious of it. The expression of shame by an offender's family members and friends, and by victims, signals the possibility of reacceptance and forgiveness. A visible sense of relief follows for victims and offenders. This is the turning point in a ceremony of reintegration.

Again, it must be emphasized that the community conference process is designed neither to amplify nor to ignore conflict, but to transform it. Thus, a community conference should quite emphatically not be a process whereby punishment is meted out on an individual by officialdom – in this case the school. Nor should a conference involve some other sort of treatment being meted out by officialdom on an individual, nor yet should it involve punishment or therapy being imposed on an individual by a collectivity on behalf of officialdom.

Rather, the community conference should allow a group of people, affected by conflict generated when one party wronged another, to tell the story of what happened, understand the consequences, and in doing so, express and share emotions, such that the ratio of negative to positive emotion is gradually transformed. When this emotional transformation reaches the point where participants feel themselves to be a single community faced with a shared problem, they can begin to work together to repair the damage and minimize further harm. A process of emotional transformation allows for transformation at the level of interpersonal relationships. Social reintegration can begin at this point.

Reintegration involves emotions of self-assessment, such as pride and guilt, and emotions that govern relations between people, such as sympathy, love, or hate. These emotions may be complex constructs, but the affective repertoire on which they are built is universal. For instance, sources of guilt have changed over time and differ between cultures, since guilt concerns the breaking of rules, and cultural rules vary enormously (see Stein and Oatley 1992; Schwartz *et al.* 1992). But the feeling of guilt involves the affect of shame, an experience which is universally recognized (Izard 1991). To see shame as bad is to blame the messenger. Like the other innate affects, shame is neither inherently good nor bad. It is 'negative' in that people seek to avoid it, but circumstances determine whether its personal and social effects are good or bad. If systems involving the unjust use of power burden people with shame, then the system is the problem. Shame is a symptom.

Just as there are optimum levels of stress at which people perform best, so it might be said that there are optimum levels at which shame is triggered. Being too easily shamed is debilitating, but feeling no shame can be dangerous. So shame performs an important function as part of the 'intangible hand' regulating social relations (Pettit 1993). Institutional arrangements should take this intangible hand into account. Well-designed institutions should favour the intangible hand of self-regulation over the command-and-control model.

The dialectic of shame and pride guiding individual development is also a sort of intangible hand. But the dialectic of shame and pride is tumultuous in adolescence. This is partly because shame is 'innately connected to the sense of self and to sexuality' (Broucek 1991: 23). Furthermore, pride, the counterpart of shame, is more complex. Pride is an emotion rather than a basic affect, an emotion built on scripts involving the affects of interest and enjoyment. This imbalance is reflected in language. The intense shame of 'humiliation' involves the rapid downward revision of one's sense of self, but the English language has no analogous construction for pride or self-respect (Taylor 1985: 19). Self-respect is developed gradually, rather than being foisted on a person in an instant. Self-respecting pride is achieved in the process of attaining goals. Striving for goals fosters the affect of interest-excitement; achieving them elicits enjoyment-joy. People with few goals are thus vulnerable to shame.

Prospects for community conferencing

A community conference is, in part, a lesson in ethics, but not a lesson for an isolated individual. It is a lesson for a group of people linked by emotional bonds. The abstract logic of a formal ethical system might be analysed with little emotion, but ethics for the real world are inextricably linked with emotion. And emotions, though subject to rational assessment, also 'supplement formal rules of rationality' (de Sousa 1987: 330; Gordon 1987). Emotions come into play in cases where no fully rational solution to a problem is available and provide 'solutions to just those problems in the management of human action that cannot be tackled by technical plans' (Oatley 1992: 15). Emotions may force a reassessment of the habits, preferences and beliefs that guide a person through reality.

Like some other successful contemporary processes employed by family therapists, educators, welfare workers and police, community conferencing emphasizes dialogue, mutual respect, and an appropriate mix of rationality and emotion. It seeks to foster empathy. And a person whose behaviour displays a lack of empathy will empathize only if they can feel for others, rather than just think about them. The truly ethical person must feel another's real needs, as well as acknowledging their abstract rights (Gilligan 1982; Pritchard 1991). In some cases, scripted responses to excessive shame may have rendered feeling difficult. The theories outlined above suggest that community conferencing offers a practical solution to this problem.

Rather than relying on the imagination of a lone individual, which often turns inward rather than outward, community conferencing encourages thinking and feeling about the self and about others. A community conference does not condone or excuse offending behaviour, but provides a lesson in apology and forgiveness within a forum for co-operation. And in the long term, communities can only survive, let alone flourish, where co-operation is preferable to litigation. But co-operating in the wake of an offence requires skill in the intricacies of apology and forgiveness (Tavuchis 1991). So, ultimately, conferencing has an educative function. As a response to patterns of victimization or serious individual incidents, a community conference may achieve far more than alternative interventions. It does not separate individuals from their community of care, rationality from the emotions, or justice from needs. Nor does it rely on the competing assessments of experts. Rather, where offending behaviour has produced an offender and a victim, it gives the community of people most affected an opportunity to respond. They have as good a chance as anyone of repairing the damage, and deserve an opportunity to do so.

Several programmes are now making that opportunity more readily available. Community conferencing in schools is providing a nexus between the desire to take a longer-term preventive approach to behaviour management, and the need to provide immediate, visible, effective responses to antisocial behaviour in schools. For example, a Pennsylvania-based organization began in 1995 to train North American educators, police, community workers and others in techniques of community conferencing.

These techniques, adopted from New Zealand and adapted in the Wagga programme, were further tailored to the needs of schools when applied in the school setting during a pilot programme in Queensland through 1995 and 1996. Nearly all schools in that trial changed their approach to the issue of behaviour management as a result of their involvement. More specific findings included those predicted on theoretical grounds in this chapter: generally very high rates of participant satisfaction with the process and outcomes; very high rates of compliance with conference agreements; low rates of reoffending; increased social support for those most directly affected by the harmful behaviour; and an appreciation of the role of the school in providing this alternative intervention (Hyndman *et al.* 1996). In 1997, our organization TJA began providing further training for teachers in Canada as part of a larger restorative justice initiative sponsored by the RCMP and Canada's Aboriginal Justice Learning Network. Other inter-agency programmes, which include schools, are now underway in North America and Australasia. These programmes will continue to be subject to internal agency evaluations. But we would encourage broader external evaluation of conferencing programmes, including longer-term follow up, wherever possible.

Evaluations should measure multiple outcomes to determine whether the programme in question is indeed managing to repair the damage caused by harmful behaviour, and minimizing further harm. Thus, measured outcomes should include:

1 participant satisfaction with the justice delivered by community conferences, where justice is an irreducibly tripartite phenomenon involving fair rules, fair play and fair outcomes;
2 measures of increased social support among participants and/or improved relations among peers;
3 reductions in the rate of (re)offending and/or behavioural problems.

Additionally, in the school setting, it is appropriate to determine whether a programme of community conferencing is producing reduced rates of suspension and exclusion.

The political significance of community conferencing is considerable, for it meets the demands of the two sides who talk past each other in debates on behaviour in schools. It meets the demands of those who argue that troublesome young people deserve greater support, since their uncivil behaviour is symptomatic of some underlying need. The process also meets the demands of those who argue for more effective, authoritative responses to uncivil behaviour, and who urge that not only schools but the broader associated communities accept some responsibility for behaviour within schools. Accepting community conferencing as an appropriate response to serious incidents of victimization, including bullying, would enable schools to transcend this fruitless debate. It would provide an alternative to the social irresponsibility of supporting escalating rates of exclusion. In the process it would teach us all a lot more about how, in an appropriate forum, pride, shame and empathy can turn conflict to positive ends, rather than simply amplifying conflict or avoiding it.

Chapter 18

Children's comments about their social skills training

Barry H. Schneider and Roland W. B. Blonk

Interventions designed to promote harmonious peer relations have a documented record of effectiveness, but not of boundless success. Reviews of the many published evaluations of social skills training indicate that well-designed interventions can engender substantial improvements in the interpersonal relations of children displaying typical as well as atypical patterns of development (Erwin and Ruane 1993; Schneider 1992; Zaragoza *et al.* 1991). Nevertheless, the benefits of social-skills training as we now know it may not be sufficient to enhance the interpersonal relationships of many of the neediest youngsters over extended periods of time: Almost all reviewers raise questions about the long-term effects of the interventions and the generalization of the benefits accrued beyond the training setting (Beelman *et al.* 1994; Ogilvy 1994; Schneider 1992). As well, many of the neediest populations, such as children with externalizing disorders, tend to profit less than others (Schneider 1992).

In contrasting the results of their meta-analysis with the more optimistic ones of earlier qualitative and quantitative reviews, Beelmann *et al.* (1994) contend that social skills training is now being asked to do more than it previously was – for example, to turn around the reputations of children who display chronic patterns of maladaptive social behaviour across settings for extended periods of time. Perhaps the unbridled enthusiasm of early proponents was unrealistic in the face of the deep-seated, multiple causes of problematic interpersonal interaction. Was it reasonable to expect that brief verbal interventions could reverse many of the results of early learning, heredity, parenting, peer reputation and social class? Schneider (1992) has argued vehemently that we should not jettison this modality of intervention, since it does bring proven benefits to many children in need, even if the gains are not always permanent and do not extend to all children who display severe difficulty. He argues that small but significant effects for at-risk groups should not be downplayed, since these often translate into considerable amelioration of the problems of some individuals. In weighing the benefits of social-skills training, one must also remember that it is relatively low in cost and that negative effects are almost unknown. Therefore, the cost–benefit ratio probably remains quite favourable. Furthermore, other modalities of intervention in common use with at-risk youngsters may not be more effective (see meta-analysis by Weiss and Weisz 1995), though they are often more costly. Furthermore, social-skills training has surely been subjected to more systematic evaluation per hour of intervention than many if not most of its 'competitors'; its reputation should not be tarnished because it has been studied so well.

The recent, sobering re-evaluation of the benefits of social skills training has resulted in several promising changes in the way interventions are conceptualized and implemented. There is a growing consensus that intervention must go beyond the scope of didactic training sessions for children, but let us emphasize that 'going beyond' does not mean abandoning. There is some evidence that social skills training will work better when accompanied by interventions directed at the families of the participants (Gettinger *et al.* 1994; Kazdin *et al.* 1992) and by components designed specifically to bring about generalization in schools (Guevremont and Foster 1993). Also, as argued by Schneider *et al.* (1995), it may be more realistic to target the skills that members of at-risk populations can use to form a small number of more intensive, intimate friendships than to attempt the mammoth endeavour of making them more popular with larger groups in which their roles are crystallized. Murphy and Schneider's (1994) data indicate the effectiveness of this approach over the short term. However, this one study is not by itself sufficient to document even the short-term benefits of a dyadic approach to intervention, and even it did not include any data pertaining to long-term effectiveness. At present, the argument for intervention at the level of the dyad is inspired by theoretical writings on the importance of friendship (e.g., Sullivan 1953), and limited, qualitative case-study data on long-term friendship-oriented dyadic pair therapy (Selman and Schultz 1990). Until further data are collected, there is not a convincing basis for arguing against teaching the skills needed to get along in large-group situations. Furthermore, even if the hypothesized benefits of dyadic interventions are eventually corroborated, it may emerge that interventions with dyadic and large-group foci are helpful in different ways.

More than a decade ago, Hymel and Franke (1985) argued that, despite the growing use of social skills training with children, almost no knowledge is available about how children themselves perceive their social skills training. Their perceptions may be regarded as part of the data useful in the current rethinking of social skills interventions. The children's feelings about their relationships are no doubt an integral part of the target problem. Perhaps more importantly, though, is the possibility that the way children perceive the intervention relates to their use of it or failure to do so. At least part of the challenge of teaching new skills that generalize outside the training setting is motivating the trainees to bring the skills with them. Perhaps they will be more energetic partners in this challenge if their impressions of the intervention are positive and if they believe it will be helpful. Trower (1984) has long argued for a shift from an 'organism approach' to social skills training in which the trainee is the passive, almost rote recipient of a series of skill components to an 'agency approach', in which the individual is helped to generate the socially competent behaviour of which he or she is capable or can be made capable. Clearly, this cannot occur without the more active intellectual participation of the target child.

The next two sections of this chapter are devoted to a portrayal of the perceptions of the participants in two social skills programmes designed for school-age children referred to professionals for deficits in social behaviour that have already been detected by their parents and/or teachers.

Study One

Study One is part of an evaluation of a school-based programme for latency-aged children referred by their teachers for social-skills training because of problematic peer-directed aggression and/or social withdrawal. These interventions were conducted in small groups of three, four or five children by trained graduate students in psychology during school time in small seminar rooms otherwise used for remedial academic lessons, speech therapy and psychological testing.

In order to be accepted into the programme, the reasons for the teacher referral had to be corroborated by peer-report measures. Each participant had to score at least one standard deviation above the mean for nomination by class peers for two of the following: (1) Liked Least sociometric nominations; (2) Revised Class Play (Morison and Masten 1991) nominations for Sensitivity/Isolation; (3) Revised Class Play nominations for Aggression–Disruption. They also had to have scored below the mean of Class Play nominations for Sociability–Leadership. In addition, the children and their parents had to agree to the children's participation.

The intervention consisted of twelve weekly sessions conducted over a four-month period from November to March, broken at the middle by a school vacation. The skill-training procedure is one that has been proved generally effective in a series of previous studies (Schneider 1991). The first half of each session was devoted to a didactic presentation of the skills targeted, which could be characterized as both cognitive and behavioural, featuring videotaped modelling. The group leaders emphasized social problem-solving, skills needed in joining a group, and appropriate interpretation of social cues. Vignettes, games, and videotaped role-play were the major teaching modalities. Free play comprised the remainder of the 70-minute intervention session. During the free-play period, the therapists prompted and reinforced the use of the skills taught using tokens that were redeemed at a makeshift 'store' that was opened just before the children went home. Tokens were also removed as fines for infractions. A session summary, reminder of key concepts, and discussion of how any incidents might have been handled, were conducted during the final five minutes.

A total of 27 children, aged 8 through 11 years, participated in the intervention condition, which was implemented in five schools in the Toronto area. They were matched with a wait-list control group of identical size by age and sex; the wait-list controls were drawn from schools where the Social Skills Training (SST) programme was not being implemented. The control group members received the intervention at their schools during the school year following the study. All but four subjects in each condition were boys. The four girls were assigned to two of the groups in order to avoid having groups in which there was only one girl. The sessions were led by three trained psychology graduate students, two male and one female, who received weekly supervision sessions from the first author of this chapter.

Quantitative indices of improvement were not entirely consistent. The teacher ratings, Class Play nominations and sociometric choice nominations were repeated in the participants' classrooms at the end of the school year and in October of the following school year (except for one child who had moved away over the summer and another whose school did not wish to participate). Analysis of covariance indicated that, in comparison with the control-group scores, the participants had made significant gains on many of the Social Skills Rating Scale teacher ratings, both at year-end follow-up and the following school year. Particularly encouraging were the very marked improvements in teacher ratings of the children's self-control, which was the topic of many of the social skills lessons. It is also noteworthy that the improvement in teacher ratings was evident the year after the training, when the teacher was less likely to be aware that the child had participated in SST. In contrast with the teacher ratings, however, there were no significant gains in Liked Most nor significant reductions in Liked Least nominations from peers at either time point; these scores were almost identical to those at pre-treatment for both the treatment group and the wait-list controls. Although the scores on each of the three scales of the Class Play indicated some improvement for the treatment group, and virtually no change for the controls, none of these gains were statistically significant at year-end. However, by October of the following school year, the treatment group had achieved significantly greater reduction in Class Play Aggression/Disruptiveness scores than the controls. It could be argued that gains are more likely to accrue in the school year after training, since the summer vacation and the turnover in classroom enrolment patterns allow for a partial 'fresh start' (Bienert and Schneider 1995).

After the first, second, sixth, and twelfth sessions, the children met with the first author of the chapter (who, it is recalled, supervised the videotaped sessions, but did not administer them and was not present during them). He conducted these interviews with the children individually. They were asked, first of all, what they would remember most about the session. They then were asked to indicate, on a 1 to 4 scale, how much they enjoyed the session (not at all, a bit, quite a bit, a lot). They were then asked to indicate, also on a 1 to 4 scale, whether they believed that the SST would be beneficial to them. After they had made their ratings, the children were asked to explain their reasons for them.

The mean enjoyment ratings were similar for groups led by the three therapists: 2.6 (out of 4), 2.8, and 2.9. Enjoyment increased over the course of the intervention, from a mean rating of 2.4 after the first session to 2.9 after the second, 2.9 at the sixth session, and 3.0 at the end. However, out of the 27 participants, six or seven gave extreme negative ratings ('1') to each session. There were four who gave the lowest enjoyment ratings at each of the four interviews. The means for the effectiveness ratings were similar, averaging 2.7, 2.8, and 3.0 (out of 4) for groups led by each of the three leaders. However, there was considerable fluctuation among effectiveness ratings obtained at each of the four interviews: means of 2.5, 3.4, 2.8 and 3.0. There were only three children who rated the intervention as unlikely to be effective for them at each of the four interviews, and only five who assigned the highest rating of effectiveness ('4') to the intervention during all four interviews.

The open-ended recollections were classified by two graduate students who were not involved in the training. They devised the classification scheme after an initial scan of the responses and discussions with the first author. They then coded all the responses; the kappa statistic for inter-rater reliability was 0.92. They were able to classify about 98 per cent of the comments.

The most frequent category, accounting for fully 42 per cent of the responses, consisted of comments about the token economy. Because of the frequency of this category, we decided *post hoc* to develop subcategories, examples of which follow. Of the 42 per cent, 10 per cent indicated enjoyment: 'It's fun to get things for doing what you're supposed to instead of being yelled at for not.' Only 3 per cent indicated disagreement with the system: 'Does he [the therapist] really think we need to get little pencils and stickers to learn how to be nice to people?' Fully 18 per cent were comments indicating that the tokens had not been distributed fairly: 'Jeff [the therapist] took a token away from me for teasing, but Melanie (name changed) teases twice as much, and Jeff never takes tokens away from her.' Another 2 per cent indicated that the reward items were not priced in proportion to their value. Most of the remaining comments about the tokens indicated that the therapists were generally too lenient (5 per cent) or two strict (2 per cent) in giving them or taking them away.

Another 19 per cent of the comments were about personal characteristics of the therapists. Virtually all of these were positive – for example, 'I hope that when I go to university I can be as nice as Elaine', or 'I wish that Jeff could be my teacher.' Ten per cent of the comments were related to being singled out for intervention: 'I don't know why they picked on me. The other kids in my group are ten times as bad'; 'OK, I should be here, but so should Mary Ann.'

Another 9 per cent were about other group members. These were about equally distributed between positive and negative comments: 'I'm glad I came to the group because I met Jason – we now get together on Saturdays'; 'The group was fine, but I wish they didn't have Jason' (name changed, but the two comments referred to the same boy).

Only 8 per cent of the comments had to do with the social skills content! Seven of the 8 per cent were positive: 'Geez, I never thought someone would just show me what I was doing wrong when I wanted to play.' Most of the comments about the problem-solving indicated that the children felt empowered by learning it: 'I would never have thought that I had real choices when I'm being bugged.' However, one participant noted that 'Jeff [the therapist] can't come to school with me – he thinks I have a lot of choice in what I do on the playground, but I really don't.'

Because of the small sample and irregular distribution of the scores, we decided to divide the treatment group into 'Clearly Improved', 'Mixed Results', 'Clearly Not Improved', in order to facilitate analysis of the global enjoyment and effectiveness ratings with nonparametric statistics. We considered subjects as 'Clearly Improved' if they had achieved improvement of at least one-half standard deviation (SD) on at least four of the seven dependent measures and no deterioration exceeding 0.1 SD on any of the others. Thirteen of the 27 treated subjects fell into this category at year-end, as did ten of the 25 subjects for whom data were available the following school year. 'Clearly Not Improved' subjects were those who had not improved by one-half SD on any of the measures, as well as any whose scores deteriorated on more measures than they improved on (except for trivial deteriorations or improvements of 0.1 SD or less). Eight of the 27 treatment-group participants were considered as clearly not improved at the end of the year, as were eight of the 25 according to the data collected the following year. The remaining subjects were classified as displaying mixed results.

The children's comments were dichotomized into Enjoyed/Did Not Enjoy and Intervention Believed Effective/Believed Ineffective in order to avoid very small cells in the chi-square analysis. A series of chi-squares was then computed in order to compare the outcome scores with, first, the positiveness of the children's feelings about the intervention, and, then, their impressions of its effectiveness. Each of these two comparisons was performed four times – once for each of the interview sessions during which the comments were gathered.

Enjoyment of the sessions was completely unrelated to improvement based on teacher and peer reports; none of the eight chi-square values even approached statistical significance. We tried several alternative groupings of the data and different analytic strategies, but in no case were there results even approaching significance. In sharp contrast with the data pertaining to the positiveness of the children's impressions, children who believed the intervention was effective were significantly more likely to belong to the Clearly Improved group in five of the eight relevant analyses, as detailed in Table 18.1. There was some correspondence between the children's reports of the enjoyment of the sessions and their impressions of its effectiveness, but the concordance was only statistically significant for the data collected at the last two of the four interview sessions (χ^2 = 4.24 and 6.10, respectively, both df = 1, both $p < 0.05$).

Study Two

Study Two was part of a larger research project on social skills training with clinically referred socially incompetent children in the Netherlands (Blonk 1996). Recently, Blonk *et al.* (1996) conducted a study on SST outcomes with 102 children referred to seven outpatient mental health centres in the Netherlands because of social relations problems, which were confirmed by parent ratings on the Child Behaviour Checklist. Their median age was 10 years (range 8–12 years) at the time of referral. All subjects manifested social adjustment disorders with a main complaint of peer relationship problems involving either social withdrawal or aggression. At the time of referral, these peer problems had endured for more than a year.

The first six sessions were devoted to the establishment of a trusting

Table 18.1 Results of chi-square analyses: Effectiveness impressions by outcome group

Time of impressions	*Time of outcome*	χ^2
Session 1	Year-end	4.07, $p < 0.05$
Session 1	Year 2 follow-up	3.11, ns
Session 2	Year-end	5.12, $p < 0.05$
Session 2	Year 2 follow-up	2.55, ns
Session 6	Year-end	7.19; $p < 0.01$
Session 6	Year 2 follow-up	1.89, ns
Session 12	Year end	8.54, $p < 0.01$
Session 12	Year 2 follow-up	3.99, $p < 0.05$

relationship with the therapist. The remaining sessions were more didactic, covering listening skills, recognition and expression of emotion, group-entry skills, reacting to criticism, and coping with bullying. The participants received 20 weekly sessions of SST, each lasting 90 minutes. The analysis of the post-treatment data revealed moderate effect sizes overall, comparable to the effect sizes reported by Schneider (1992) and Beelmann *et al.* (1994). This SST trial with clinically referred children proved to be effective in enhancing social behaviour and in improving peer relationships, as measured by nominations for social acceptance by their peers at school and by parent and teacher reports. These improvements were sustained over a period of five months. As well, social anxiety and negative self-evaluation were reduced at five-month follow-up. The reader is referred to the detailed English-language report of the quantitative results by Blonk *et al.* (1996).

The participants were followed for two-and-a-half years after treatment. It was hypothesized that treatment effects in terms of social behaviour, social anxiety and negative self-evaluation would be maintained. In order to augment the quantitative results, the children were asked to answer two open-ended questions about how they experienced their social skills training. The programme developers hoped that these answers might reveal important insights useful in enhancing the impact of SST with children in the future. The sample for the present follow-up study consisted of 72 children (45 boys and 27 girls). Fourteen of the original parents and/or children either had moved and were not traceable or refused to cooperate. Four other children did not answer the open-end questions; one additional subject answered only one of the two questions. Therefore, 53 children (74 per cent) remained for the analyses reported herein.

We focus here on the two open-end questions that were part of a follow-up questionnaire administered to the children at the two-and-a-half year follow-up. The questions were: (1) What do you think of the social skills training you received? and (2) Did you learn anything from it?

The majority of the responses (66 per cent) were positive. Although the children were not specifically asked to report the reasons for their impressions, most provided some spontaneous elaboration. In the vast majority of cases, they used adjectives such as 'nice', 'pleasant' and 'enjoyable' in a general way to describe the overall feeling that they had retained. There were also several references to the other group members:

'Sometimes I wish to meet the other children again to talk about how things have gone on.'

'I enjoyed it and I liked the other children.'

'Pleasant, sometimes a bit boring, nice children.'

Only two of the responses contained any reference to the therapists, and these were less specific than those of the Canadian participants in Study One. For example:

> 'And I like the people who helped with that too'.
> 'Pleasant, nice children and coaches.'

In contrast, the responses to the second question, pertaining to what they learned, seemed very articulate. Most of these described improvements. Interestingly, about half of them indicated the ways in which the participants themselves changed:

> 'I gained in self-confidence and stick up more for myself.'
> 'Yes, I can get along better with friends and I dare to look boys right in the face. I get along better with them.'
> 'I changed a lot at home and at school. I learned how to behave.'
> 'I learned how to make friends.'
> 'Yes, I behave more like normal. I am more even tempered. I am less often angry.'
> 'Yes, formerly I did not dare to go up to other children; now I do.'
> 'Yes, I have become much more confident.'
> 'Yes, I stand up more for myself and I am able to make clear what I mean to others.'
> 'Yes, because I am different from two years ago.'

A smaller but substantial number of the reponses were third-person references to things that had changed, though not necessarily because the participant's behaviour had changed:

> 'Yes I am bullied less and have more friends.'
> 'It is more fun at high school than at elementary school.'
> 'It has improved a lot. I don't know whether this was caused by the training or by a change of school.'

About half of the non-positive responses (17 per cent out of 34 per cent) could be classified as mixed in tone, but not as decidedly negative. A number of the critical elements in these responses had more to do with the outcome than with the process:

'On the one hand yes, on the other hand no. I still don't talk very loudly.'
'I did not really enjoy it but, on the other hand, I didn't dislike it either. Not much changed for me at school.'
'Sometimes it was pleasant, however at times it was not. I learned something from it, but my problem did not disappear completely.'
'I enjoyed it but I lost all my spare time. I do not think about it a lot, so I can't say [if I learned anything].'
'Yes, I have learned not to hit others. However, I am still bullied.'

Other participants (17 per cent) held negative opinions of their SST. There were several negative themes, none of which predominated. Some had to do with the general tone of the impressions. With one exception (an unelaborated 'not pleasant'), these referred to boredom rather than active hostility:

'It was dull and boring.'
'No, I kept myself quiet and the homework assignments were so boring that I just wrote anything down.'
'Boring and honestly speaking a bit of a waste of time.'

Several former trainees indicated that the content of the intervention was artificial:

'So so. Reality did not come up.'
'I think that the things we learned were too vague. One should react in one's own way. Otherwise one would behave in an artificial way.'
'The training dealt only with stupid theory which had nothing to do with day-to-day life.'
'No, not really. We learned how to ask for a pencil; however I knew that already and that was not the point.'

Other negative comments pertained to a lack of results:

'There was no change in how I behaved before and after the training.'
'No, nothing changed at school.'
'I think I did not really learn anything from the training.'

A few of the interviewees indicated that they had not profited from the intervention because 'the problem' was caused by external agents:

> 'No. Things changed because I moved to another school and not because of the training.'
> 'No, it was not my problem.'
> 'No, my problems were caused by the school.'

Finally, a few of the remarks were specific to the way the groups were conducted or organized:

> 'It was OK, but it is a downright shame that they spy on you from behind a one-way screen.'
> 'The group consisted of children who were younger than me.'

In order to faciliate quantitative analysis, we divided the children's comments in response to the second question (Did you learn from the SST?) into three categories: (1) comments that were definitely negative (DN), (2) comments that were definitely positive (DP) and (3) comments in between these two extremes (IB). Next, a series of ANOVAs was performed to compare children whose comments belonged to these categories in terms of the following outcome measures: self-reported negative self-evaluation (NSE), self-reported social anxiety (SA), self-reported peer relationships (SRP), parent-reported peer relationships (PRP), parent-reported socially withdrawn behaviour (SWB), parent-reported socially aggressive behaviour (SAB), and four parent-report Child Behaviour Checklist subscales: social competence (SC), internalizing behaviour problems (INT), externalizing behaviour problems (EXT) and total behaviour problems (TOT).

Scores were first analysed using the two-and-a-half-year follow-up data. ANOVA yielded significant results at $p < 0.05$ for only two of the 11 variables. Differences in the positivity of responses to Question 2 were only evident in their scores for negative self-evaluation and social anxiety ($F(2,49) = 4.19$ and $F(2,49) = 3.67$ respectively; see Table 18.2 for descriptive statistics). Children whose responses were characterized as definitely negative were those with more negative self-evaluations and higher social anxiety than the children in the other categories. A closer look at the data revealed that the mean score on these dependent measures was also higher than the population mean for NSE and SA. Thus, the children whose impressions of the training were negative tended to display near-extreme scores for negative self-evaluation and social anxiety.

Table 18.2 Means (SDs) of children whose comments were definitely negative (DN), in between (IB), and definitively positive (DP) for negative self-evaluation and social anxiety

	DN (*n* = *10*)	*IB* (*n* = *16*)	*DP* (*n* = *26*)
Negative self-evaluation	9.70 (5.68)	4.50 (5.25)	4.92 (4.28)
Social anxiety	3.70 (2.87)	1.13 (2.39)	1.65 (2.23)

Next, the data were analysed using residual gain scores computed from pre-test and the two-and-a-half year follow-up. No significant differences were found whatsoever among the residual gain scores (computed from pre-test to post-test) of children whose impressions of SST were clearly positive, clearly negative, or intermediate, in terms of any of the 11 variables. Thus, the children's impressions were clearly unrelated to outcome.

Discussion

The first, and perhaps most important, caveat is that the participants in both studies were selected specifically because they were already manifesting peer-relations problems that were sufficient enough to prompt the adults in their environments to refer them for help. This population is likely to be more resistant to any form of intervention. Perhaps more than those of other participants, their comments about the training may reflect the long-standing negative character of their relations with others and their bitterness about them. Both studies represent challenges that 'test the limits' of SST rather than typical experiences – and did so with considerable success. Although it could be argued that the training time might have been better spent with less dysfunctional trainees, it must be remembered that conduct disorder in childhood poses a high risk for maladjustment across the lifespan. Parents, educators and mental-health professionals have little choice but to attempt to assist this population, even if they must often be content with less effectiveness than with other groups.

These two studies provide complementary perspectives of the children's experience of social skills training. The questions used to elicit the comments in Study One were more detailed, and were administered more frequently. Therefore, they provide more detail. On the other hand, Study Two was conducted with a larger number of children who were involved in social skills training for a longer period of time. The larger sample is more suitable for learning how representative certain opinions are of the population of behaviour-disordered children participating in social skills training. As detailed below, the results of the two studies were similar in many ways. In contemplating what inconsistencies there were among the results of the two studies, we remind the reader that, aside from the geographic differences (Netherlands vs Canada), the participants for Study Two were mostly older than their counterparts in Study One at the time of follow-up (though not at the times of referral and training), and had been participants in their SST for a much longer time. The more articulate nature of their reponses is probably attributable to their ages.

The detail of the Study One responses indicates that children often focus on aspects of the training that the adults who planned and implemented the sessions considered peripheral. For example, the programme developers saw the token economy/response cost system as an adjunct designed to facilitate decorum during the sessions and to reinforce the use of newly learned skills. However, the token economy dominated the children's comments to the extent that we wonder how much the cognitive skills on which the therapists spent so much time had penetrated the children's awareness. Adjunct token reinforcement is well established in social skills training and cognitive-behavioural therapy with children. Some researchers have determined through systematic studies that meaningful generalization across contexts and maintenance of skill learning sometimes only occur when systematic, tangible reinforcement is added (Bierman *et al.* 1987; Storey *et al.* 1994). Therefore, we do not think that the children's comments should be construed as indicating that token reinforcement not be used as an 'adjunct' to social skills training. However, those who use this means of facilitating transfer and maintenance should be cognizant of the fact that this component of the training cannot realistically be relegated to peripheral, 'adjunct' status.

There were also many comments about other children, about the general atmosphere of the sessions, and about how different the children felt from their therapists. Thus, many of the children seemed to be more caught up in the group experience than in the content of the lessons, which were presented to them using primarily a didactic format in both studies. This suggests that more attention might be paid to different ways of presenting social skills to trainees. For example, Elias and Allen (1991) tried three different ways of delivering a preventive social problem-solving to children, and found clear benefits for both a discovery-learning and a directed-learning approach over a standard social problem-solving skills curriculum. Importantly, the benefits of these more novel methods were particularly salient in the data obtained from at-risk children.

The results of both these studies indicate that children hold mixed feelings about being participants in social skills training. The proportions of positive comments are strikingly similar across the two studies: at least half the comments are positive. Since both authors enjoy conducting and organizing social skills training, we none the less find the size of the negative minority opinion something of a surprise.

Some of the results from Study Two suggest that the negative comments may come from participants who themselves are socially anxious and prone to feelings of inferiority. Their negative feelings about themselves may be projected onto others and to potential change agents. They might feel as negative about other modalities of intervention that might be tried with them, although we have no basis in our data for finding out.

Perhaps part of the reason for the children's divided opinion about SST is that youngsters with behaviour problems may develop unrealistic perceptions of their own social skills and peer acceptance (Zabriski and Coie 1996; Kupersmidt and Patterson 1991) in order to protect themselves from the harshness of the reality. If that is the case, they may see little need for the intervention and may resent being singled out for it – as was clear from some of their comments. For example, several participants in Study Two said that SST was not appropriate because they were not the problem; the problem was the school they were attending.

The common thread running throughout the literature and in the data from both studies reported above is that children's perceptions of their own social competence – and of changes in it – may often differ sharply from the perceptions of others. This reality might be interpreted in a number of ways. Some might see children's self-perceptions as a domain that is separate from the perceptions of others, but of value in its own right. Taking such reasoning one step further, it could be argued that SST should be deemed effective if and only if the children participating in it consider it effective. Given the number of negative comments we received from a substantial minority of trainees, it might seem difficult to achieve change in the trainees' perceptions of SST. However, the impression obtained from Forness and Kavale's (1996) meta-analytic review of social skills training with learning-disabled children is the opposite. They conclude that measures obtained directly from the trainees displayed the most change, unlike the very modest results documented by information obtained from teachers and peers.

The child participants in social skills training might be seen as the consumers of a service. Accordingly, their perceptions as consumers should be an important measure of outcome, if not the most important. Another reason for emphasizing improvement in children's perceptions of SST is that the end goal of this modality is to enhance interpersonal relationships. The participants in the relationships at the dyadic level are probably far better informants about them than the adults who provide the bulk of the outcome data in many studies, and very possibly better than the large group of their classroom peers. In any event, the information obtained by most researchers from adults and peers to evaluate SST does not usually pertain to relationships directly, but to overt behaviour at school and global reputation.

Furthermore, it could be argued – but probably not proved – that the participants are unlikely to implement what they have learned in contexts other than the training session if their perceptions of the experience are not positive. The data from both studies suggest that the children's impressions may be anchored in their own subjective feelings or impressions of the training rather than in any reading of their own social relations before and after. If this is the case, and if one assigns considerable value to the self-perceptions, it becomes incumbent on proponents of SST to work to improve the trainees' global feelings about this enterprise, perhaps by making SST more enjoyable, by tailoring it to the needs of the individual child, or by redoubling efforts to identify which children profit from it in terms of both their own and others' perceptions.

On the other hand, some might see their perceptions of the intervention as irrelevant. Data from both studies and from much of the literature available highlight the gap between children's perceptions of their social behaviour and the information one can gather from all other sources – peers, parents, teachers, direct observation. Hawkins (1991) has argued that 'consumer satisfaction' data often do not predict the consumer's own behaviour or the 'habilitative validity' of the intervention in question. 'Habilitative validity' refers to the degree to which the 'individual behavioural repertoire maximizes the overall rewards, and minimizes the costs, to that individual and to others, including family, peers, and society' (Hawkins 1991: 206). The fact that children's perceptions of SST in both our studies seem to be based on factors other than its effects on social behaviour underscores Hawkins's arguments. Hawkins also maintains that clients may not be the best judges of the benefits of an intervention because they do not have the awareness of the alternatives to it, among other reasons.

We ourselves believe that it is important for SST to be enjoyed and considered effective by its participants, and to be effective in an objective sense. However one perceives the importance of children's perceptions, it is difficult to see how an intervention can be effective without overcoming the resistance of any participants who harbour negative feelings about it and the scepticism of any participants who may not believe in it. The behavioural tradition that was highly instrumental in the emergence of SST has little room for such phenomena as resistance or counter transference. In looking at the content of some of the children's comments, we find that the skills trainer and the children's relationship with him/her was far more predominant than the developers of social skills curricula might expect. However, it would come as little surprise to practitioners of other forms of therapy that clients might pay more attention to the personality of the therapist than to the content of the therapy. The preponderance of comments about the adult group leaders need not suggest that formal social skills training should be abandoned in favour of relationship therapy. Problem-solving skills training and relationship therapy have been compared directly in a very well-designed study conducted by Kazdin *et al.* (1987) with psychiatric inpatient children aged 7 through 13 years; the results indicate the clear superiority of problem-solving skills training.

Therapists trained in non-behavioural models would also not be astonished that children may not wish to own up to their problems, may not enjoy having attention paid to their shortcomings, and may project blame for their problems onto others. The results of both studies indicate that there was only modest correspondence between children's impressions of enjoyment and of effectiveness. Furthermore, only the effectiveness data were linked to outcome in any way. This may mean that a certain amount of pain may be associated with gain in children's social skills training as in many other endeavours.

Perhaps, in order to achieve its own aims, SST will have to incorporate more of what is known from other schools of therapy, and, more generally, about the dynamics of influencing people to change. Hopefully, this will lead to more consistent long-term results with populations that are difficult to work with. However, it is also possible that the negative comments of the minority of the children we interviewed are the voice of a subgroup of trainees that are unlikely to respond to anything resembling current forms of social skills training. This may mean that we have taken children's social skills training about as far as we can. Just as children rejected by their peers sometimes have to learn to cope with a certain amount of rejection that cannot be eliminated, social skills trainers may have to face the fact that the benefits of this form of helping, though not negligible, are not unlimited.

References

Aboud, F.E. (1977) 'Interest in ethnic information: a cross-sectional developmental study', *Canadian Journal of Behavioural Science*, 9: 134–146.

Aboud, F.E. (1988) *Children and Prejudice*, Oxford: Blackwell.

Aboud, F.E. and Mitchell, F.G. (1977) 'Ethnic role taking: the effects of preference and self-identification', *International Journal of Psychology*, 12: 1–7.

Abramovitch, R., Stanhope, L., Pepler, D. and Corter, C. (1987) 'The influence of Down's syndrome in sibling interaction', *Journal of Child Psychology and Psychiatry*, 28: 865–879.

Achenbach, T.M., McConaughy, S.H. and Howell, C.T. (1987) 'Child/adolescent behavioral and emotional problems: implications of cross-informant correlations for situational specificity', *Psychological Bulletin*, 101: 213–232.

Adams, G., Schvaneveldt, J., Jenson, G. and Jones, R. (1982) 'Sociometric research with adolescents: in search of a self-report alternative with evidence of psychometric validity', *Adolescence*, 17: 905–909.

Ahmad, Y. and Smith, P.K. (1994a) 'Bullying in schools and the issue of sex differences', in J. Archer (ed.) *Male Violence*, London: Routledge.

Ahmad, Y. and Smith, P.K. (1994b) 'Behavioural measures: bullying in schools', *Newsletter of the Association for Child Psychiatry and Psychology*, 12: 26–27.

Akerley, M. (1974) 'The near-normal autistic adolescent', *Journal of Autism and Childhood Schizophrenia*, 4: 348–355.

Akerley, M.S. (1992) 'The last bird', in E. Schopler and G.B. Mesibov (eds) *High-functioning Individuals with Autism*, New York: Plenum Press, 266–275.

Alexander, R.D. (1987) *The Biology of Moral Systems*, New York: A. De Gruyter.

Allport, G.W. (1954) *The Nature of Prejudice*, Reading, Mass.: Addison-Wesley.

American Psychiatric Association (1994) *Diagnostic and Statistical Manual of Mental Disorders: Fourth Edition*, Washington, DC: APA.

Arabie, P., Boorman, S.A. and Levitt, P.R. (1978) 'Constructing blockmodels: how and why', *Journal of Mathematical Psychology*, 17: 21–63.

Asher, S. and Dodge, K. (1986) 'Identifying children who are rejected by their peers', *Developmental Psychology*, 22: 444–449.

Asher, S.R., Hymel, S. and Renshaw, P.D. (1984) 'Loneliness in children', *Child Development*, 55: 1456–1464.

Asher, S.R., Singleton, L.C., Tinsley, B.R. and Hymel, S. (1979) 'A reliable sociometric measure for preschool children', *Developmental Psychology*, 15: 443–444.

Athens, L.H. (1989) *The Creation of Dangerous Violent Criminals*, London: Routledge.

Attar, B.K., Guerra, N.G. and Tolan, P.H. (1994) 'Neighbourhood disadvantage, stressful life events, and adjustment in urban elementary-schoolchildren', *Journal of Clinical Child Psychology*, 23: 391–400.

Australian Children's Television Foundation (1985) *Top Kid*, Tarman, NSW (video).

Australian Education Council (1994) *A Statement on Health and Physical Education for Australian schools*, Carlton, Victoria: Curriculum Corporation.

Axelrod, R. (1984) *The Evolution of Cooperation*, New York: Basic Books.

Balda, S. (1998) 'Socialization experiences and preschool-aged children's social problem-solving skills in Australia and India: a cross-cultural study', Unpublished doctoral dissertation, Queensland University of Technology, Centre for Applied Studies in Early Childhood, Brisbane, Australia.

Balda, S. and Irving, K. (1996) 'Parental beliefs and practices regarding young children's friendships: how similar are Australian and Indian families?', in *Footsteps to the Future: Equity and Excellence in Early Childhood*, proceedings of the Crèche and Kindergarten Association of Queensland Early Childhood Conference, Brisbane: Crèche and Kindergarten Association of Queensland.

Balda, S. and Irving, K. (1997) 'Social problem solving skills in Australian and Indian children: a comparative study', Paper presented at the 5th Annual Conference of Australian Research in Early Childhood Education, Canberra, January.

Banks, W.C. and Rompff, W.J. (1973) 'Evaluative bias and preference in Black and White children', *Child Development*, 44: 776–783.

Barber, B.K. (1996) 'Parental psychological control: revisiting a neglected construct', *Child Development*, 67: 3296–3319.

Barkow, J.H., Cosmides, L. and Tooby, J. (eds) (1992) *The Adapted Mind: Evolutionary Psychology and the Generation of Culture*, Oxford: Oxford University Press.

Baron-Cohen, S. (1989a) 'The autistic child's theory of mind: a case of specific developmental delay', *Journal of Child Psychology and Psychiatry*, 30, 2: 285–297.

Baron-Cohen, S. (1989b) 'Critical notice: thinking about thinking: how does it develop?', *Journal of Child Psychology and Psychiatry*, 30, 6: 931–933.

Baron-Cohen, S. (1991) 'The theory of mind deficit in autism: how specific is it?', *British Journal of Developmental Psychology*, 9: 301–314.

Baron-Cohen, S. (1992) 'Out of sight or out of mind? Another look at deception in autism', *Journal of Child Psychology and Psychiatry*, 33, 7: 1141–1155.

Baron-Cohen, S. (1993) 'From attention–goal psychology to belief–desire psychology: the development of a theory of mind, and its dysfunction', in S. Baron-Cohen, H. Tager-Flusberg and D. Cohen (eds) *Understanding other Minds: Perspectives from Autism*, Oxford: Oxford University Press, 59–82.

Baron-Cohen, S. and Howlin, P. (1993) 'The theory of mind deficit in autism: some questions for teaching and diagnosis', in S. Baron-Cohen, H. Tager-Flusberg and D. Cohen (eds) *Understanding other Minds: Perspectives from Autism*, Oxford: Oxford University Press, 466–480.

Baron-Cohen, S., Leslie, A.M., and Frith, U. (1985) 'Does the autistic child have a "theory of mind"?', *Cognition*, 21: 37–46.

Baron-Cohen, S., Leslie, A.M. and Frith, U. (1986) 'Mechanical, behavioural and intentional understanding of picture stories in autistic children', *British Journal of Developmental Psychology*, 4: 113–125.

Basch, M.F. (1988) *Understanding Psychotherapy: The Science Behind the Art*, New York: Basic Books.

Batsche, G.M. and Knoff, H.M. (1994) 'Bullies and their victims: understanding a pervasive problem in the schools', *School Psychology Review*, 23, 2: 165–174.

Baumrind, D. (1996) 'The discipline controversy revisited', *Family Relations*, 45: 405–414.

Bayer, J. (1996) 'Social competence and social skills training for children and adolescents: a literature review', *Australian Journal of Guidance and Counselling*, 6: 1–13.

Beelman, A., Pfingsten, U. and Losel, F. (1994) 'Effects of training social competence in children: a meta-analysis of recent studies', *Journal of Clinical Child Psychology*, 23: 260–271.

Bell. R.Q. and Chapman, M. (1986) 'Child effects in studies using experimental or brief longitudinal approaches to socialization', *Developmental Psychology*, 22: 595–603.

Belle, D. (1989) 'Gender differences in children's social networks and supports', in D. Belle (ed.) *Children's Social Networks and Supports*, New York, Wiley: 173–188.

Belsky, J. (1984) 'The determinants of parenting: a process model', *Child Development*, 55: 83–96.

Benenson, J.F. (1990) 'Gender differences in social networks', *Journal of Early Adolescence*, 10: 472–495.

Bennett, A. and Derevensky, J. (1995) 'The medieval kingdom typology: peer relations in kindergarten children', *Psychology in the Schools*, 32: 130–141.

Bennett, D. (1994) 'Depression among children with chronic medical problems: a meta-analysis', *Journal of Pedriatric Psychology*, 19, 2: 149–169.

Berdondini, L. and Smith, P.K. (1996) 'Cohesion and power in families of children involved in bully/victim problems at school: an Italian replication', *Journal of Family Therapy*, 18: 99–102.

Berg, M. and Medrich, E.A. (1980) 'Children in four neighbourhoods: the physical environment and its effect on play and play patterns', *Environment and Behavior, 12: 320–348.*

Berkowitz, L. (1993) *Aggression. Its Causes, Consequences, and Control.* New York: McGraw-Hill.

Berndt, T.J. and Keefe, K. (1995) 'Friends' influence on adolescents' adjustment to school', *Child Development*, 66: 1312–1329.

Berndt, T.J. and Ladd, G.W. (1989) *Peer Relationships in Child Development*, New York: Wiley.

Berry, J.W. (1989) 'Imposed etics-emics-derived etics: the operalization of a compelling idea', *International Journal of Psychology*, 24: 721–735.

Besag, V.E. (1989) *Bullies and Victims in Schools: A Guide to Understanding and Management*, Milton Keynes: Open University Press/Bristol: Oxford University Press.

Bhavnagri, N. and Parke, R.D. (1985) 'Parents as facilitators of preschool children's peer relationships', paper presented at the biennial meeting of the Society for Research in Child Development, Toronto, April.

Bhavnagri, N. and Parke, R.D. (1991) 'Parents as direct facilitators of children's peer relationships: effects of age of child and sex of parent', *Journal of Social and Personal Relationships*, 8: 423–440.

Bienert, H. and Schneider, B.H. (1995) 'Deficit-specific social skills training with peer nominated aggressive-disruptive and sensitive-isolated preadolescents', *Journal of Clinical Child Psychology*, 24: 287–299.

Bierman, K.L. and Furman, W. (1984) 'The effects of social skills training and peer involvement on the social adjustment of preadolescents', *Child Development*, 55: 151–162.

Bierman, K.L and McCauley, E. (1987) 'Children's descriptions of their peer interactions: useful information for clinical child assessment', *Journal of Clinical Child Psychology*, 16: 9–18.

Bierman, K.L., Miller, C.L. and Stabb, S.D. (1987) 'Improving the social behavior and peer acceptance of rejected boys: effects of social skills training with instructions and prohibitions', *Journal of Consulting and Clinical Psychology*, 55: 194–200.

Bishop, D.V.M. (1989) 'Autism, Asperger's syndrome and semantic-pragmatic disorder: where are the boundaries?', *British Journal of Disorders of Communication*, 24: 107–121.

Björkqvist, K. and Niemelä, P. (1992) 'New trends in the study of female aggression', in K. Björkqvist and P. Niemalä (eds) *Of Mice and Women: Aspects of Female Aggression*, Orlando, Fla.: Academic Press.

Björkqvist, K., Ekman, K. and Lagerspetz, K.M.J. (1982) 'Bullies and victims: their ego-picture, ideal ego-picture, and normative ego-picture', *Scandinavian Journal of Psychology*, 23: 281–290.

Björkqvist, K., Lagerspetz, K.M.J. and Kaukiainen, A. (1992a) 'Do girls manipulate and boys fight? Developmental trends regarding direct and indirect aggression', *Aggressive Behavior*, 18: 117–127.

Björkqvist, K., Österman, K. and Kaukiainen, A. (1992b) 'The development of direct and indirect aggressive strategies in males and females', in K. Björkqvist and P. Niemelä (eds) *Of Mice and Women: Aspects of Female Aggression*, Orlando, Fla.: Academic Press.

Björkqvist, K., Österman, K. and Hjelt-Bäck, M. (1994) 'Aggression among university employees', *Aggressive Behavior*, 20: 173–184.

Black, B. and Logan, A. (1995) 'Links between communication patterns in mother–child, father–child, and child–peer interactions and children's social status', *Child Development*, 66: 255–271.

Black, D., Harris-Hendriks, J. and Kaplan, T. (1992) 'Father kills mother: post-traumatic stress disorder and the children', *Psychotherapy and Psychosomatics*, 57: 152–157.

Black, H.D. (1987) 'Ethnocentrism in a pluralist society: children's perspectives', *Curriculum and Teaching*, 2: 41–47.

Blechman, E., McEnroe, M.J., Carella, E.T. and Audette, D.D. (1986) 'Childhood competence and depression', *Journal of Abnormal Psychology*, 95, 3: 223–237.

Blonk, R.W.B. (1996) 'Self-efficacy and treatment of childhood social incompetence', Unpublished doctoral dissertation, University of Amsterdam, Netherlands.

Blonk, R.W.B., Prins, P.J.M., Sergeant, J.A., Ringrose, J. and Brinkman, A.G. (1996) 'Cognitive-behavioral group therapy for socially incompetent children: short-term and maintenance effects with a clinical sample', *Journal of Clinical Child Psychology*, 25: 215–224.

Bloom, B.L. (1985) 'A factor analysis of self-report measures of family functioning', *Family Process*, 24: 225–239.

Bloom, B.L. and Naar, S. (1994) 'Self-report measures of family functioning: extensions of a factorial analysis', *Family Process*, 33: 203–216.

Bornstein, M., Bellack, A. and Hersen, M. (1977) 'Social skills training for unassertive children: a multiple baseline analysis' *Journal of Applied Behavior Analysis*, 5: 443–454.

Bost, K. (1995) 'Mother and child reports of preschoolchildren's social support networks: network correlates of peer acceptance', *Social Development*, 4: 149–164.

Bottroff, V. and Duffield, V. (1997) 'Concepts and development of friendships in individuals with autism/Asperger syndrome', Paper presented at the National Autism Conference, Sydney, Australia, March.

Boulton, M.J. and Smith, P.K. (1994) 'Bully/victim problems in middle school children', *British Journal of Developmental Psychology*, 12: 315–329.

Boulton, M.J. and Underwood, K. (1992) 'Bully/victim problems among middle school children', *British Journal of Educational Psychology*, 62: 73–87.

Bowers, L., Smith, P.K. and Binney, V. (1994) 'Perceived family relationships of bullies, victims, and bully/victims in middle childhood', *Journal of Personal and Social Relationships*, 11, 215–232.

Boyce, G. and Barnett, W. (1993) 'Siblings of persons with mental retardation: a historical perspective and recent findings', in Z. Stoneman and P. Berman (eds) *The Effects of Mental Retardation, Disability, and Illness on Sibling Relationships: Research Issues and Challenges*, Baltimore, Md.: Brookes Publishing, 145–184.

Boyce, G., Barnett, S. and Miller, B. (1991) 'Time use and attitudes among siblings: a comparison in families of children with and without Down's syndrome', Poster presented at the Biennial Meeting of the Society for Research in Child Development, Seattle, Washington, April.

Braha, V. and Rutter, D.R. (1980) 'Friendship choice in a mixed-race primary school', *Educational Studies*, 6: 271–223.

Braithwaite, J. (1989) *Crime, Shame, and Reintegration*, Cambridge: Cambridge University Press.

Braithwaite, J. and Mugford, S. (1994) 'Conditions of successful reintegration ceremonies: dealing with young offenders', *British Journal of Criminology*, 32, 2.

Brand, E.S., Ruiz, R.E. and Padilla, A.M. (1974) 'Ethnic identification and preference', *Psychological Bulletin*, 81: 860–890.

Breslau, N. (1983) 'The psychological study of chronically ill and disabled children: are healthy siblings appropriate controls?' *Journal of Abnormal Child Psychology*, 11: 379–391.

Breslau, N. and Davis, G.C. (1986) 'Chronic stress and major depression', *Archives of General Psychiatry*, 43: 309–314.

Bristol, M.M., Gallagher, J.J. (1986) 'Research on fathers of young handicapped children', in J.J. Gallagher and P.M. Vietze (eds) *Families of Handicapped*

Persons: Research, Programs and Policy Issues, Baltimore, Md.: Paul Brookes, 81–100.

Brodie-Tyrell, J. and Ahang, S. (1991) *Towards Success: A Success-Oriented Classroom*, Adelaide: Education Department of South Australia.

Brody, G. and Stoneman, Z. (1986) 'Contextual issues in the study of sibling socialization', in J.J. Gallagher and P.M. Vietze (eds) *Families of Handicapped Persons: Research, Programs and Policy Issues*, Baltimore, Md.: Paul Brookes, 197–219.

Brody, G.H.M. (1987) 'Family system and individual child correlates of sibling behavior', *American Journal of Orthopsychiatry*, 57: 561–569.

Broucek, F.J. (1991) *Shame and the Self*, New York: The Guilford Press.

Brown, D.E. (1991) *Human Universals*, New York: McGraw-Hill.

Brown, G.A. (1973) 'An exploratory study of interaction amongst British immigrant children', *British Journal of Social and Clinical Psychology*, 12: 159–162.

Brown, R. (1995) *Prejudice: Its Social Psychology*, Oxford: Blackwell.

Bryant, B. (1985) 'The neighborhood walk: sources of support in middle childhood', *Monographs of the Society for Research in Child Development*, 50, 3 (Serial No. 210).

Bryant, B.K. and DeMorris, K.A. (1992) 'Beyond parent–child relationships: potential links between family environments and peer relations', in R.D. Parke and G.W. Ladd (eds) *Family–Peer Relationships: Modes of Linkage*, Hillsdale, N.J.: Erlbaum.

Buckingham, D. (ed.) (1993) *Reading Audiences: Young People and the Media*, Manchester: Manchester University Press.

Bukowski, W.M. and Hoza, B. (1989) 'Popularity and friendship: issues in theory measurement and outcome', in T.J. Berndt and G.W. Ladd (eds) *Peer Relationships in Child Development*, New York: Wiley, 15–45.

Bukowski, W.M., Gauze, C., Hoza, B. and Newcomb, A.F. (1993) 'Differences and consistency between same-sex and other-sex peer relationships during early adolescence', *Developmental Psychology*, 29: 255–263.

Burgess, R.L. (1981) 'Relationships in marriage and the family', in S. Duck and R. Gilmour (eds) *Personal Relationships 1: Studying Personal Relationships*, New York: Academic.

Burgess, R.L. and Huston, T.L. (eds) (1979) *Social Exchange in Developing Relationships*, New York: Academic.

Burke, J., Borus, J., Burns, B., Millstein, K. and Beaslet, M. (1982) 'Changes in children's behavior after a national disaster', *American Journal of Psychiatry*, 139: 1010–1014.

Buss, A.H. (1961) *The Psychology of Aggression*, New York: Wiley.

Buss, A.H., and Durkee, A. (1957) 'An inventory for assessing different kinds of hostility', *Journal of Consulting Psychology*, 21: 343–349.

Buss, A.H. and Perry, M. (1992) 'The aggression questionnaire', *Journal of Personality and Social Psychology*, 63: 452–459.

Cadman, D., Boyle, M. and Offord, D. (1988) 'The Ontario Child Health Study: social adjustment and mental health of siblings of children with chronic health problems', *Developmental and Behavioral Pediatrics*, 9: 117–121.

Cairns, R.B. and Cairns, B.D. (1991) 'Social cognition and social networks: a developmental perspective', in D. Pepler and K. Rubin (eds) *The Development and Treatment of Childhood Aggression*, Hillsdale, N.J.: Lawrence Erlbaum, 249–278.

Cairns, R.B. and Cairns, B.D. (1994) *Lifelines and Risks: Pathways of Youth in Our Time*, Cambridge: Cambridge University Press/New York: Harvester Wheatsheaf.

Cairns, R.B., Perrin, J.E. and Cairns, B.D. (1985) 'Social structure and social cognition in early adolescence: affiliative patterns', *Journal of Early Adolescence*, 5: 339–355.

Cameron, R.J., Gersch, I., M'Gadzah and Moyse, S. (1995) 'Educational psychologists and post-trauma stress management', *Educational and Child Psychology*, 12: 5–12.

Camp, B. (1977) 'Verbal mediation in young aggressive boys', *Journal of Abnormal Psychology*, 86: 145–153.

Campbell, S.B. (1995) 'Behavior problems in preschoolchildren: a review of recent research', *Journal of Child Psychology and Psychiatry*, 36: 113–149.

Campbell, S.B., Pierce, E.W., March, C.L., Ewing, L.J. and Szumowski, E.K. (1994) 'Hard-to-manage preschool boys: symptomatic behavior across contexts and time', *Child Development*, 65: 836–851.

Cantrell, S. and Prinz, R.J. (1985) 'Multiple perspectives of rejected, neglected, and accepted children: relationship between sociometric status and behavioral characteristics', *Journal of Consulting and Clinical Psychology*, 53: 884–889.

Caplan, M., Bennetto, L. and Weissberg, R. (1991) 'The role of interpersonal context in the assessment of social problem-solving skills', *Journal of Applied Developmental Psychology*, 12: 1103–1114.

Carapetis, G. and Robinson, J.A. (1995) 'Peer preferences among preschool children from different ethnic backgrounds', Paper presented at the annual meeting of the Australian Psychological Society, Perth.

Carithers, M.C. (1970) 'School desegregation and racial cleavage, 1954–1970: a review of the literature', *Journal of Social Issues*, 26: 25–47.

Cassidy, J. (1994) 'Emotion regulation: influences of attachment relationships', in N.A. Fox (ed.) 'The development of emotion regulation: Biological and behavioural considerations', *Monographs of the Society for Research in Child Development*, 59, 240 (no. 2–3): 228–249.

Cauce, A.M., Reid, M., Landesman, S. and Gonzales, N. (1990) 'Social support in young children: measurement, structure and behavioral impact', in B.R. Sarason, I.G. Sarason and G.R. Pierce (eds) *Social Support: An Interactional View*, New York: Wiley.

Cavell, T.A. (in press) *Working with Parents of Aggressive Children: A Practitioner's Guide*, Washington, DC: American Psychological Association.

Chao, R.K. (1994) 'Beyond parental control and authoritarian parenting style: understanding Chinese parenting through the cultural notion of training', *Child Development*, 65: 1111–1119.

Chao, R.K. (1996) 'Chinese and European American mothers' beliefs about the role of parenting in children's school success', *Journal of Cross-Cultural Psychology*, 27: 403–423.

Charles, C.M. (1996) *Building Classroom Discipline: From Models to Practice* (5th edn), New York: Longman.

Chen, X. (in press) 'Peer relationships and networks and socio-emotional adjustment: a Chinese perspective', in B. Cairns and T. Farmer (eds) *Social Networks from a Developmental Perspective*, New York: Cambridge University Press.

Chen, X. and Rubin, K. (1992) 'Correlates of peer acceptance in a Chinese sample of six-year-olds', *International Journal of Behavioral Development*, 15: 259–273.

Chen, X., Dong, Q. and Zhou, H. (1997) 'Authoritative and authoritarian parenting and social practices and school performance in Chinese children', *International Journal of Behavioral Development*, 21: 855–873.

Chen, X., Rubin, K.H. and Li, B. (1995a) 'Social and school adjustment of shy and aggressive children in China', *Development and Psychopathology*, 7, 2: 337–349.

Chen, X., Rubin, K. and Li, B. (1995b) 'Social functioning and adjustment in Chinese children: a longitudinal study', *Developmental Psychology*, 31: 531–539.

Cicirelli, V. (1995) *Sibling Relationships Across the Lifespan*, New York: Plenum Press.

Cilleson, A.H., van Ijzendoorn, H.W., van Lieshout, C.F. and Hartup, W.W. (1992) 'Heterogeneity among peer-rejected boys: subtypes and stabilities', *Child Development*, 63: 893–905.

Cochran, M. and Brassard, J. (1979) 'Child development and personal social networks', *Child Development*, 50: 601–616.

Cochran, M. and Riley, D. (1988) 'Mothers' reports of children's personal networks: antecedents, concomitants, and consequences', in S. Salzinger, J. Antrobus and M. Hammer (eds) *Social Networks of Children, Adolescents, and College Students*, Hillsdale, N.J.: Lawrence Erlbaum Associates, 113–148.

Cohen, R. and Siegel, A. (1991) *Context and Development*, Hillsdale, N.J.: Lawrence Erlbaum.

Cohn, D.A., Patterson, C. and Christopoulos, C. (1991) 'The family and children's peer relations', *Journal of Social and Personal Relationships*, 8: 315–346.

Coie, J. (1985) 'Fitting social skills intervention to the target group', in B.H. Schneider, K.H. Rubin and J.E. Ledingham (eds) *Children's Peer Relations: Issues in Assessment and Intervention*, New York: Springer-Verlag, 15–45.

Coie, J.D. and Dodge, K.A. (1983) 'Continuities and changes in children's social status: a five-year longitudinal study', *Merrill-Palmer Quarterly*, 29: 815–829.

Coie, J., Dodge, K. and Coppotelli, H. (1982) 'Dimensions and types of social status: a cross-age perspective', *Developmental Psychology*, 18: 557–570.

Coie, J., Dodge, K. and Kupersmidt, J. (1990) 'Peer group behavior and social status', in S. Asher and J. Coie (eds) *Peer Rejection in Childhood*, New York: Cambridge University Press, 17–59.

Coie, J.D., Dodge, K.A., Terry, R. and Wright, V. (1991) 'The role of aggression in peer relations: an analysis of aggression episodes in boys' play groups', *Child Development*, 62: 812–826.

Cole, P.M., Michel, M.K. and Teti, L.O. (1994) 'The development of emotion regulation and dysregulation: a clinical perspective', in N.A. Fox (ed.) 'The development of emotion regulation: biological and behavioural considerations', *Monographs of the Society for Research in Child Development*, 59, 240 (No. 2–3), 73–100.

Coley, R.L. and Hoffman, L.W. (1996) 'Relations of parental supervision and monitoring to children's functioning in various contexts: moderating effects of families and neighborhoods', *Journal of Applied Developmental Psychology*, 17: 51–68.

Conway, M. (1990) *Autobiographical Memory*, Milton Keynes: Open University Press.

Coplan, R.J. and Rubin, K.H. (1998) 'Exploring and assessing nonsocial play in the preschool: the development and validation of the preschool behavior scale', *Social Development*, 7: 72–91.

Coplan, R.J., Rubin, K.H., Fox, H.A., Calkins, S.D. and Stewart, S.L. (1994) 'Being alone, playing alone, and acting alone: distinguishing among reticence and passive and active solitude in young children', *Child Development*, 65: 129–137.

Corsaro, W.A. (1994) 'Discussion, debate and friendship processes: peer discourse in US and Italian nursery schools', *Sociology of Education*, 67: 1–26.

Costanzo, P. (1991) 'Morals, mothers, and memories: the social context of developing social cognition', in R. Cohen amd A. Siegel (eds) *Context and Development*, Hillsdale, N.J.: Lawrence Erlbaum.

Cowen, E.L., Pederson, A., Babigian, H., Izzo, L.D. and Trost, M.A. (1973) 'Long-term follow-up of early detected vulnerable children', *Journal of Consulting and Clinical Psychology*, 41: 438–446.

Cowie, H. and Sharp, S. (1994) 'Tackling bullying through the curriculum', in P.K. Smith and S. Sharp (eds) *School Bullying: Insights and Perspectives*, London: Routledge.

Crick, N. and Grotpeter, J.K. (1995) 'Relational aggression, gender, and social–psychological adjustment', *Child Development*, 66: 710–722.

Crick, N.R., Casas, J.F. and Mosher, M. (1997) 'Relational and overt aggression in preschool', *Developmental Psychology*, 33: 579–588.

Crnic, K.A. and Greenberg, M.T. (1990) 'Minor parenting stresses with young children', *Child Development*, 61: 1628–1637.

Crockett, A.J., Ruffin, R.E., Schembri, D.A. and Alpers, J.H. (1986) 'The prevalence rate of respiratory symptoms in schoolchildren for two South Australian rural communities', *Australian and New Zealand Journal of Medicine*, 16: 653–657.

Crowley, S.L. and Taylor, M.J. (1994) 'Mothers' and fathers' perceptions of family functioning in families having children with disabilities', *Early Education and Development*, 5: 211–225.

Cummings, E.M. (1994a) 'Marital conflict and children's functioning', *Social Development*, 3: 16–36.

Cummings, E.M. (1994b) *Children and Marital Conflict: The Impact of Family Dispute and Resolution*, New York: Guilford.

Dale, R.R. (1991) 'Mixed versus single-sex schools', in M. Elliott (ed.) *Bullying: A Practical Guide to Coping for Schools*, Glasgow: Longman, 146–153.

Damico, S.B., Bell-Nathaniel, A. and Green, C. (1981) 'Effects of school organizational structure on interracial friendships in middle schools', *Journal of Educational Research*, 74: 388–393.

Daniels, D., Miller, J.J., Billings, A.G. and Moos, R.H. (1986) 'Psychosocial functioning of siblings of children with rheumatic disease', *The Journal of Pediatrics*, 109: 279–383.

Danziger, K. (1971) *Socialization*, Harmondsworth: Penguin.

Darling, N. and Steinberg, L. (1993) 'Parenting style as context: an integrative model', *Psychological Bulletin*, 113: 487–496.

Darwin, C.E. (1981[1871]) *The Descent of Man and Selection in Relation to Sex*, Princeton: Princeton University Press.

Darwin, C.E. (1969[1872]) *The Expression of the Emotions in Man and Animals*, Chicago: Chicago University Press.

Davey, A.G. (1983) *Learning to be Prejudiced*, London: Edward Arnold.

Deaux, K. (1984) 'From individual differences to social categories: analysis of a decade's research on gender', *American Psychologist*, 39: 105–116.

De Blasio, T. (1994) 'Children's social support: Its relationship to parenting style and self-esteem', Unpublished Honours dissertation, The Flinders University of South Australia.

Degler, C.N. (1991) *In Search of Human Nature: The Decline and Revival of Darwinism in American Social Thought*, New York: Oxford University Press.

Denham, S.A., Zoller, D. and Couchoud, E.A. (1994) 'Socialization of preschoolers' emotion understanding', *Developmental Psychology*, 30: 928–936.

DeRosier, M.E., Kupersmidt, J.B. and Patterson, C.J. (1994) 'Children's academic and behavioral adjustment as a function of the chronicity and proximity of peer rejection', *Child Development*, 65: 1799–1813.

Deseret News (1994) 'L.A. aims to quell fears in wake of boy's slaying', *Deseret News Archives*, 10 September.

Deseret News (1995) 'Teacher gunned down at school parking lot', *Deseret News Archives*, 25 May.

Desguin, B.W., Holt, I.J. and McCarthy, S.M. (1994) 'Comprehensive care of the child with a chronic condition. Part 1: Understanding chronic conditions in childhood', *Current Problems in Pediatrics*, July: 199–218.

De Sousa, R. (1987) *The Rationality of Emotion*, Cambridge, Mass.: MIT Press.

De Vries, D.L. and Slavin, R.E. (1978) 'Teams-Games-Tournaments (TGT): review of ten classroom experiments', *Journal of Research and Development in Education*, 12: 28–38.

Diabetes Control and Complications Trial Research Group (1993) *New England Journal of Medicine*, 329: 977–986.

Diehl, V.A., Zea, M.C. and Espino, C.M. (1994) 'Exposure to war violence, separation from parents, post-traumatic stress and cognitive functioning in Hispanic children', *Review of Interamerican Psychology*, 28: 25–41.

Dishion, T. (1990) 'The family ecology of boys' peer relations in middle childhood', *Child Development*, 61: 874–892.

Dix, T. (1991) 'The affective organization of parenting: adaptive and maladaptive processes', *Psychological Bulletin*, 110: 3–25.

Dix, T., Ruble, D.N. and Zambarano, R.J. (1989) 'Mothers' implicit theories of discipline: child effects, parent effects, and the attribution process', *Child Development*, 60: 1373–1391.

Dodge, K.A. (1983) 'Behavioral antecedents of peer social status', *Child Development*, 54: 1386–1399.

Dodge, K.A. (1986) 'A social information processing model of social competence in children', in M. Perlmutter (ed.) *Cognitive Perspectives on Children's Social and Behavioral Development*, The Minnesota Symposia on Child Psychology (vol. 18), Hillsdale, N.J.: Lawrence Erlbaum.

Dodge, K. and Coie, J. (1987) 'Social–information–processing factors in reactive and proactive aggression in children's peer groups', *Journal of Personality and Social Psychology* 53, 6: 1146–1158.

Dodge, K.A., Coie, J.D., Pettit, G.S. and Price, J.M. (1990) 'Peer status and aggression in boys' groups: developmental and contextual analyses', *Child Development*, 61: 649–665.

Dodge, K.A., McClaskey, C.L. and Feldman, E. (1985) 'Situational approach to the assessment of social competence in children', *Journal of Consulting and Clinical Psychology*, 53: 344–353.

Dodge, K.A., Murphy, R.R. and Buchsbaum, K. (1984) 'The assessment of intention-cue detection skills in children: implications for developmental psychopathology', *Child Development*, 55: 163–173.

Dodge, K.A., Pettit, G.S., McClaskey, C.L. and Brown, M.M. (1986) 'Social competence in children', *Monograph of the Society for Research in Child Development* (Serial No. 213), vol. 51, 2.

Donald, M. (1991) *Origins of the Modern Mind: Three Stages in the Evolution of Culture and Cognition*, Cambridge, Mass.: Harvard University Press.

Donaldson, M. (1992) *Human Minds: An Exploration*, London: Allen Lane.

Downey, G. and Coyne, J.C. (1990) 'Children of depressed parents: an integrative review', *Psychological Bulletin*, 108: 50–76.

Doyle, A.-B. (1982) 'Friends, acquaintances and strangers: the influence of familiarity and ethnolinguistic background on social interaction', in K.H. Rubin and H.S. Ross (eds) *Peer Relationships and Social Skills in Childhood*, New York: Springer-Verlag.

Dreidger, L. (1976) 'Ethnic self-identity: a comparison of ingroup evaluations', *Sociometry*, 39: 131–141.

Drotar, D. (1981) 'Psychological perspective of chronic childhood illness', *Journal of Pediatric Psychology*, 6, 3: 211–228.

Dunn, J. (1988) *The Beginnings of Social Understanding*, Oxford: Blackwell.

Dunn, J. (1992) 'Sisters and brothers: current issues in developmental research', in F. Boer and J. Dunn (eds) *Children's Sibling Relationships: Developmental and Clinical Issues*, Hillsdale, N.J.: Erlbaum, 1–17.

Dunn, J., Brown, J. and Beardsall, L. (1991) 'Family talk about feelings states and children's later understanding of others' emotions', *Child Development*, 27: 448–455.

Durkin, K. (1985) *Television, Sex Roles and Children*, Philadelphia: Open University Press.

Durlak, J. (1983) 'Social problem solving as a primary prevention strategy', in R. Felner, L. Jason, J. Moritsugo and S. Farber (eds) *Preventive Psychology*, New York: Pergamon, 31–48.

Durojaiye, M.O.A. (1970) 'Patterns of friendship in an ethnically-mixed junior school', *Race*, 12: 189–200.

Dyson, L. (1989) 'Adjustment of siblings of handicapped children: a comparison', *Journal of Pediatric Psychology*, 14: 215–229.

Dyson, L., Edgar, E. and Crnic, K. (1989) 'Psychological predictors of adjustment by siblings of developmentally disabled children', *American Journal on Mental Retardation*, 94, 3: 292–302.

Eagly, A.H. and Steffen, V.J. (1986) 'Gender and aggressive behavior. A meta-analytic review of social psychological literature', *Psychological Bulletin*, 100: 309–330.

Economist (1994) 'Evo-economics: biology meets the dismal science', Dec. 25–Jan. 7: 91–93.

Edelman, G. (1992) *Bright Air, Brilliant Fire: On The Matter of The Mind*, New York: Basic Books.

Education Department of South Australia (1990) *Educating for the 21st Century: A Charter for Public Schooling in South Australia*, Adelaide: Education Department of South Australia.

Edwards, C.P. (1992) 'Cross-cultural perspectives on family–peer relations', in R.D. Parke and G.W. Ladd (eds) *Family–peer Relationships: Modes of Linkage*, Hillsdale, N.J.: Erlbaum, 285–316.

Eisenberg, N. (1986) *Altruism, Emotion, Cognition, and Behavior*, Hillsdale, N.J.: Erlbaum.

Eisenberg, N., Fabes, R.A., Carlo, G., Troyer, D., Speer, A.L., Karbon, M. and Switzer, G. (1992) 'The relations of maternal practices and characteristics to children's vicarious emotional responsiveness', *Child Development*, 63: 583–602.

Eisenberg, N., Fabes, R.A., Murphy, B., Maszk, P., Smith, M. and Karbon, M. (1995) 'The role of emotionality and regulation in children's social functioning: a longitudinal study', *Child Development*, 66: 1360–1384.

Eisenmajer, R. and Prior, M. (1991) 'Cognitive linguistic correlates of "theory of mind" ability in autistic children', *British Journal of Developmental Psychology*, 8: 351–364.

Eiser, J.R. and Van der Pligt, J. (1984) 'Attitudinal and social factors in adolescent smoking: in search of peer group influence', *Journal of Applied Social Psychology*, 14: 348–363.

Elardo, P.T. and Caldwell, B.M. (1979) 'The effects of an experimental social development program in children in the middle childhood period', *Psychology in the Schools*, 16: 93–100.

Elbedour, S., Ten Besel, R. and Muruyama, G.M. (1993) 'Children at risk: psychological coping with war and conflict in the Middle East', *International Journal of Mental Health*, 22: 33–52.

Elias, M. and Allen, G.J. (1991) 'A comparison of instructional methods for delivering a preventive social competence/social decision-making program to at-risk, average, and competent students', *School Psychology Quarterly*, 6: 251–272.

Elias, N. (1978[1939]) *The Civilising Process: I. The History of Manners*, Oxford: Basil Blackwell.

Elias, N. (1982[1939]) *The Civilising Process: II. State Formation and Civilisation*, Oxford: Basil Blackwell.

Elliott, M. (1992) 'Bullies, victims, signs, solutions', in M. Elliott (ed.) *Bullying: A Practical Guide to Coping for Schools*, Harlow, Essex: Longman.

Elliott, S.N. and Busse, R.T. (1991) 'Social skills assessment and intervention with children and adolescents', *School Psychology International*, 12: 68–83.

Ellis, S., Rogoff, B. and Cromer, C.C. (1981) 'Age segregation in children's social interactions', *Developmental Psychology*, 17: 399–407.

Epstein, J.L. (1986) 'Choice of friends over the life-span: developmental and environmental influences', in E.C. Mueller and C.R. Cooper (eds) *Process and Outcome in Peer Relations,* New York: Academic Press, 129–160.

Eron, L. (1987) 'The development of aggressive behavior from the perspective of a developing behaviorism', *American Psychologist,* 42: 435–442.

Erwin, P. (1993) *Friendship and Peer Relations in Children,* Chichester: John Wiley and Sons.

Erwin, P.G. and Ruane, G.E. (1993) 'Effectiveness of social skills training with children: a meta-analytic study', *Counselling Psychology Quarterly,* 7: 305–310.

Fagan, J.F. and Singer, L.T. (1979) 'The role of simple feature differences in infants' recognition of faces', *Infant Behavior and Development,* 2: 39–45.

Fein, D., Pennington, B., Makowitz, P., Braveman, M. and Waterhouse, L. (1986) 'Toward a neuropsychological model of infantile autism: are the social deficits primary?', *Journal of American Academy of Child Psychiatry,* 25: 198–212.

Feiring, C. and Lewis, M. (1988) 'The child's social network from three to six years: the effects of age, sex, and SES', in S. Salzinger, J. Antrobus, M. Hammer (eds) *Social Networks of Children, Adolescents, and College Students,* Hillsdale, N.J.: Erlbaum, 93–112.

Feiring, C. and Lewis, M. (1989) 'The social networks of girls and boys from early through middle childhood', in D. Belle (ed.) *Children's Social Networks and Social Supports,* New York: John Wiley and Sons, 119–150.

Ferguson, D.M., Horwood, L.J. and Lynskey, M. (1994) 'The childhoods of multiple problem adolescents: a 15-year longitudinal study', *Journal of Child Psychology and Psychiatry,* 35: 1123–1140.

Ferraresi, L. (1988) 'Identita sociale, categorizzazione e pregiudizio', Tesi di Laurea, University of Bologna (cited in Brown 1995).

Feshbach, N. (1969) 'Sex differences in children's modes of aggressive responses toward outsiders', *Merrill-Palmer Quarterly of Behavior and Development,* 15: 249–258.

Feshbach, N.D. (1988) 'Television and the development of empathy', in S. Oskamp (ed.) *Television as a Social Issue: Applied Social Psychology Annual 8,* Newbury Park, Calif.: Sage.

Feshbach, N. and Sones, G. (1971) 'Sex differences in adolescents' reactions toward newcomers', *Developmental Psychology,* 4: 381–386.

Field, T. (1995) 'Psychologically depressed parents', in M.H. Bornstein (ed.) *Handbook of Parenting: Vol. 4. Applied and Practical Parenting,* Mahwah, N.J.: Erlbaum, 85–99.

Fine, G.A. (1981) 'Friends, impression management and preadolescent behaviour', in S.R. Asher and J.M. Gottman (eds) *The Development of Children's Friendships,* New York: Cambridge University Press, 29–52.

Finkelhor, D. (1988) 'The trauma of child sexual abuse. Two models', in G. Wyatt and G. Powell (eds) *Lasting Effects of Child Sexual Abuse,* Newbury Park, Calif. and London: Sage, 61–84.

Finkelstein, N.W. and Haskins, R. (1983) 'Kindergarten children prefer same-color peers', *Child Development,* 54: 502–508.

Finnie, V. and Russell, A. (1988) 'Preschoolchildren's social status and their mothers' behavior and knowledge in the supervisory role', *Developmental Psychology,* 24: 789–801.

Flannagan, D. (1996) 'Mothers' and kindergarteners' talk about interpersonal relationships', *Merrill-Palmer Quarterly*, 42: 519–536.

Flannagan, D. and Baker-Ward, L. (1996) 'Relations between mother–child discussions of children's preschool and kindergarten experiences', *Journal of Applied Developmental Psychology*, 17: 423–437.

Follain, M. (1996) 'Frame acts on school violence', *The Times*, 5 April.

Foot, H.C., Morgan, M.J. and Shute, R.H. (1990) (eds) *Children Helping Children*, Chichester: Wiley.

Foreman, P. (ed.) (1996) *Integration and Inclusion in Action*, Harcourt Brace: Sydney, NSW.

Forness, S.R. and Kavale, K. (1996) 'Treating social skill deficits in children with learning disabilities: a meta-analysis of the research', *Learning Disability Quarterly*, 19: 2–13.

Fox, N.A., Coplan, R.J., Rubin, K.H., Porges, S.W., Calkins, S.D., Long, J.M., Marshall, T.R. and Stewart, S. (1995) 'Frontal activation asymmetry and social competence at four years of age', *Child Development*, 66: 1770–1784.

Fox, R. (1989) *The Search for Society: Quest for a Biosocial Science and Morality*, New Brunswick: Rutgers University Press.

Frank, N. (1996) 'Helping families support siblings', in P.J. Beckman (ed.) *Strategies for Working with Families of Young Children with Disabilities*, Baltimore, Md.: Paul H. Brookes Publishing Co., 169–188.

Frank, R. (1988) *Passions With Reason: The Strategic Role of the Emotions*, New York: W.W. Norton.

French, D. (1988) 'Heterogeneity of peer-rejected boys: aggressive and non-aggressive subtypes', *Child Development* 59: 976–985.

French, D. (1990) 'Heterogeneity of peer rejected girls', *Child Development*, 61: 2028–2031.

French, D.C., Setiono, K. and Eddy, J.M. (in press) 'Bootstrapping through the cultural comparison minefield: childhood social status and friendship in the United States and Indonesia', in W.A. Collins and B. Laursen (eds) *Relationships as Developmental Contexts: A Tribute to Willard W. Hartup*, Mahwah, N.J.: Lawrence Erlbaum.

Frith, U. (1991) 'Asperger and his syndrome', in U. Frith (ed.) *Autism and Asperger Syndrome*, Cambridge: Cambridge University Press, 1–36.

Frodi, A., Macaulay, J. and Thome, P.R. (1977) 'Are women always less aggressive than men?', *Psychological Bulletin*, 84: 634–660.

Frost, L. (1992) 'A primary school approach – what can be done about the bully?', in M. Elliot (ed.) *Bullying: A Practical Guide to Coping for Schools*, Harlow, Essex: Longman.

Furman, W. (1984) 'Enhancing children's peer relations and friendships', in S. Duck (ed.) *Personal Relationships 5: Repairing Personal Relationships*, London: Academic Press, 103–126.

Furman, W. and Buhrmester, D. (1985) 'Children's perceptions of the personal relationships in their social networks', *Developmental Psychology*, 21: 1016–1024.

Furman, W.C. (1993) 'Contemporary themes in research on sibling relationships of nondisabled children', in Z. Stoneman and P.W. Berman (eds) *The Effects of Mental Retardation, Disability, and Illness on Sibling Relationships: Research Issues and Challenges*, Baltimore, Md.: Paul H. Brookes Publishing, 31–50.

Gallo, A. and Knafl, K. (1993) 'Siblings of children with chronic illness: a categorical and noncategorical look at selected literature', in Z. Stoneman and P. Berman (eds) *The Effects of Mental Retardation, Disability, and Illness on Sibling Relationships: Research Issues and Challenges*, Baltimore, Md.: Brookes Publishing, 215–234.

Gamble, W. and McHale, S. (1989) 'Coping with stress in sibling relationships: a comparison of children with disabled and nondisabled siblings', *Journal of Applied Developmental Psychology*, 10: 353–373.

Gamble, W. and Woulbroun, E.J. (1993) 'Measure considerations in the identification and assesment of stressors and coping strategies', in Z. Stoneman and P.W. Berman (eds) *The Effects of Mental Retardation, Disability, and Illness on Sibling Relationships: Research Issues and Challenges*, Baltimore, Md.: Paul Brookes Publishing, 287–319.

Garbarino, J. (1982) *Children and Families in the Social Environment*, New York: Aldine.

Garcia Coll, C.T., Meyer, E.C. and Brillon, L. (1995) 'Ethnic and minority parenting', in M.H. Bornstein (ed.) *Handbook of Parenting: Vol. 2. Status and Social Conditions of Parenting*, Mahwah, N.J.: Lawrence Erlbaum, 189–209.

Garfinkel, H. (1956) 'Conditions of successful degradation ceremonies', *American Journal of Sociology*, 61: 420–424.

Gath, A. (1972) 'The mental health of siblings of a congenitally abnormal child', *Journal of Child Psychology and Psychiatry*, 13: 211–218.

Gath, A. (1973) 'The school-age siblings of mongol children', *British Journal of Psychiatry*, 123: 161–167.

Gazzaniga, M. (1992) *Nature's Mind: The Biological Roots of Thinking, Emotions, Sexuality, Language, and Intelligence*, New York: Basic Books.

Geller, J. and Johnston, C. (1995) 'Predictors of mothers' responses to child noncompliance: attributions and attitudes', *Journal of Clinical Child Psychology*, 24: 272–278.

George, D.M. and Hoppe, R.A. (1979) 'Racial identification, preference, and self-concept', *Journal of Cross-Cultural Psychology*, 10: 85–100.

Gerrull, S. and Atkinson, L. (eds) (1994) *National Conference on Juvenile Justice*, Canberra: AIC.

Gettinger, M., Doll, B. and Salmon, D. (1994) 'Effects of social problem solving, goal setting, and parent training on children's peer relations', *Journal of Applied Developmental Psychology*, 15: 141–163.

Giles, H. (ed.) (1977) *Language, Ethnicity and Intergroup Relations*, London: Academic.

Gillberg, C. (1991) 'Clinical and neurobiological aspects of Asperger syndrome in six family studies', in U. Frith (ed.) *Autism and Asperger Syndrome*, Cambridge: Cambridge University Press, 122–146.

Gillberg, C. (1995) 'Autism and its spectrum disorders. Epidemiology and neurobiology', *National Autism Conference: Building Bridges Proceedings*, (Feb. 24–26), Brisbane: Autism Children's Association of Queensland (Inc.), 101–140.

Gilligan, C. (1982) *In a Different Voice: Psychological Theory and Women's Development*, Cambridge, Mass.: Harvard University Press.

Glynn, T. (1992) 'Discipline is for the whole school', in K. Wheldall (ed.)

Discipline in Schools: Psychological Perspectives on the Elton Report, London: Routledge.

Goldfried M.R. and d'Zurilla T.J. (1969) 'A behavioral analytic model for assessing competence', in C.D. Spielberger (ed.) *Current Topics in Clinical and Community Psychology* (Vol. 1), New York: Academic Press, 151–196.

Gordon, R.M. (1987) *The Structure of Emotions: Investigations in Cognitive Philosophy*, New York: Cambridge University Press.

Gottfredson, M.R. and Hirschi, T. (1990) *A General Theory Of Crime*, San Francisco, Calif.: Stanford University Press.

Gottman, J. (1983) 'How children become friends', *Monographs of the Society for Research for Child Development*, 48, Serial No. 201: 3.

Gottman, J., Gonso, J. and Schuler, P. (1976) 'Teaching social skills to isolated children', *Journal of Abnormal Child Psychology*, 4: 179–197.

Gottman, J.M., Katz, L.F. and Hooven, C. (1996) 'Parental meta-emotion philosophy and the emotional life of families: theoretical models and preliminary data', *Journal of Family Psychology*, 10: 243–268.

Graetz, B. and Shute, R. (1995) 'Assessment of peer relationships in children with asthma', *Journal of Pediatric Psychology*, 20, 2: 205–216.

Graziano, W.G. and Musser, L.M. (1982) 'The joining and parting of the ways', in S. Duck and R. Gilmour (eds) *Personal relationships 4: Dissolving Personal Relationships*, New York: Academic Press.

Green, A. (1983) 'Dimensions of psychological trauma in abused children', *Journal of American Academy of Child Psychiatry*, 22: 231–237.

Green, L., Richardson, D. and Lago, T. (1996) 'How do friendship, indirect, and direct aggression relate?', *Aggressive Behavior*, 22: 81–86.

Gresham, F.M. (1981) 'Validity of social skills measures for assessing social competence in low-status children: a multivariate investigation', *Developmental Psychology*, 17: 390–398.

Gresham, F.M. (1982) 'Misguided mainstreaming: the case for social skills training with handicapped children', *Exceptional Children*, 48, 5: 422–433.

Gresham, F.M. (1985) 'Utility of cognitive-behavioural procedures for social skills training with children: a review', *Journal of Abnormal Child Psychology*, 13: 411–423.

Gresham, F.M. (1986a) 'Conceptual and definitional issues in the assessment of children's social skills: implications for classification and training', *Journal of Clinical Psychology*, 15: 16–25.

Gresham, F.M. (1986b) 'Conceptual issues in the assessment of social competence in children', in P.S. Strain, M.J. Guralnick and H.M. Walker (eds) *Children's Social Behavior*, New York: Academic Press, 143–180.

Gresham, F.M. (1988) 'Social skills: conceptual and applied aspects of assessment, training, and social validation', in J.C. Witt, S.N. Elliott and F.M. Gresham, *Handbook of Behavior Therapy in Education*, New York: Plenum Press, 523–546.

Gresham, F.M. and Elliott, S.N. (1990) *Social Skills Rating System Manual*, Circle Pines, Minn.: American Guidance Service.

Gresham, F.M. and Nagle, R.J. (1980) 'Social skills training with children: responsiveness to modelling and coaching as a function of peer orientation', *Journal of Consulting and Clinical Psychology*, 48: 718–729.

Groeblinghoff, D. and Becker, M. (1996) 'A case study of mobbing and the clinical treatment of mobbing victims', *European Journal of Work and Organisational Psychology*, 5: 277–294.

Grusec, J.E. and Goodnow, J.J. (1994) 'Impact of parental discipline methods on the child's internalization of values: a reconceptualization of current points of view', *Developmental Psychology*, 30: 4–19.

Grych, J.H. and Fincham, F.D. (1993) 'Children's appraisals of marital conflict: Initial investigations of the cognitive–contextual framework', *Child Development*, 64: 215–230.

Guerney, L.F. and Guerney, B.G., Jr. (1987) 'Integrating child and family therapy', *Psychotherapy*, 24: 609–614.

Guevremont, D.C. and Foster, S.L. (1993) 'Impact of social problem-solving training on aggressive boys: skill acquisition, behavior change, and generalization', *Journal of Abnormal Child Psychology*, 21: 13–27.

Gunter, B. and McAleer, J.L. (1990) *Children and Television: The One Eyed Monster?*, London: Routledge.

Guralnick, M.J., Connor, R.T., Hammond, M.A., Gottman, J.M. and Kinnish, K. (1996) 'The peer relations of preschoolchildren with communication disorders', *Child Development*, 67: 471–489.

Hallinan, M.T. and Williams, R.A. (1990) 'Students' characteristics and the peer-influence process', *Sociology of Education*, 63: 122–132.

Hanson, C.L. (1992) 'Developing systemic models of the adaptation of youths with diabetes', in A.M. La Greca, L.J. Siegel, J.L. Wallander and C.E. Walker (eds) *Stress and Coping in Child Health*, New York: Guilford Press.

Hargreaves, D. (1973) *Social Relations in a Secondary School*, London: Routledge and Kegan Paul.

Harkness, S. and Super, C. (1995) 'Culture and parenting', in M.H. Bornstein (ed.) *Handbook of Parenting: Vol 3. Status and Social Conditions of Parenting*, Mahwah, N.J.: Lawrence Erlbaum.

Harris, P.L. (1985) 'What children know about the situations that provoke emotion', in M. Lewis and C. Saarni (eds) *The Socialisation of Emotions*, New York: Plenum Press, 161–185.

Harris, P., Olthof, T. and Meerum Terwogt, M. (1981) 'Children's knowledge of emotion', *Journal of Child Psychology and Psychiatry*, 22: 247–261.

Harrist, A.W., Pettit, G.S., Dodge, K.A. and Bates, J.E. (1994). 'Dyadic synchrony in mother–child interaction: relations with children's subsequent kindergarten adjustment', *Family Relations*, 43: 417–424.

Hart, C.H., DeWolf, M.D., Wozniak, P. and Burts, D.C. (1992) 'Maternal and paternal disciplinary styles: relations with preschoolers' playground behavioral orientations and peer status', *Child Development*, 63: 879–892.

Hart, C.H., McGee, L. and Hernandez, S. (1993) 'Themes in the peer relations literature: correspondence to playground interactions portrayed in children's literature', in C.H. Hart (ed.) *Children on Playgrounds: Research Perspectives and Applications*, Albany: State University of New York Press, 371–416.

Hart, C.H., Olsen, S.F., Robinson, C.C. and Mandleco, B.L. (1997) 'The development of social and communicative competence in childhood: review and a model of personal, familial, and extrafamilial processes', in B.R. Burleson (ed). *Communication Yearbook*, 20: 305–373.

Hart, C.H., Nelson, D.A., Robinson, C.C., Olsen, S.F. and McNeilly-Choque,

M.K. (1998a) 'Overt and relational aggression in Russian nursery-school-age children: parenting style and marital linkages', *Developmental Psychology*, 34: 687–697.

Hart, C.H., Yang, C., Nelson, L.J., Jin, S., Olsen, J.A., Nelson, D.A., Wu, P., Robinson, C.C. and Porter, C. (1998b) 'Peer acceptance in early childhood and subtypes of socially withdrawn behavior in China, Russia, and the United States', Paper presented at the XVth Biennial International Society for the Study of Behavioral Development Meetings, Berne, Switzerland, July.

Hart, C.H., Yang, C., Nelson, D.A., Jin, S., Robinson, C.C. and McNeilly-Choque, M.K. (1998c) 'Subtypes of aggression and victimization in Chinese, Russian and US preschoolers: sex and peer status linkages'. (Manuscript submitted for publication.)

Hart, C.H., Nelson, D.A., Robinson, C.C., Olsen, S.F., McNeilly-Choque, M.K. and McKee, T.R. (in press) 'Russian parenting styles and family processes: linkages with subtypes of victimization and aggression' in K.A. Kerns, J.M. Contreras and A. Neal-Barnett (eds) *Family and Peers: Linking Two Social Worlds*, Westport, Conn.: Praeger.

Harter, S. (1983) 'Developmental perspectives on the self-esteem', in E.M. Hetherington (ed.) *Handbook of Child Psychology: Vol. 4. Socialization, Personality, and Social Development* (4th. edn), New York: John Wiley and Sons, 275–385.

Hartup, W.W. (1976) 'Peer interaction and the behavioral development of the individual child', in E. Schopler and R.J. Reichler (eds) *Psychopathology and Child Development*, New York: Plenum, 203–218.

Hartup, W.W. (1983) 'Peer relations', in E.M. Hetherington (ed.) *Handbook of Child Psychology, Vol. 4, Socialization, Personality and Social Development* (4th edn), New York: Wiley.

Hartup, W.W (1992) 'Peer relations in early and middle childhood', in V. Van Hasselt and M. Hersen (eds) *Handbook of Social Development: A Lifespan Perspective*, New York: Plenum Press.

Hartup, W.W. and Laursen, B. (1993) 'Conflict and context in peer relations', in C.H. Hart (ed.) *Children on Playgrounds: Research Perspectives and Applications*, Albany: State University of New York Press, 44–84.

Hartup, W.W. and Sancilio, M.F. (1986) 'Children's friendships', in E. Schopler and G.B. Mesibov (eds) *Social Behavior in Autism*, New York: Plenum Press, 61–78.

Hawkins, J.D. and Weiss, J.G. (1983) 'The Social Development Model: an integrated approach to delinquency prevention', in R.J. Rubel (ed.) *Juvenile Delinquency Prevention: Emerging Perspectives of The 1980s*, San Marcos, Tex.: Institute of Criminal Justice Studies, South West Texas State University.

Hawkins, R.P. (1991) 'Is social validity what we are interested in? Argument for a functional approach', *Journal of Applied Behavior Analysis*, 24: 205–213.

Hazen, N.L. and Black, B. (1989) 'Preschool peer communication skills: the role of social status and interaction context', *Child Development*, 60: 867–876.

Hazen, N.L., Black, B. and Fleming-Johnson, F. (1984) 'Social acceptance', *Young Children*, 4: 26–35.

Heaman, D.J. (1995) 'Perceived stressors and coping strategies of parents who have children with developmental disabilities: a comparison of mothers with fathers', *Journal of Pediatric Nursing*, 10: 311–320.

Heider, F. (1958) *The Psychology of Interpersonal Relations*, New York: Wiley.

Heinnemann, P.P. (1972) *Mobbning-gruppvald barn och vuxna*, Stockholm: Natur och Kultur.

Heller, M. (1987) 'The role of language in the formation of ethnic identity', in J.S. Phinney and M.J. Rotheram (eds) *Children's Ethnic Socialization*, Newbury Park, Calif.: Sage.

Hill, T. (1989) 'Neglected and rejected children: promoting social competence in early childhood settings', *Australian Journal of Early Childhood*, 14, 1: 11–16.

Ho, D.Y.F. (1986) 'Chinese pattern of socialization: a critical review', in M.H. Bond (ed.) *The Psychology of the Chinese People*, New York: Oxford University Press, 1–37.

Ho, M. (1995) 'Sociolinguistic and metalinguistic skills of preschool children from non-English speaking backgrounds', Unpublished Honours thesis, Flinders University of South Australia.

Hobson, R.P. (1992) 'Social perception in high-level autism', in E. Schopler and G.B. Mesibov (eds) *High-functioning Individuals with Autism*, New York: Plenum Press, 157–184.

Hobson, R.P. (1993) *Autism and the Development of Mind*, Sussex: Lawrence Erlbaum Associates.

Hodgkinson, P. and Stewart, M. (1991) *Coping with Catastrophe. A Handbook of Disaster Management*, London: Routledge.

Hops, H. (1982) 'Social-skills training for socially isolated children', in P. Karoly and J.J. Steffen (eds) *Improving Children's Competence: Advances in Child Behavioral Analysis And Therapy: (Volume One)*, Toronto: Lexington Books, 39–97.

Hops, H. and Greenwood, C.R. (1988) 'Social skill deficits', in E.J. Mash and L.G. Terdal (eds) *Behavioral Assessment of Childhood Disorders* (2nd edn), New York: Guilford Press, 263–314.

Horowitz, E.L. (1936) 'The development of attitude towards the Negro', *Archives of Psychology*, 194: 5–47.

Howe, G.W. (1993) 'Siblings of children with physical disabilities and chronic illnesses: studies of risk and social ecology', in Z. Stoneman and P.W. Berman (eds) *The Effects of Mental Retardation, Disability, and Illness on Sibling Relationships: Research Issues and Challenges*, Baltimore, Md.: Paul Brooks Publishing, 185–213.

Howes, C. (1983) 'Patterns of friendship', *Child Development*, 54: 1041–1053.

Howes, C. (1988) *Peer Interaction of Young Children*, Monographs of the Society for Research in Child Development 53 (Serial No. 217).

Howes, C. and Phillipsen, L.C. (1992) 'Gender and friendship: relationships within peer groups of young children,' *Social Development*, 1: 231–242.

Howes, C., Droege, K. and Phillipsen, L. (1992) 'Contribution of peers to socialization in early childhood', in M. Gettinger, S. Elliott, and T. Kratochwill (eds) *Preschool and Early Childhood Treatment Directions*, Hillsdale, N.J.: Lawrence Erlbaum.

Hraba, J. and Grant, G. (1970) 'Black is beautiful: a reexamination of racial preference and identification', *Journal of Personality and Social Psychology,* 16: 398–402.

Huesmann, L.R. (1986) 'Psychological processes promoting the relation between exposure to media violence and aggressive behavior by the viewer', *Journal of Social Issues,* 42: 125–139.

Huesmann, L.R., Eron, L.D., Klein, R., Brice, P. and Fischer, P. (1983) 'Mitigating the imitation of aggressive behaviors by changing children's attitudes about media violence', *Journal of Personality and Social Psychology,* 44: 899–910.

Hughes, T. (1968 [1856]) *Tom Brown's School Days*: New York: Airmont Publishing Co.

Hume, D. (1969[1739–40]) *A Treatise of Human Nature,* Harmondsworth: Penguin.

Hurtig, A.L. and White, L.S. (1986) 'Psychosocial adjustment in children and adolescents with sickle cell disease', *Journal of Pediatric Psychology,* 11: 241–247.

Hyde, J.S. (1984) 'How large are gender differences in aggression? A developmental meta-analysis', *Developmental Psychology,* 20: 1120–1134.

Hymel, S. and Asher, S.R. (1977) 'Assessment and training of isolated children's social skills', paper presented at the biennial meeting of The Society for Research In Child Development, New Orleans (ERIC Document Reproduction Service No. ED 136 930).

Hymel, S. and Franke, S. (1985) 'Children's peer relations: Assessing self-perceptions', in B. Schneider, K.H. Rubin, J.E. Ledingham (eds) *Children's Peer Relationships: Issues in Assessment and Intervention,* New York: Springer-Verlag, 75–92.

Hymel, S., Woody, A. and Bowker, A. (1993) 'Social withdrawal in childhood: considering the child's perspective', in K.H. Rubin and J.B. Asendropf (eds) *Social Withdrawal, Inhibition and Shyness in Childhood,* Hillsdale, N.J.: Lawrence Erlbaum Associates, 237–262.

Hymel, S., Woody, E., Ditner, E. and Le Mare, L. (1988) 'Children's self perceptions in different domains: are children consistent across measures, do they see what others see?', Paper presented at the biennial University of Waterloo Conference on Child Development, Waterloo, Ontario.

Hyndman, M., Thorsborne, M. and Wood, S. (1996) *Community Accountability Conferencing: Trial Report,* Brisbane: Department of Education.

Irving, K. (1994) 'Maternal beliefs, young children's peer contacts and social problem solving skills', in K. Oxenberry, K. Rigby and P. Slee (eds) *Children's Peer Relations: Cooperation and Conflict,* Conference Proceedings, Adelaide: Institute of Social Research, University of South Australia.

Irving, K. and Balda, S. (1996) 'Parental beliefs, parenting practices and young children's social competence in two cultures', Paper presented at the XIVth Biennial Meeting of the International Society for the Study of Behavior and Development, Quebec City, August.

Isabella, R.A. and Belsky, J. (1991) 'Interactional synchrony and the origins of infant-mother attachment: a replication study,' *Child Development,* 62: 373–384.

Iwaniec, D. (1995) *The Emotionally Abused and Neglected Child,* Chichester: John Wiley and Sons.

Izard, C.E. (1991) *The Psychology of Emotions,* New York: Plenum Press.

Jaffe, M.L. (1997) *Understanding Parenting* (2nd edn), Boston, Mass.: Allyn and Bacon.

Jelinek, M.M. and Brittan, E.M. (1975) 'Multiracial education 1: inter-ethnic friendship patterns', *Educational Research,* 18: 42–53.

Johnson, D.W. and Johnson, R. (1986) 'Impact of classroom organisation and instructional methods on the effectiveness of mainstreaming', in C.J. Meisal (ed.) *Mainstreaming Handicapped Children: Outcomes, Controversies and New Directions*, Hillsdale, N.J.: Lawrence Erlbaum, 219–250.

Johnson, D.W. and Johnson, R.T. (1995) 'Relations between black and white students in intergroup cooperation and competition', *Journal of Social Psychology,* 125: 421–428.

Johnson, S.B. (1985) 'The family and the child with chronic illness', in D.C. Turk and R.D. Kerns (eds) *Health, Illness and Families*, New York: Wiley.

Jones, J.C. and Barlow, D.H. (1990) 'The etiology of post-traumatic stress disorder', *Clinical Psychology Review,* 10: 299–328.

Jones, R.W. and Peterson, L.W. (1993) 'Post-traumatic stress disorder in a child following an automobile accident', *Journal of Family Practice*, 36: 223–225.

Kanner, L. (1943) 'Autistic disturbances of affective contact', *Nervous Child,* 2: 217–250.

Kaplan, R.M. and Toshima, M.T. (1990) 'The functional effects of social relationships on chronic illness and disability', in B.R. Sarason, I.G. Sarason and G.R. Pierce (eds) *Social Support: An Interactional View*, New York: Wiley.

Kaplan, R.M., Chadwick, M.W. and Schimmel, L.E. (1985) 'Social learning intervention to promote metabolic control in Type 1 diabetes mellitus: private experiment results', *Diabetes Care,* 8: 152–155.

Karniol, R. (1978) 'Children's use of intention cues in evaluating behavior', *Psychological Bulletin*, 85,1: 76–85.

Katz, L.F. and Gottman, J.M. (1994) 'Patterns of marital interaction and children's emotional development', in R.D. Parke and S.G. Kellam (eds) *Exploring Family Relationships Within Other Social Contexts*, Hillsdale, N.J.: Erlbaum, 49–74.

Kaukiainen, A., Björkqvist, K., Österman, K. and Lagerspetz, K.M.J. (1996) 'Social intelligence and empathy as antecedents of different types of aggression', in G. Ferris and T. Grisso (eds) *Understanding Aggressive Behavior in Children,* (*Annals of the New York Academy of Sciences*, vol. 794): 364–366.

Kaukiainen, A., Björkqvist, K., Lagerspetz, K.M.J., Österman, K., Salmivalli C., Forsblom, S. and Ahlbom, A. (in press) 'The relationships between social intelligence, empathy, and three types of aggression', *Aggressive Behaviour.*

Kawwa, T. (1968) 'Three sociometric studies of ethnic relations in London schools', *Race*, 10: 173–180.

Kazac, A.E. (1992) 'The social context of coping with chronic childhood illness: family systems and social support', in La Greca, A.M., Siegel, L.J., Wallander, J.L. and Walker, C.E. (eds) *Stress and Coping in Child Health*, New York: Guilford.

Kazdin, A.E., Siegel, T.C. and Bass, D. (1992) 'Cognitive problem-solving skills training and parent management training in the treatment of antisocial behavior in children', *Journal of Consulting and Clinical Psychology,* 60: 733–747.

Kazdin, A.E., Esveldt-Dawson, K., French, N.H. and Unis, A.S. (1987) 'Problem-solving skills training and relationship therapy in the treatment of antisocial child behavior', *Journal of Consulting and Clinical Psychology*, 55: 76–85.

Kennedy, J. (1992) 'Relationship of maternal beliefs and childrearing strategies to social competence in preschoolchildren', *Child Study Journal*, 22: 39–60.

Kids Helpline (1996) *Newsletter*, December Issue.

King, A.Y.C. and Bond, M.H. (1985) 'The Confucian paradigm of man: a sociological view', in W.S. Tseng and D.Y.H. Wu (eds) *Chinese Culture and Mental Health*, San Diego, Calif.: Academic Press, 29–45.

Kochanska, G. (1997) 'Mutually responsive orientation between mothers and their young children: implications for early socialization', *Child Development*, 68: 94–112.

Kochenderfer, B.J. and Ladd, G.W. (1996) 'Peer victimization: Cause or consequence of school maladjustment?', *Child Development*, 67: 267–283.

Kohn, M. (1977) *Social Competence, Symptoms and Underachievement in Childhood: A Longitudinal Perspective*, Washington, DC: Winston.

Konner, M. (1982) *The Tangled Wing: Biological Constraints on the Human Spirit*, New York: Henry Holt.

Krappman, L. (1989) 'Family relationships and peer relationships in middle childhood', in K. Kreppner and R.M. Lerner (eds) *Family Systems and Life-span Development*, Hillsdale, N.J.: Erlbaum, 93–104.

Krappman, L. (1996) 'Amicitia, drujba, shin-yu, phila, Freundschaft, friendship: on the cultural diversity of a human relationship', in W.M. Bukowski, A.F. Newcomb and W.W. Hartup (eds) *The Company They Keep: Friendship in Childhood and Adolescence*, New York: Cambridge University Press, 19–40.

Kriger, S.F. and Kroes, W.H. (1972) 'Child-rearing attitudes of Chinese, Jewish, and Protestant mothers', *Journal of Social Psychology*, 86: 205–210.

Kuczynski, L. (1984) 'Socialization goals in mother–child interaction: strategies for long-term and short-term compliance', *Developmental Psychology*, 20: 1061–1073.

Kupersmidt, J. and Coie, J. (1990) 'Preadolescent peer status, aggression, and school adjustment as predictors of externalizing problems in adolescence', *Child Development*, 61: 1350–1362.

Kupersmidt, J. and Patterson, C. (1991) 'Childhood peer rejection, aggression, withdrawal, and perceived competence as predictors of self-reported behavior problems in preadolescence', *Journal of Abnormal Child Development*, 19: 427–429.

Kupersmidt, J.B., Coie, J.D. and Dodge, K.A. (1990) 'The role of poor peer relationships in the development of disorder', in S.R. Asher and J.D. Coie (eds) *Peer Rejection In Childhood*, Cambridge: Cambridge University Press, 274–305.

Kupersmidt, J.B., Griesler, P.C., DeRosier, M.E., Patterson, C.J. and Davis, P.W. (1995) 'Childhood aggression and peer relations in the context of family and neighborhood factors', *Child Development*, 66: 360–375.

La Greca, A.M. (1990) 'Social consequences of pediatric conditions: fertile areas for future investigations and interventions?', *Journal of Pediatric Psychology*, 15: 285–307.

La Greca, A.M. (1992) 'Peer influences in pediatric chronic illness: an update', *Journal of Pediatric Psychology*, 17, 6: 775–784.

La Greca, A.M. (1993) 'Social skills training with children. Where do we go from here?' *Journal of Clinical Child Psychiatry*, 22, 1: 288–298.

La Greca, A.M. and Santogrossi, D. (1980) 'Social skills training with elementary school students: a behavioral group approach', *Journal of Consulting and Clinical Psychology*, 48: 220–227.

La Greca, A.M., Auslander, Greco, Spetter, Fisher and Santiago (1995) 'I get by with a little help from my family and friends: adolescents' support for diabetes care', *Journal of Pediatric Psychology*, 20, 4: 449–476.

Ladd, G.W. (1981) 'Effectiveness of a social learning method for enhancing children's social interaction and peer acceptance', *Child Development*, 52: 171–178.

Ladd, G.W. (1985) 'Documenting the effects of social skill training with children: process and outcome assessment', in B.H. Schneider, K.H. Rubin and J.E. Ledingham (eds) *Children's Peer Relations: Issues in Assessment and Intervention*, New York: Springer-Verlag.

Ladd, G.W. (1990) 'Having friends, keeping friends, making friends, and being liked by peers in the classroom: predictors of early school adjustment?' *Child Development*, 61: 312–331.

Ladd, G.W. (1992) 'Themes and theories: perspectives on processes in family–peer relationships', in R.D. Parke and G.W. Ladd (eds) *Family–Peer Relationships: Modes of Linkage*, Hillsdale, N.J.: Erlbaum, 3–34.

Ladd, G.W. and Asher, S.R. (1985) 'Social skill training and children's peer relations', in L. L'Abate and M. Milan (eds) *Handbook of Social Skills Training and Research*, New York John Wiley, 219–244.

Ladd, G.W. and Golter, B.S. (1988) 'Parent's management of preschoolers' peer relations: Is it related to children's social competence?', *Developmental Psychology*, 24: 109–117.

Ladd, G.W. and Hart, C.H. (1992) 'Creating informal play opportunities: are parents' and preschoolers' initiations related to children's competence with peers?', *Developmental Psychology*, 28: 1179–1187.

Ladd, G.W. and Kochenderfer, B.J. (1996) 'Linkages between friendship and adjustment during early school transitions', in W.M. Bukowski, A.F. Newcomb, W.W. Hartup (eds) *The Company They Keep: Friendship in Childhood and Adolescence*, New York: Cambridge University Press, 322–345.

Ladd, G.W. and Le Sieur, K.D. (1995) 'Parents' and children's peer relationships', in M. Bornstein (ed.) *Handbook of Parenting: Vol. 4. Applied and Practical Parenting*, Hillsdale, N.J.: Erlbaum, 377–410.

Ladd, G.W. and Price, J. (1987) 'Predicting children's social and school adjustment following the transition from preschool to kindergarten', *Child Development*, 57: 446–460.

Ladd, G.W., Kochenderfer, B.J. and Coleman, C.C. (1996) 'Friendship quality as a predictor of young children's early school adjustment', *Child Development*, 67: 1103–1118.

Ladd, G.W., Profilet, S.M. and Hart, C.H. (1992) 'Parents' management of children's peer relations: facilitating and supervising children's activities in the peer culture', in R.D. Parke and G.W. Ladd (eds) *Family–Peer Relationships: Modes of Linkage*, Hillsdale, N.J.: Erlbaum, 215–253.

Ladd, G.W., Hart, C.H., Wadsworth, E.M. and Golter, B.S. (1988) 'Preschoolers' peer networks in nonschool settings: relationship to family characteristics and school adjustment', in S. Salzinger, J. Antrobus and M. Hammer (eds) *Social*

Networks of Children, Adolescents, and College Students, Hillsdale, N.J.: Erlbaum, 61–92.

Lagerspetz, K.M.J. and Björkqvist, K. (1993) 'Indirect aggression in boys and girls', in R. Huesmann (ed.) *Aggressive Behavior: Current Perspectives*, New York: Plenum Press.

Lagerspetz, K.M.J., Björkqvist, K., Peltonen, T. (1988) 'Is indirect aggression typical of females? Gender differences in aggressiveness in 11 to 12 year old children', *Aggressive Behavior*, 14: 403–414.

Lagerspetz, K.M.J., Björkqvist, K., Berts, M. and King, E. (1982) 'Group aggression among schoolchildren in three schools', *Scandinavian Journal of Psychology*, 23: 45–52.

Laird, R.D., Pettit, G.S., Mize, J., Brown, E.G. and Lindsey, E. (1994) 'Mother–child conversations about peers: contributions to competence', *Family Relations*, 43: 425–432.

Lambert, M.C., Knight, F., Taylor, R. and Newell, A.L. (1993) 'Further comparisons of teacher and parent ratings of behavior and emotional problems in Jamaican children', *International Journal of Intercultural Relations*, 17: 1–18.

Lancelotta, G. and Vaughn, S. (1989) 'Relation between types of aggression and sociometric status: peer and teacher perceptions', *Journal of Educational Psychology*, 81: 86–90.

Landry, S.H. and Loveland, K.A. (1988) 'Communication behaviours in autism and developmental language delay', *Journal of Child Psychology and Psychiatry*, 29: 621–634.

Langer, E. (1978) 'Rethinking the role of thought in social interactions', in J. Harvey, W.K. Wickes and R. Kidd (eds) *New Directions in Attribution Research* (Vol. 2), Hillsdale, N.J.: Erlbaum, 36–58.

Larsen, A. and Olson, D.H. (1990) 'Capturing the complexity of family systems: integrating family theory, family scores, and family analysis', in T.W. Draper and A.C. Marcos (eds) *Family Variables: Conceptualization, Measurement, and Use*, Newbury Park, Calif.: Sage, 19–47.

LeClere, F. and Kowalewski, B. (1994) 'Disability in the family: the effects on children's well-being', *Journal of Marriage and the Family*, 56: 457–468.

Lederberg, A.R., Chapin, S.L., Rosenblatt, V. and Vandell, D.L. (1986) 'Ethnic, gender and age preferences among deaf and hearing preschool peers', *Child Development*, 57: 375–386.

LeMare, L. and Rubin, K.H. (1987) 'Perspective taking and peer interactions: structural and developmental analyses', *Child Development*, 58: 306–315.

Leslie, A.M. and Frith, U. (1988) 'Autistic children's understanding of seeing, knowing and believing', *British Journal of Developmental Psychology*, 6: 315–324.

Lever, J. (1978) 'Sex differences in the complexity of children's play and games', *American Sociological Review*, 43: 471–483.

Lewis, M. (1992) *Shame: The Exposed Self*, New York: Free Press.

Lieberman, A.F. (1977) 'Preschoolers' competence with peers: Relations with attachment and peer experience', *Child Development*, 48: 1277–1287.

Lin, C.C. and Fu, V.R. (1990) 'A comparison of child-rearing practices among Chinese, immigrant Chinese, and Caucasian-American parents', *Child Development*, 61: 429–433.

Lindman, R. and Sinclair, S. (1988) 'Social roles and aspirations of bullies and victims', Paper presented at the 8th World Biennial ISRA Conference, Swansea, Wales, 2–6 July.

Lindsey, E.W., Mize, J. and Pettit, G.S. (1997) 'Mutuality in parent–child play: consequences for children's peer competence', *Journal of Social and Personal Relationships*, 14: 523–538.

Lipovsky, J.A. (1991) 'Post-traumatic stress disorder in children', *Family Community Health*, 14: 42–51.

Livingstone, S. (1990) 'Interpreting a television narrative: how different viewers see a story', *Journal of Communication*, 40: 72–85.

Lobato, D. (1990) *Brothers, Sisters, and Special Needs: Information and Activities for Helping Young Siblings of Children with Chronic Illness and Developmental Disabilities*, Baltimore, Md.: Paul Brookes.

Lobato, D., Faust, D. and Spirito, A. (1988) 'Examining the effects of chronic disease and disability on children's sibling relationships', *Journal of Pediatrics*, 13: 389–407.

Lobato, D., Barbour, L., Hall, L.J. and Miller, C.T. (1987) 'Psychosocial characteristics of preschool siblings of handicapped and nonhandicapped children', *Journal of Abnormal Child Psychology*, 15: 329–338.

Lollis, S.P., Ross, H.S. and Tate, E. (1992) 'Parents' regulation of children's peer interactions: direct influences', in R.D. Parke and G.W. Ladd (eds) *Family–Peer Relationships: Modes of Linkage*, Hillsdale, N.J.: Erlbaum, 255–284.

Loomis, C.P. (1943) 'Ethnic cleavages in the Southwest as reflected in two high schools', *Sociometry*, 6: 7–26.

Lorenz, K.Z. (1965) *Evolution and Modification of Behavior*, Chicago: University of Chicago Press.

Maag, J.W. (1990) 'Social skills training in school', *Special Services in the School*, 6, 1–2: 1–19.

McCandless, B.R. and Marshall, H.R. (1957) 'A picture sociometric technique for preschoolchildren and its relation to teacher judgements of friendship', *Child Development*, 28: 139–147.

Maccoby, E.E. (1992) 'The role of parents in the socialization of children: an historical overview', *Developmental Psychology*, 28: 1006–1017.

Maccoby, E.E. and Jacklin, C.N. (1974) 'Sex differences in aggression. a rejoinder and reprise', *Child Development*, 51: 964–968.

McCubbin, M.A. and McCubbin, H. (1989) 'Theoretical orientations to family stress and coping', in C.R. Figley (ed.) *Treating Stress in Families*, New York: Brunner/Mazel, 3–44.

McCubbin, M.A. and McCubbin, H. (1992) 'Families coping with illness: the resiliency model of family stress, adjustment, and adaptation', in C.B. Danielson, B. Hamel-Bissell and P. Winstead-Fry (eds) *Families, Health, and Illness*, St. Louis: Mosby, 21–63.

McDonald, J.M. and Moore, D.B. (1995) 'Achieving the "Good Community": a local police initiative and its wider ramifications', in K. Hazlehurst (ed.) *Perceptions of Justice: Issues in Indigenous and Community Empowerment. (Justice and Reform, vol. 2*), Aldershot: Avebury.

McDonald, J.M., Moore, D.B., O'Connell, T.A. and Thorsborne, M.T. (1995) *Real Justice Training Manual: Coordinating Family Group Conferences*, Pipersville, Pa.: The Piper's Press.

MacDonald, K.B. (1987) 'Parent–child physical play with rejected, neglected, and popular boys', *Developmental Psychology*, 23: 705–711.
MacDonald, K.B. and Parke, R. (1984) 'Bridging the gap: parent–child play interaction and peer interactive competence', *Child Development*, 55: 1265–1277.
McFall, R.M. and Dodge, K.A. (1982) 'Self management and interpersonal skills learning', in P. Karoly and F.H. Kanfer (eds) *Self Management and Behavior Change*, New York: Pergamon, 353–392.
McGovern, L.P. (1976) 'Dispositional social anxiety and helping behaviour under three conditions of threat', *Journal of Personality*, 44: 84–97.
McGrath, H. (1996a) 'The importance of social skills', Conference paper, Adelaide, May.
McGrath, H.L. (1996b) 'An evaluation of three school-based whole-class social skills intervention programs', Unpublished Ph.D. manuscript, Monash University.
McGrath, H.L. and Francey, S. (1988) 'An evaluation of a school-based social skills training program', Paper presented at the Bicentennial Conference of the Australian Behaviour Modification Association, Adelaide, South Australia, May.
McGrath, H.L. and Francey, S. (1991) *Friendly Kids, Friendly Classrooms*, Melbourne: Longman Cheshire.
McGrath, H. and Noble, T. (1993) *Different Kids, Same Classroom*, Melbourne: Longman.
McGregor, J. (1993) 'Effectiveness of role playing and antiracist teaching in reducing student prejudice', *Journal of Educational Research*, 86: 215–226.
McHale, S.M. and Gamble, W.C. (1987) 'Sibling relationship and adjustment of children with disabled brothers and sisters', in F.F. Schachter and R.K. Stone (eds) *Practical Concerns about Siblings: Bridging the Research–Practice Gap*, New York: The Hawthorne Press, 131–158.
McHale, S. and Gamble, W. (1988) 'The social networks of children with disabled and nondisabled siblings', in S. Salzinger, J. Antrobus and M. Hammer (eds) *Social Networks of Children, Adolescents, and College Students*, Hillsdale, N.J.: 149–167.
McHale, S.M. and Gamble, W.C. (1989) 'Sibling relationships of children with disabled and nondisabled brothers and sisters', *Developmental Psychology*, 25: 421–429.
McHale, S. and Harris, V. (1992) 'Children's experiences with disabled and non-disabled siblings: links with personal adjustment and relationship evaluation', in F. Boer and J. Dunn (eds) *Children's Sibling Relationships*, Hillsdale, N.J.: Erlbaum.
McLeer, S.V., Deblinger, E.B., Henry, D. and Orvaschel, H. (1992) 'Sexually abused children at high risk of post-traumatic stress disorder', *Journal of the American Academy of Child & Adolescent Psychiatry*, 31: 875–879.
McMahon, R.J. and Forehand, R. (1984) 'Parent training for the noncompliant child: treatment outcome, generalization, and adjunctive therapy procedures', in R.F. Dangel and A. Polster (eds) *Parent Training: Foundations of Research and Practice*, New York: Guilford Press, 298–328.
MacMullin, C.E. (1988) 'Assessment of children's social skills: identifying social

situations that are problematic for children in school', Unpublished Ph.D. thesis, University of Connecticut.

MacMullin, C.E. (1996) 'A situational approach to assessing children's social skills at school', *Australian Journal of Guidance and Counselling*, 6 (special edition).

MacMullin, C., Aistrope, D., Brown, J.L., Hannaford, D. and Martin, M. (1992) *Sheidow Park Social Problem Solving Program*, Flinders University, Adelaide, South Australia.

McNally, R.J. (1991) 'Assessment of post-traumatic stress disorder in children', *Psychological Assessment*, 3: 531–537.

McNally, R.J. (1993) 'Stressors that produce post-traumatic stress disorder in children', in J.R.T. Davidson and E.B. Foa (eds) *Post-traumatic Stress Disorder DSM-IV and Beyond*, Washington, DC: American Psychiatric Press, 57–74.

McNeilly-Choque, M.K., Hart, C.H., Robinson, C.C., Nelson, L.J. and Olsen, S.F. (1996) 'Overt and relational aggression on the playground: correspondence among different informants', *Journal of Research in Childhood Education*, 11: 47–67.

Magrab, P. and Calcagno, P. (1978) 'Psychological impact of chronic pediatric conditions', in P.R. Magrab (ed.) *Psychological Management of Pediatric Problems*, Baltimore, Md.: University Park Press, 3–14.

Magwaza, A.S. Killian, B.J., Petersen, I. and Pillay, Y. (1993) 'The effects of chronic violence on preschoolchildren in South African township', *Child Abuse and Neglect*, 17: 795–803.

Maine, S. (1996) 'Are peer preferences of preschoolchildren influenced by skin colour, ethnicity, and/or mutual play interests', Unpublished Honours thesis, Flinders University of South Australia.

Maines, B. and Robinson, G. (1992) *Michael's Story: The No Blame Approach*, Bristol: Lame Duck Publishing (video and handbook).

Marchione, K., Michelson, L. and Mannarino, A. (1983) 'Behavioral, cognitive, combined treatments for socially maladjusted school children, Unpublished manuscript, University of Pittsburgh.

Marsh, A. (1970) 'Awareness of racial differences in West African and British children', *Race*,11: 289–302.

Marsh, H.W., Smith, I.D. and Barnes, J. (1983) 'Multitrait-multimethod analyses of the self-description questionnaire', *American Educational Research Journal*, 20: 333–357.

Martin, J. and Ross, H. (1995) 'The development of aggression within sibling conflict', *Early Education and Development*, 6: 335–358.

Mastropieri, M.A. and Scruggs, T.E. (1985–1986) 'Early intervention for socially withdrawn children', *Journal of Special Education*,19: 429–441.

Mattson, A. (1972) 'Long-term physical illness in childhood: a challenge to psychosocial adaptation', *Pediatrics*, 50: 801–811.

Medrich, E.A., Roizen, J.A., Rubin, V. and Buckley, S. (1982) *The Serious Business of Growing Up: A Study of Children's Lives Outside School*, Berkeley: University of California Press.

Mesch, D., Lew, M., Johnson, D. and Johnson, R. (1986) 'Positive interdependence, academic and collaborative-skills, group contingencies and isolated students', *American Educational Research Journal*, 23, 3: 476–488.

Mesibov, G. (1984) 'Social skills training with verbal autistic adolescents and adults: a program model', *Journal of Autism and Developmental Disorders,* 14, 4: 395–404.

Mesibov, G. (1992) 'Treatment issues with high-functioning adolescents and adults with autism', in E. Schopler and G.B. Mesibov (eds) *High-functioning Individuals with Autism,* New York: Plenum Press, 143–155.

Meyer, D. and Vadasy, P. (1994) *Sibshops: Workshops for Siblings of Children with Special Needs,* Baltimore, Md.: Brookes Publishing.

Michelson, L. and Mannarino, A.T. (1986) 'Social skills training with children: research clinical application', in P.S. Strain, J.M. Guralnick and H. Walker (eds) *Children's Social Behavior: Development, Assessment and Modification,* New York: Academic Press, 373–406.

Middleton, D. and Edwards, D. (eds) (1990) *Collective Remembering,* London: Sage.

Miedzianik, D. (1986) *My Autobiography,* Nottingham: University of Nottingham, Child Development Research Unit.

Miller, P., Danaher, D. and Forbes, D. (1986) 'Sex-related strategies for coping with interpersonal conflict in children aged five to seven', *Developmental Psychology,* 22: 543–549.

Mize, J. (1995) 'Coaching preschoolchildren in social skills: a cognitive–social learning curriculum', in G. Carteledge and J.F. Milburn (eds) *Teaching Social Skills to Children and Youth: Innovative Approaches* (3rd edn), Boston, Mass: Allyn and Bacon, 237–261.

Mize, J. and Abell, E. (1996) 'Encouraging social skills in young children: tips teachers can share with parents', *Dimensions of Early Childhood,* 24: 15–23.

Mize, J. and Ladd, G.W. (1990) 'A social–cognitive learning approach to social skill training with low-status preschoolchildren', *Developmental Psychology,* 26: 388–397.

Mize, J. and Pettit, G.S. (1997) 'Mothers' social coaching, mother–child relationship style, and children's peer competence: is the medium the message?', *Child Development,* 68: 291–311.

Mize, J., Pettit, G.S., and Brown, E.G. (1995) 'Mothers' supervision of their children's peer-play: relations with beliefs, perceptions and knowledge', *Developmental Psychology,* 31: 311–321.

Modell, A. (1990) *Other Times, Other Realities,* Cambridge, Mass.: Harvard University Press.

Moore, D.B. (1993) 'Shame, forgiveness, and juvenile justice', *Criminal Justice Ethics,* 12: 3–25.

Moore, D.B and Forsythe, L. (1995) *A New Approach to Juvenile Justice: An Evaluation of Family Group Conferencing in Wagga Wagga*', Wagga Wagga: Centre for Rural Social Research.

Moore, R. and Young, D. (1978) 'Children outdoors: toward a social ecology of the landscape', in I. Altman and J.F. Wohlwill (eds) *Children and the Environment,* New York: Plenum, 83–130.

Morgan, M.J. and Eiser, J.R. (1990) 'Smoking education and peer group influence', in H.C. Foot, M.J. Morgan and R.H. Shute (eds) *Children Helping Children,* Chichester: Wiley.

Morison, P. and Masten, A. (1991) 'Peer reputation in middle childhood as a predictor of adaptation in adolescence: a seven-year follow-up', *Child Development,* 62: 991–1007.

Morland, J.K. (1969) 'Race awareness among American and Hong Kong Chinese children', *American Journal of Sociology,* 75: 360–374.

Morland, J.K. and Hwang, C.-H. (1981) 'Racial/ethnic identity of preschool children', *Journal of Cross-Cultural Psychology,* 12: 409–424.

Mrazek, D.A. (1986) 'Childhood asthma: two central questions for child psychiatry', *Journal of Child Psychiatry,* 27: 1–5.

Mundy, P. and Sigman, M. (1989) 'Specifying the nature of the social impairment in autism', in G. Dawson (ed.) *Autism: Nature, Diagnosis, and Treatment*, New York: Guilford Press, 3–21.

Mundy, P., Sigman, M. and Kasari, C. (1993) 'The theory of mind and joint-attention deficits in autism', in S. Baron-Cohen, H. Tager-Flusberg and D. Cohen (eds) *Understanding Other Minds: Perspectives from Autism*, Oxford: Oxford University Press, 181–203.

Mundy, P., Sigman, M., Ungerer, J. and Sherman, T. (1986) 'Defining the social deficits of autism: the contribution of non-verbal communication measures', *Journal of Child Psychology and Psychiatry,* 27, 5: 657–669.

Murphy, K. and Schneider, B. (1994) 'Coaching socially rejected early adolescents regarding behaviors used by peers to infer liking: a dyad specific intervention' *Journal of Early Adolescence,* 14 (1): 83–95. (Special issue: *Canadian Research on Early Adolescene*).

Nadar, K.O. and Fairbanks, L.A. (1994) 'The suppression of reexperiencing: impulse control and somatic symptoms in children following traumatic exposure. Special issue: War and stress in the Middle East', *Anxiety, Stress & Coping,* 7: 229–239.

Nathanson, D.L. (ed.) (1987) *The Many Faces Of Shame,* New York: Guilford Press.

Nathanson, D.L. (1992) *Shame and Pride: Affect, Sex and the Birth of the Self,* New York: W.W.Norton.

Nathanson, D.L. (ed.) (1996) *Knowing Feeling,* New York: W.W. Norton.

Nelson, G. and Carson, P. (1988) 'Evaluation of a social problem-solving skills program for third and fourth grade students', *American Journal of Community Psychology,* 16, 1: 79–97.

Nelson, L.J., Hart, C.H., Robinson, C.C., Olsen, S.F. and Rubin, K.H. (1998) 'Relations between sociometric status and three subtypes of withdrawn behavior in preschool children: a multi-method perspective', Paper presented at the Society for Research in Child Development meetings, Washington, DC, April. (Manuscript submitted for publication.)

Newcomb, A.F. and Bukowski, W.M. (1984) 'A longitudinal study of the utility of social preference and social impact classification schemes', *Child Development,* 55: 1434–1447.

Newcomb, A.F., Bukowski, W.M. and Pattee, L. (1993) 'Children's peer relations: a meta-analytic review of popular, rejected, neglected, controversial and average sociometric status', *Developmental Psychology,* 19: 856–867.

Newman, C.J. (1976) 'Children of disaster: clinical observations at Buffalo Creek', *American Journal of Psychiatry,* 133: 306–312.

Newman, M.A., Liss, M.B., and Sherman, F. (1983) 'Ethnic awareness in children. Not a unitary concept', *Journal of Genetic Psychology,* 143: 103–112.

New Zealand Police (1992) *Kia Kaha*, Wellington, New Zealand.

Noble, G. (1975) *Children in Front of the Small Screen*, London: Constable.

Noll, R.B., LeRoy, S., Bukowski, W., Rogosch, F.A. and Kulkarni, R. (1991) 'Peer relationships and adjustment in children with cancer', *Journal of Pediatric Psychology*, 16: 307–326.

Oakes, P.J., Haslam, A. and Turner, J.C. (1994) *Stereotyping and Social Reality*, Oxford: Blackwell.

Oatley, K. (1992) *Best Laid Schemes: The Psychology of Emotions*, New York: Cambridge University Press.

Oden, S.L. and Asher, S.R. (1977) 'Coaching children in social skills for friendship making', *Child Development*, 48: 495–506.

Ogilvy, C.M. (1994) 'Social skills training with children: a review of the evidence on effectiveness', *Educational Psychology*, 14: 73–83.

Okin, S.M. (1989) *Justice, Gender, and the Family*, New York: Basic Books.

Olweus, D. (1972) *Personality Factors and Aggression – with Special Reference to Violence within the Peer Group*, Reports from the Institute of Psychology, University of Bergen, Norway.

Olweus, D. (1973) *Hackkycklingar Och Oversittare Forskring om Skolmobbning*, Stockholm: Almqvist and Wicksell.

Olweus, D. (1978) *Aggression in Schools: Bullies and Whipping Boys*, Washington, DC: Hemisphere Press.

Olweus, D. (1989) 'Bully/victim problems among schoolchildren: basic facts and effects of a school-based intervention programme', in K. Rubin and D. Pepler (eds) *The Development and Treatment of Childhood Aggression*, Hillsdale, N.J.: Erlbaum.

Olweus, D. (1991) 'Bully/victim problems among schoolchildren: basic facts and effects of a school based intervention program', in D.J. Pepler and K.H. Rubin (eds) *The Development and Treatment of Childhood Aggression*, Hillsdale, N.J.: Erlbaum.

Olweus, D. (1993a) *Bullying at School: What We Know and What We Can Do*, Oxford: Blackwell.

Olweus, D. (1993b) *Bullying at School*, Cambridge, Mass.: Harvard University Press.

O'Moore, A.M. and Hillery, B. (1989) 'Bullying in Dublin schools', *Irish Journal of Psychology*, 10: 426–441.

O'Moore, A.M. and Hillery, B. (1991) 'What do teachers need to know?', in M. Elliott (ed.) *Bullying, a Practical Guide to Coping for Schools*, Harlow: Longman, 56–69.

Osofsky, J.D., Cohen, G. and Drell, M. (1995) 'The effects of trauma on young children: a case of 2-year-old twins', *International Journal of Psychoanalysis*, 76: 595–607.

Owens, L. (1996) 'Sticks and stones and sugar and spice: girls' and boys' aggression in schools', *Australian Journal of Guidance and Counselling*, 6: 45–57.

Parke, R.D. (1994) 'Epilogue: unresolved issues and future trends in family relationships with other contexts', in R.D. Parke and S.G. Kellam (eds) *Exploring Family Relationships within other Social Contexts*, Hillsdale, N.J.: Erlbaum, 215–229.

Parker, J.G. and Asher, S. (1987) 'Peer relations and later personal adjustments: are low accepted children at risk?', *Psychological Bulletin*, 102: 357–389.

Parker, J.G. and Gottman, J.M. (1989) 'Social and emotional development in a relational context: friendship interaction from early childhood to adolescence', in T.J. Berndt and G.W. Ladd (eds) *Peer Relationships in Child Development*, New York: Wiley, 95–132.

Parker, J. and Randall, P. (1996) 'Post-traumatic stress disorder in children: the social work challenge', *Journal of Social Work Practice*, 10, 1: 71–81.

Parker, J., Watts, H. and Allsopp, M.R. (1995a) 'Post-traumatic stress symptoms in children and parents following a school-based fatality', *Child Care, Health and Development*, 21: 183–189.

Parker, J.G., Rubin, K.H., Price, J.M. and DeRosier, M.E. (1995b) 'Peer relationships, child development and adjustment: a developmental psychopathological perspective', in D. Cicchetti and E. Cohen (eds) *Developmental Psychopathology: Vol. 2: Risk, Disorder and Adaptation*, New York: Wiley.

Parpal, M. and Maccoby, E.E. (1985) 'Maternal responsiveness and subsequent child compliance', *Child Development*, 56: 1326–1334.

Patterson, G.R. (1986) 'Performance models for antisocial boys', *American Psychologist*, 41: 432–444.

Patterson, G.R., Reid, J.B. and Dishion, T.J. (1992) *Antisocial Boys*, Eugene, Oreg.: Castalia.

Pattison, P. (1993) *Algebraic Models for Social Networks*, Cambridge: Cambridge University Press.

Peery, C. (1979) 'Popular, amiable, isolated, rejected. A reconceptualisation of socio-metric status in pre-school children', *Child Development*, 50: 1231–1234.

Pelligrini, D.S. and Urbain, E.S. (1985) 'An evaluation of interpersonal cognitive problem solving training with children', *Journal of Child Psychology and Psychiatry*, 26, 1: 17–41.

Pepler, D., Craig, W., Ziegler, S. and Charach, A. (1993) 'A school-based anti-bullying intervention: preliminary evaluation', in D. Tattum (ed.) *Understanding and Managing Bullying*, Oxford: Heinemann.

Pepler, D.J. and Slaby, R.G. (1995) 'Theoretical and developmental perspectives on youth and violence', in L.D. Eron, J.H. Gentry and P. Schlegel (eds) *Reason to Hope: A Psychosocial Perspective on Violence and Youth*, Washington, DC: APA.

Perry, D.G., Kusel, S.J. and Perry, L.C. (1988) 'Victims of peer aggression', *Developmental Psychology*, 24: 807–814.

Petersen, K. and Petersen, S. (1993) 'Creating safe and caring elementary schools', *School Safety*, Fall: 11–15.

Petersen, L. and Gannoni, A.F. (1989) *Teachers' Manual for Training Social Skills While Managing Student Behaviour*, St Marys, South Australia: Stop Think Do Pty Ltd.

Petersen, L.M. and Gannoni, A.F. (1992) *Manual for Social Skills Training in Young People with Parent and Teacher Programmes*, Victoria: ACER.

Pettit, G.S., Harrist, A.W., Bates, J. and Dodge, K. (1991) 'Family interaction, social cognition and children's subsequent relations with peers at kindergarten', *Journal of Social and Personal Relationships*, 8: 383–402.

Pettit, G.S. and Harrist, A.W. (1993) 'Children's aggressive and socially unskilled behavior with peers: origins in early family relations', in C.H. Hart (ed.)

Children on Playgrounds: Research Perspectives and Applications, Albany: State University of New York Press, 240–270.

Pettit G.S. and Mize, J. (1993) 'Substance and style: understanding the ways in which parents teach children about social relationships', in S. Duck (ed.) *Understanding Relationship Processes. Vol. 2: Learning About Relationships*, Newbury Park, Calif.: Sage, 118–151.

Pettit, P. (1993) *The Common Mind: An Essay in Psychology, Society, and Politics*, New York: Oxford University Press.

Pikas, A. (1975) *Så stoppar vi mobbning*, Stockholm: Prisma.

Pikas, A. (1989a) 'The common concern method for the treatment of mobbing', in E. Roland and E. Munthe (eds) *Bullying: An International Perspective*, London: David Fulton.

Pikas, A. (1989b) 'A pure concept of mobbing gives the best results for treatment', *School Psychology International*, 10: 95–104.

Porter, B. and O'Leary, D. (1980) 'Marital discord and childhood behavior problems', *Journal of Abnormal Child Psychology*, 8: 287–295.

Porter, J.D.R. (1971) *Black Child, White Child: The Development of Racial Attitudes*, Cambridge, Mass.: Harvard University Press.

Porter, L. (1996) *Student Behaviour: Theory and Practice for Teachers*, Sydney: Allen and Unwin.

Powell, T.H. and Gallagher, P.A. (1993) *Brothers and Sisters – A Special Part of Exceptional Families*, Baltimore, Md.: Paul H. Brookes Publishing Co.

Premack, D. and Woodruff, G. (1978) 'Does the chimpanzee have a theory of mind?', *The Behavioral and Brain Sciences*, 4: 515–526.

Prinstein, M.J. (1997) 'Maternal social competence, mothers' social management behavior, and children's social competence: a mediational model', Unpublished doctoral dissertation, University of Miami, Coral Gables, Florida.

Prior, M., Sanson, A. and Oberklaid, F. (1989) 'The Australian Temperament Project', in G. Kohnstamm, J. Bates and M. Rothbart (eds) *Temperament in Childhood*, Chichester: Wiley.

Prior, M., Sanson, A., Smart, D. and Oberklaid, F. (1997) 'Psychological disorders and their correlates in an Australian sample of pre-adolescent children', Paper submitted for publication.

Prior, M., Smart, D., Sanson, A. and Oberklaid, F. (1993) 'Sex differences in psychological adjustment from infancy to eight years', *Journal of the American Academy of Child and Adolescent Psychiatry*, 32: 291–304.

Pritchard, M.S. (1991) *On Becoming Responsible*, Lawrence, Kans.: Kansas University Press.

Profilet, S.M. and Ladd, G.W. (1994) 'Do mothers' perceptions and concerns about preschoolers' peer competence predict their peer-management practices?', *Social Development*, 3: 205–221.

Profilet, S.M. and Ladd, G.W. (1996) 'Relations between maternal consulting about kindergarten children's peer relationships and children's peer competence', Paper presented at the annual meeting of the American Educational Research Association. New York.

Pulkkinen, L. and Pitkänen, T. (1993) 'Continuities in aggressive behaviour from childhood to adulthood', *Aggressive Behavior*, 19: 249–263.

Putallaz, M. (1983) 'Predicting children's sociometric status from their behavior', *Child Development*, 54: 1417–1426.

Putallaz, M. (1987) 'Maternal behavior and children's sociometric status', *Child Development*, 58: 324–340.

Pynoos, R.S. (1990) 'Post-traumatic stress disorder in children and adolescents', in B.D. Garfinkel, G.A. Carlson, and E.B. Weller (eds) *Psychiatric Disorders in Children and Adolescents*, Philadelphia, Pa.: Saunders.

Pynoos, R.S. and Eth, S. (1985) 'Children traumatised by witnessing acts of personal violence: homicide, rape and suicide behavior', in S. Eth and R.S. Pynoos (eds) *Post-traumatic Stress Disorder in Children*, Washington, DC: American Psychiatric Press.

Pynoos, R.S. and Nadar, K. (1988) 'Children who witness the sexual assault of their mothers', *Journal of the American Academy of Child and Adolescent Psychiatry*, 27: 567–572.

Pynoos, R.S., Goenjian, A. and Tashjian, M. (1993) 'Post-traumatic stress reactions in children after the 1988 Armenian earthquake', *British Journal of Psychiatry*, 163: 239–247.

Pynoos, R.S., Fredrick, C., Nadar, K. and Arroyo, W. (1987) 'Life threat and post-traumatic stress disorder in school-age children', *Archives General Psychiatry*, 44: 1057–1063.

Radloff, L.S. (1977) 'The CES-D Scale: a self-report depression scale for research in the general population', *Applied Psychological Measurement*, 3: 385–401.

Ramsey, P.G. (1983) 'Young children's responses to racial differences: sociocultural perspectives', Paper presented at the biennial meeting of the Society for Research in Child Development, Detroit (cited in Ramsey 1987).

Ramsey, P.G. (1985) 'Early ethnic socialization in a mono-racial community', Paper presented at the biennial meeting of the Society for Research in Child Development, Toronto (cited in Ramsey 1987).

Ramsey, P.G. (1987) 'Young children's thinking about ethnic differences', in J.S. Phinney and M.J. Rotheram (eds) *Children's Ethnic Socialization*, Newbury Park, Calif.: Sage.

Ramsey, P. (1995) 'Changing social dynamics in early childhood classrooms', *Child Development*, 66: 764–773.

Randall, P.E. (1996) *A Community Approach to Bullying*, Stoke-on-Trent: Trentham Books.

Randall, P.E. (1997) *Adult Bullying*, London: Routledge.

Random House Dictionary (1978) New York: Ballantine.

Raver, C.C. (1996) 'Relations between social contingency in mother-child interaction and 2-year-olds' social competence', *Developmental Psychology*, 32: 850–859.

Renshaw, P.D. and Brown, P.J. (1993) 'Loneliness in middle childhood: concurrent and longitudinal predictors', *Child Development*, 64: 1271–1284.

Rey, J.M., Schrader, E. and Morris-Yates, A. (1992) 'Parent–child agreement on children's behaviors reported by the Child Behavior Checklist (CBCL)', *Journal of Adolescence*, 15: 219–230.

Richard, B.A. and Dodge, K.A. (1982) 'Social maladjustment and problem solving in school-aged children', *Journal of Consulting and Clinical Psychology*, 50: 226–233.

Richards, R.J. (1987) *Darwin and the Emergence of Evolutionary Theories of Mind and Behavior*, Chicago: Chicago University Press.

Richardson, S.A. and Green, A. (1971) 'When is black beautiful? Coloured and white children's reactions to skin colour', *British Journal of Educational Psychology*, 41: 62–69.

Rickel, A.U. and Burgio, J.C. (1982) 'Assessing social competencies in lower income preschoolchildren', *American Journal of Community Psychology*, 10: 635–647.

Ridley, C.A. and Vaughn, S.R. (1982) 'Interpersonal problem solving: an intervention program for preschoolchildren', *Journal of Applied Developmental Psychology*, 3: 177–190.

Rigby, K. (1994) 'An evaluation of strategies and methods for addressing problems of peer abuse in schools', in M. Tainish and J. Izard (eds) *Widening Horizons: New Challenges, Directions and Achievements*, Canberra: ACER.

Rigby, K. (1995a) 'New thinking about bullying in schools', *Independent Education*, New South Wales Education Union, Sydney, July: 3–6.

Rigby, K. (1995b) 'Peer victimization and gender among Australian school children', Paper presented at the 4th European Congress of Psychology, Athens, Greece, 5 July.

Rigby, K. (1996a) *Bullying at School and What to Do About It*, Melbourne: ACER.

Rigby, K. (1996b) *Technical Manual for the Peer Relations Questionnaire. The Professional Reading Guide*, Point Lonsdale, Victoria, Australia.

Rigby, K. (1996c) *Technical Manual for the Peer Relations Questionnaire:* Adelaide: University of South Australia.

Rigby, K. (1996d) 'What should we do with school bullies?', *Australian Journal of Guidance and Counselling*, 6: 71–76.

Rigby, K. (1997a) *Bullying in Schools – And What To Do About It*, London: Jessica Kingsley.

Rigby, K. (1997b) 'Attitudes and beliefs about bullying among Australian schoolchildren', *Irish Journal of Psychology*, 18 (2): 202–220.

Rigby, K. and Slee, P.T. (1991) 'Bullying among Australian schoolchildren: reported behaviour and attitudes to victims', *Journal of Social Psychology*, 13: 615–627.

Rigby, K. and Slee, P.T. (1992) *Bullying in Schools* (a video), Melbourne: ACER.

Rigby, K. and Slee, P.T. (1993a) 'Dimensions of inter-personal relating among Australian school children and their implications for psychological well-being', *Journal of Social Psychology*, 133: 33–42.

Rigby, K. and Slee, P.T. (1993b) 'Children's attitudes towards victims', in D. Tattum (ed.) *Understanding and Managing Bullying*, Oxford: Heinemann, 119–135.

Rigby, K. and Slee, P.T. (1993c) *The Peer Relations Questionnaire (PRQ)*, Adelaide: University of South Australia.

Rigby, K., Cox, I. and Black, G. (1997) 'Cooperativeness and bully/victim problems among Australian schoolchildren', *The Journal of Social Psychology*, 137: 357–368.

Rivers, I. and Smith, P.K. (1994) 'Types of bullying behavior and their correlates', *Aggressive Behavior*, 20: 359–368.

Rivers, M. (1978) *Manipulating Freedom in Groups: Two Months Hell, Ten Months Heaven*, Adelaide: Education Department of South Australia.

Robbins, L.N. (1966) *Deviant Children Grown Up*, Baltimore, Md.: Williams and Wilkins.

Robinson, J.A. (1994) 'Patterns of play and communication between children from different ethnic backgrounds: the influence of language', in K. Oxenberry, K. Rigby, P. Slee (eds) *Children's Peer Relations: Co-operation and Conflict*, Adelaide: Institute of Social Research, University of South Australia.

Rocissano, L., Slade, A. and Lynch, A. (1987) 'Dyadic synchrony and toddler compliance', *Developmental Psychology*, 23: 698–704.

Roff, J.D. and Wirt, R.D. (1984) 'Childhood aggression and social adjustment as antecedents of delinquencies', *Journal of Abnormal Child Psychology*,12: 111–126.

Roland, E. and Munthe, E. (eds) (1989) *Bullying: An International Perspective*, London: David Fulton.

Rolf, J. (1972) 'The social and academic competence of children vulnerable to schizophrenia and other behavior pathologies', *Journal of Abnormal Psychology*, 80: 225–243.

Romney, D.M., Brown, R.I. and Fry, P.S. (1994) 'Improving the quality of life: recommendations for people with and without disabilities', in D.M. Romney, R.I. Brown and P.S. Fry (eds) *Improving the Quality of Life: Recommendations for People with and without Disabilities*, Boston, Mass.: Kluwer Academic Publishers, 237–272.

Rosenberg, M. and Simmons, P.G. (1971) *Black and White Self-Esteem: The Urban School Child*, Washington, DC: American Sociological Association.

Rosenfield, D. and Stephan, W.G. (1981) 'Intergroup relations among children', in S.S. Brehm, S.M. Kassin and F.X. Gibbons (eds) *Developmental Social Psychology*, Oxford: Oxford University Press.

Rosenthal, D.A. and Hrynevich, C. (1985) 'Ethnicity and ethnic identity: a comparative study of Greek-, Italian-, and Anglo-Australian adolescents', *International Journal of Psychology*, 20: 723–742.

Rubin, K.H. (1980) *Children's Friendships*, Cambridge, Mass.: Harvard University Press.

Rubin, K.H. (1985) 'Socially withdrawn children: an "at risk" population?', in B.H. Schneider, K.H. Rubin and J.E. Ledingham (eds) *Peer Relationships and Social Skills in Childhood: Issues in Assessment and Training*, New York: Springer-Verlag.

Rubin, K.H. (1988) *The Social Problem Solving Test – Revised*, Waterloo, Canada: The University of Waterloo.

Rubin K.H. and Rose-Krasnor, L. (1986) 'Social–cognitive and social behavioral perspectives on problem solving', in M. Perlmutter (ed.) *Cognitive Perspectives on Children's Social and Behavioral Development*, Minnesota Symposium on Child Psychology (vol. 18), Hillsdale, N.J.: Lawrence Erlbaum.

Rubin, K.H. and Coplan, R.J. (1992) 'Peer relationships in childhood', in M.H. Bornstein and M.E. Lamb (eds) *Developmental Psychology: An Advanced Textbook*, Hillsdale, N.J.: Erlbaum, 519–578.

Rubin, K.H. and Mills, R.S.L. (1992) 'Parent's thoughts about children's socially adaptive and maladaptive behaviors: stability, change and individual differences', in I. Sigel, J. Goodnow and A. McGillicuddy-DeLisi (eds) *Parental Belief Systems*, Hillsdale, N.J.: Erlbaum, 41–68.

Rubin K.H. and Rose-Krasnor, L. (1992) 'Interpersonal problem solving and social competence in children', in V. Van Hasselt and M. Hersen (eds) *Handbook of Social Development: A Lifespan Perspective*, New York: Plenum Press.

Rubin, K.H., Daniels-Beirness, T. and Hayvren, M. (1982) 'Social and social-cognitive correlates of sociometric status in preschool and kindergarten children', *Canadian Journal of Behavioral Science*, 14: 338–348.

Rubin, K.H., Fein, G.G. and Vandenberg, B. (1983) 'Play', in P.H. Mussen (series ed.) and E.M. Hetherington (vol. ed.) *Handbook of Child Psychology: Vol. 4, Socialization, Personality, and Social Development* (4th edn), New York: John Wiley and Sons, 693–774.

Rubin, K.H., Daniels-Beirness, T. and Bream, L. (1984) 'Social isolation and social problem-solving: a longitudinal study', *Journal of Consulting and Clinical Psychology*, 52: 17–25.

Rubin, K.H., Mills, R.S.L. and Rose-Krasnor, L. (1989) 'Parental beliefs and children's social competence', in B. Schneider, G. Atilli, J. Nadel and R. Weissberg (eds) *Social Competence in Developmental Perspective*, Dordrecht, Netherlands: Kluwer, 313–331.

Rubin, K.H., Le Mare, L.J. and Lollis, S. (1990) 'Social withdrawal in childhood: developmental pathways to peer rejection', in S.R. Asher and J.D. Coie (eds). *Peer Rejection in Childhood*, Cambridge: Cambridge University Press, 217–249.

Rubin, K.H., Stewart, S.I. and Coplan, R.J. (1994) 'Social withdrawal in childhood: conceptual and empirical perspectives', in T. Ollendick and R. Prinz (eds) *Advances in Clinical Child Psychology*, Vol. 17, New York: Plenum.

Rubin, K.H., Stewart S.L. and Chen, X. (1995) 'Parents of aggressive and withdrawn children', in M. Bornstein (ed.) *Handbook of Parenting: Vol. 1. Children and Parenting*, Hillsdale, N.J.: Erlbaum, 255–284.

Rubin, K.H., Bukowski, W. and Parker, J.G. (1998) 'Peer interactions, relationships, and groups', in W. Damon (series ed.) and N. Eisenberg (vol. ed.) *Handbook of Child Psychology: Vol, 3, Social, Emotional, and Personality Development*, New York: Wiley, 619–700.

Rubin, Z. (1980) *Children's Friendships*, Boston Mass.: Harvard University Press.

Rubin, Z. and Sloman, J. (1984) 'How parents influence their children's friendships', in M. Lewis (ed.) *Beyond the Dyad*, New York: Plenum Press, 223–250.

Rule, B.G. and Ferguson, T.J. (1986) 'The effects of media violence on attitudes, emotions and cognitions', *Journal of Social Issues*, 42: 29–50.

Russell, A. and Finnie, V. (1990) 'Preschool children's social status and maternal instructions to assist group entry', *Developmental Psychology*, 26: 603–611.

Russell, A., Pettit, G.S. and Mize, J. (in press) 'Horizontal qualities in parent-child relationships: their nature and possible effects', *Developmental Review*.

Rutter, M. (1994) 'Family discord and conduct disorder: cause, consequence, or correlate?', *Journal of Family Psychology*, 8: 170–186.

Rutter, M., Tizard, J. and Whitmore, K. (1970) *Education, Health and Behaviour*, London: Longmans.

Salmivalli, C. (1992) 'Bullying as a group process: typical bullying situations, pupils' roles, and status hierarchy in school classes', Unpublished Masters thesis. Department of Psychology, University of Turku, Finland.

Salmivalli, C. (1995) *Participant Role Questionnaire (Revised)*, Department of Psychology, University of Turku, Finland.

Salmivalli, C., Karhunen J. and Lagerspetz, K.M.J. (1996a) 'How do victims respond to bullying?', *Aggressive Behavior*, 22, 2: 99–109.

Salmivalli, C., Lagerspetz, K.M.J., Björkqvist, K., Österman, K. and Kaukiainen, A.

(1996b) 'Bullying as a group process: participant roles and their relations to social status within the group', *Aggressive Behavior,* 22, 1: 1–15.

Salmivalli, C., Huttunen, A. and Lagerspetz, K.M.J. (1997) 'Peer networks and bullying in schools', *Scandinavian Journal of Psychology,* 38, 4: 305–12.

Salmivalli, C., Lappalainen, M. and Lagerspetz, K.M.J. (1998) 'Stability and change of behaviour in connection with bullying in schools', *Aggressive Behaviour,* 24, 3: 205–218.

Sancilio, M.F., Plumert, R. and Hartup, W.W. (1989) 'Friendship and aggressiveness as determinates of conflict outcomes in middle childhood', *Developmental Psychology,* 25, 5: 812–819.

Sanson, A., Kennedy, G., Matjacic, E., Reid, K. and Smart, D. (1994) 'Children's peer relationships: associations between peer status, friendship, behavioural adjustment and conflict resolution styles', in K. Oxenberry, K. Rigby and P. Slee (eds) *Children's Peer Relations: Cooperation and Conflict*, Adelaide: Institute of Social Research.

Sapon-Shevin, M. (1994*) Playing Favorites: Gifted Education and the Disruption of the Community,* New York: State University of New York Press.

Scherer, K. (1992) *Justice: Interdisciplinary Perspectives,* Cambridge: Cambridge University Press.

Schneider, B.H. (1991) 'A comparison of skill-building and desensitization strategies for intervention with aggressive children', *Aggressive Behavior,* 17: 301–311.

Schneider, B.H. (1992) 'Didactic methods for enhancing children's peer relations: a quantitative review', *Clinical Psychology Review,* 12: 363–382.

Schneider, B.H. (1993) *Children's Social Competence In Context*, New York; Pergamon Press.

Schneider, B.H., and Byrne, B.M. (1985) 'Children's social skills training: a meta-analysis', in B.H. Schneider, K.H. Rubin and J.E. Ledingham (eds) *Children's Peer Relations: Issues in Assessment and Peer Intervention*, New York: Springer-Verlag, 175–190.

Schneider, B.H., Barr, D.J., Nakkula, M.J. and Udvari, S. (1995) 'Helping behaviour-disordered children make friends who are not also their foes', *Exceptionality Education Canada,* 5: 137–156.

Schneider, C.D. (1977) *Shame, Exposure, and Privacy,* Boston, Mass.: Beacon.

Schofield, J.W. (1979) 'The impact of positively structured contact on intergroup behavior: does it last under adverse conditions?', *Social Psychology Quarterly,* 42: 280–284.

Schofield, J.W. (1986) 'Black–white contact in desegregated schools', in M. Hewstone and R. Brown (eds) *Contact and Conflict in Intergroup Encounters,* Oxford: Basil Blackwell.

Schwartz, D., Dodge, K., Pettit, G. and Bates, A. (in press) 'The early socialisation and adjustment of aggressive victims of bullying', *Child Development.*

Schwartz, E.D. and Kowalski, J.M. (1991) 'Malignant memories: PTSD in children and adults after a school shooting', *Journal of the American Academy of Child and Adolescent Psychiatrics,* 30: 936–944.

Schwartz, T., White, G.M. and Lutz, C.A. (eds) (1992) *New Directions in Psychological Anthropology,* Cambridge: Cambridge University Press.

Selman, R.L. (1980) *The Growth of Interpersonal Understanding: Developmental and Clinical Analyses*, New York: Academic Press.

Selman, R. and Schultz, L.H. (1990) *Making a Friend in Youth: Developmental Theory and Pair Therapy*, Chicago: University of Chicago Press.

Seymour, J. (1988) *Dealing With Young Offenders*, Sydney: Law Book Company.

Shank, R.C. (1990) *Tell Me a Story*, New York: Scribners.

Sharp, S. and Cowie, H. (1994) 'Empowering pupils to take positive action against bullying', in P.K. Smith and S. Sharp (eds) *School Bullying: Insights and Perspectives*, London: Routledge, 108–132.

Sharp, S. and Thompson, D. (1994) 'The role of whole-school policies in tackling bullying behaviour in schools', in P.K. Smith and S. Sharp (eds) *School Bullying: Insights and Perspectives*, London: Routledge.

Shaw, M.E. (1973) 'Changes in sociometric choices following forced integration of an elementary school', *Journal of Social Issues*, 29: 143–157.

Shure, M.B. and Spivack, G. (1972) 'Means-end thinking, adjustment, and social class among elementary schoolaged children', *Journal of Consulting and Clinical Psychology*, 38: 348–353.

Shure, M. and Spivack, G. (1978) *Problem Solving Techniques in Childrearing*, San Francisco, Calif.: Jossey-Bass.

Shute, R. (1994) 'Peer support in chronic childhood illness', in K. Oxenberry, K. Rigby and P. Slee (eds) *Children's Peer Relations: Cooperation and Conflict*, Adelaide: Institute of Social Research.

Shute, R.H. and Paton, D. (1990) 'Childhood illness: the child as helper', in H.C. Foot, M.J. Morgan and R.H. Shute (eds) *Children Helping Children*, Chichester: Wiley.

Silverman, I. and Shaw, M.E. (1973) 'Effects of sudden mass school desegregation on interracial interaction and attitudes in one Southern city', *Journal of Social Issues*, 29: 133–142.

Simeonsson, R. and Bailey, D. (1986) 'Siblings of handicapped children', in J. Gallagher and P. Vietze (eds) *Families of Handicapped Persons: Research, Programs, and Policy Issues*, Baltimore, Md.: Brooks Publisher, 67–77.

Simonds, J.F. (1979) 'Emotions and compliance in diabetic children', *Psychosomatics*, 20: 544–551.

Simpson, S. (1994) 'An evaluation of group relaxation therapy for children with asthma', Unpublished Master of Psychology (Clinical) dissertation, The Flinders University of South Australia.

Sinclair, J. (1992) 'Bridging the gaps: an inside-out view of autism (or, do you know what I don't know?)', in E. Schopler and G.B. Mesibov (eds) *High-functioning Individuals with Autism*, New York: Plenum Press, 294–302.

Sinclair, J.J., Pettit, G.S., Harrist, A.W., Dodge, K.A. and Bates, J.E. (1994) 'Encounters with aggressive peers in early childhood: frequency, age differences, and correlates of risk for behavior problems', *International Journal of Behavioral Development*, 17: 675–696.

Singer, J.A. and Salovey, P. (1993) *The Remembered Self: Emotion and Memory in Personality*, New York: The Free Press.

Singleton, L.C. and Asher, S.R. (1979) 'Racial integration and children's peer preferences: an investigation of developmental and cohort differences', *Child Development*, 50: 936–941.

Siperstein, G.N. and Gale, M.E. (1983) 'Improving peer relationships of rejected children', Paper presented at the Society for Research in Child Development, Detroit.

Slavin, R.E. (1983) 'When does cooperative learning increase student achievement?', *Psychological Bulletin*, 94: 429–445.

Slee, P.T. (1993) 'Bullying: a preliminary investigation of its nature and the effects of social cognition', *Early Child Development and Care*, 87: 47–57.

Slee, P.T. (1994) 'Situational and interpersonal correlates of anxiety associated with peer victimisation', *Child Psychiatry and Human Development*, 25: 97–107.

Slee, P.T. (1996) 'Family climate and behavior in families with conduct disordered children', *Child Psychiatry and Human Development*, 26: 255–266.

Slee P.T. (1997) *The P.E.A.C.E. Pack: a Programme for Reducing Bullying in Our Schools*, Adelaide: Flinders University.

Slee, P.T. and Rigby, K. (1993) 'The relationship of Eysenck's personality factors and self-esteem to bully–victim behaviour in Australian school boys', *Personality and Individual Differences*, 14: 371–373.

Smetana, J.G. (1994) 'Parenting styles and beliefs about parental authority', *New Directions for Child Development*, 66: 21–36.

Smets, A.C. and Hartup, W.W. (1988) 'Systems and symptoms: family cohesion/adaptability and childhood behavior problems', *Journal of Abnormal Child Psychology*, 16: 233–246.

Smith, A. (1982 [1759]) *A Theory of Moral Sentiments* Indianapolis: Liberty.

Smith, P.K. (1994) *Bullying, Don't Suffer in Silence: An Anti-bullying Pack for Schools*, London: HMSO.

Smith, P.K., Cowie, H., Berdonolini, L. (1994) 'Cooperation and Bullying', in P. Kutnick and C. Rogers (eds) *Groups in Schools*, London: Cassell.

Smith, P.K. and Sharp, S. (eds) (1994) *School Bullying. Insights and Perspectives*, Routledge: London.

Smith, P.K. and Thompson, D. (1991) *Practical Approaches to Bullying*, London: David Fulton.

Stainback, S. and Stainback, W. (1996) *Inclusion: A Guide for Educators*, Baltimore: P.H. Brooks.

Stanger, C. and Lewis, M. (1993) 'Agreement among parents, teachers and children on internalizing and externalizing behavior problems', *Journal of Clinical Child Psychology*, 22: 107–115.

Steffenburg, S. and Gillberg, C. (1989) 'The etiology of autism', in C. Gillberg (ed.) *Diagnosis and Treatment of Autism*, New York: Plenum Press.

Stein, N. and Oatley, K. (eds) (1992) *Basic Emotions* (Special Issue of Cognition and Emotion), Hove: Lawrence Erlbaum.

Stephan, W.G. and Rosenfield, D. (1978) 'Effects of desegregation on racial attitudes', *Journal of Personality and Social Psychology*, 36: 795–804.

Stewart, S.L. and Rubin, K.H. (1995) 'The social problem-solving skills of anxious–withdrawn children', *Development and Psychopathology*, 7: 323–336.

Sticks and Stones: Report on Violence in Australian Schools (1994) Canberra: Australian Government Publishing Service.

St. John, N.H. and Lewis, R.G. (1975) 'Race and the social structure of the elementary classroom', *Sociology of Education*, 48: 346–368.

Stockfelt-Hoatson, B.-I. (1979) *Training of Immigrant Children in Pre-school in*

Norrkoping, Linkoping Studies in Education Dissertations No. 8, Linkoping, Sweden.

Stoneman, Z. (1989) 'Comparison groups in research on families with mentally retarded members: a methodological and conceptual review', *American Journal on Mental Retardation*, 94: 195–215.

Stoneman, Z. (1993) 'Common themes and divergent paths', in Z. Stoneman and P.W. Berman (eds) *The Effects of Mental Retardation, Disability, and Illness on Sibling Relationships: Research Issues and Challenges*, Baltimore, Md.: Paul Brookes Publishing, 355–365.

Stoneman, Z. and Brody, G. (1993) 'Sibling relations in the family context', in Z. Stoneman and P. Berman, (eds) *The Effects of Mental Retardation, Disability, and Illness on Sibling Relationships: Research Issues and Challenges*, Baltimore, Md.: Brookes Publishing, 3–30.

Stoneman, Z., Brody, G. and Davis, C. (1989) 'Role relations between children who are mentally retarded and their older siblings: observations in three in-home contexts', *Research in Developmental Disabilities*, 10: 61–77.

Storey, K., Danko, C.D., Ashworth, R. and Strain, P.S. (1994) 'Generalization of social skills intervention for preschoolers with social delays', *Education and Treatment of Children*, 17: 29–51.

Stormshak, E.A., Bellanti, C.J. and Bierman, K.L. (1996) 'The quality of sibling relationship and the development of social competence and behavioral control in aggressive children', *Developmental Psychology*, 32: 79–89.

Strain, P.S. (1981) 'Modification of sociometric status and social interaction with mainstreamed mild developmentally disabled children', *Analysis and Intervention in Developmental Disabilities*, 1: 157–169.

Strauss, C.C., Lahey, B.B., Frick, P., Frame, C.L. and Hynd, G.W. (1988) 'Peer social status of children with anxiety disorders', *Journal of Consulting and Clinical Psychology*, 56: 137–141.

Strentz, T. (1995) 'Crisis intervention and survival strategies for victims of hostage situations', in A.R. Roberts (ed.) *Crisis Intervention and Time-Limited Cognitive Treatment*, Thousand Oaks, London, New Delhi: Sage, 127–147.

Stuber, M.L. and Nader, K.O. (1995) 'Psychiatric sequelae in adolescent bone marrow transplantation survivors: implications for psychotherapy', *Journal of Psychotherapy Practice and Research*, 4: 30–42.

Sullivan, B.J. (1979) 'Adjustment in diabetic adolescent girls. 1: Development of the diabetic adjustment scale', *Psychosomatic Medicine*, 41: 119–138.

Sullivan, H.S. (1953) *The Interpersonal Theory of Psychology*, New York: Norton.

Tabachnik, B.G. and Fidell, L.S. (1983) *Using Multivariate Statistics*, New York: Harper.

Tajfel, H., Jahoda, G., Noneth, C., Rim, Y., and Johnson, N. (1972) 'Devaluation by children of their own national or ethnic group: two case studies', *British Journal of Social and Clinical Psychology*, 11: 235–243.

Tavuchis, N. (1991) *Mea Culpa: A Sociology of Apology and Reconciliation*, Stanford, Calif.: Stanford University Press.

Taylor, G. (1985) *Pride, Shame, and Guilt: Emotions of Self-Assessment*, Oxford: Clarendon.

Taylor, L., Zuckerman, B., Harik, V. and Groves, B.M. (1994) 'Witnessing violence by young children and their mothers', *Journal of Developmental and Behaviour Procedures*, 15: 120–123.

Terr, L.C. (1979) 'Children of Charchilla: study of psychic trauma', *Psychoanalytic Study of the Child*, 34: 547–623.

Terr, L.C. (1989) 'Treating psychic trauma in children: a preliminary discussion', *Journal of Traumatic Stress*, 2: 3–20.

Thompson, R.A. (1994) 'Emotion regulation: a theme in search of definition', in N.A. Fox (ed.) 'The development of emotion regulation: biological and behavioral considerations', *Monographs of the Society for Research in Child Development*, 59, 240 (No. 2–3): 25–52.

Tisak, M.S. and Tisak, J. (1996) 'My sibling's but not my friend's keeper: reasoning about responses to aggressive acts', *Journal of Early Adolescence*, 16: 324–339.

Tomkins, S.S. (1962/63/91/92) *Affect/Imagery/Consciousness* (4 vols), New York: Springer.

Tomkins, S.S. (1987) 'Shame', in D.L. Nathanson (ed.) *The Many Faces of Shame*, New York: Guilford Press.

Tonge, B., Bartak, L., Bottroff, V. and Langford, P. (1993) 'A comparative study of social cognitive skills in adolescents with autism, non-autistic adolescents with developmental delays and those developing normally', in *International Conference Proceedings, Autism: A World of Options*, Texas: Future Education, 195–198.

Torrey, E.F. (1992) *Freudian Fraud: The Malignant Effect of Freud's Theory on American Theory and Culture*, New York: HarperCollins.

Treiber, F., Mabe, P.A. and Wilson, G. (1987) 'Psychological adjustment of sickle cell children and their siblings', *Children's Health Care*, 16: 82–88.

Tritt, S. and Esses, L. (1988) 'Psychosocial adaptation of siblings of children with chronic medical illnesses', *American Journal of Orthopsychiatry*, 58: 211–219.

Trower, P. (1984) 'A radical critique and reformulation: from organism to agent', in P. Trower (ed.) *Radical Approaches to Social Skills Training*, London: Croom Helm, 47–88.

Tryon, A.S. and Keane, S.P. (1991) 'Popular and aggressive boys' initial social interaction patterns in co-operative and competitive settings', *Journal of Abnormal Child Psychology*, 19: 395–406.

Tulloch, M. (1995) 'Gender differences in bullying experiences and attitudes to social relationships in high school students', *Australian Journal of Education*, 39, 3: 279–293.

Tyler, T.R. (1990) *Why People Obey The Law*, New Haven, Conn.: Yale University Press.

Ugiris, I.C. and Raeff, C. (1995) 'Play in parent–child interactions,' in M.H. Bornstein (ed.) *Handbook of Parenting. Vol 4: Applied and Practical Parenting*, Mahwah, N.J.: Lawrence Erlbaum Associates, 353–376.

Urbain, E.S. (1980) 'Interpersonal problem-solving training and social perspective-taking with impulsive children via modeling, roleplay, and self-instruction', Doctoral dissertation, University of Minnesota.

Urbain, E.S. and Kendall, P.C. (1980) 'Review of social–cognitive problem-solving interventions with children', *Psychological Bulletin*, 88: 109–143.

Van Avermaet, E. and McClintock, L.G. (1988) 'Intergroup bias and fairness among children', *European Journal of Social Psychology,* 18: 407–427.

Van der Meer, A. (1996) 'First friendships', *Sesame Street Parents,* October: 29–30, 32–35.

Van Parys, M. (1983) 'Preschoolchildren's understanding and use of race and gender', Paper presented at the biennial meeting of the Society for Research in Child Development, Detroit (cited in Ramsey 1987).

Vaughan, G. (1964) 'The development of ethnic attitudes in New Zealand school children', *Genetic Psychology Monographs,* 70: 135–175.

Vaughan, G. (1987) 'A social psychological model of the ethnic identity development', in J.S. Phinney and M.J. Rotheram (eds) *Children's Ethnic Socialization,* Newbury Park, Calif.: Sage.

Wahler, R.G. and Bellamy, A. (1997) 'Generating reciprocity with conduct problem children and their mothers: the effectiveness of compliance training and responsive parenting', *Journal of Social and Personal Relationships,* 14: 549–564.

Walker, H.M., Colvin, G. and Ramsey, E. (1995) *Antisocial Behavior in Schools: Stages and Best Practices,* Monterey, Calif.: Brooks-Cole.

Wallander, J.L., Varni, J.W., Babani, L.V., Banis, H.T. and Wilcox, K.T. (1989) 'Family resources as resistance factors for psychological maladjustment in chronically ill and handicapped children', *Journal of Pediatric Psychology,* 14: 157–173.

Wasserman, S. and Faust, K. (1994) *Social Network Analysis: Methods and Applications,* Cambridge: Cambridge University Press.

Weiland, A. and Coughlin, R. (1979) 'Self-identification and preferences: a comparison of White and Mexican-American first and third graders', *Journal of Cross-Cultural Psychology,* 10: 356–365.

Weisner, T. (1984) 'Ecocultural niches of middle childhood: a cross-cultural perspective', in W.A. Collins (ed.) *Development During Middle Childhood: Years 6 to 12,* Washington, DC: National Academy of Sciences Press.

Weiss, B. and Weisz, J. (1995) 'Relative effectiveness of behavioral versus non-behavioral child psychotherapy', *Journal of Consulting and Clinical Psychology,* 63: 317–320.

Weiss, B., Dodge, K.A., Bates, J.E. and Pettit, G.S. (1992) 'Some consequences of early harsh discipline: child aggression and a maladaptive social information processing style', *Child Development,* 63: 1321–1335.

Weissberg, R.P. (1985) 'Designing effective social problem solving programs for the classroom', in B.H. Schneider, K.H. Rubin and K.E. Ledingham (eds) *Children's Peer Relations: Issues in Assessment and Intervention,* New York: Springer-Verlag.

Weissberg, R.P. and Allen, J.P. (1986) 'Promoting children's social skills adaptive interpersonal behavior', in B.A. Edelstein and L. Michelson, *Handbook of Prevention,* New York: Plenum Press, 153–175.

Weissberg, R.P. and Gesten, E.L. (1982) 'Considerations for developing effective school-based problem-solving (SPS) training programs', *School Psychology Review,* 11: 56–63.

Weissberg, R.P., Gesten, E.L., Carnike, C.L., Toro, P.A., Rapkin, B.D., Davidson, E. and Cowen, E.L. (1981a) 'Social problem-solving skills training: a competence-building intervention with second to fourth grade children', *American Journal of Community Psychology,* 9: 411–424.

Weissberg, R.P., Gesten, E.L., Liebenstein, N.L., Schmid, K.D. and Hutton, H. (1980) *The Rochester Social Problem Solving Program*, Rochester, N.Y.: Centre for Community Study.

Weissberg, R.P., Gesten, E.L., Rapkin, B.P., Cowen, E.L., Davidson, E., Flores De Apodaca, R. and McKim, B.J. (1981b) 'Evaluation of a social-problem-solving training program for suburban and inner-city third grade children', *Journal of Consulting and Clinical Psychology*, 49: 251–261.

Wetherby, A.M. and Prutting, C.A. (1984) 'Profiles of communication and cognitive–social abilities in autistic children', *Journal of Speech and Hearing Research*, 27: 364–377.

Wheldall, K. (1992) *Discipline in Schools: Psychological Perspectives on the Elton Report*, London: Routledge.

White, J.W. (1983) 'Sex and gender issues in aggression research', in R.G. Geen and E.I. Donnerstein (eds) *Aggression: Theoretical and Empirical Reviews* (Vol. 2), New York: Academic Press, 1–26.

Whitley, B.E., Snyder, H.N. and Schofield, J.W. (1984) 'Peer preferences in a desegregated school: a round robin analysis', *Journal of Personality and Social Psychology*, 46: 799–810.

Whitney, I. and Smith, P.K. (1993) 'A survey of the nature and extent of bullying in junior/middle and secondary schools', *Educational Research*, 35: 3–25.

Williams, D. (1994) *Somebody Somewhere*, London: Doubleday.

Williams, G.A. and Asher, S.R. (1987) 'Peer- and self-perceptions of peer rejected children: issues in classification and subgrouping', Paper presented at the biennial meeting of the Society for Research in Child Development, Baltimore.

Williams, J.E. and Morland, J.K. (1976) *Race, Color, and the Young Child*, Chapel Hill, N.C.: University of North Carolina Press.

Williams, T.I. (1989) 'A social skills group for autistic children', *Journal of Autism and Developmental Disorders*, 19, 1: 143–155.

Wilson, B.J. and Gottman, J.M. (1995) 'Marital interaction and parenting', in M. Bornstein (ed.) *Handbook of Parenting: Vol. 4. Applied and Practical Considerations of Parenting*, Hillsdale, N.J.: Erlbaum, 33–56.

Wilson, J.Q. (1993) *The Moral Sense*, New York: The Free Press.

Wilson, N., Brodie, R., Carey, M., Dale, A., Lafleur, C., Johnson, B. and Young, T. (1979) *Developing the Classroom Group: Research Report*, Adelaide: Education Department of South Australia.

Wilton, K. and Renaut, J. (1986) 'Stress levels in families with intellectually handicapped preschoolchildren and families with nonhandicapped preschool children', *Journal of Mental Deficiency Research*, 30: 163–169.

Winer, B.J. (1971) *Statistical Principles in Experimental Design*, New York: McGraw-Hill.

Wing, L. (1989) 'The diagnosis of autism', in C. Gillberg (ed.) *Diagnosis and Treatment of Autism*, New York: Plenum Press, 5–22.

Wing, L. (1991) 'The relationship between Asperger's syndrome and Kanner's autism', in U. Frith (ed.) *Autism and Asperger Syndrome*, Cambridge: Cambridge University Press, 93–121.

Winson, J. (1985) *Brain and Psyche: The Biology of the Unconscious*, New York: Anchor Press.

Wispé, L. (1991) *The Psychology of Sympathy*, New York: Plenum Press.

Witt, J.C. and Elliott, S.N. (1985) 'Acceptability of classroom intervention strategies', in T.R. Kratochwill (ed.) *Advances in School Psychology* (Vol. 4), Hillsdale, N.J.: Erlbaum, 251–288.

Wortman, C.B. and Dunkelshetter, C. (1987) 'Conceptual and methodological issues in the study of social support', in A. Baum and J.E. Singer (eds) *Handbook of Psychology and Health, 5*, Hillsdale, N.J.: Erlbaum.

Wright, R. (1994) *The Moral Animal – Why We Are The Way We Are: The New Science of Evolutionary Psychology,* New York: Pantheon.

Wright, S. and Cowen, E.L. (1982) 'Student perception of school environment and its relationship to mood, achievement, popularity and adjustment', *American Journal of Community Psycholgy,*10, 6: 687–703.

Wu, D. (1985) 'Child training in Chinese culture', in W.S. Tseng and D. Wu (eds) *Chinese Culture and Mental Health,* Orlando, Fla.: Academic Press, 3–13.

Wu, X., Hart, C.H. and Draper, T.W. (1998) 'Peer and teacher sociometrics for preschoolchildren: cross-informant concordance, temporal stability and reliability, and validity', Paper submitted for publication.

Yang, B., Ollendick, T.H., Dong, Q., Xia, Y. and Lin, L. (1995) 'Only children and children with siblings in the People's Republic of China: levels of fear, anxiety, and depression', *Child Development,* 66: 1301–1311.

Yeats, K.O. and Selman, R.L. (1989) 'Social competence in the schools: towards an integrative developmental model for intervention', *Developmental Review,* 9: 64–100.

Yee, M.D. and Brown, R.J. (1988) *Children and Social Comparisons,* Final report to the ESRC, University of Kent (cited in Brown 1995).

Yirmiya, N., Sigman, M.D., Kasari, C. and Mundy, P. (1992) 'Empathy and cognition in high-functioning children with autism', *Child Development,* 63: 150–160.

Yule, W. (1992) 'Post-traumatic stress disorder in child survivors of shipping disasters: the sinking of the "Jupiter"', *Psychotherapy and Psychosomatics,* 57: 200–205.

Zabriski, A.L. and Coie, J.D. (1996) 'A comparison of aggressive-rejected and non aggressive-rejected children's interpretations of self-directed and other-directed rejection', *Child Development,* 67: 1048–1070.

Zahn-Waxler, C., Cummings, E.M., McKnew, D.H. and Radke-Yarrow, M. (1984) 'Altruism, aggression, and social interactions in young children with a manic-depressive parent', *Child Development Development,* 55, 112–122.

Zahn-Waxler, C., Denham, S., Iannotti, R.J. and Cummings, E.M. (1992) 'Peer relations in children with a depressed caregiver', in R.D. Parke and G.W. Ladd (eds) *Family–Peer Relationships: Modes of Linkage,* Hillsdale, N.J.: Erlbaum, 317–344.

Zaragoza, N., Vaughn, S. and McIntosh, R. (1991) 'Social skills interventions and children with behavior problems: a review', *Behavioral Disorders,* 16: 260–275.

Name index

Subject index